Catalonia's Advocates

Studies in Legal History

Published by the University of North Carolina Press in association with the American Society for Legal History

∾ DANIEL ERNST and THOMAS A. GREEN, *editors*

Catalonia's Advocates
LAWYERS, SOCIETY, AND POLITICS IN BARCELONA, 1759–1900

Stephen Jacobson

THE UNIVERSITY OF NORTH CAROLINA PRESS
Chapel Hill

Publication of this book was aided by grants from the Universitat Pompeu Fabra (MEC HUM2006-07328) and the Program for Cultural Cooperation between Spain's Ministry of Culture and United States Universities.

© 2009 The University of North Carolina Press
All rights reserved

Designed and set by Rebecca Evans
in Arno Pro and Fling

Manufactured in the United States of America

The paper in this book meets the guidelines for permanence and durability of the Committee on Production Guidelines for Book Longevity of the Council on Library Resources.

The University of North Carolina Press has been a member of the Green Press Initiative since 2003.

Library of Congress Cataloging-in-Publication Data
Jacobson, Stephen, PhD
Catalonia's advocates : lawyers, society, and politics in Barcelona, 1759–1900 / Stephen Jacobson.
   p. cm.—(Studies in legal history)
Includes bibliographical references and index.
ISBN 978-0-8078-3297-4 (cloth : alk. paper)
1. Law—Spain—Catalonia—History. 2. Law—Spain—Barcelona—History. 3. Lawyers—Spain—Catalonia—History. 4. Practice of law—Spain—Catalonia—History. I. Title.
KKT6071.A197.J33 2009
349.46'7—dc22   2009009384

13 12 11 10 09   5 4 3 2 1

THIS BOOK WAS DIGITALLY PRINTED.

To MARINA *and* GABRIEL

Contents

Acknowledgments xi
Significant Dates in Spanish History xiii
Note on Style xv

1 Introduction
   LAWYERS AND THE CITY 1

2 The Modern Profession
   OLD REGIME AND ENLIGHTENMENT 28

3 The Liberal Profession
   WAR, REVOLUTION, AND REPRESSION 68

4 The Conservative Profession
   INSTITUTIONS, LEADERS, AND THE LAW 107

5 The Corporate Profession
   BACKGROUNDS, TRAINING, AND PRACTICE 151

6 The Nationalist Profession
   LAW AND CATALANISM 198

7 Conclusion and Epilogue
   THE SILVER AGE OF THE PROFESSION 239

Notes 257
Bibliography 299
Index 327

Tables, Figures, and Illustrations

TABLES

1. Lawyers per 10,000 Inhabitants in Barcelona 31
2. Social Origins of Bar Applicants to the Barcelona Audiencia, 1823–1833 38
3. Social Origins of the Barcelona Bar, 1857 and 1897 159

FIGURES

1. Civil Decisions Issued by the Barcelona Audiencia 118
2. Litigation at Catalan Audiencias and District Courts 193

ILLUSTRATIONS

"Barcelona Seen from Above the Mataró-North Train Station" 12

"Barcelona Seen from the Fortress of Don Carlos" 19

Entrance to the Audiencia Palace 20

"The Heroism of Barcelona Authorities on the 9th of April of 1809" 80

Portrait of Manuel Duran i Bas 131

Maurici Serrahima at thirty-five 160

Women in a lawyer's office 189

Acknowledgments

THIS LONG-OVERDUE BOOK has gathered many intellectual debts over the years. Numerous scholars have offered insightful comments at conferences and seminars in the United States, Britain, and Spain. The Universitat Pompeu Fabra and King's College London have provided stimulating atmospheres that any academic would envy. Archivists and librarians have graciously, and at times enthusiastically, lent their expertise and time. Acknowledging everyone is simply not possible. A general thanks must suffice, even though it is simply insufficient to express the depth of my gratitude to all.

A few scholars have been involved with this project from its conception, while others offered their expertise along the way without full knowledge of the extent to which I would abuse their goodwill. José Álvarez Junco, Jim Amelang, John Butt, Josep Maria Fradera, Albert Garcia Balañà, and Enric Ucelay-Da Cal all read drafts at various stages. Some may be surprised at how the manuscript has evolved, although all will recognize their invaluable comments reflected in the text. My colleagues Federico Bonaddio, Josh Goode, Marició Janué, Isabel Juncosa, Dan Kowalsky, Diego Muro, Quim Puigvert, Martín Rodrigo, Elena Roselló, Xon de Ros, and Chris Schmidt-Nowara have shared conference panels, pub tables, stress, and ideas. At the University of North Carolina Press, Charles Grench, Ron Maner, Brian MacDonald, and Katy O'Brien smoothly guided the manuscript through the submission, approval, editing, and production processes with characteristic professionalism. The anonymous referees subsequently agreed to have their names released: I am grateful to Ken Ledford and Gary Wray McDonogh, who eyed theoretical angles and made numerous suggestions, ensuring that the book realized its potential. Most of all, I am indebted to Tom Green, the series editor, who shepherded the manuscript through the revision stage with a steady and experienced hand. His close readings and detailed comments were surpassed only by the ease of his affable manner.

I would like to thank my parents, Paul and Bev, for their support. The book is dedicated to my wife, Marina, and my son, Gabriel.

Significant Dates in Spanish History

OLD REGIME AND ENLIGHTENMENT (1759–1808)

- 1759–1777 Reign of Charles III
- 1788–1808 Reign of Charles IV
- 1793–1796 War against the French Convention

REVOLUTION AND REACTION (1808–1843)

- 1808–1813 War of Independence or Peninsular War
- 1810–1813 Cortes of Cadiz
- 1814–1820 Absolutism restored under Ferdinand VII
- 1820–1823 Constitutional Triennium
- 1823–1833 The "Ominous Decade": Absolutism again restored under Ferdinand VII
- 1833–1840 Regency of Maria Christina and the First Carlist War
- 1841–1843 Regency of General Espartero

ISABELINE SPAIN (1844–1868)

- 1844–1854 The Moderate Decade
- 1854–1856 Progressive Biennium
- 1857–1866 Era of the Liberal Union

THE DEMOCRATIC SEXENNIUM (1868–1874)

- 1868 Revolution of 1868
- 1870–1872 Monarchy of Amadeo de Saboya
- 1872–1875 Second Carlist War
- 1873 First Republic

THE RESTORATION (1875–1923)

- 1875 Restoration of the Bourbon Monarchy, Alphonse XII
- 1885 Death of Alphonse XII
- 1885–1902 Regency of Maria Christina de Habsburgo

Note on Style

Foreign Expressions and Translation Techniques

Necessarily subjective choices must be made when deciding what language to employ for proper names. Both Catalan and Spanish (Castilian) were used in eighteenth- and nineteenth-century Catalonia depending upon whether a person was speaking or writing, who was speaking or writing, and in what context. Whenever possible, English translations are preferred. When it is necessary to refer to an original expression, the following choices have been made.

NAMES OF PERSONS. The language used for the names of Catalan lawyers varied depending on the document and the time period. For example, printed material always lists lawyers' names in Spanish, while most baptismal certificates list them in Catalan. Other documents, such as handwritten tax records, vary. For the sake of simplicity, Catalan names are used in the text, except for those persons who were not Catalan natives. Modern spelling and accent techniques of Catalan names are employed. However, names in the footnotes and bibliography appear exactly as they did in the sources themselves.

For the sake of simplicity, I refer to an individual by his given name and first surname and omit the second surname. An exception is made for the cases of sons and nephews, when both surnames will be used in order to distinguish them from their fathers and uncles. For example, the nephew of the university professor Vicenç Rius is referred to by both surnames, Francesc Rius i Taulet. Another exception will be made for well-known names in Spanish history (e.g., Francesc Pi i Margall, Manuel Alonso Martínez). For the reader's information, first and second surnames, when they are known, can be found in the index.

COLLOQUIAL EXPRESSIONS. Because Catalan was the language ordinarily used for informal conversation, I refer to colloquial expressions in Catalan. For example, to describe the Catalan collaborators with the French during the Spain's War of Independence against Napoleon, I use the expression *afrancesats* instead of *afrancesados*.

NAMES OF INSTITUTIONS, ASSOCIATIONS, OFFICIAL TITLES, AND POLITICAL PARTIES. In the eighteenth and nineteenth centuries, public institutions, official titles, and private institutions and associations were referred to in all publications in Spanish and are left in Spanish (e.g., *alcalde mayor*, Audiencia).

NAMES OF PLACES. Names of places are translated into English when possible. For example, I use Seville, Cadiz, Navarre, Aragon, Cordoba, Castile, and Catalonia instead of Sevilla, Cádiz, Navarra, Aragón, Córdoba, Castilla, and Cataluña/Catalunya. Outdated English names of places are not used (e.g., Saragossa). Otherwise, Catalan places are left in Catalan, while other places in Spain are in Spanish.

Capitalization

Normal rules of capitalization are used. Note that political parties appear in uppercase, while general ideological descriptions appear in lowercase. For example, "liberal" and "conservative" are general descriptions, whereas a "Liberal" or "Conservative" refers to a member of the Liberal or Conservative Party.

1 Introduction
LAWYERS AND THE CITY

OVER THE COURSE OF what has been termed the "long nineteenth century," lawyers throughout much of Europe accomplished something rather remarkable. In the late eighteenth century, they constituted an order of experts, modestly comfortable within the privileged universe of the Old Regime. In the new century, however, unlike other professionals, they not only survived political and industrial revolution but thrived. Their feat can be appreciated when compared to others. The physician saw his practice threatened and overturned by educated and popular surgeons, barbers, and other healers more effective at cures.[1] It would take some time before doctors would expand their practices beyond diagnosis; incorporate surgical methods and blend with surgeons; overhaul medical knowledge; and, by so doing, reestablish and, in fact, augment their prestige, authority, and monopoly. The secular and especially the regular clergies witnessed their influence dwindle. The difficult fit between sacred ideas and the scientific needs of an industrializing society made men of religion expendable; in Catholic countries, legislators auctioned off the properties of a bloated landowning church to service the national debt and to put farms in the hands of owners capable of increasing productivity.[2] But lawyers were different. During the fall of the Old Regime and the consolidation of the constitutional state, they spectacularly augmented their influence in law, politics, and business. Just about everywhere, the nineteenth century was a renewed era of splendor for the bar.

Among historians, this ascendancy has been taken for granted when it has not been ignored. Others enter and exit the stage — the aristocracy, the bourgeoisie, the proletariat, the crown, the army, the church — but the bar is often assumed to be part of the scenery, a seemingly (and perhaps regrettably) endemic feature of the Western condition rather than a critical agent of social and political change. Not all periods have suffered from such neglect. Histories of the Middle Ages treat the rise of lawyers, the rediscovery of Roman law, and the making of a Western legal tradition as a defining feature of the epoch.[3] Lawyers multiplied in numbers, penetrated high politics, and brought royal justice to much of the population during the early modern period, a phenomenon that has also attracted ample scholarly attention.[4] With respect to modern Europe, there are many fine studies but also noticeable lacunae. Although the London bar has been the subject of thorough scholarly inquiry, only limited comparative lessons can be drawn: Education, training, and practice at the Inns of Court had few parallels elsewhere; what is more, the division of tasks between English barristers and solicitors was quite different from that which existed between continental advocates and proctors.[5] With respect to the continent, lucid monographs have addressed crucial periods — the Enlightenment, the French and Russian revolutions, the decades leading up to fascism in Germany and Hungary.[6] These have covered the late eighteenth and the early twentieth centuries, but a conspicuous gap remains in the middle. Missing is a social history of a continental bar during the long nineteenth century when political and industrial revolutions, the rise of the liberal state, and the advent of nationalism radically rearranged society and politics.[7] A proper understanding of how an Old Regime profession gained renewed prominence and flourished in the modern age remains a pending challenge. This study seeks to fill part of that void.

Barcelona provides an attractive setting in which to undertake such a social history. It was a liberal, revolutionary, and industrial city that experienced the full gamut of changes associated with what was once commonly referred to as the Great Transformation.[8] In the mid-eighteenth century, the bar consisted of a few dozen practitioners who went about their business, litigating in royal courts without attracting too much attention. But over the course of the ensuing century, lawyers dramatically augmented their influence. During the Enlightenment, they entered new forums, contributed to the creation of a public sphere, abandoned a myopic intellectual preoccupation with Roman and ecclesiastical law, elevated practical jurisprudence to scholarly prestige, and intermixed legal reasoning with modest doses of philosophy and economy. They shed their nostalgic attachment to urban nobility; embraced a professional ethos of probity, reason, and independence; and stressed the utility of advocacy in society. In the early nineteenth century, they emerged as liberal elites amid revolutionary scenarios, forging key compromises that helped establish a constitutional order. During the middle decades of the century, they resurrected the humanist heritage of the bar and built puissant corporate associations. Many became political leaders in a burgeoning and conflictive metropolis undergoing industrial takeoff, demographic boom, urban renovation, social dislocation, and intense episodes of political violence. At the outset of the twentieth century, lawyers headed a nascent nationalist movement demanding home rule for Catalonia. Obviously, the goal is not to tell a lineal, triumphal story of success but to treat the history of lawyers with the same critical attention afforded to other powerful social actors.

To highlight points of inquiry, it is best to start with sociological theories, which, in the absence of social histories, have squarely addressed the question of why lawyers and other professionals became so prominent in the modern age. Many historians have critiqued these for being deterministic, for ignoring the medieval and early modern past, for asserting a simplistic symbiosis between law and capitalism (or law and social class), and for failing to appreciate regional and national diversity.[9] In an attempt to find a middle ground, some historians, sympathetic with sociological methods, and some sociologists, sympathetic with historical methods, have posited that lawyers in different states have undergone similar but distinctive "paths of professionalization." This approach, although informative, has dwelled on education, the regulatory framework, degrees of professional autonomy, and institutional structures and, for the most part, has ignored the real-life experiences of lawyers and their practices.[10] Aside from this methodological concern, there is another reason why it would be a poor strategy to bracket off a new path of professionalization for lawyers in Barcelona: the Barcelona bar could not be said to be representative of those in either Spain or southern Europe. Although located on the Mediterranean, the city of Barcelona went down a path of industrialization more typical of northern Europe; although part of the Spanish state, the region of Catalonia housed a semiautonomous legal tradition with its roots in the medieval principality. To be sure, it is best to keep the comparative lens opened wide and focused on western Europe as a whole. Nor should institutions and regulations be at the center of attention. Instead, the focus is on individuals and associations, and their ideas and actions, with the purpose of discussing the relationship between the bar and major phenomena of the long nineteenth century: enlightenment, revolution, liberalism, industrialism, and nationalism.

In spite of critique, seminal sociological theories frame large questions that serve as crucial points of departure and can be revisited from time to time to highlight areas of theoretical interest. The preoccupation with law and lawyers can be found at the very foundation of the field itself. Max Weber dedicated an ample section of his *Economy and Society* to developing the first sociology of law. To Weber, lawyers and judges were indispensable agents of modernity who oversaw the maintenance of laws and procedures that ensured predictability, protected private property and individual security, promoted liberty, and sustained the juridical framework for capitalism. Formal, abstract, and rational rules were said to distinguish the West from the rest of the world, where substantive and charismatic forms of justice were said to have dominated.[11] Later, a Marxist gloss was added. Magali Sarfatti Larson and Pierre Bourdieu contended that the professions served to reproduce bourgeois hegemony by allowing children of the middle classes to avoid the brutality of an unregulated market by pursuing secure and predictable career tracks; education and professionalization inculcated dominant class values, endowed with scientific legitimacy, to elites as well as newcomers.[12] To Larson and many Marxists, lawyers have been "inescapably conservative" because they lay down "stable and defensible foundations for hegemonic power, whose justice need go no further than that law."[13] These theories were inspired by Antonio Gramsci and Louis Althusser, who had posited that "organic intellectuals" and professionals were to the bourgeoisie what the clergy had been to the aristocracy — learned men who supported "ideological apparatuses" that routinized, reified, and reproduced the dominant means of production.[14]

In the past decade, another approach has shifted emphasis away from the market and toward the state. In Terence Halliday and Lucien Karpik's edited volume *Lawyers and the Rise of Western Political Liberalism*, the introductory essay reinforces the central thesis that "Western legal professions have historically been engaged in 'political projects' that constitute political liberalism."[15] In one respect, these authors resurrect the ideas of Montesquieu and Tocqueville, who are often bundled together to buttress the familiar principle that an independent bar, in tandem with an autonomous judiciary, ensures stability, moderation, balance of powers, and good government within a constitutional order. In a similar vein, Émile Durkheim stressed that professional associations buffer governments from potential excesses resulting from an unmediated connection between society and politics.[16] While recognizing the continued validity of these perspectives, Haliday and Karpik add a Weberian gloss, reasoning that a "lawyer's liberal core centres on proceduralism."[17] The axiom that underlies this contention is that procedural consistency naturally brooks conceptions of liberty and equality. Resolving conflicts on the basis of the immutable validity of law — rather than the identity, status, or power of the litigant or instinctive or moral conceptions of fairness — made lawyers intuitively liberal. This volume brought together studies that divided countries into those in which lawyers were said to have successfully defended liberal institutions (Britain, France) and those in which they failed to do so (Germany).

When read together, these theories are functionalist insofar as they explain that lawyers made a successful transition from the Old Regime to the industrial age because capitalism, the bourgeoisie, and the liberal state demanded it. Capitalism had to preserve the monopoly of experts on juridical knowledge in order to ensure predictability, which in turn guaranteed that markets functioned properly. An identifiable body of licensed experts gave clients access to representation without having to spend unnecessary transaction costs to distinguish qualified practitioners from charlatans. The bourgeoisie needed the professions to provide secure career paths for their children and to sustain a meritocratic ethos in which the best and the brightest were said to succeed. Parliamentary systems required an autonomous bar and judiciary for stability. For these reasons, while many corporations of the Old Regime perished, the bar triumphed. Whereas the guilds were said to be an impediment to the smooth functioning of capitalism and contrary to the liberal ethos of equality of opportunity, lawyers were deemed guardians of essential rules that allowed markets to flourish and the state to remain stable.

Although these theories are intellectually coherent and indeed convincing, they must be tested against history. This does not mean, however, that one should adopt the approach of scholars who "deconstruct" normative theories by harping on the fact that generalizations obscure meaningful particularities. Asserting that not all individual lawyers in history fit the mold would hardly be revealing. Instead, it is wise to avoid gratuitous remarks reflective of disciplinary rivalry and instead engage with sociological literature in a respectful, though critical, fashion. Chapter titles such as the "modern profession," "the liberal profession" and the "conservative profession" emphasize that such theories possess significant explanatory power, and cannot be dismissed simply because history is riddled with paradox and exception. As we shall see, Barcelona lawyers constituted a "modern" profession in which practitioners were dependent on their livelihoods for their families' welfare. As a group, lawyers emerged as elitist liberals amid the political convulsions of the early nineteenth century. Conservative advocates representative of big business and agriculture came to dominate associations during the industrial era. The bar furnished a predictable career path for intelligent and hardworking children of the middle classes, while doubling as a relatively meritocratic place open to motivated and intelligent youth from humble backgrounds seeking to better their station in life. Of course, it is easy to point to numerous cases of diversity and dissent and to highlight that the path toward modernity was sinuous rather than straight. Still, there is no reason to tear down an entire edifice simply because particular elements are not in harmony with the overall scheme.

At the same time, some serious critiques to sociological approaches are in order. The chief problem with functionalist theories is that they strip lawyers of agency. Lawyers are assumed to be instruments of a commercial and agrarian bourgeoisie and guardians of rules that protect private property and promote capitalism. However, this relationship was not unidirectional, in which client guided practitioner; rather, it was a symbiotic one in which the ideas and interests of lawyers, especially when it came to politics, frequently prevailed over — and, at the very least, served to mold — the opinions of men of commerce. To be clear, the argument is not only that the bourgeoisie is an unwieldy concept, which must be broken down into its component parts before deciding whether to reassemble it or not. The argument is also that lawyers were pivotal players in the history of modern Europe whose motivations, ideas, interests, and actions need to be understood in order to comprehend the emergence, content, and contradictions of major ideologies — liberalism, conservatism, and nationalism. Another problem with Marxist theories, in particular, is that they have argued that industrialization provided the impetus to professionalization. With respect to lawyers, this chronology is off by a century. It was in the eighteenth century when the bar began to reorganize and "professionalize" after having suffered decline under the absolutist state. Just as the economic historian Jan de Vries has contended that the "industrious revolution" rather than the "industrial revolution" ushered Europe into the modern age, the bar also became enlightened and industrious in the eighteenth century.[18]

With respect to the literature that has stressed a symbiotic link between lawyers and liberalism, a policy of respectful though critical engagement is again followed here. On the one hand, it is true that many lawyers in Barcelona — and throughout western and southern Europe — were quintessential representatives of liberalism. On the other hand, it is false that their ideological preferences naturally blossomed out of the seeds of procedural rationality planted in the fields of Western law. Throughout history, the strict adherence to procedure has been the mantra of various regimes of multiple ideologies. Absolutists in the eighteenth century, liberals in the nineteenth, and authoritarians in the twentieth — to name but a few — all recurred to the imperatives of "procedure" to justify decisions that were unjust, immoral, and even murderous. For this reason, it is best to abandon the Weberian path of proceduralism and instead follow Tocqueville who reasoned that the liberal-elitist inclinations of lawyers grew out of their hostile relationship with the absolutist state and their awareness of the enormous rewards to be reaped under a constitutional one. In other words, in order to explain why the bar came to be identified with liberalism, it is necessary to analyze lawyers as human actors in history rather than just viewing them as extensions of a theoretical-idealistic conception of the law.

The legal profession evolved from liberalism to conservatism to corporatism during the nineteenth century. This analytical framework not only describes the history of lawyers in Barcelona but, with the help of comparative literature, can also be applied to those in western continental Europe. The book begins with the foundation of the modern profession during the Enlightenment (chapter 2) and continues with the emergence of a liberal profession during the revolutionary era (chapter 3). It then demonstrates how a conservative leadership built corporate associations, resurrected the humanist heritage of the bar, defended the legal tradition from legislative intrusion, and articulated a historical memory that anchored the origins of the bar in the Middle Ages and Rome (chapter 4). During the second half of the century, young lawyers embraced bourgeois culture but became increasingly corporatist, bonded through education, training, and the shared stresses of developing a private practice within a competitive and overcrowded environment. By the later decades of the century, many lawyers called for home rule for Catalonia, which, among its various attractions, promised to build and to center a Catalan bureaucracy in Barcelona; self-government would provide increased opportunities in the judiciary and administration for men with law degrees who faced difficult prospects breaking into private practice (chapter 5). Lawyers sparked nascent nationalism by defending the Catalan civil law when confronted with the coming of the Spanish Civil Code (chapter 6).

This last subject — the appearance of "juridical nationalism" — could be seen to undermine the contention that Barcelona can serve as a case study for the profession elsewhere. On one level, Barcelona was an industrial city with a distinguished legal tradition and, for this reason, constitutes an ideal vantage point from which to observe the history of a modern legal profession. On another level, its lawyers departed from the script where local bars voluntarily, or helplessly, stood by as regional law became absorbed into, or overrun by, a unified and uniform civil code of the state. Furthermore, the political defense of Catalan civil law provided momentum to a nationalist movement demanding home rule for Catalonia. In other places, religious or linguistic tensions gave rise to nationalism, but Catalonia was the only region in Europe where a juridical conflict took off in this direction.

All the same, when viewed from a broad perspective, juridical nationalism was not so exceptional. Throughout all of Europe, lawyers portrayed themselves as curators of the customs and mores of the nation, while also stressing the importance of an independent bar and judiciary to the success and stability of constitutional systems. By relying on authors such as Montesquieu and Savigny, Catalan jurists reasoned, as did many others elsewhere, that law evolved in harmony with history, custom, geography, and climate and hence reflected the "spirit" of the people. It is also worth underscoring that this juridical nationalism shared some characteristics with the corporatist behavior of various European bars that came under the spell of nationalist, if not xenophobic and misogynist, ideas when confronted with overcrowding in the early decades of the twentieth century. In any case, the conclusion (chapter 7) thoroughly discusses questions of exceptionalism and normativity and reviews the major theoretical questions posed. Barcelona lawyers, like those of any city, were not without their peculiarities — ideal types are easier to manufacture than to find. The study of the Barcelona bar, however, offers a fine perspective on the evolution of a profession in western Europe as a whole.

The City of Barcelona

The capsule history of Barcelona can appear to be a romantic narrative of how an old medieval capital recaptured its prominence during the industrial era.[19] During the High Middle Ages, the Catalans were a crusading and commercial power that colonized much of the western Mediterranean. The counts of the House of Barcelona were the kings of the Crown of Aragon, and by the fifteenth century they governed one of the most extensive empires in Europe. Their suzerainty stretched over Naples, Sicily, Malta, Sardinia, the Balearic Islands, Valencia, Aragon, and Catalonia. During the middle of the century, however, the kingdom became riddled with dynastic conflict and descended into civil war. In 1469 the crowns of Castile and Aragon were united by marriage, which brought stability to Catalonia and gave rise to what became the country of Spain. Over the course of the ensuing century, the colonization of the Americas and the successful exploitation of New World silver enabled

Castile to emerge as the senior partner. Madrid, the capital of the monarchy, and Seville, the chief point of contact with the Americas, grew to be more populous and prosperous than Barcelona. During the early modern period, Barcelona remained a capital of one of the various Spanish kingdoms, but it had lost its preeminence. Its population actually decreased from some 40,000 persons in the mid-fourteenth century to approximately 30,000 by the outset of the eighteenth.[20]

Because the House of Barcelona ruled such a vast empire when written Western law reemerged in the Mediterranean, it is not surprising that Catalonia developed a renowned and distinguished legal tradition. Barcelona's oldest compilation of royal orders, the *Usatges*, was one of the first charters of feudal law anywhere, some of its provisions dating to the mid-eleventh century. An early twentieth-century nationalist scholar bragged that it predated England's Magna Carta by almost a century and a half.[21] The *Consolat del Mar* (1260–70), written in Catalan and subsequently translated into Latin and a number of other languages, was a milestone of legal history. Applied in commercial tribunals throughout the world, it was to the mercantile law what Justinian's *Institutes* was to private law, the *Libri Feudorum* to feudal law, and the *Decretals* to canon law.[22] The chief compiler of the *Decretals*, incidentally, was the Catalan lawyer, Ramon de Penyafort, one of Europe's great juridical minds of the thirteenth century. The *Usatges* and the *Consolat* were the showpieces of a deep corpus that included compilations of municipal customs, statutory laws or "constitutions" of the parliament (Corts), and volumes of scholarly commentary. Interestingly, the decline of Barcelona in the early modern period was not paralleled by juridical decadence. Upon the unification of the crowns in 1474, Catalonia maintained its parliamentary institutions and its traditional body of laws. During the seventeenth century, its jurists achieved international fame for their Roman law expertise. They published their treatises, written in Latin, in Venice, Frankfurt, Lyon, Antwerp, and Geneva, from where they were distributed throughout the continent.[23] To draw a rough parallel, Joan Pere Fontanella (1575–1649) — the most prolific of Catalonia's seventeenth-century jurists — is held with similar veneration at the Barcelona bar today as Coke in England, Grotius in Holland, and Bodin in France.

Catalonia did eventually succumb to juridical decadence. The immediate cause was the War of Spanish Succession (1702–14), an international conflagration in which the Catalans came out on the losing side. This was the second major defeat in less than a century, for the Catalan Estates had also revolted during the Reapers' War (1623–40), an outgrowth of the Thirty Years' War. In 1716 Spain's first Bourbon king, Philip V, promulgated the New Foundation (Nueva Planta), a seminal document that implanted absolutism in Catalonia. It abolished autonomous institutions, including the parliament (the Corts), the standing commission of the parliament (the Diputació), and Barcelona's municipal council (the Consell de Cent). Although the New Foundation left private law intact, there was no lawmaking body empowered to enact new laws or keep old ones up-to-date. As a result of this and subsequent reforms, Spanish became the official language of the courts and all officialdom, many persons from outside Catalonia were appointed magistrates and judges in the region, and Castilian legal texts gradually gained increasing authority in Catalan courts. Interestingly, economic regeneration, underway since the late seventeenth century, followed on the heels of institutional and juridical decline. During the eighteenth century, Barcelona embarked upon an era of outstanding growth. By the mid-nineteenth century, it was the most industrialized city in Spain and on the Mediterranean.

The reemergence of Barcelona as one of Europe's great cities can be read as a romantic tale, but it was obviously not a teleological phenomenon in which inhabitants magically awoke to a preordained mission to reclaim glories of the past. Rather, the chief reason behind renewed prominence was economic rather than spiritual. In the eighteenth century, a productive agrarian economy and a profitable proto-industrial cotton industry lifted the region out of centuries of demographic and economic slumber. Barcelona entered a period of boom while other Spanish cities languished in what was often portrayed as systemic or even racial decadence. In 1786 the bishop of Barcelona counted more than 100 cotton factories in the city, many of which employed more than 100 workers.[24] In 1787 the British economist Arthur Young observed, "The manufactories at Barcelona are considerable. There is every appearance as you walk the streets of great and active industry: you move no where without hearing the creak of stocking engines."[25] In 1789 the Chevalier de Bourgoanne wrote, "Few of the reproaches alleged against the Spaniards are applicable to the Catalonians. When we cross their cultivated province, and see it full of manufacturers of various kinds, we find it difficult to believe it belongs to Spain."[26] From the French Revolution through Spain's liberal revolution of the 1830s, the economy slowed, but the arrival of steam power in the early 1830s spurred mechanized industrial takeoff. By the mid-1840s, the city housed approximately 250 factories, averaging more than 50 workers in each. In 1856, one industrial engineer counted some 21,000 cotton textile workers and reported another 50,000 men and women engaged in other forms of skilled and unskilled labor. Barcelona and its environs not only produced cotton goods but also housed smaller industries in wool, silk, chemicals, paper, cork, and metals.[27]

Along with industry, trade with the Americas propelled economic growth. In 1778 the enlightened monarch Charles III ended the monopoly of Cadiz (the Atlantic port city downriver from Seville) on colonial commerce and allowed Barcelona merchants to send and receive ships to and from the Americas. Spain lost most of its colonies by the mid-1820s, but productive commercial relationships with Latin America continued thereafter. Not to be forgotten, Spain retained a small but profitable empire in the Philippines, Puerto Rico, and Cuba. Of the three, the jewel of the crown was Cuba, arguably the most economically valuable colony of any European power in the nineteenth century. Here, slave plantations produced some 42 percent of the world's sugarcane supply by the 1870s.[28] One of the more lucrative enterprises among Barcelona merchants was importing Brazilian and United States cotton to feed city looms. Ships departed Barcelona destined for Buenos Aires, Montevideo, Rio de Janeiro, Recife, Cartagena, Veracruz, Havana, San Juan, Charleston, New Orleans, Mobile, and various other ports. Some went straight to the Americas while others stopped on the western coast of Africa to engage illegally in the slave trade. Upon reaching the Americas, they would exchange African slaves and Catalan liqueurs, wines, paper, and textiles for raw materials. In the last leg of the journey, Cuban sugar, Argentine beef jerky (used to feed slaves in Brazil, Cuba, and the United States), and numerous other metropolitan and colonial products were swapped for cotton. This was not the only "triangular" trade route. Ships also returned with other goods such as sugar, coffee, chocolate, tobacco, and rum, but the routes that supplied cotton were key to the march of industry.[29]

Industrialization spurred population growth. In 1760 Barcelona numbered some 80,000 persons, and when the city tore down its medieval walls in the mid-1850s, it had more than doubled in size. Migrants from the Catalan countryside, many of whom fled rural poverty to work in factories, were the major source of new labor.[30] Not only did immigrants flood into the city, but some settled in adjacent towns, which became gradually absorbed into the urban fabric. Barcelona was not a single manufacturing dot on an agrarian landscape; rather, it was the center of a large enclave thoroughly transformed by industry. Beyond the small mountain range enclosing Barcelona (called the Collserola), another set of small cities — Terrassa, Sabadell, Igualada, Mataró

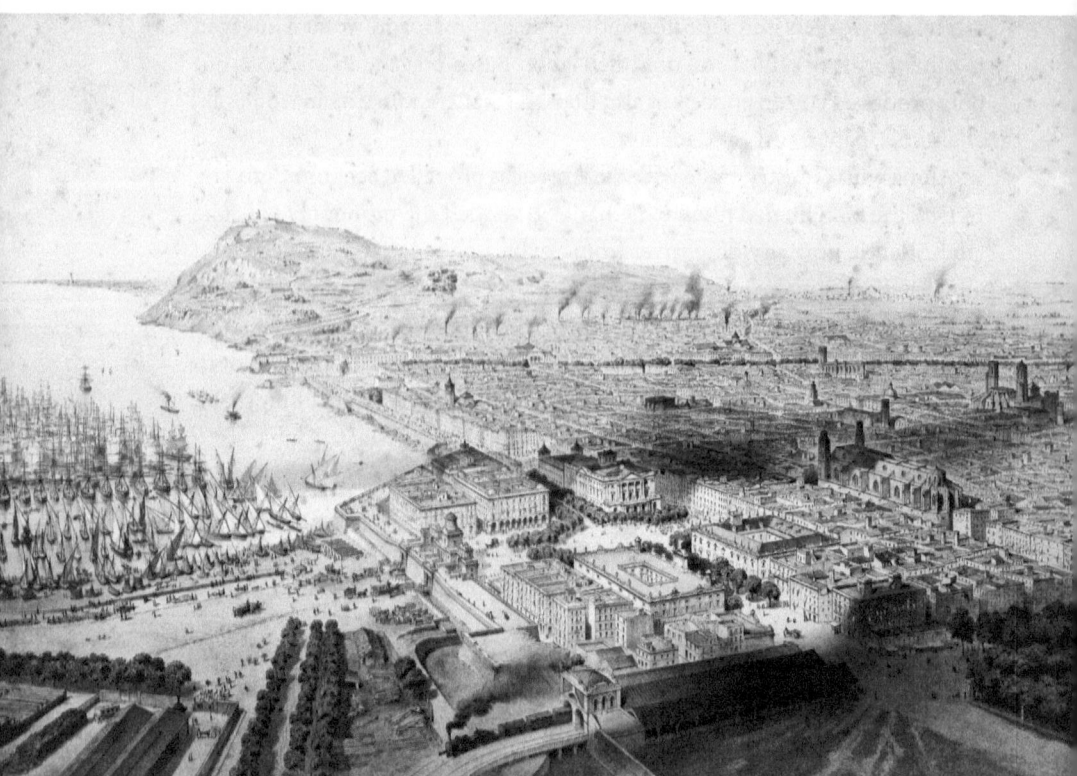

"Barcelona Seen from Above the Mataró-North Train Station" (1850s). Notice the railroad in the foreground, the small steamships in the harbor, and the smokestacks in the Raval neighborhood. The city's walls have not yet been torn down. (Lithograph by A. Guesden, Institut de Cultura, Arxiu Històric de la Ciutat, Barcelona)

and Vilanova — formed the nodes of an industrial belt. Industry sprang up in rural towns as well, especially along rivers where water mills continued to drive small factories even in the age of coal. South along the coast, Sitges, Vilanova, and Tarragona also carried on thriving commercial business with the Americas. Picturesque northern ports along the rocky Costa Brava were fishing villages with scattered trade and shipbuilding. Further in the interior, Reus, Catalonia's second largest city, was a regional center for commerce and industry, although its population (26,000 at century's end) paled in comparison to that of Barcelona. By 1897 the population of Barcelona had exceeded 500,000, and that of the province of Barcelona had surpassed 1 million. The other three Spanish provinces that composed Catalonia — Girona,

Tarragona, and Lleida — together added an additional 1 million. At the time, Catalonia comprised eleven percent of the country's population.³¹ But its economic importance far exceeded its demographic weight. To cite two telling statistics, in 1905 42 percent of all Spanish imports came into Catalan ports and 26 percent of exports left through them.³²

Barcelona was not only an industrial city but also a revolutionary and liberal one. Engels had once famously declared that its barricades rose with greater frequency than anywhere in the world. The age of revolution opened in Spain, as in much of the continent, with the Napoleonic Wars. The French invasion of 1808 ignited more than three decades of political instability, as Spain underwent alternating periods of revolution and repression and was plagued by urban revolt and rural civil war. Along with Madrid and Cadiz, Barcelona was a focal point of Spain's "liberal revolution." Lawyers who doubled as revolutionary elites carried on a delicate balancing act. Riding waves of popular mobilization, they collaborated with other liberal notables to bury the Old Regime, to weaken the power of the church, and to establish a viable constitutional monarchy. At the same time, they also maneuvered to ensure that Spain did not slide into the uncontrolled democracy of the French Revolution, which, among its various consequences, had wrought havoc on the bar itself. Committed to parliamentary monarchy and wary of extremist ideologies from the republican Left to the absolutist Right, lawyers filled vacuums of power, framed and channeled popular demands, searched out compromises, and guided violence toward orderly ends. Obviously, the bar did not consist of men with homogeneous opinions. A few politicized practitioners were faithful to the absolutist Right and others were attracted to the radical Left. Moreover, the bulk of established practitioners strove to avoid politics, attempting to continue their livelihoods amid tumultuous times. However, the most dynamic members of the bar emerged as quintessential representatives of liberalism during the early decades of the nineteenth century. Later, Barcelona underwent further revolutionary waves from 1854 to 1856 and from 1868 to 1874. During these periods, democrats attempted to open what had become an elitist constitutional system with a restricted franchise to wider participation. By this time, however, lawyers were no longer associated with revolution. Although a few led, joined, and sympathized with the goals of democratic revolutionaries, most were content with the established elitist, liberal order.

Politics, commerce, and industry transformed the structure of the bar. Following the establishment of a constitutional order in the 1830s, juridical reforms provided civil litigants and criminal defendants with more rights, which, in turn, gave lawyers greater room for maneuver and granted them easier access to proceedings and forums where their presence had been previously resisted. The bar underwent two major changes. The first was the rise of mercantile lawyers into positions of authority. They shared preeminence with top civil lawyers whose staple business of inheritance and property disputes was fueled by a booming property market and a productive agrarian economy. The civil and mercantile law converged, as a successful law practice tended to combine both types of work. The second major change was that an increasing percentage of the bar became occupied with criminal defenses. Industrialization created social dislocation and spiraling levels of inequality, driving crime rates higher. Much of this work was scooped up by novices, who either worked for free as public defenders or charged nominal fees in order to gain courtroom expertise. Over the course of the nineteenth century, a group of lawyers that had been chiefly dedicated to civil lawsuits became transformed into a plural bar, consisting of men with different orientations in their practices, not to mention diverse social origins and religious beliefs. Opportunities in business and politics tempted many to abandon full-time practice in favor of parallel or alternative careers. The bar was galvanized by associations — the College of Lawyers and the Academy of Jurisprudence — that defended collective interests. Diversity, in fact, fomented corporatism. As the bar became larger, more diverse, and potentially fissiparous, the shared experiences of training and apprenticeship, the culture of youthful camaraderie and middle-aged collegiality, the participation in associations, and the Catalan law itself reinforced cohesion, solidarity, common purpose, and corporate identity.

The impression should not be given that the history of Barcelona, Catalonia, or its bar was equivalent to the inexorable and successful march of liberalism and industry. With regard to politics, liberalism never won the hearts and minds of those excluded from its small franchise; it was ultimately consolidated through military victory over absolutists in civil wars. It is probable that Catalonia witnessed higher levels of political violence than any other region in Europe during the first three decades of the nineteenth century. The agrarian world was the chief source of instability. Along with the Basque Country, rural Catalonia was the locus of the "Spanish Vendée." Beyond the industrial belt were the foothills of the Pyrenees, where free trade destroyed uncompetitive economies and where revolutionary laws disentailing and auctioning off church and municipal lands wrought havoc on property relations, causing massive social dislocation. Some towns in this region were strongholds for counterrevolutionaries who waged civil wars against liberal regimes in defense of throne and altar. After succumbing to an absolutist revolt and a French invasion in the early 1820s, the Spanish army triumphed over absolutists during the First Carlist War from 1833 to 1839 and again during the Second Carlist War from 1872 to 1875. Aside from these large civil wars, Catalonia also experienced two localized peasant jacqueries with rather picturesque names — the War of the Malcontents (1827) and the War of the Early Risers (1846–49) — in addition to other smaller disturbances. Even in times of peace, the constitutional regime needed to be maintained by a standing army. Throughout the century, a disproportionate number of Spanish troops were stationed in Catalonia, where disenfranchised rural and urban popular classes were not adverse to resorting to revolutionary and reactionary violence.[33] Very few lawyers sympathized with absolutism, the ideological leadership of which was associated with another professional group: priests and monks.

The economy also experienced serious problems. In the long run, Catalan textiles were unable to compete on international markets. Britain, Germany, and France simply produced cheaper goods in larger, more-efficient factories, leaving Catalan industrialists dependent on high tariff walls and colonial monopolies to ensure outlets for their finished products. Compounding the problem of poor competitiveness was a lack of economic diversity. Devoid of coal or iron, Catalonia possessed meager mineral resources, a limitation that hindered the emergence of a sizable metallurgical industry. Capital investment followed tight, personal, and often interfamilial networks between country and city, which stymied the development of a mature banking system able to assume risks needed to branch out into diverse businesses. Many pioneering midcentury banks descended into sluggishness and bankruptcy during the worldwide economic crisis of the 1860s. Others appeared in their wake, but by the mid-1880s, Catalan banks entered a gradual phase of contraction, outpaced by larger institutions centered in Madrid and Bilbao, the latter the steel capital of Spain. In Barcelona, the paternalistic attitudes of factory owners, coupled with poor pay, long hours, and dangerous working conditions, poisoned industrial relations and fomented anarchosyndicalism.[34] As far as lawyers were concerned, however, the structural problems of the economy did not have a devastating effect on their practices. If top lawyers eventually lost out on the lucrative opportunities available to their counterparts in Madrid and Bilbao, where big banking and heavy industry were more capital intensive, they had no trouble filling the courts with lawsuits and continued to minister to the needs of a growing economy.

To put things in perspective, this list of problems did not cause either economic turmoil or chronic political instability. During the second half of the nineteenth century, the Catalan economy expanded steadily. High tariff walls allowed industry to flourish. Raw cotton imports to Catalonia rose from 15 million kilograms per year in 1863 to a whopping 142 million by 1887, an increase that provides a convenient measurement of the growth of manufactured textiles. Another telling indicator was the vitality of the wine business, the chief good of exchange used to bring American cotton to Catalan looms. Over the same period, wine exports grew from 57 million liters to 260 million per year.[35] Even when textiles began to sputter because of falling demand during the worldwide depression of the 1890s, the electrical industry spurred recovery by reducing dependency on imported coal.[36] Railroad construction, which had begun in the mid-1840s, although hamstrung by the lack of domestic capital and the absence of a large metallurgical industry, eventually connected Barcelona with major cities in Spain and France. Insurance companies, steamship lines, mortgage, deposit, agrarian-credit, and investment banks, and numerous other ventures attracted investors. With respect to politics, Spain's constitutional system suffered from endemic problems of oligarchy and corruption, and the frequent intervention of the army in politics, but in spite of revolutionary interludes, it remained durable.[37] In 1923 a coup d'état by Miguel de Primo de Rivera, then captain general of Catalonia, put an end to some ninety years of liberal constitutionalism. In the aftermath of the First World War, industrial violence in Barcelona made the country ungovernable. Until this occurred, however, Spain was a working constitutionalist monarchy with typical problems characteristic of much of southern Europe.

With regard to economy and society, however, Barcelona is more often compared to northern than to southern Europe. As the economic historian Jordi Maluquer has poignantly observed, "The Catalan economy was the only one in the Mediterranean area that aligned itself successfully with the 'first-comers' of industrialization." By the mid-nineteenth century, levels of steam power mechanization in Catalonia were lower than in Belgium or Germany but higher than in France or Czechoslovakia.[38] Not only have comparisons with northern Europe been made with the benefit of hindsight, but persons living at the time were conscious of similarities. To textile workers, Lancashire was the closest parallel to Catalonia. At least this was the opinion of the largest trade union, the Three Classes of Steam Power, which in 1889 sent a study group on a pilgrimage to Manchester with the mission to survey ways to alleviate industrial strife. It returned with an exhaustive list of recommendations to improve production, competitiveness, wages, and working conditions.[39]

To the cultivated, however, Paris — rather than Manchester — was always the exemplar. Visitors first observed parallels in the late eighteenth century. This was hardly surprising: Barcelona was only a few hours on horseback from the French border, and Paris had exerted a spell over all of continental high culture since the reign of Louis XIV. In 1772 Joseph Marshall depicted Barcelona as a "very fine place, admirably situated, carrying on a brisk and extensive commerce, and having all the appearance of wealth and industry." The city had "as great an appearance of activity as any in France."[40] In 1787 another British traveler, Arthur Young, wrote, "I have been at no city since we left Paris, whose approach carries such a face of animation and cheerfulness; and considering Paris as the capital of a great Kingdom, and Barcelona as that of a province only, the latter is more striking beyond all comparison."[41] During his visit, he attended the Principal Theater, where he took in a Spanish comedy followed by an Italian opera. Surprised to find "clergymen in every part of the house; a circumstance never seen in France," he also remarked that "every well dressed person was in the French fashion."[42] Henry Swinburne, another Englishman, also attended the Principal Theater in 1787, where he enjoyed a musical adaptation of the Spanish epic poem *The Cid*. "A pretty ballad was sung by a woman, in the smart dress of a *maja* or a coquette: she wore her hair in a scarlet net, with tassels; a striped gauze handkerchief crossed over her breast; a rich jacket, flowered apron, and brocade petticoat. I observed the pit was crowded with clergymen."[43]

Elegant style and dress, together with a love for theater and music, were the cultural hallmarks of an eminently self-conscious bourgeoisie. During the nineteenth century, numerous theaters staged comedies, musicals (*zarzuelas*), historic dramas and tragedies, and even small circus acts. The dissolution of the monasteries following the Revolution of 1835 caused the number of clergy to dwindle, and, in any case, few attended the theater. Spectacles catered to a diverse public, including artisans and workers. The most splendorous theater was the Liceu Opera House, constructed between 1844 and 1847. It was promoted in part by Manuel Girona, the most prominent banker in Barcelona at the time, who convinced others to buy shares in the house as they had in railroads, mines, maritime insurance companies, and banks. It was built up the street from the Principal Theater on the Ramblas, the widest and most luxurious city boulevard. Here, high society could garishly show off its grandeur while basking in the sonorous voices of Europe's star performers.[44] In 1887 the Russian writer Isaac Pavlovski remarked, "The Catalans are passionate lovers of music and theater. The Barcelona Liceu could be more prestigious than the *Royal* of Madrid." He added, "Perhaps the public does not possess a vast music education, but it does distinguish itself for its fine ear. . . . One false note and it is capable of flooding the hall with a veritable storm of whistles and indignant cries."[45]

As was the case with so many other cities, urban planners also regarded Paris as a model. Urban renovation came to be considered an urgent priority following the Revolution of 1854 when an outbreak of cholera had prompted desperate residents to take picks and axes to medieval walls. Built within the walls, factories were concentrated in the Raval quarter and along the high and low streets branching out from the parish of Sant Pere de les Puelles, the traditional location of the cloth industry. Unsanitary conditions, sewage problems, and overcrowding caused average life expectancy in the city to dwindle to an abominable twenty-five years.[46] Outside the walls, tracts of farmland stretched to nearby towns and were ripe for development. To this end, the municipality recommended an urban plan inspired by Haussmann's Paris, in which intersecting grand boulevards would emanate from of a series of plazas that would fan out around an enlarged city center. The Spanish government, though, ignored the suggestion and in 1857 approved a rival design in which a meticulously planned urban grid, the "Eixample" (Extension) wrapped itself around the old city.[47] Although the Eixample more closely resembled Charles L'Enfant's utopian-republican design of Washington, D.C., it also incorporated Parisian grand boulevards and plazas. Its central boulevard, the Passeig de Gràcia, replaced the Ramblas as the fashionable destination for the palaces of the rich. Two World Fairs — the first in 1888 and the second in 1929 — gave further boosts to urban development. Visitors who attended the first fair marveled at industry, architecture, and urban planning, much of which was still a work in progress; by the second, they were able to witness the result of decades of construction and expansion, including much crowding and some sprawl, while taking in the vaunted creations of Barcelona's "modernist" architects — Lluís Domènech, Antoni Gaudí, and Josep Puig. An eclectic intellectual community took root. The young artist from Malaga, Pablo Picasso, attended art school in the 1890s, learning his trade by painting the brothels around the port before moving on to survey those of

"Barcelona Seen from the Fortress of Don Carlos." Aerial view with the winning design for the Citadel park in the foreground (early 1870s). (Lithograph by A. Castelucho, Institut de Cultura, Arxiu Històric de la Ciutat, Barcelona)

the French capital. The dreams of the bourgeoisie were self-fulfilling. If the midcentury city had resembled Manchester, with its stench, disease, and low life expectancy, by the outset of the twentieth century, Barcelona had earned the title "Paris of the South."[48]

The vast majority of lawyers lived in the physical center of the old city, the locus for civil and ecclesiastical justice and administration. Their homes were close to Catalonia's highest court, the Audiencia, located in the Palace of the Deputation (today the Palace of the Generalitat) on the Plaça Sant Jaume. The Audiencia was only a few paces away from the cathedral, the Ecclesiastical Palace, the town hall, and the jail. From this neighborhood, it was a short walk to the port and the Pla de Palau, the center for commercial life, where the majestic Llotja Palace housed the Chamber of Commerce and the Commercial Tribunal. In previous centuries, the neighborhood surrounding the Audiencia had been more sparsely populated than the commercial and

Entrance to the Audiencia Palace. The artist depicts St. George's Day, when the public was allowed to visit. (Engraving by R. Puiggari, Institut de Cultura, Arxiu Històric de la Ciutat, Barcelona)

manufacturing zones and hence must have been propitious for quiet legal practice. However, it had become increasingly dense and suffered from all the strains of the industrial age.[49] In spite of cramped conditions, lawyers were reluctant to relocate because they needed to remain close to proctor and notary offices, banks, commercial enterprises, the courts, and the prison. In the 1880s, a few prescient individuals migrated to more comfortable homes in the Eixample quarter, but they were not followed by their colleagues in droves. Only after the completion of the New Model Prison (1904) and the Judicial Palace (1911) did the gravity of legal practice gradually shift out of the old city and into the Eixample.[50] In 1924 the College of Lawyers — the bar association for Barcelona lawyers — moved its headquarters from the Archdeacon's Palace (facing the cathedral) to the palace it today occupies on the Carrer Mallorca.

Legal practice resembled that of similarly sized cities. Any continental advocate visiting midcentury Barcelona would have found its law offices, courts, university, and associations recognizable. They were perhaps smaller and more claustrophobic compared to large metropolises, such as London and Paris, where relationships were theoretically less personal, financial enterprise existed on a grander scale, the halls of justice were more majestic, and juridical etiquette was more rigid and pretentious. But, for the most part, lawyers practiced in a typical ambience. They were immersed in everyday legal problems — from murders to petty theft, from major bankruptcies to minor fraud, from inheritance battles to marital separations, from property sales to rents and evictions. Although there was no civil code, lawyers used guidebooks written in the style of codes, coherently organized into books, titles, and articles. Most lawyers who entered politics helped sustain an oligarchic liberal system, although a handful of leftist advocates joined republican ranks and a few even counseled trade unions. It was common for lawyers to double as businessmen, journalists, intellectuals, poets, satirists, novelists, and playwrights. Some pious men of the law dutifully flocked to mass on Sundays and a handful of freethinkers attended Mason meetings, while most of the others were less zealous and regarded orthodoxies with skepticism. The judicial corps provided jobs for judges, prosecutors, and court secretaries. Others used their law degree to secure positions as estate administrators or secretaries to private and public enterprise, or to manage their personal wealth. Many held a law degree for show. Some lawyers were rich, others were middling, and still others struggled to make ends meet.

With such an extensive period to be covered, it is not possible to address all species of legal professionals. The focus is on the lawyer, also known as the "advocate" in western continental Europe. Significantly less attention, in fact hardly any at all, will be paid to the "proctor," often referred to in English as an "attorney" or "solicitor."[51] These experts in procedure undertook the clerical administration of lawsuits by filing relevant papers, liaising with advocates and court secretaries, and steering cases through the judicial system. Invaluable men of technical expertise, they worked closely with lawyers. However, with the exception of a few, they were not educated at university. Nor did they share the same cultural, political, or intellectual spaces or command the same pay or prestige as lawyers. In their social lives, proctors intermixed with artisans, shopkeepers, and fellow lower-rung professionals, such as clerks and white-collar employees. The third legal professional, the "notary," is discussed from time to time, given that many notaries held law degrees and some were active within juridical associations, but they do not receive the detailed attention as lawyers. The vast majority of Catalonia's notaries resided in the rural world where they dedicated themselves to conveyancing, marriages, wills, and rural credit.[52] Although notaries were enormously effective at defending corporate privileges, and many wielded ample power in the towns, their political influence in the city of Barcelona was negligible.[53] Finally, in order to concentrate on society and politics, it is necessary to sacrifice an in-depth exploration of the courtroom. The evolution of procedures, symbols, etiquettes, dress, and ritual in civil, criminal, commercial, and ecclesiastical courts is a fascinating but complementary field for which further research in Spain and Europe is needed.

"Catalanism" and Catalan Nationalism

To round out this introductory chapter, it will be helpful to provide some background on Catalan nationalism. Because of the popularity of the study of nationalism, it might be expected that the subject would feature prominently from the start, but it is not addressed until the later chapters. The reason is simply chronology. A cultural and legal renaissance did not get underway until the 1860s, and, even when it did, it was initially void of political pretensions. "Catalanism" — as "protonationalism" was called — did not emerge until the early 1880s. For most of the century, Catalans possessed dual identities as Catalans and Spaniards, which were routinely regarded as mutually reinforcing rather than problematic or antagonistic. As the Catalan economic historian and constitutional scholar Antoni de Capmany wrote during the Napoleonic Wars, "What would become of Spaniards, if there were no Aragonese, Valencians, Murcians, Asturians, Galicians, Extremadurans, Catalans, Castilians, etc. Each one of these names shines bright and looms large. These small nations make up the mass of the Great Nation."[54] In the mid-nineteenth century, most enfranchised Catalans voted for liberal parties — the Progressives and Moderates. By the early 1880s, these parties had evolved into the Liberals and the Conservatives (technically called the Liberal-Conservatives). Those dissatisfied with these "dynastic" options could vote for leftist republicans or rightist absolutists, but a regionalist party did not appear on the ballot in Barcelona until 1901.

Barcelona became internationally renowned for many things — industry, revolution, and urban design. It did not, however, achieve a reputation as a hotbed of political regionalism until the nineteenth century was drawing to a close. Controversies pitting Catalan elites against the central government were not initially a feature of the political landscape. For example, the division of Catalonia into the four provinces of Barcelona, Lleida, Girona, and Tarragona, first undertaken in 1822, did not create friction even though nationalists would later consider this measure equivalent to the carving up of the ancient principality.[55] In the 1840s and 1850s, the Moderate Party emulated Bonapartist legislative models by centralizing administration, taxation, education, and public safety around the ministries in Madrid, which operated through delegations in the provincial deputations. These sweeping reforms reduced Barcelona from the capital of Catalonia to the administrative capital of a single province, but no organized protest surfaced. While nationalists pushed forth demands throughout Europe during revolutions in 1848 in Frankfort, Budapest, Prague, and Rome, the insurrectional wave did not cross the Pyrenees. Barcelona remained silent. Controversies between Barcelona and Madrid first took place during the 1850s and 1860s when Catalan lawyers and politicians expressed dissatisfaction over a series of legislative initiatives. In retrospect, these conflicts foreshadowed the appearance of nationalist tensions, but at the time, they were seen as ordinary disagreements in which regional conservatives and centralist modernizers wrangled over the scope of reform.

With the benefit of hindsight, however, it is evident that the midcentury bar prepared the groundwork for Catalanism even if its members initially had no explicit intention of doing anything of the sort. The first major conflict of regionalist overtones took place when Catalan lawyers and property owners successfully defeated a proposal to promulgate a uniform code of civil laws for all of Spain. Had the draft civil code of 1851 been enacted, it would have wiped out all Catalan law and radically transformed the organization of family and property in Catalonia. In the early 1860s, Catalan parliamentary deputies inveighed against the Law of Mortgages (1861) and the Notarial Law (1862), insisting that these reforms ran roughshod over perfectly viable native laws. Even though these disputes did not produce any immediate political fallout, lawyers became aware that they needed to pay closer attention to their native legal regime or else it would be doomed to extinction. Many wrote pamphlets and newspaper articles that stressed the symbolic and material importance of the Catalan legal tradition; in the meantime, jurists published guidebooks and manuals so that laws could be easily applied in court. Confronted with the threat of piecemeal reform and the looming prospect of full codification, the university professor and commercial lawyer Manuel Duran imported and popularized Friedrich von Savigny's "historical-school" jurisprudence, a legal philosophy that held that law evolved in harmony with custom and reflected the spirit of the people (*Volksgeist*). As legal culture became rife with historicism and romanticism, it would become fertile ground for budding Catalanists.

The first group to demand parallel legislative authority for Catalonia, however, was not made up of conservatives defensive of traditional laws. This honor belonged to the Federal-Republicans, members of a revolutionary and democratic party founded in the 1850s with its stronghold in Barcelona. Representative of disenfranchised lower-middle classes and critical of the notorious elitism of liberal parties, Federalists believed that Spain should be organized along the lines of Switzerland or the United States, democratic republics in which component states possessed autonomous legislatures with ample lawmaking authority. The party's founder, the Barcelona lawyer Francesc Pi i Margall, moved to Madrid, where he ran a thriving law practice and became president of the short-lived Republic of 1873. In 1876, he published *Nationalities*. To Pi i Margall, the "nation" (Spain) consisted of a free union of citizens; a federation would "establish unity without destroying variety."[56] With time, however, many leading Federalists in Barcelona grew less interested in Spain and more concerned with Catalonia. In 1881 many members left the party to found the Catalan Center (Centre Català), the first political association dedicated to achieving home rule. Others remained faithful to the party but collaborated with Catalanists in various projects. Indeed, Federalists were among the most ardent defenders of Catalan law during the protests against the coming of the Spanish Civil Code (1889).

The cultural renaissance, which emerged hand in hand with legal renaissance, was another source from which a nationalist political movement would draw inspiration. In the 1850s romanticists began to publish poetry and produce theater in Catalan. In so doing, they revived a language had not been considered appropriate for literary purposes for centuries, even though it had always remained the preferred medium for daily conversation among natives. By the 1870s these literati expanded their repertoire by turning their attentions toward history, archaeology, folklore, and other cultural topics. By the 1880s Catholic groups sponsored ambitious projects to restore monasteries and other religious shrines deemed representative of the spiritual soul of the medieval principality. In the early years, revivalists did not throw into question the legitimacy or organization of the state: the rebirth of Catalan culture was considered essential to rediscovering the diversity and beauty of

Spain. All the same, literary — as well as legal — romanticism made future generations susceptible to the nationalist message then tearing through Europe. In 1870 a group of romanticist intellectuals founded "Young Catalonia," which took its name from organizations with explicit nationalist objectives, such as Young Italy, Young Poland, and Young Ireland. In 1871 this group launched the first Catalan-language literary magazine, called *La Renaixensa*. "Renaixença" — meaning rebirth — later came to be used as a label to describe the entire literary movement.

The Renaixença was a bridge between revivalism and the appearance of organized political pressure groups. Participants comprised an array of people, ranging from dilettantes determined to keep literary endeavor pure of the corrupting influence of politics to militants within mainstream parties who wrote poetry, history, short stories, and folklore in Catalan as an escapist distraction to remember bygone days with nostalgic affection. The most dynamic sector, however, consisted of a clutch of political activists, many of whom were lawyers, who asserted that cultural revival should lead to the resurrection of autonomous political institutions. In the late 1870s, Josep Pella, a lawyer, and Josep Coroleu, a legally trained historian, suggested that it was not enough that Catalan private law be saved; they posited that the region's lost public law could be recuperated and reassembled in order to construct a legal foundation upon which political autonomy would rest. The once-independent Crown of Aragon, they reasoned, had agreed to unite with Spain only upon being promised that the Catalan parliament would be conserved. Accordingly, the New Foundation (1716), which had abolished Catalonia's representative bodies and mandated the exclusive use of Spanish for administration and justice, was an egregious and illegal violation of the original union agreement.[57]

In 1881 Valentí Almirall, a lawyer and leader of the Federalist Party in Barcelona, founded the Catalan Center. Blessed with ample family wealth, he abandoned courtroom practice to dedicate himself to journalism, politics, and propaganda.[58] Almirall broke with Federalists in three ways. First, Catalanism was neither revolutionary nor antimonarchical but sought to court comfortable middle classes, appeal to persons of various ideological beliefs, and incorporate conservative participants in the literary renaissance. Second, he and his colleagues were not concerned with proposals to reform the rest of Spain, which they considered to be so riddled with corruption and oligarchy as to be a burden that could only impede Catalonia from realizing its potential. In *Lo catalanisme* (1886), he argued that Catalonia — like

Hungary — should be granted its own elected, self-governing legislature because of its "particular" or privileged status. Third, while federalism was undergirded by philosophical principles that promised to bring democracy closer to the people, Catalanism derived its legitimacy from law, history, culture, and economy: Catalonia deserved to recapture its ancient liberties, which had been illegally violated by Philip V; economic ascendancy mandated the creation of institutions consonant with the technological needs of industry; and the vitality of law, language, culture, and custom made the region deserving of political autonomy.[59] During much of the 1880s, Almirall and his followers collaborated with juridical associations and other pressure groups to defend Catalan law. They did not instantaneously convince colleagues to abandon dynastic parties and to flock to the Catalan Center, but the civil-code conflicts made Catalanism respectable and popularized it for future generations.

As occurred with nationalism throughout Europe, Catalanism migrated from the Center-Left to the Center-Right. This shift took place during the second half of the 1880s when conflicts over the coming of the Spanish Civil Code, paired with tariff disputes, drew prominent individuals and associations to the cause. In 1886 a group of conservatives, many of whom were active within literary circles, split from the Catalan Center, which they felt was too secular and democratic, and launched the Catalan League (Lliga de Catalunya). These men shared affinities with "regionalism," a doctrine that sought to return political life to local communities and Catholic values in order to regenerate a society corrupted by the dehumanizing effects of industrialization and political centralization. The most dynamic new presence, however, was the Catalanist Student Center (Centre Escolar Catalanista), an organization led by law students and also founded in 1886. Although most of its members hailed from the political Right, not all were traditionalists. Many latched onto novel theories of race and degeneration then running rampant in Europe. During the first decade of the twentieth century, veterans of the Student Center popularized the term "nationalism." Nationalism was like "Catalanism," insofar as it supported home rule, but it fortified romanticist claims with the potent formula of Herderian national self-determination mixed with anthropological and biological theories of ethnicity. As such, Catalonia deserved political autonomy not only because of historic, cultural, and economic reasons but also because Catalans were ethnically distinct from and — according to a few imaginative souls — more European and Aryan than other Spaniards.[60] Like Catalanism, nationalism remained divided between a republican Left and a regionalist Right. There was one crucial point, though, upon which most agreed: its maximalist demand remained self-government rather than outright separation or independence.

The history of Catalanism is obviously more complex than this overview suggests. As elsewhere, the vexed question of origins has generated virulent, and at times acrid, debates.[61] Rather than taking a side, the purpose of this summary has been to provide background, to outline the various sources from which modern nationalism sprung, to foreshadow the crucial contribution of the bar, and to underscore that a formal and identifiable political movement emerged late. In order to avoid misinterpretation, the emphasis on late emergence is not meant to cast doubt upon nationalism's legitimacy but only to warn against viewing the rich history of Barcelona as merely a precursor. It is hoped that the analysis of how law and identity became interlaced in Catalonia will open the door to further study in Europe. Barcelona lawyers worked with texts and sources from a Catalan legal tradition, came to embrace historicist and organicist ideas about law and society, and formed a robust corporate group able to confront an oligarchic state over the civil law. Many lawyers and students imported jural ideas into the political sphere and doubled as early ideologues and organizers; their vibrant leadership of protonationalist organizations was a major reason behind the movement's widening appeal and growing strength. However, other subjects are given equal weight. The book concludes with nationalism, but it opens with enlightenment and revolution.

2 *The Modern Profession*
OLD REGIME AND ENLIGHTENMENT

> As this used to be a career in which one could regularly achieve the most honorable positions, many young nobles and rich persons dedicated themselves to the study of practical jurisprudence and the practice of law to the great benefit of a public concerned that such men be of honor and decorum. But now it is rare that this class applies itself to lawyering, as a vulgar mode of thinking has come to prevail in these reigns that equates the practice of law with the practice of the poor.
> ∾ *Representation to King Charles III from Deputies from the Crown of Aragon* (1760)

> In order to depopulate a kingdom, there is no better means than to increase the number of nobles, of state employees, of lawyers, notaries, proctors, agents, and others. To populate it, there is nothing better than a reform of the classes.
> ∾ Francesc Romà i Rosell, *Signs of Happiness in Spain and the Means to Bring Them into Fruition* (1768)

> Let us say to them, sirs, to those men who dare insult our profession: without civil laws no people can live who are not barbarous; without a class of citizens occupied in knowing them, interpreting them, and defending them, nothing can reign except despotism or anarchy and disorder.
> ∾ Manuel Barba i Roca, *A Discourse on Lawsuits* (1781)

WHEN DID THE modern profession emerge? This question, once the focus of an entrenched debate, is worth resuscitating because it has not been satisfactorily answered with regard to the legal profession. At one time, sociologists confidently contended that industrialization and the rise of a modern bureaucratic state were the handmaidens of professionalism. Under the Old Regime, professionals were depicted as gentlemanly practitioners dependent on elite patronage and organized into closed, uncompetitive, privileged corporations. The foundation of state-sponsored systems of education, teaching "scientific" disciplines and awarding degrees on the basis of competitive examination, were said to have made the professions more accessible, and made services more widely available, to a broader sector of the populace.[1] In contrast, historians of early modern and medieval Europe have stressed that many characteristics associated with professionalism were present centuries before invention of the steam engine or the civil-service exam. With respect to lawyers, it was as early as the eleventh or twelfth century when violent, sacred, and ritualistic means of private dispute resolution became less frequent, and courts of normative justice began to settle down and operate with received Roman law. Thereafter, the continental advocate evolved into a university-educated, fee-charging practitioner with clients ranging from peasant communities to artisans to merchants to aristocrats to various corporations, from the smallest guild to the mighty Roman Catholic Church.[2]

With time, this debate has waded into the tepid waters in which reasonable minds have agreed to recognize the dialectical forces of change and continuity. On the one hand, it is accepted that lawyers constitute a slowly evolving and resilient profession that has maintained a monopoly over a discrete body of knowledge, namely the law, for centuries; on the other hand, it is also acknowledged that enormous changes in recruitment and training, client profiles, and professional culture took place in modern times.[3] Although this balanced analysis sounds reasonable, its terms are still too loose. It is still necessary to locate the emergence of the modern profession and to identify its salient attributes. This chapter does this by examining the rise of professionalism in the eighteenth century when the bar overcame a crisis in litigation, prestige, influence, and numbers; abandoned its attachment to urban nobility; integrated Enlightenment thought into legal reasoning; raised practical jurisprudence to scholarly heights; and adopted the lineaments of a professional ethos suited to the needs of private practitioners representing middle-class clients in a competitive environment.[4]

To be sure, the eighteenth century was the key period of transformation. Sociological perspectives are correct insofar as they have emphasized that the professions underwent a fundamental change in the modern era. However, with respect to the bar, this did not occur in the nineteenth century, at the behest of the bourgeoisie and as a consequence of industrialization, but in the eighteenth century when lawyers took advantage of preindustrial economic growth, responded to their loss of status under absolutism, and adopted a modern professional ethic that would later be borrowed by other groups seeking to emulate their success and to carve out new areas of expertise. Shifting the birth of modern professionalism from industrialization to the Enlightenment is no chronological nuance but is crucial to understanding subsequent events. For the bar embarked on the nineteenth century not as an obstreperous corporation dependent on elite patronage and privilege but as a relatively meritocratic and moderately enlightened place consisting of practitioners from a range of family backgrounds, with diverse clienteles, who were aware — perhaps to a greater degree than any other group — of the tremendous tensions existing in society on the verge of the disintegration of the Old Regime. As we shall see in the following chapter, lawyers were well positioned and brilliantly equipped to take advantage of opportunities in the age of revolution. Again, the goal is not to tell a triumphal story of success but to explain why lawyers became so prominent in the modern era.

The historian Christopher Brooks has characterized the eighteenth century as a period of "decline and rise" of the bar.[5] Although his study is limited to England, the description also fits continental trends. In concrete terms, the old bar declined, and a modern one emerged. In the sixteenth and seventeenth centuries, lawyers had represented a range of clients with civil disputes from a wide swath of society, and litigation had been a more regular occurrence, a more general and less exceptional manner of dispute resolution than it ever had been or would be in history. However, at some point in the early modern period, in some places earlier and in others later, the volume and diversity of legal business dried up and litigation rates fell.[6] The reasons for this were not uniform and need to be studied on a case-by-case basis, but with respect to Catalonia, and other places on the continent, absolutism was the cause. Bureaucratic bodies increasingly made law, resolved conflicts, and mediated disputes in lieu of courts. Lawyers no longer worked as political counselors and intermediaries to the extent that they had in the past, and no longer spent as much time engaged in jurisdictional jockeying between municipal, regional, and royal bodies, and between the numerous corporations of the Old Regime.[7] Yet, amid falling rates of litigation and an attendant decline in status, Catalan lawyers reorganized, adjusted their practices to changing circumstances, and opened new frontiers.

In Barcelona, a statistical perspective of this "decline and rise" can be gained by measuring the number of lawyers per inhabitant. Table 1 shows that, following the implantation of absolutism under Philip V in 1716, the number of lawyers in the city decreased sharply. After bottoming out, the bar

Table 1. Lawyers per 10,000 Inhabitants in Barcelona

Year	Total Number of Lawyers	Approximate Population	Lawyers per 10,000 Inhabitants
1389	39	40,000	10
1589	130	35,000	37
1716	165	30,000	55
1759	109	75,000	15
1802	215	115,000	19
1847	329	160,000	21
1887	653	270,000	24

Sources: For figures running between 1359 and 1716, see Amelang, "Barristers and Judges," 1269. For population figures after 1716, see Figuerola, *Estadística de Barcelona en 1849*, 34–37, and CPE (1887). For numbers of lawyers after 1716, see ACA, RA, legs. 139, 154, 159; and LACB (1847, 1887).

gradually recovered. Beginning in the second half of the eighteenth century and continuing into the nineteenth, the number increased in both absolute and relative terms. The table also contextualizes the extent of the recovery: lawyers would never constitute as large a percentage of population as they did during the early modern period, just as litigation would never be such a routine manner of dispute resolution among the populace as a whole. Statistics obviously do not tell the whole story, but the drastic decline in the density of lawyers in the eighteenth century, followed by a steady resurgence, clearly indicates that the bar was amid a significant period of transformation.

The rest of this chapter examines what was behind these numbers by discussing the characteristics of legal practice, the reception of a modern professional ethic, and the influence of the Enlightenment on juridical culture. Before doing this, however, it is helpful to review the doldrums in which the bar found itself at midcentury when it was at its historical nadir. In order to understand the direction in which the bar was heading, it is necessary to examine from where it came.

The Bar at a Historical Nadir

Visitors to eighteenth-century Barcelona were more impressed by the city than its bar. The city was amid an era of prosperity, but lawyers were no longer as prominent as they had once been. A burgeoning cotton calico–printing industry, one of the largest in Europe, was the motor force of a dynamic economy. Catalans were then earning the reputation of an "industrious people," a description often juxtaposed to other Spaniards, stereotypically thought to be pretentious and slothful.[8] In 1787 the English traveler Henry Swinburne described Catalans as a "hardy, active, industrious race."[9] In addition to mercantile activity, he was struck by the heavy fortifications, the size of the army, and of the massive Citadel Fortress, constructed by Philip V following the War of Spanish Succession (1702–14) to ensure that the rebellious city would never again raise arms against the crown: "Seven thousand men form the garrison of Barcelona, of which four thousand two hundred are guards; the rest Swiss and dragoons."[10] In 1786 and 1787, another traveler, Joseph Townsend, undertook a meticulous appraisal of activities, detailing religious practices, farming, medicine, and the techniques of printers, chocolatiers, and cotton, silk, and wool manufactures. Upon visiting the Audiencia, the region's highest court, he was more impressed by the palace's architecture than the activities of those inside. He dryly recorded there were "199 advocates" and that "the process is by written evidence, and the only parties visible in court are the judges and the pleaders."[11]

Lawyers went about their business without generating much commotion. Juridical life had not always been so dull. On the contrary, elite jurists had once been at the epicenter of politics. During the seventeenth century, they had sat on assemblies representative of the estates and had served as counselors for multiple corporations of the Old Regime — from the guilds to the municipalities to the estates to the crown — where they had engaged in jurisdictional jockeying under the "constitutions" of Catalonia. Ongoing disputes between crown and principality over taxation, conscription, and royal succession had grown acrid, leading to the outbreak of two wars, both of which Catalonia lost.[12] The second, the War of Spanish Succession, brought lasting consequences. Philip V, Spain's first Bourbon king, implanted absolutism in Catalonia, and abolished all representative bodies, hence suppressing platforms from where elite jurists had wielded influence and power. In prerevolutionary France, a few lawyers published briefs, which doubled as political pamphlets and wrought havoc on royal, aristocratic, and ecclesiastical authority.[13] In Barcelona, jural pamphleteering had occurred in the seventeenth century when constitutional disputes had sparked political crises; but in the eighteenth century, brief publishing was prohibited without official permission.[14] Even if this had not been the case, few were worthy of attention. The courts were, for the most part, clogged with lawsuits involving inheritance, property, contract, and other matters that were heavy on facts and rarely touched on controversial points of law, not to mention politics.

In addition to falling numbers, another sign of decline was the dwindling presence of nobility at the bar. In the early modern period, many distinguished or well-connected jurists had obtained the title "honored citizen" (*ciutadà honrat*) and by the seventeenth century had come to form the bulwark of a *noblesse de robe* that dominated representative posts on municipal and regional political assemblies. It has been estimated that as much as 10 percent of the bar held titles of nobility.[15] The Bourbons, however, ceased to award this title to lawyers with the same frequency as their predecessors, the Habsburgs. From 1719 to 1795, records reveal that out of more than 1,100 calls to the Catalan bar, court scribes registered only 32 honored citizens, while an additional 8 held the title of knight (*cavaller*) and 1 was described as a *hidalgo infanzón*.[16] This is not a definitive count as there were other whiffs of nobility around: some lawyers came from families in which an older brother or cousin held a patent; a few inherited or acquired one later in life; and court notaries may not have recorded all titles. Nonetheless, the days in which elite lawyers were prominent members of an urban aristocracy had become a memory of yesteryear. In 1589 a local chronicler, Hieronim de Jorba, had observed that "lawyers are in this city very principal persons."[17] By the eighteenth century, it did not cross anyone's mind to utter such (reluctantly) glowing terms. Complements were reserved for those representatives of the industrious and entrepreneurial spirit. As the French diplomat Jean François Peyron pithily observed in 1772, "The citizens are all merchants, tradesmen, or manufacturers."[18]

Decline was not a gradual phenomenon only to be appreciated by hindsight. Lawyers were themselves conscious that better days lay in the past and, when given the chance, expressed frustration over their deteriorating status. This chance came in 1759 when the enlightened monarch Charles III ascended to the throne and, in a sign of goodwill, convoked what he called "Cortes." He invited notables from the various Spanish kingdoms to air complaints and to offer suggestions on how to improve royal administration. In response, the enlightened lawyer Francesc Romà, the public defender at the Barcelona Audiencia, authored, in whole or in part, a polemical declaration known as the *Representation to Charles III*.[19] It consisted of a list of grievances from the Crown of Aragon, in which those of Barcelona lawyers featured prominently. Under normal circumstances, Romà would never have dared write such a damning condemnation of royal justice. The Spanish monarchy did not tolerate public criticism, and the Inquisition had the power to censor materials deemed heretical and treasonous. But the royal invitation granted the enlightened advocate a rare license to voice discontent to an enlightened monarch who had turned a sympathetic ear. The ferocity of the language revealed the presence of deep-seated frustrations. That Romà was recognized to write on behalf of the Crown of Aragon indicates that his words must have had widespread support among colleagues at the bar.

The *Representation* beseeched Charles III to abandon the ways of his Bourbon predecessors and to return to the Habsburg policy in which native lawyers and clerics had possessed a monopoly on appointments to the bench and the pulpit within the Crown of Aragon. Under the Bourbons, natives were not barred from achieving these coveted positions, but it was more difficult than before. Spain's first two Bourbon kings, Philip V and Ferdinand VI, preferred to mix natives with outsiders, a policy based on the supposition that candidates born and bred in distant locales were less dependent on local networks of power and patronage, less prone to venality, and more faithful to the crown. The framers of the *Representation*, however, were not convinced by this principle of Bourbon statecraft, which was applied not only in the Crown of Aragon but in many of the other kingdoms as well. Although the reasoning was sound, the authors maintained that royal appointees were themselves notoriously corrupt and routinely solicited and accepted bribes. The document depicted royal judges (*alcaldes mayores*) as a "troop of young men with the university degree of lawyer" who "confused the good men with the bad." In order to finance their gluttonous life-styles, they dispatched their bailiffs "not to remedy abuse but to come to an understanding with the guilty provided they were not poor."[20]

In addition to the atrocious quality of judges and the widespread presence of corruption, the authors complained that royal authorities treated candidates from the Crown of Castile with blatant favoritism. They pointed out that some two-thirds of magistrates at the *audiencias* in the Crown of Aragon came from other kingdoms in Spain, but only one Valencian, two Aragonese, and not a single Catalan were among the more than one hundred high peninsular magistrates found in other kingdoms.[21] Aggravating the situation, appointments in Spanish America were just as discriminatory.[22] In order to redress this grievance, the authors did not request that more Crown of Aragon natives ascend to judicial offices elsewhere. Instead, the goal was to convince Charles III to return to the way things once were when judges and magistrates were natives, "understood perfectly the native language," and were versed in the laws and customs of the region.[23] To top things off, the framers contended that the cumulative effect of Bourbon reforms had caused the bar to lose prestige and become a less-attractive career destination. They histrionically decried that what had once been a calling of "nobles and rich persons... of honor and decorum" had deteriorated into the province of the "poor."[24]

From all perspectives, then, and even in their own words, the bar was at a historical nadir. The days of a *noblesse de robe* were long gone, distinguished advocates no longer served as venerated counselors to political bodies, talented forensic minds did not ascend to the bench with the frequency of the past, and the bar had become a career destination for the so-called poor. No doubt, a few advocates felt suffocated within a walled city, rapidly expanding in population, where royal appointees and army officers — many recruited from outside the region and ignorant of local laws, customs, and language — dominated positions of authority and political power. Under absolutism, the army had replaced the bar, not only in Spain but in Europe as a whole, as the chief place for the recruitment of royal bureaucrats.[25] What is more, things did not improve, for the *Representation* fell on deaf ears. Although Charles III and his enlightened ministers would eventually win over much of the Barcelona legal community, appointment policies remained unchanged. Nonnative judges and magistrates, unfamiliar with local laws, customs, and language in Catalonia, continued to garner coveted positions.[26] Moreover, royal justice remained subject to virulent criticism, as accusations of corruption became a common refrain. In the early nineteenth century, one Catalan jurist asserted that the chief reason why much of the populace had joined revolutionary causes was because so many had suffered at the hands of cruel and arbitrary judges (*alcaldes mayores*), the public face of royal authority in the large towns.[27] One pamphlet from the 1820s inveighed against judges and mayors who, in order to satiate their anger and line their wallets, would take advantage of "one legal transgression of a head of household to confiscate his wealth and leave his family on the street."[28]

From a comparative perspective, the saga of Catalan lawyers was by no means exceptional, as the decline of the bar under absolutism was a common theme throughout continental Europe. In many respects, Barcelona lawyers were undergoing in the eighteenth century something similar to what French lawyers had been experiencing for a longer time. In the *Dialogue of the Advocates of the Paris Parliament* (1602), Parisian lawyers had famously complained that prejudicial royal policies had led to "lowering of the honor of lawyers."[29] The situation in France was different. In search of revenue, the French monarchy had made magisterial and other public offices venal and heritable, a policy that, in the long run, prevented elite lawyers from being appointed to the *parlements* and high public office and hence impeded their entrance into the magistracy and nobility. During the seventeenth and eighteenth centuries, French lawyers intermittently but insistently griped about poor treatment and loss of noble status. By so doing, they exaggerated the extent to which lawyers had been noble in the past.[30] In contrast, the Catalan bar began its decline at a later date and suffered less severely. Even in the late eighteenth century, a few lawyers were noble and it was still possible to be appointed to the bench. However, it is clear that in Catalonia and France, and surely many other places as well, absolutism had taken a toll on the bar.

The Catalan bar would recover from these doldrums and cease to yearn for a return to the past. Although the *Representation* appears to have been unceremoniously shelved at the royal court, the Barcelona bar overcame the source of its discontent. Economic and demographic growth generated more legal business, and advocates became as industrious as merchants and manufacturers. Crucially, the ability to ascend to judgeships became less important to acquiring prestige. Although lawyers surely continued to grouse privately about discriminatory appointment policies, they ceased to wish for a return to the halcyon days of urban nobility. This was not a conscious process where spokesmen acted as directors of an enterprise who adjusted strategies and their corporate ethos to take advantage of favorable market conditions. Something of the sort did occur, although the process of adaptation was not the result of an abrupt shift in opinion. Rather, it took place gradually. Lawyers followed the market, sought out diverse clienteles, pursued opportunities in multiple forums, directed intellectual energies toward practical jurisprudence, and embraced a new "professional" ideology. As in the rest of Europe, rising numbers of advocates, and their conspicuous assertiveness, provoked ardent debates: opinions differed over whether they were friend or foe to monarchical authority and good governance.

Lawyers and Their Practices

Even at the bar's ebb, lawyers should not be taken at their own words. Few would qualify as "poor" by today's standards. When the authors of the *Representation* complained that many practitioners were "poor," they did not mean genuinely indigent. Rather, they referred to persons without personal fortunes whose success and status were dependent on the fruits of their labors — in other words, the practice of law. According to an urban guidebook for 1787, the majority of lawyers lived in the physical center of the city, a close walking distance to the Plaça Sant Jaume where the Audiencia Palace was located. This was a neighborhood of moderate-to-high property values where families associated with royal, municipal, and ecclesiastical administration resided. Within the winding streets, an advocate frequently crossed paths with colleagues from the bar, and the numerous notaries, proctors, clerks, scribes, magistrates, councillors, and other officials who staffed the Audiencia, the Ecclesiastical Palace, the Inquisition, the Intendencia (tax authority), the municipality, and other such bodies. Lawyers did not tend to live on streets of the highest property values where much of the nobility traditionally resided: Carrer Montcada, Carrer Ample, and the streets surrounding the splendorous parish of Santa Maria del Mar and the Royal Palace. Nor did many live in manufacturing zones where the bulk of the truly indigent dwelled. Judging by the locations of their homes, lawyers were firm if not quintessential members of the juridical and administrative middle classes.[31]

Another perspective on the place of lawyers in society can be gained by examining social origins. Unfortunately, we do not have access to information for the eighteenth century, given that the Audiencia did not conserve notarized copies of baptismal certificates of bar applicants until the 1820s. It is worth examining the available data at this point, however, because the structure supporting the local society and economy in the 1820s had not changed significantly since the late eighteenth century. Steam power had not yet come to Barcelona, so the city still had a proto-industrial economy. Furthermore, economic and demographic growth had stagnated from the 1790s to the late 1820s because of the reverberations of the French Revolution followed by the devastating effects of the war against Napoleon. For this reason, social mobility had probably not increased (or decreased) significantly. The guilds and the rest of Old Regime society, though on their last legs, were still in place. Table 2 provides a rough idea of the preindustrial composition of the bar, or, at the very least, the direction it was heading.

Table 2 should be regarded as providing a general guide rather than a precise assessment. Although based on data of aspirants who sought admission more than a half a century after the publication of the *Representation*, it bears out the observation that the profession had ceased to be the province of the wealthy and had become a destination for persons without vast familial riches attempting to maintain or better their station in life. Precise conclu-

Table 2. Social Origins of Bar Applicants to the Barcelona Audiencia, 1823–1833

Father's Occupation	Number of Applicants (%)
Noble	10 (14)
Peasant	14 (19)
Lawyer	7 (9)
Other professionals and royal officials	10 (14)
Commerce/manufacture	15 (20)
Artisan	18 (24)
Total	74 (100)

Source: ACA, RA, exps. (1823–33), cajas 56–140. Some 125 men applied for bar examinations during this period. Of these applications, 74 contained descriptions of the father's occupation or status within the baptismal certificate.

sions should not be drawn from this information alone, for descriptions were often vague. For example, the broad category "peasant" includes the *pagès*, who could be any sort of farmer. A member of the gentry, who did not have a title but was still considered a "baron," was sometimes called a *pagès*; at the same time, the description could include someone with a secured tenancy, a freeholder, or even a sharecropper, also sometimes called *pagès labrador* or just *labrador* (worker). In a like manner, men of commerce — usually *del comerç* or *comerciant* — ranged from rich colonial capitalists, to currency traders, to wholesalers, to smaller brokers and dealers. Artisans include velvet makers, silk makers, and silversmiths, some of whom were among the city's wealthiest men, to humble tailors, bottle makers, roofers, carpenters, or handrail makers. With these considerations in mind, it is worth taking note that almost 25 percent of the sample came from artisan families, while many of those persons described as peasants and merchants were probably not from families with vast wealth. The considerable percentage of lawyers from popular origins would continue throughout the nineteenth century. To be sure, the preindustrial bar was already open to children from ascending families seeking social advancement.

Aside from the vagueness of some of the descriptions, the data have another important limitation. They include only applicants who took qualifying exams at the Barcelona Audiencia but not the many who took them in Madrid at the Royal Council, the highest court in Spain. A candidate who passed in Barcelona became a "Lawyer of the Royal Audiencia" and was permitted to practice throughout the Audiencia jurisdiction, which included all royal courts located within Catalonia. By qualifying in Madrid, however, a candidate received the prestigious title "Lawyer of the Royal Councils" and was granted a license to appear in any of the kingdoms on the peninsula or in the empire. Because the horizons of persons who chose this latter route extended beyond Catalonia, it is likely that a greater percentage of them came from wealthy, mobile, or at least status-conscious families. Given this omission, Table 2 may understate the proportion of lawyers who came from society's upper echelons. On balance, advocates were recruited from an ample swath of society. They were scions of lawyers, notaries, royal officials, army officers, merchants, agrarian gentry, enterprising farmers and sharecroppers, and upwardly mobile artisan families. For the most part, they were neither noble nor "poor" (as we understand the term today) but from families of middling social status.

The road to the bar was clearly mapped out. To prepare a son for law, parents first needed to provide him with an education in Latin and Spanish grammar, after which he could study for a university degree. The University of Cervera, a day's trip by horseback and two or three days by foot from Barcelona, was the sole university in Catalonia. Many students attended one of the others in the Crown of Aragon — Huesca, Zaragoza, and Valencia — and even a few went to universities in the Crown of Castile, such as Salamanca or Alcalá de Henares. It was common for students to rotate between universities, beginning study at one and then packing up and trying their luck elsewhere, mixing and matching courses to piece together a degree. A bachelor's degree could be obtained in as few as four years while a doctorate took a minimum of six. Rules for bar admission, approved in 1771, obliged all aspirants to pass through an apprenticeship stage — four years for bachelors and two for doctors. As such, eight years was the minimum amount of time a student needed to dedicate to study and training before he could take the bar exam.[32] At university, a student studied "scholarly jurisprudence," which, for the most part, was synonymous with "Roman law" or the *ius commune*. As an apprentice, he would learn "practical jurisprudence," which included procedure as well as royal and municipal law, the *ius proprium*.[33] An apprentice "dedicated himself to the study and practice of local law and procedure, spending time reading cases and practical and forensic books." He was immersed in "the study of practical authors and the drafting of different kinds of documents." He helped his mentor in "managing and dispensing of all sorts of judicial matters, civil as well as criminal."[34]

Bar examination was a "baptism by fire" rather than a means to weed out the unqualified. Once a candidate had obtained a degree and had undertaken a stint as an apprentice, either in one office or in a number of offices, as was often the custom, it was assumed he would pass the exam. Beginning in 1771, all applicants were required to suffer a preliminary exam before a board of practicing lawyers in Barcelona, who were periodically appointed by the regent, the chief magistrate of the Audiencia. In theory, the board was supposed to act as a filter and approve only those candidates ready to pass, so as not to waste the magistrates' time. The afternoon before the Audiencia exam an aspirant would visit the examining magistrates in their homes, the last being the most junior, who would hand him papers of a sample lawsuit. The candidate would then toil by candlelight preparing a full written legal analysis, which he would deliver orally in front of a panel of seven magistrates the following morning. The exam consisted of a single question: "What sentence would you give if you were a judge in this case?" Afterward, the weary-eyed and nerve-wracked applicant waited outside chambers: if he heard a bell ring, this meant success, after which he would be administered the oath; if silence reigned, the panel set a retake date.[35] This process could be repeated a number of times until a candidate passed or, on the rare occasion, gave up trying, at least in Barcelona. The Audiencia exam did not undergo major changes until it was abolished in 1837, when liberal reformers deemed that a university degree was itself equivalent to a license to practice. Thereafter, graduates were given the right to appear in courts in Spain without having to undergo a bar exam.[36]

As the bar began to swell in size, magistrates, under royal pressure, became more exacting. In 1790 they voiced discontent over the quality of the candidates that the practicing lawyers' board ferried over to the Audiencia for final examination.[37] Failure could give rise to pathetic pleas for leniency. In 1786 an applicant named Joan Soler failed the exam twice, each time suffering from shortness of breath or hyperventilation (*sufocación*). He begged the magistrates to pass him anyway, observing that an exception had been made in "similar cases." Unconvinced, they ordered him to retake the exam for a third time.[38] In 1790 another candidate failed, also unable to utter a word, having been made nervous by the "impression of solemnity of the Court." After denying the request to be examined "privately in his house," the magistrates instructed him to return in four months time.[39] Some excuses were more original than others. Josep Estany requested an instant retake because he would suffer unbearable "shame" upon having to convey the bad news to his aged parents. Josep Matas, in an altogether pedestrian attempt at emotional blackmail, implored the examining magistrates to let him try again: "His seven-month pregnant wife is in the city, and he would be unable to tell her the outcome, which, if she should be made aware, would put her in risk of a miscarriage to which she has a propensity upon hearing any bad news."[40] In 1801 the regent again admonished the board of examining lawyers for sending over ill-prepared candidates "only capable of presenting weak exams," causing them to fail "in prejudice to their honor, interests, and family."[41]

Once a candidate had passed the exam, he was theoretically free to represent clients in court. Barcelona did not have a guild of lawyers or any sort of numerical ceiling, so after an applicant had taken the oath, he instantly became a full-fledged member of the tribe. It is unlikely that many aspiring practitioners immediately headed off on their own; most probably continued to work under the tutelage of a mentor for some time. Lawyers were known as *letrados* (men of letters), as they had been for centuries, or *profesores*, although this latter description would fall out of use by the early nineteenth century. In some years, Audiencia magistrates attempted to limit calls to the bar. This occurred in 1780 when they carried out a policy "not to admit anyone unless they intended to apply themselves to another calling."[42] Yet young men were never kept out for very long. Rising numbers of university graduates showed up with certificates in hand, demanding to be let into the club; a year of low enrollment, perhaps a result of ad hoc if not arbitrary Audiencia measures, was often followed by an abnormally high one.

In many countries, judicial power was riddled with numerous special courts with overlapping and competing jurisdictions. This was not the case in Catalonia where the New Foundation of 1716 had overhauled and rationalized judiciary and had imposed a rather intelligible hierarchy. At the top of the pyramid was the Audiencia. Presided over by a regent, the highest royal appointee in Catalonia next to the captain general, it housed one penal and two civil chambers, each of which comprised five magistrates. Civil magistrates were known as "hearers" (*oidores*) while criminal ones were called "crime mayors" (*alcaldes de crimen*). The Audiencia heard appeals coming from lower royal courts, presided over by judges (*alcaldes mayores*), as well as from seigneurial courts. This intelligible structure, however, was complicated by the fact that the Audiencia also exercised original jurisdiction in many instances; moreover, upon petition, it could assume the jurisdiction of — or "evoke" — a case that had commenced in front of a lower royal court.

The Audiencia was obliged to hear cases in first instance or by "evocation" when a victim or litigant was a royal or ecclesiastical official or institution, a pauper, or someone vulnerable to having the scales of justice tipped against him or her in local courts because of lack of status. This latter category included minors, widows, rape and rapture victims, invalids, and orphans. In 1769 the organization of justice in Barcelona underwent a major change to accommodate rising populations. The crown ordered criminal magistrates, who apparently were not busy enough (as criminal appeals must have been cursory affairs), to double as municipal judges and to adjudicate criminal and civil cases in the first instance.[43]

In spite of widespread accusations of incompetence and corruption expressed in the *Representation*, it would be a mistake to assume that courts dispensed rough justice without regard to form or style. Although *alcaldes mayores* were accused of being avaricious men who had received their jobs through the notorious system of spoils and patronage centered in Madrid, they held law degrees. If their decisions did not exude brilliance and avoided going into great depth on the mysteries and nuances of law, they did convey the impression of competence. Insofar as accusations of corruption and abuse of power were aired, these tended to concern the realm of criminal justice. In the case of civil litigants able to afford evenly matched counsel, judges were not the targets of stinging criticism. The blame for the poor quality of civil justice was usually leveled at lawyers, who had a vested interest in hunting down lawsuits and dragging out cases in order to boost profits. Pleading was undertaken by filing paper motions, and judges interviewed witnesses in the privacy their chambers using interrogatories and counterinterrogatories prepared by council. When hearings were held, sometimes only advocates were present. At court, paperwork was carefully ordered and meticulous attention was paid to procedural detail. Justice was not a public "spectacle" as it was in France and England; aside from annual opening ceremonies, there was little pageantry.[44]

Although lawsuits often involved dramatic disputes — in which passions could be at play, vendettas were sometimes pursued, and suitors had much to gain or lose — legal practice could be dull. Quotidian tasks were mostly tedious and often grueling. Procedure dominated over substance, and questions of fact were more common than questions of law. One can only imagine the delight that a scholarly practitioner must have felt when presented with a borderline legal conundrum that would allow him to delve into commentary in order to fashion a novel legal argument and hence make use of his education. Most of the time, however, advocates and their apprentices were inundated with paperwork, much of which would be quite familiar to the contemporary practitioner. A lawyer frequently met with clients, witnesses, notaries, and proctors; strategic decisions constantly needed to be taken with respect to content and timing of complaints, answers, motions, interrogatories, and briefs. An advocate and a proctor were immersed in constant procedural conversations: what forum to choose, whether to petition to evoke a case to the Audiencia, whether additional parties should be joined or separated, which motions to file and when, which allegations should be asserted, what defenses should be invoked, which witnesses should be called (expert as well as material), how to frame interrogatories, how property should be valued, and so on and so forth.

Civil procedure was intensely bureaucratic. A complaint was followed by answers, responses, and counterresponses. The addition and subtraction of parties caused motions to be repeated. Identifying the parties, and each of their respective allegations and defenses, could take months. Afterward, the case would move to a probatory phase, consisting of the presentation of evidence and the interview of witnesses. There was no examination or cross-examination, but each side would file a series of questions with the judge, who would then depose each witness, in secret and without the presence of lawyers, using these prepared interrogatories. The judge would publish the answers, and then each side filed "articles" and sometimes responses to articles. Here, counsel could seek to modify or rebut what a witness, or a group of witnesses, had offered by asking the judge to examine additional evidence, interview other witnesses, or take into account countervailing factors. After witnesses had been deposed and all evidence presented, a judge would sometimes ask lawyers to file briefs and then counterbriefs, but he often passed by this process when issues of law were not involved and moved straight to oral argument. He would then publish a decision, which could be appealed. Throughout the case, motions and other obstacles frequently delayed or even derailed a case.

Civil appeals were not that different from cases in the first instance. At the Audiencia, a board of magistrates often repeated procedures and reviewed similar evidence. It would take note of what the lower court had done and then, after entertaining motions and responses, examine new witnesses and evidence that each side proposed with the aim to convince them to overturn, confirm, or modify a decision. Then came briefs and rebuttal briefs, more common on appeal than in first instance. Oral argument, if deemed necessary, followed. The Audiencia used internal procedures for ruling on "supplications" (appeals of a point of law), and it was not out of the ordinary for more than one supplication to be raised in a single suit.[45] If a party had a decision reversed because of a supplication, he or she was allowed to bring a "second supplication" to the "Chamber of the One Thousand Five Hundred" at the Royal Council in Madrid. The latter name derived from the fact that supplicants had to deposit 1,500 doblas of gold in order to have the pivotal point of law adjudicated. The exorbitant cost was designed to limit second supplications to instances in which the party was sufficiently convinced of a favorable outcome that he or she was willing to foot the hefty bill.[46] Appeals could delay a lawsuit interminably, and once appealed, it was not uncommon for a case to end up in front of an *alcalde mayor* for one reason or another. First-instance cases often lasted only a few months or, at the most, a few years, but once appealed, months and years could go by for a case to be heard, given backlogs, and more months or years to be resolved. The end of one suit could give rise to another, and complications inevitably arose during the execution of judgments. Cases strung out over the course of a decade were not uncommon and a few dragged on for more than two.

Lawyers took on penal defenses, although their maneuverability was seriously restricted. Criminal procedure was divided into summary and plenary procedures, in which the investigating and sentencing judge was one in the same person. In the summary phase, the judge carried out an investigation. He would interview and interrogate witnesses, collect evidence, and eventually confront the accused with the evidence with the goal to elicit a confession. If unsatisfied with a response, a judge could use torture to extract one. Although the use of torture was on the decline and may have disappeared in some jurisdictions by the second half of the eighteenth century, judges were still at liberty to use it.[47] By the time a case moved to the plenary phase and a lawyer was allowed to enter the process, he was usually facing a situation in which the defendant had already confessed to a crime. Procedure in the plenary phase was similar to that of a civil case. A lawyer could file motions, interrogatories, articles, briefs, and responses, requesting a judge to examine further witnesses and evidence, to reexamine old witnesses and evidence, to pursue a different theory of the case, or to look into mitigating circumstances. Once a sentence was delivered, cases could be appealed to the Audiencia, although there was no appeal for serious crimes such as sedition, treason, heresy, simony, rapture, counterfeiting, and violent crimes resulting in death.

Lawyers were also permitted to appear on the accusatory side, representing a victim or his or her aggrieved family.[48]

As with civil suits, penal appeals went to the Audiencia. Supplication followed similar procedures, although there were no second supplications, so all cases ended in Barcelona. At the Audiencia, either a private lawyer or the public defender (*abogado de pobres*) represented the defendant, while a prosecutor (*fiscal de lo criminal*) pleaded the crown's case. A defendant's lawyer could try to reduce the offense, lower the punishment, or win an acquittal; a prosecutor could ask the magistrates to uphold the verdict, look into additional crimes, or even stiffen sentences. Neither criminal nor civil cases were public trials but ongoing paper proceedings in which lawyers jostled over what evidence and which witnesses would be examined by a judge in the secrecy of his chambers. After a judge had issued the witness responses and his evaluation of the evidence, they then argued over what decision he should arrive at. When Napoleonic troops occupied Barcelona from 1808 to 1814 and commenced plans to integrate Catalonia into France, they were scandalized by the density of this bureaucracy: "Lawyers, in general, are poorly prepared and will not become easily accustomed to public pleading. This litigation style requires study and training that would require them to abandon the habit of pleading by filing multiple papers which confuse matters and assure that cases are needlessly prolonged. This, in turn, assures lawyers of a secure and inflated profit."[49]

In addition to royal courts, lawyers were active in other forums. The Ecclesiastical Palace, located down the street from the Audiencia adjudicated disputes among clergy and also heard various matters involving laymen and women. Some priests and monks held law degrees. Such hybrid professionals — men of the robe and the cloth — were often ecclesiastical-law specialists, but to appear as counsel a person needed only a degree in "canons" and was not obliged to have uttered sacramental vows. A small but important percentage of the bar held degrees in "laws" and "canons," colloquially referred to as "both laws" (*ambos derechos*). During the course of the nineteenth century, royal courts came to usurp many of the functions of ecclesiastical ones, but until this occurred, the church brandished a long jurisdictional arm. A guidebook from 1787 lists four courts at the palace with overlapping personnel: one adjudicated conflicts over feudal domains and tithes; another dealt with sacramental matters such as clergy, marriages, and separations; a third dispensed annulments, absolutions, and excommunications; and a fourth heard disputes over charitable and testamentary gifts.[50] Another court — the Tribunal del Breve — resolved jurisdictional conflicts between royal and ecclesiastical courts.[51] For its part, the Inquisition allowed the accused access to counsel, although, as was the case with criminal matters, an advocate's formal actions were seriously restricted.[52]

Located in the majestic Llotja Palace on the Pla de Palau, the Commercial Consulate was the single forum that lawyers were most eager to exploit. Commerce was booming, and disputes between merchants offered succulent opportunities. Prying open consular courts was one of the great conquests of lawyers everywhere, and this occurred around the globe. In Barcelona, the consulate held jurisdiction over all licensed merchants in Catalonia, adjudging claims arising on land and at sea. The presence of counsel represented a major change from traditional practice. Since their foundation in the Middle Ages, these tribunals were designed to remain insulated from royal and ecclesiastical authority and oversight. Boards of judges, elected from members of a merchant corporation, were left to arbitrate disputes and to decide cases according to the written and customary international laws, practices, and ethics of men of commerce rather than the scholarly law of jurists. In addition to applying their own body of law, bristling with its peculiar features and complicated instruments, consulates also operated with their own philosophy. Although they were committed to upholding fixed rules to foster smooth business relations, they balanced this concern with the need to distribute substantive justice in order to maintain harmony within a closed merchant community. By the mid-eighteenth century, however, things were changing rapidly. Barcelona merchants, no longer grouped into a closed guild, now belonged to a more open chamber of commerce. As business relationships became more complex and anonymous, consular independence was winding to an end. The tribunal employed advocates as full-time consultants (*asesores*), as it had for some time. More importantly, disputants relied on lawyers eager to inject procedures and rules that were thought to deliver a greater degree of fairness and predictability. Advocates represented clients, wrote motions and briefs, and advised judges, even though they were sometimes prohibited from appearing in hearings.[53]

Eager to extend the reach of royal justice and pressured by lawyers, Audiencia magistrates also contributed to the "lawyerization" of mercantile law.[54] By the late eighteenth century, the Audiencia increasingly heard mercantile disputes by routinely invoking special procedures originally designed for exceptional circumstances when evidence of gross corruption had been present within a consular proceeding.[55] To some, this oversight brought a higher quality of justice to a creaking system that had long been corrupt: a web of intersecting business relationships between dominant commercial houses meant that conflicts of interest abounded within an adjudicatory board whose members could negotiate the outcome of a dispute in tandem with future business deals. To others, such creeping judicial interventionism, ever rampant and so characteristic of the era, augmented the problem of litigiousness. As one deputy complained at the legislative convention called by Spanish partisans of Napoleon in Bayonne in 1809, "All businessmen have to resort to a lawyer in order to formulate their defenses, and every mercantile tribunal needs a lawyer to direct its hearings."[56] In the end, lawyers were able to fend off resistance against their assertiveness. In 1830 the Code of Commercial Procedure definitively allowed counsel to represent clients in matters before consular courts.[57]

Most law school graduates wishing to pursue a career as practicing advocates migrated to Barcelona to seek out apprenticeships. For such men, the goal was to open a private practice that would feed off lawsuits at the Audiencia, the courts of first instance, the Commercial Consulate, and the Ecclesiastical Palace. From the late eighteenth to the end of the nineteenth century, between three and four of every six practicing Catalan advocates resided in the city.[58] If a lawyer preferred to practice outside Barcelona, he usually set up residence in a town that was a capital of a jurisdiction known as a *corregimiento*. In these towns, lawyers represented clients in front of the *alcaldes mayores*, worked as prosecutors, and served as "advisers." *Alcaldes mayores*, ordinary mayors, and even seigneurs and their judicial agents often farmed out matters to an adviser if the resolution of a legal question was beyond their expertise, time consuming, or simply too intricate to be bothered with. Not to be overlooked, seigneurial justice was extensive: it encompassed the vast majority of Catalonia, 75 percent of all municipalities and some 55 percent of the population.[59] The seigneurs — or "barons" as they were called in Catalonia — held civil and criminal jurisdiction within their domains.[60] Although a baron or his agent often served as judge for a penal or minor matter, it was advisable that a lawyer be contracted to "instruct" or preside over an important civil or feudal case. Because many of the decisions of baronial courts could be appealed to the Audiencia, it was necessary that magistrates receive orderly paperwork containing coherent arguments grounded in law.[61]

Seigneurial jurisdictions covered much of the agrarian world where lawsuits were less frequent than in royal ones. During the late eighteenth century, however, baronial courts generated a bevy of lawsuits arriving at courts of royal justice, as peasants and their lawyers contested jurisdictions and appealed decisions. At the time, Catalonia, like much of France, was undergoing what historians have labeled an "aristocratic reaction." The rural nobility and the church, faced with declining real value of rents, were trying to reestablish old feudal domains, collect forgotten or new rents and tithes, and charge other lucrative dues. In response, the peasantry did not passively sit by but met such claims with resistance. Many peasants were not only reluctant to assume additional obligations but also eager to establish alodial ownership over secure tenancies that their families had farmed for generations and hence confirm their status as freeholders independent of feudal authority.[62] To use precise terminology, most of these lawsuits were technically not *feudal* but *emphyteutic*. According to the law of emphyteusis in Catalonia and other places in Europe, the "direct" rights of seigneurs, monasteries, convents, and cathedrals, as well as the "usufructory" rights of peasants, were not only passed down from one generation to the next (as feudal obligations were) but could also be bought, sold, divided, and sometimes mortgaged (as contractual rights could). To make matters more complicated, infeudated properties were often subinfeudated or farmed by contractual sharecropping. To be sure, the legal regime of emphyteusis consisted of a confusing hybrid of feudal and contractual forms. Whether it should continue, or how it should be reformed, was to remain one of the most divisive issues in juridical circles throughout the nineteenth and well into the twentieth century.

As might be expected, lawyers appeared on both sides of these lawsuits. Nobles, barons, monasteries, convents, and cathedral chapters contracted advocates to bring and adjudge claims. Peasants holding usufructuary rights were not always hapless victims or even small farmers who worked alone or with the help of family members or a farmhand or two. Many were wealthy and enterprising men with secure tenures, some of whom even subinfeudated their properties or used contractual sharecropping to exploit parcels and, hence, were seigneurs themselves. In short, many could afford to hire lawyers and vigorously fight cases. If a peasant decided to contest a claim, his lawyer would sometimes not bother to conduct a defense in a baronial forum; instead, he would contest jurisdiction in a court of ordinary jurisdiction or appeal a decision to the Audiencia, or both. In an ordinary case, a baron's or an ecclesiastical body's lawyer would produce notarial deeds and sworn statements attesting to the existence of "direct ownership," while the peasant would usually present conflicting documents and testimony. Common defenses were that the seigneur (or ecclesiastical body) did not have jurisdiction or could not establish such property rights; or that the peasant (or his ancestors) had not been bound by, or had not purchased the interest from someone bound by, an emphyteutic agreement; or that the agreement had been modified; or the property was different.[63] Lawyers were neither appendages of the nobility or the church nor spirited activists fomenting peasant resistance. They found themselves smack in the middle of feudal disputes during the waning years of feudalism.

Diverse but recognizable types of lawsuits filled a lawyer's office. Inheritance constituted the most common source of business as issues of testate and intestate succession frequently overlapped with tutelage, trusts, marriage contracts, dowries, and widowhood. In addition to emphyteutic claims, lawyers were deluged with other property matters: sales, rents, evictions; grazing, timber, and water rights; and the use of common mills, easements, and servitudes. Contractual disputes arose when transactions went sour or joint projects unraveled. Unpaid loans, legal and medical fees, and gambling debts were prevalent. The guilds, eager to protect monopolies and capture new forms of business, sued (or were sued by) rival guilds, interlopers, and rebellious members. At the Commercial Consulate, lawyers were immersed in sales, credit, debt, breaches, bankruptcies, partnership disputes, fraud, commercial paper, and insurance. Canon-law specialists took on cases involving legitimacy, marriage, separation, annulment, adoption, tithes, feudal dues, and ecclesiastical crimes. Client profiles were similar to lawyer origins. Litigants were heterogeneous, but for the most part came from middle classes — merchants, artisans, shopkeepers, professionals, and peasants — fighting over property, inheritance, contract, credit, and debt. The corporations of the Old Regime — the church, the nobility, municipalities, peasant corporations, and guilds — provided a large chunk of business, much of it well paying, but did not generate as many lawsuits as commoners.[64]

Lawyer and client were free to negotiate a fee, called an "honorarium." In Catalonia, the traditional rule had been that a lawyer for a given case earned double the fee of the proctor and half of that of the magistrate. Although this law was abolished in 1734, it can be taken as a rough guide to relative earnings: the average lawyer tended to earn much more than the average proctor and much less than an Audiencia magistrate. According to Roman law, lawyers were technically prohibited from charging contingency fees, but a Catalan custom said to exist since "time immemorial," called a *palmari*, allowed lawyer and client to agree upon an additional monetary award if the lawsuit was won. This could have been the typical instance where the exception devoured the rule, although the *palmari*, by the sound of it, was probably a fixed bonus rather than a percentage of the winnings.[65] Whatever the case, it would be naive to think that contingency fees, or some form of them, perhaps disguised as *palmaris*, were not charged. A common species of lawsuit featured a poor plaintiff (or a group of plaintiffs) who disputed an inheritance in which the property in question could be extremely valuable. A poor litigant — or a group of disgruntled and disinherited family members (widows, siblings, and in-laws) — could become instantaneously rich, or quite well-off, if a suit was won. The high stakes of inheritance battles made them theoretically vulnerable to contingency-fee arrangements as did other types of lawsuits with similar characteristics.[66]

A general idea of comparative earnings can be ascertained through tax records. The crown charged each member of a guild or corporation a tax, called a *contribución*. Persons of the wealthiest occupations, such as licensed merchants or currency traders, paid the highest amounts, while those of humbler callings, such as tailors, shoemakers, or coopers, contributed less. Because lawyers did not have a guild, and possibly because they nominally qualified as "noble" for taxation purposes, they were exempt. In the early 1820s, however, lawyers were required to contribute. By this time, a system of gradations had been implemented: a guild was charged a fixed amount based on an average tax per head; this net amount was then redistributed along a sliding scale so that high-earning individuals were charged more and low earners less. Examining tax records for 1823 shows that the average lawyer paid 9,000 reales a year, whereas the average merchant or currency trader paid around 13,000; the average doctor, notary, silversmith, or velvetier contributed 6,000; and a tailor or shoemaker, 3,000. There was much overlap: wealthy artisans — such as the single richest silversmith or velvet maker — were charged about 45,000 reales, roughly the same amount as the top four or five lawyers. The lowest-earning lawyers, many of whom had recently passed their bar exams, contributed 1,000 reales, an amount considerably more than the average tailor or shoemaker.[67] On balance, lawyers had little reason to complain. Only traders, merchants, lenders, and brokers were better off.

The Ethos of Professionalism

As lawyers multiplied in numbers and pushed their way into new forums, their assertiveness did not go unnoticed. Justice was a paramount concern for absolutist monarchs, whether enlightened or not, in all of Europe. Royal ministers, self-styled *philosophes*, and pamphleteers discussed whether and how the legal profession should be reformed. There was never a single "enlightened" view on what the optimal organization of the profession should be. Rather, conflicting opinions were present. On the one hand, admirers of the judicial systems of England and France favored an independent judiciary and bar. The ministers of Charles III seem to have held this belief. The architect of royal policy on lawyers, as well as guilds, was Pedro Rodríguez de Campomanes, whose writings bore the firm imprint of Montesquieu. A commoner from the region of Asturias, he had risen from ordinary litigator to crown counselor (*fiscal*) at the Royal Council through hard work and a ferocious forensic talent.[68] His early reforms — the creation of a board of examiners and the requirement that university doctorates undertake an apprenticeship stage of two years (1771) — had the combined effect of augmenting the corporate power of the Barcelona bar. In 1777 Campomanes sanctioned the creation of a Royal Academy of Practical and Theoretical Jurisprudence in Barcelona as he had in Madrid, Valencia, and Zaragoza. The academies endowed lawyers with an associational presence, promoted practical jurisprudence, and served as moderately enlightened forums.

In contrast, others viewed the independence of the bar and the proliferation of lawyers as a social ill. Prussia represented a different model from those of England or France. Here, the monarchy had fused the advocate and proctor into a single professional — called the "attorney" — who carried out the dual tasks of procedure and pleading. Prussian monarchs had capped numbers, converted attorneys into state functionaries, regulated fees, and submitted their corporate bodies to royal oversight.[69] Such policies came to be considered consistent with the credo of enlightened absolutism, which, among its various tenets, held that constricting the autonomy of lawyers — like limiting the power of the aristocracy — would reduce litigiousness, waste, and inefficiency. These opinions were echoed in Barcelona, where Francesc Romà, an admirer of Frederick the Great, in a rather pretentious display of self-deprecation bundled lawyers and proctors together with nobles as representatives of the "unproductive classes." As others at the time, he suggested that their numbers should be limited.[70]

Lawyers were neither immune to criticism nor ignorant of the presence of debates taking place in associations, in academies, and at the royal court over their future. The type of unscrupulous behavior in which they could become involved was public knowledge. As in all of Europe, Audiencia regulations prohibited advocates from filing frivolous claims or motions, repeating issues on appeal that had been resolved in first instance, discussing a case with the other side, divulging secrets, abandoning clients, switching sides, bribing witnesses, using privileged information for personal gain, charging contingency fees, or padding briefs.[71] These were normal regulations present in tribunals since anyone could remember, reflective of the timeless belief that the adversarial nature of the judicial process offered ample incentive for a lawyer to engage in dilatory tactics and to manipulate procedures. No one would deny that there was a real need for such regulations. Lawyers were entrepreneurial. In their private dealings, they voraciously hunted down business wherever they could, truculently forced their way into multiple forums whether welcome or not, and flirted with the limits of propriety to win. To counteract accusations of greed and sharp practice, the bar strove to present a public face of honor and decorum. During the eighteenth century, however, this public face was changing.

The bar's traditional claim to prestige had rested upon the lofty ideal of a noble profession. When confronting criticism or attempting to assert authority, lawyers instinctively clutched these laurels. In the *Representation to Charles III* (1760), the framers had voiced the wish to return to a golden age when "nobles and rich men" had populated the bar.[72] Five years later, Valencia lawyers published a *Summary of the Privileges, Virtues, and Prerogatives of Spanish Lawyers*, in which they also asserted that lawyers, like judges, should be considered "ministers" of the crown and enjoy full privileges of nobility, including the right to bear arms and to be exempt from taxation and conscription.[73] By the late eighteenth century, however, this appeal reeked of nostalgia and rang false. The monarchy no longer granted noble titles to lawyers as in times past, and only a few could boast distinguished lineages. As everyone was aware, many came from peasant, artisan, and merchant families where children were weaned on entrepreneurial habits more reflective of modern capitalism than classical virtue. The disappearance of Latin was another telltale sign of the decline of Renaissance humanism at the bar. In 1768 Charles III abolished the custom that judicial decisions be published in Latin, requiring them to be published in Spanish. He further mandated that all primary and secondary education take place in Spanish and recommended that university professors follow suit.[74] These measures accelerated the already dwindling use of Latin in legal practice and pedagogy.

Appealing to the tired notion of nobility not only ill suited practitioner profiles but proved to be treacherous discursive terrain. This rhetorical device could be turned around and redeployed against the bar itself. In 1782 the Madrid lawyer Juan Pérez published *A Dissertation on the Free Proliferation of Lawyers*, a pamphlet designed to persuade royal advisers to take strident measures to reduce the size of the bar. The author entertained the suggestion, then being mooted in court circles, that only nobles should be allowed to practice, but in the end he considered this too restrictive. Nonetheless, he recommended that children of ordinary or poor families be prevented from enrolling in the bar. If only wealthy men with independent incomes were granted a license to practice, the assumption was, the quality of advocacy would improve. An advocate who did not depend on his practice for his family's survival or even comfort would have less incentive to be swayed by profit and hence be less tempted to act unscrupulously.[75] Derogatory characterizations peppered the pamphlet: "There are many more bad than there are good lawyers." "It is a shame to see such a noble profession in the hands of many who treat her like a vile whore."[76] The use of "nobility" in this fashion continued. In 1818 Audiencia magistrates issued a circular to clamp down on overzealous criminal defenses. They excoriated lawyers whose briefs were "so prolonged that they were disgusting to read" and accused them of "scandalously abusing and discrediting such a noble profession."[77]

Lawyers were in a difficult position. The hard realities of competitive legal practice in a bustling city made it inevitable that they would face increasing criticism in an age when enlightened minds petitioned monarchs to implement decisive measures aimed at reforming recalcitrant corporations of the Old Regime. Faced with this situation, lawyers abandoned their nostalgic attachment to nobility and embraced a new ethos. This was not an original endeavor, for all lawyers in Europe were undergoing similar stresses and adopting like strategies. Barcelona advocates simply emulated conventions developed elsewhere. Symbolically, they switched manuals. In previous centuries, Coluccio Salutati's *On the Nobility of Law and Medicine* (1399) had provided the central arguments for the aristocratic status of lawyers. In this book, first published in 1542, the Florentine humanist had famously reasoned that nobility was not dependent on lineage but on virtue. In 1693, however, Henri D'Aguesseau's published speech, *The Independence of a Lawyer*, abandoned the obsession with nobility (a logical move because few advocates were noble in France) and set forth a new behavioral code. To D'Aguesseau, lawyers needed to adopt common personality traits designed to defend their moral integrity. They needed to make clear to the public that their sole concern was the pursuit of justice rather than profits, power, or vanity.[78] In order to do this, virtue was no longer enough. In 1785 Antoni Puig, the criminal-law instructor at the Barcelona Royal Academy of Jurisprudence, published a Spanish-language translation of the speech.[79] D'Aguesseau's advocate belonged to a "profession" and strove to display reason, independence, disinterestedness, and incorruptibility. The implication was clear: jurists could no longer derive authority solely from texts, titles, robes, symbols, or etiquette. Being able to speak and write Latin and emulate the rehearsed mannerisms of Renaissance aristocrats had ceased to convey the charisma of times past. In order to justify his utility in society, a lawyer needed to present a studied image that conveyed confidence, independence, probity, integrity, and expertise.

From the speeches at the Academy of Jurisprudence, it is evident that Barcelona lawyers had been absorbing the ethos of their French counterparts by osmosis long before the publication of the translation. This did not mean that lawyers ceased to refer discursively to the virtues of a "noble profession," but they did avoid making explicit arguments in which their authority rested on their noble status. In 1781 the most enlightened lawyer of his generation, Manuel Barba, implored his colleagues to improve the quality of justice in concert with other sciences, so that lawsuits could be resolved quickly and equitably. He admonished them to "listen to the voice of reason that speaks to you from the depths of your own being" and, shamelessly imitating Voltaire, urged them to make clear the "difference between the savage of America and a rich Barcelona citizen." Responding to critics and cynics, he declared: "To those men who dare insult our profession: without civil laws no people can live who are not barbarous; without a class of citizens occupied in knowing them, interpreting them, and defending them, nothing can reign except despotism or anarchy and disorder."[80] In this formulation, lawyers were "a class of citizens" rather than a privileged nobility.

In his speech, Barba referred to the mandates of the "Enlightenment" and of a "a happy revolution that no longer looks for sterile truths but for knowledge useful to society."[81] A few years later, the Audiencia magistrate Miquel Magarola delivered a more conservative address at the academy in which he intentionally avoided mention of telltale markers such as "Enlightenment" or "revolution." Instead, he anchored the attributes of the "perfect lawyer" in the timeless Christian ideals of "honor" and "god, truth, and language." The eminent jurist ignored D'Aguesseau and sought guidance from classical advocates, philosophers, saints, and kings such as Plutarch, Aristotle, Cicero, Justinian, Saint Ambrose, and Jesus Christ (who successfully defended Mary Magdalene from the charge of adultery). At the same time, Magarola also voiced the typical worry of the age — the need to maintain dignity and reinforce honesty. He criticized those lawyers whose "voices serve more to cloud than to clarify" and upbraided "tricky lawyers" whom he described as "errant comets and not the fixed stars of our jurisprudence."[82] What is most striking about the speech, though, is that even Magarola, a traditional rather than an "enlightened" magistrate, depicted lawyers as representative of the *learned* — and not the *noble* — estate. "Jurisprudents, Saints, Jurisconsults, Priests, and Savants" shared the mission to succor individuals "who because of their ignorance cannot assert their rights and their reason, nor defend themselves from the strategic machinations of their adversaries." Although he made passing reference to the "dignity and nobility of advocacy," he consciously chose to avoid making explicit mention of lawyers as nobles and drew no parallels to the aristocracy.[83]

In the late eighteenth century, Barcelona lawyers began to refer to themselves as "professionals" and, by so doing, imported terminology that had long been present in Britain and France but was just then penetrating Spain.[84] The reception of this nomenclature was telling. In the late eighteenth century, lawyers were sometimes grouped into what were called the "classes," an umbrella description that encompassed all persons who lived off the fruits of their labors, be they intellectual or manual. Priests, clerics, doctors, artisans, agrarian day workers, and domestic servants were lumped into the category.[85] This would not do. Lawyers were willing to relinquish their increasingly tenuous, nostalgic, and rhetorical claim on nobility, but they were not content to be relegated to the level of the classes. It would be perhaps too reductionist to argue that the appearance of the word "profession" is proof positive of the coming of modern "professionalism." However, it is no coincidence. During the late eighteenth century, lawyers no longer considered themselves members of either the nobility or the classes but, emulating their counterparts in France, carved out an intermediate space as learned "professionals."[86] As Manuel Barba proclaimed, "We make it a profession to defend it [the truth] and to teach it to men."[87]

Lawyers and the Enlightenment

During the Enlightenment, new forms of public sociability changed the way lawyers held themselves in society. Lenard Berlanstein, in his study of the eighteenth-century bar at the *parlement* in nearby Toulouse, has observed that advocates ceased to limit their intellectual pursuits to law but broadened their horizons and raised their profiles by participating in royal academies, frequenting private salons, entering essay and poetry competitions, and dabbling in literary and scientific endeavor. With respect to politics, they were broadly constitutionalist; some were versed in the *philosophes*, from Montesquieu to Rousseau; and most saw the need to reform penal law and to abolish torture. Yet open-mindedness had its limits: lawyers did not espouse radical ideas questioning the structure of the Old Regime and their privileged place in it.[88] Similarly, studies of the English bar have found that some London barristers were involved in movements of political radicalism and religious dissent, but David Lemmings has shown that the bar "turned its back on substantive enlightenment," resisted calls to reorganize the Inns of Court, and even ignored Blackstone's, not to mention Bentham's, proposal to provide order, structure, and philosophical coherence to the English common law.[89]

In Barcelona, the bar was similarly Janus-faced. Some enlightened advocates engaged in broad cultural pursuits, but the average litigator, occupied with the drudgery of harvesting lawsuits and garnering judgments, was content to wade through Roman law and customary sources and to conduct his practice in the society from which he came and within the institutions with which he was familiar. The University of Cervera, as well as other universities in the Crown of Aragon, harbored a professoriate that ardently defended the Roman-ecclesiastical tradition and exerted a lasting influence on students who passed through its classrooms. Leading law professor Josep Finistres and his colleagues equated literary renaissance not with secular or scientific knowledge but, like many in Spain, with a revival of Jesuit learning.[90] When Charles III expelled the Jesuits from Spain in 1767, the conservatism of Cervera professors was only exacerbated. As university rector, Finistres fought off an enlightened reform of the law school curriculum, promoted by Campomanes and other courtiers, taking place in much of Spain during the 1770s. Unlike universities such as Seville or Salamanca, Cervera did not teach "novel" subjects such as natural law or legal history.[91]

If Cervera was the bastion of traditionalism in Catalonia, then Barcelona was the locus of the Enlightenment. The official Enlightenment could be found in associations sanctioned by royal authority: the Chamber of Commerce, the Royal College of Surgery, the Royal Military College of Mathematics, the Economic Friendly Society, and the Royal Academies of Natural Sciences and Arts, Medicine, Good Letters, and Jurisprudence. In these places, merchants, army surgeons and engineers, lawyers, doctors, aristocrats, literate artisans, and even some clerics digested and debated philosophical ideas. Because no detailed study of the academies exists, we do not have quantitative or qualitative profiles of their participants. Anecdotal information, however, reveals that distinguished lawyers were among the city's most publicly enlightened men. The one with the highest profile was Francesc Romà, who, in addition to serving as public defender, was the founder of the Royal Conference on Physics and Agriculture. Similarly, Manuel Barba was a member of the Academy of Natural Sciences and Arts.[92] Another jurist who moved within such circles was Manuel Sisternes, a Jansenist from Valencia and crown counsel (*fiscal de lo civil*) at the Audiencia in the 1760s and 1770s. In tandem with Romà, Sisternes petitioned royal officials to move the university from Cervera to Barcelona in order to make it more accessible to students, and — although he did not say so directly — to extricate it from its traditional professoriate and endow it with a more enlightened curriculum.[93] Although his exhortation fell on deaf ears, nineteenth-century liberals would carry forth this quest. The university would be moved to Barcelona, first in the early 1820s and definitively in the 1830s.

At the same time, one must be careful not to exaggerate the reach of the Enlightenment in Barcelona. After all, Barcelona was better known for being "industrious" rather than "enlightened." It was no Naples or Edinburgh, and it never came to house any thinkers near the international stature of Giambattista Vico or David Hume.[94] It is revealing that Barcelona's two most prolific enlightened writers — Antoni de Capmany and Francesc Romà — left the city for greener pastures. Capmany, an economic historian and constitutional scholar, headed off to Seville where he joined the intellectual circle of Pablo de Olavide and then went to Madrid where he penetrated the court. For his part, Romà ended up as regent of the Audiencia in Mexico City, perhaps the highest judicial appointment in the empire.[95]

Meanwhile in Barcelona, intense religious devotion coexisted with scientific and practical knowledge. During his visit, Joseph Townsend was shocked to see more than 100,000 people from the city and surrounding areas, exhibiting a feverish devotion, descend onto the streets during Holy Week. At the same time, he praised places dedicated to the dissemination of science: the nautical school, the military academy, the museum of natural history, and the four public libraries, three of which belonged to ecclesiastical bodies and one of which was dedicated to medicine and surgery.[96] There was no public law library. The nineteenth-century historian Josep Coroleu portrayed a similar ambience in a fictionalized account of the city's history. He recounted that some citizens in the 1790s were so pious that upon hearing church bells they would immediately cease conversation and stop dead in their tracks to recite the *Angelus Domini*. Every Saturday evening, the Dominican monks undertook a fantastic procession carrying torches, chanting the rosary, and attracting devout multitudes. In the meantime, others mixed belief with skepticism and met behind closed doors in private *tertulias* where they discussed banned authors such Voltaire, Dupuis, and Volney, hoping to have taken the necessary precautions to avoid the (somewhat benign) gaze of the Inquisition.[97]

The Inquisition was no longer the fearsome tribunal of the Counter-Reformation. Henry Swinburne remarked that "the proceedings of the Inquisition are grown very mild,"[98] while Arthur Young recounted that the Holy Office was chiefly occupied with clamping down on café life and prosecuting persons of "notorious ill fame."[99] First offenders were usually given a warning, and, although the court did imprison repeat offenders, it was conscious of the need to steer clear of controversial prosecutions of prominent men and women. By the eighteenth century, the Inquisition had long ceased to search out crypto-Jews, but was in the business of censorship. Within its unofficial ranking of heretical materials, law was never considered as corrosive as politics or, even worse, novels, which were deemed universally licentious. As far as law was concerned, the Inquisition frequently dispensed licenses to readers wishing to consult banned authors such as Grotius, Pufendorf, Vattel, and Montesquieu, a policy that indicated mild tolerance toward quiet circulation.[100] It was less permissive with respect to Beccaria, given that *Of Crimes and Punishments* contained a virulent condemnation of the Spanish and Portuguese Inquisitions. But the book had been translated into Spanish in 1771, three years before it had been banned, and had achieved a wide readership.[101] One leading Spanish author had incorporated Beccaria's philosophy into his own, so the central issues of enlightened penal-law reform were easily accessible, and presumably often debated, by anyone interested.[102] In Barcelona, the library at the Dominican Convent contained an apartment filled with banned books, and these could be consulted by anyone who could work his connections to secure a license. To dissuade passers-by from perusing them and to discourage permitted readers from being persuaded by their contents, the Dominicans decked the walls with graphic images of devils sodomizing sinners.[103]

Lawyers were limited about what they could write to a greater extent than what they could read or talk about. Veiled references to prohibited authors in published speeches indicate that discussions routinely took place in private.

On the printed page, though, it was safer to refer to ideas and avoid names. The framers of the *Representation to Charles III* (1760), for example, aped Montesquieu's *Spirit of Laws* but avoided citing author or source: "Prudence and natural reason dictate that given that the climates of the provinces and the spirit of their inhabitants are different, their laws should also be different."[104] Even though Voltaire was banned, lawyers were familiar with his reputation. In a speech at the Academy of Jurisprudence in 1781, Manuel Barba praised a "monarch, of whom it is said has seated philosophy on the throne,"[105] a clear allusion to the relationship between Frederick the Great and Voltaire. Although Voltaire's works had been banned for almost two decades, the audience easily caught the reference. Ramon de Dou, a traditionalist university professor, demonstrated knowledge of prohibited authors in his writings on penal law. With respect to capital punishment, a debate raging in Spain at the time, he came down on the side of keeping it.[106] Yet, like many of his colleagues, Dou supported an absolute ban on torture and addressed the "need for moderation in all types of punishment" and for "proportionality of punishments to crimes," verbatim language introduced by Montesquieu and later repeated by Beccaria. The eminent Dou made reference to the lessons of "critics and philosophers of the times."[107] Hesitant to cite prohibited authors, he was confident that his readership knew to whom he referred.

The lineaments of the legal theories of Voltaire, Montesquieu, and Beccaria were broadly known in legal circles (even to those who had never read them), but it would be a mistake to gauge the influence of the Enlightenment by solely tracking the reception of *philosophes*. It is also necessary to explore less polemical trends that contributed to the transformation of jural culture. Perhaps the most important feature of the "moderate" jural enlightenment was the rise of practical jurisprudence to scholarly status. This represented a noticeable change. In the eyes of traditional scholars, practical jurisprudence — the royal laws of Spain and the regional and municipal laws of Catalonia — was thought to be a vocational pursuit to be learned on the job. When university professors taught royal and municipal law, they relied heavily on the *ius commune*, in other words, Roman-canonical texts, glosses, and commentaries. Ramon de Dou's nine-volume *Institutions of General Public Law of Spain with Particular Notice of Catalonia and the Principal Rules that Govern Any State* (1800–1803) endowed practical jurisprudence with prestige. A gargantuan achievement reflective of the "encyclopedian" spirit of the age, it covered subjects not taught at university but necessary for practice: judicial power, penal law and procedure, and civil and ecclesiastical procedure.[108]

One of the chief characteristics of the Enlightenment was a growing interest in the practical. In philosophy, Immanuel Kant had famously grounded morality in "practical" rather than "pure" knowledge. In law, the pure (Roman law) was also rapidly ceding ground to the practical (royal, municipal, and customary law).

One did not have to be a distinguished professor such as Ramon de Dou to write on practical jurisprudence. Jaume Tos's *Treatise on the Recognition of Emphyteutic Domains according to the Law and Style of the Principality of Catalonia* (1784) did not aspire to reach scholarly heights but was a fine example of how lawyers could share acquired expertise with colleagues, who in turn welcomed that quotidian needs were being addressed by practically minded men concerned with everyday legal problems. This short volume was essentially a "how-to" manual, containing sample forms, that instructed advocates on how to enforce and defend emphyteutic claims. Instead of plowing through the Latin and Catalan works of early modern jurists, whom Tos had glossed and distilled, a practitioner could turn to this handy volume, written in Spanish, the language of the courts, which contained ready-made citations. Novel at the time, this method of legal writing would become standard in the next century. The lawyer for the largest aristocratic house in Catalonia, the Duke of Medinaceli, Jaume Tos was not an enlightened man. His *Treatise* avoided all references to the "lights" (*las luces*). Nonetheless, the book inaugurated a new method of exposition, in which practitioners could address their colleagues without having to conform to ornate convention.

Another characteristic of the moderate jural enlightenment was the use of "soft" philosophical ideas to argue for the continuation, reform, or abolition of legal institutions. Nowhere was this trend more noticeable than in debates revolving around emphyteusis. As far as published opinion was concerned, Catalan commentators trumpeted its virtues. What must be highlighted, though, is that even traditional jurists did not cling to the predictable intellectual defense of feudalism — the infallibility and sacrosanctity of law. Rather, they appealed to happiness and wealth — in other words, utility and economy. Jaume Tos, for example, contended that emphyteusis benefited the peasantry as much as the nobility: "By this means, an errant, poor, and hopeless family can better its fortune and find a fixed home. It can escape its miserable state, and achieve, if not wealth and abundance, at least a happy medium of honor and splendor."[109] Ramon de Dou later contended, albeit not very convincingly, that Adam Smith's theories on free trade could be read, or slightly modified, to justify the continuity of emphyteusis.[110] The two enlightened lawyers Manuel Sisternes and Francesc Romà proposed that emphyteusis should not only be maintained in Catalonia but extended throughout Spain. They argued that it was far superior to systems of property exploitation present in the center and the south where nobles resisted granting usufructory rights (for fear of losing ownership), hence leaving large tracts of land barren or poorly farmed by salary labor. In his treatise on agrarian legal reform, Manuel Sisternes boasted that he had "worked for the public cause" and "attempted to contribute his enlightened knowledge and education ... to the benefit of the Realm."[111]

Given censorship, Barcelona advocates avoided writing on politics with one notable exception. Francesc Romà published the most influential political tract within the court of Charles III of any Spanish author. His *Signs of Happiness in Spain and the Ways to Bring Them to Fruition* (1768) contained an impressive catalog of socioeconomic reform proposals, calling for public education, the free circulation of goods, and property reform. It was highly influenced by Baron von Bielfeld's *Political Institutions*, a book popular in the courts of Frederick the Great, Charles III, and other enlightened despots throughout Europe.[112] Romà disputed Montesquieu's view that aristocracy was the ideal governing class. Without mentioning the French magistrate by name, he contended that aristocracy subjected people to a "multitude of immoderate sovereigns" and formed "bonds that make those who govern slaves to themselves." Instead, he lauded government that was "absolute, moderate, and enlightened" and a "Monarchy in which everything is subordinated to a single person who has the goodness to measure his orders by the natural laws of the people and the state."[113] Ostentatious praise of Charles III and his ministers was common at the bar. In a speech to the Academy of Jurisprudence in 1779, another lawyer besought his audience: "Raise your eyes gentlemen to the high offices of this monarchy. Admire the decisions and appointments of the great prince who governs us. Absorb his commands, while all of posterity prepares to celebrate them and to commemorate this period of Spanish grandeur and the rise of its jurisprudence."[114]

It is difficult to gauge the extent to which radical ideas were present at the bar. Censorship prevented anyone from airing subversive opinions in public. Barcelona lawyers never did anything as bold as the College of Lawyers of Madrid, which in 1770 directly challenged nothing less than the divine right of kingship and papal infallibility, contending that "all laws and decrees, be they ecclesiastic or temporal, are neither obligatory nor enforceable unless accepted by the people."[115] Although it was not possible that Madrid lawyers could have unanimously agreed with this statement, it is clear that a good number of lawyers throughout Spain and indeed Europe, including Barcelona, shared the belief. Not surprisingly, a law professor from the University of Cervera published the official reply, which was little more than unvarnished absolutist orthodoxy, reading as if it had come from the pen of Richelieu himself: "Subjects who resist the law resist the divine order, the Potestas of the Prince or Legislator."[116] To be sure, the epochal question of whether sovereignty resided with the people or the prince was one of those common subjects of discussion, endlessly heard in private and even public circles, but which, given censorship, had trouble making its way into print.

In theory, feudal lawsuits could have been open to politicization. The large quantity of emphyteutic litigation was clearly a jural precursor to revolutionary uprisings of the early nineteenth century, when disputes over property rights would give rise to antiseigneurial and anticlerical violence. Litigators, though, went to great lengths to hide any radical beliefs they may have harbored. Although published opinion consistently sang the virtues of emphyteusis, it would be naive to think that a unanimous consensus existed. No doubt, many advocates representing peasants in courtrooms believed that the barons and the church were unjustifiably dredging up old domains that had grown obsolete or were seeking to enforce feudal obligations that had fallen into desuetude or had never existed. A handful probably agreed with French revolutionaries who sought to abolish emphyteusis in an attempt to grant freeholds to the peasantry. Yet advocates did not dare publish such arguments and, in fact, went to great lengths to sap suits of any drama. Lawyers have been frequently accused of exaggerating the significance of a minor crime or family squabble by suggesting that a legal decision could create a precedent-setting rule conditioning widespread behavior. More often, though, they did the opposite. They took potentially explosive matters, indicative of deep social divisions, and diffused them into dull lawsuits, buried in reams of paper, the outcome of which depended on making sense out of series of facts or, in rare cases, resolving a technical point of law.

Take the case of a peasant named Magí Planas, a respondent at the Audiencia in the auspicious year of 1789. Planas had refused to pay the tithe or recognize the feudal domain of the Cathedral of Barcelona, which claimed jurisdiction over his farm in the town of Hospitalet, a few kilometers outside city walls. In most cases, a peasant usually refused to pay a tithe because his or her family had not paid it for some time. Yet resistance to succumb to renewed pressure was also indicative of the simple truth that many peasants neither feared purgatory nor believed that the church held the keys to salvation. In this case, as in so many others, Planas's lawyer sidestepped sensitive ideological and religious ground and did not dare cite philosophical sources. Instead, the advocate argued that the cathedral did not have "ecclesiastical jurisdiction over the land where it wishes to charge the tithe" and presented notarized evidence that Planas's grandfather had purchased the entire interest (including the right to charge the tithe) from a noble. The cathedral countered with a notarized writing from the grandfather recognizing the church's domain and with testimony from neighboring peasants who swore to having paid the tithe since time immemorial. As was probably the case with most such suits arriving at the Audiencia, the peasant lost.[117]

The extent to which radical opinions were present at the bar, or in all of society for that matter, remains an open question: censorship prevented the content of private conversations from reaching the printed page. What is evident, however, is that advocates were divided over the extent to which philosophy should be allowed to condition jurisprudence. On the one hand, traditionalists were open to the notion that Roman law studies could be complemented by courses on practical jurisprudence, but they resisted the incorporation of "philosophical" or natural law into the university curriculum. To such individuals, some philosophical arguments could be blended into political debates over the viability of legal institutions without altering the foundations of jurisprudence. Whether a specific legal institution augmented utility and hence the happiness of the people or whether it was conducive to increasing population and wealth was the extent to which their inquiries reached. On the other hand, a few felt that philosophy and economy mandated a wholesale reorganization of jural knowledge and university education. No Barcelona lawyer showed in-depth familiarity with the natural-law tradition of Grotius, Pufendorf, and Thomasius, a school of legal thought based on the axiom that all law could be derived from reason alone. But enlightened lawyers were familiar with Voltaire's instructions to follow the guidance of such authors. Manuel Barba, for example, proposed that the entire legal tradition should be replaced by a uniform set of laws that would govern the entire world. With Voltaire in mind, he suggested that this would be "the work of a philosopher who from a distance observes men not as they are but how they should be."[118] Miquel Magarola disagreed: such a simple and idealistic solution "opened the door to fraud, confusion, the masking of truth, and injustice."[119]

The brief history of the Royal Academy of Practical and Theoretical Jurisprudence evidenced the presence of cleavages between traditionalists and the enlightened. Like other royal academies in Spain, it was most likely an outgrowth of a *tertulia* of young lawyers who had reached adulthood during the optimistic days characteristic of the first decade of Charles III's reign.[120] In 1776 they petitioned Madrid for permission to create an academy where curious minds "could engage in enlightened interchange with one another."[121] According to its foundational articles, it was also a place to train city apprentices, who were required to attend classes on practical jurisprudence two days a week (except for summer months) where they would be tutored in forensic skills, royal and Catalan law, and civil and criminal law and procedure.[122] These lofty goals, however, were never met. The founders saw their original hopes deflated, as elders and traditionalists usurped leadership roles and took over the reins of the academy. In a letter to a colleague, Manuel Barba vented his frustrations: the academy was "servilely tied to the laws of seniority," unaware that "the oldest are not always the best"; its leaders "lived isolated among their glossators of Roman law"; their "ridiculous and very indulgent love toward past centuries makes them forget the present."[123] Nor were those who ran the academy pleased. In 1786 officers complained "that the number of apprentices who attend the Academy is not equal to those who practice in the city."[124] Its activities soon fizzled out. In 1788 Charles IV inherited the throne, looked on the bar with a mixture of fear and disdain, and ceased to sponsor these academies. The academy may have continued to hold scattered sessions until the Napoleonic invasion of 1808, but, if they existed, they must have been infrequent.[125]

With the ascension of Charles IV, the relative harmony between crown and bar evaporated. Royal policies did not become patently "unenlightened," but they tended to follow the line of thought that regarded the proliferation of lawyers as a social ill. As was the case with so many aspects of his reign, the king was influenced by events in revolutionary France, where almost half the representatives of the Third Estate to the National Assembly and more than two-thirds of the deputies of the Constituent Assembly were men of law.[126] If he harbored any doubts over whether lawyers were dangerous, these were put to rest in 1793 when a fiery advocate and judge from Arras, named Robespierre, ministered to the execution of the French royal family, kinsmen of the Spanish Bourbons. In 1794 Charles went to war against the Directory and prohibited the teaching of natural law. This had little effect in Cervera, where professors had refused to teach the subject anyway. Royal officials, though, were suspicious of Barcelona lawyers. The king instructed Audiencia magistrates to discipline "those professors [lawyers] who deviate from true studies and dedicate their time to reading risky and pernicious works, which imbue them with false ideas and seductive doctrines."[127]

This warning shot was accompanied by a straightforward attempt to limit the size of the bar. In 1794 the Royal Council ordered that the number of lawyers in Madrid be gradually reduced to two hundred, and soon thereafter Barcelona was given a more Draconian cap of one hundred. Other high-court seats received similar limitations.[128] In addition, legal education was to be made longer and more arduous. In 1802 the monarchy deemed that a four-year "bachelor's degree" would no longer be sufficient for lawyers to start their apprenticeships, but insisted that all lawyers receive the "licentiate" (*licenciado*), which now took a minimum eight years of study. In 1807 this was extended to the astronomical, and punitive, sum of ten years.[129] The theory was that a lengthy legal education would be accessible only to children of rich families. It was also believed that men who spent eight to ten years in the university classroom, under the supervision of a traditional professoriate, would be less prone to radical ideas than those who spent a mere four years before moving to the cities to pursue apprenticeships.[130] Not surprisingly, many resented these laws. In 1811 Spanish liberals, meeting at the constitutional convention in Cadiz, criticized the "absurd curriculum," reflective of "despotism" and "prejudicial to the monopoly of lights." The attempt to limit the number of lawyers "impeded the flourishing of knowledge and the arrival of new talent." If allowed to stand, such laws would mean that "this illustrious profession would not be open to anyone except ignoramuses and simpletons."[131] It is worth noting that by this time, the expression "illustrious profession" was preferred to "noble profession."

Charles IV's measures, designed to prevent Spanish lawyers from becoming like their French counterparts and to shape the bar into a smaller group of richer and more conservative men, seem to have had little effect. Although it is possible that education reforms did put a law degree out of the reach of some children from popular classes and hence slowed growth, the size of the bar did not shrink. The royal order instituting a *numerus clausus* in Barcelona was shelved, as magistrates at the Audiencia exercised a right of remonstration that did not exist on paper but apparently in practice.[132] On the eve of the Napoleonic invasion of 1808, the number of Barcelona lawyers on court rolls had swelled to an all-time high of 245.[133] This script seems to have been played out elsewhere: the Royal Council also attempted to impose a limit of one hundred in Valencia, again without success.[134] As might be expected, lawyers did not cease to read "risky and pernicious works" either in Barcelona or anywhere in Spain. The Buenos Aires revolutionary Manuel Belgrano recalled that he had become politically awakened while a law student in Salamanca. "Since I was in Spain in 1789," he wrote, "at a time when the French Revolution was causing a change of ideas particularly among the men of letters with whom I associated, the ideas of liberty, equality, security, and property, took a firm hold on me."[135]

On the Eve of the Napoleonic Invasion

When Napoleonic troops occupied Catalonia in 1808, they assessed the quality of justice in order to implement reforms and smooth the annexation of the principality to France. In their opinion, the state of affairs was depressing. In 1812 a Bonapartist official reported that the Audiencia and the lower courts were so infested with venality that customary procedures existed for assassins to purchase verdicts. He observed that "the majority of lawyers do not have independent means and are forced to search out a living by meddling in conflicts between families and individuals. The widespread corruption of the courts does not permit the belief that lawyers could be immune to the general contagion."[136]

These accusations must be read in their historical context. The French expressed a notorious disdain for much of what they found in Spain. Influenced by a "black legend," forged by Richelieu and reiterated by Montesquieu, they considered Spaniards superstitious, obscurantist, despotic, cruel, and racially inferior. Although Catalans were considered ethnically different (they had at least some Frankish blood) and were thought to be more practical and industrious, the French depicted them as a stingy, litigious, recalcitrant, and rebellious lot, who had historically manipulated the principality's special laws in order to defend petty interests and resist taxation.[137] Napoleonic authorities sought to overhaul substantive law and judicial organization; hence, they had ample incentive to justify their endeavors, and confirm their prejudices, by inflating the extent of the corruption. Still, their observations should not be dismissed solely as a product of preconceptions and ulterior motives. Rampant judicial corruption was an old song, but it is worth pointing out that even the French, who thought themselves advanced, were uncomfortable with the fact that many lawyers did not have "independent means" but were dependent on lawsuits to make a living. To be sure, much of what was deemed "corruption" was, in many respects, justice as we know it today.

Lawyers were motivated by profit, and at the turn of the nineteenth century, this truism, itself a hallmark — or perhaps an unbleachable stain — of the modern profession, scandalized many observers. Enlightenment skepticism held that truth was not absolute but a matter of perspective. Consequently, justice was no longer something to be distributed charitably by kings and nobles but asserted aggressively by commoners.

On the eve of the Napoleonic invasion in 1808, lawyers had come a long way from the nostalgic wishes expressed in the *Representation to Charles III* (1760) when they had all but requested the monarch to restore them miraculously to their former grandeur and noble status. During the eighteenth century, they had overcome a crisis in litigation, had come to terms with their popular origins, and courted and were courted by middle-class clients. They had greatly expanded their activities in the commercial law. Not all lawyers were "enlightened." Nor did they march to a single tune. Some clung to traditional ideas, others injected philosophical and economic reasoning into legal knowledge, and a few advocated a radical overhaul of jurisprudence; most went about their business, though, convinced of, and eager to defend when necessary, the utility of their calling. Having abandoned their attachment to nobility, they embraced a professional ethos of talent, merit, probity, and expertise. Void of a guild or order, they worked within a judicial system that, however bureaucratic and corrupt, was relatively free of suffocating ritual. On balance, they entered the era of political and industrial revolution remarkably well equipped to handle the massive challenges that awaited them. Although the rumblings of the French Revolution were not far off, they had no idea just how violent and cataclysmic these challenges were to be. As elsewhere, the Enlightenment was the calm before the storm.

3 The Liberal Profession
WAR, REVOLUTION, AND REPRESSION

Do you swear in the form of law to God, our father, and his four evangelical saints to defend the Conception of our matron and the poor for free, and that you will use and proceed correctly in your office, and comply with all that is contemplated by the honorable magistrates in the Ordinances of this Royal Audiencia and other Orders and Royal Pragmatics?
~ Oath administered to lawyers during the Old Regime (1744–1808, 1813–20)

Do you swear to God, our father, through his four evangelical saints, to defend the Immaculate Conception of the Virgin Mary, our mother and matron, and to defend the political Constitution of the Monarchy, be faithful to the King, to practice correctly and faithfully the profession of Lawyer, to defend the poor for free, and to comply with the superior orders, decrees, and Ordinances of this Court?
~ Oath administered to lawyers during the Constitutional Triennium (1820–23)

Do you swear by God and by the evangelical Saints to defend the Immaculate Conception of the Virgin our matron: that you do not belong or have ever belonged to any Lodge or secret society of whatever denomination and that you do not Recognize the absurd principle that the People are arbiters who can vary the forms of established government; to be faithful to the King; to defend his right of Sovereignty; to undertake correctly and legally your office and to serve the Poor for free?
~ Oath administered to lawyers during the Ominous Decade (1823–33)

THE STUDY OF LAWYERS AND REVOLUTION has thus far focused exclusively on the French Revolution.[1] Tocqueville first tried to solve the puzzle of why lawyers who had the "tastes and habits of aristocracy" and an "instinctive penchant for order" had "contributed singularly to overturning the French monarchy." Although advocates had enjoyed a high status under absolutism, he reasoned, they had been excluded from political power. When such a disjuncture occurs, "lawyers will be very active agents of revolution."[2] To Tocqueville, this rule applied not only to France but to other places as well; lawyers headed rebellions against authority when they did not have a role in making the laws they studied and used. Contemporary research has confirmed this depiction of a revolutionary bar with some qualification. Historians have discovered that the majority of high advocates, the practitioners in the seats of the *parlements*, were bewildered by events and either disappeared from public life or sidled into midlevel bureaucratic positions as a means of survival. A few became prominent political figures, but they were the exception. In contrast, the middle and lower rungs of the bar appear to have been more enterprising. Numerous lawyers and judges from district courts took advantage of opportunities, vaulted into positions of power, sat on local and national assemblies, continued litigating, and accessed coveted judgeships from which they had previously been barred.[3]

By focusing on Barcelona, we can add another building block to this intriguing, though understudied, subject. As a group, Barcelona lawyers were also revolutionary and exhibited a similar cleavage between less-prominent and younger men prone to activism and older and established advocates who, with much exception, tended to avoid becoming embroiled in politics. However, the history was not the same from one country to the next. While lawyers elected to the French National Assembly got caught up in the revolutionary moment — or the "ideal of the sublimity of the nation"[4] — and legislated against the interest of their own profession, events in Barcelona, and in all of Spain, never took off in such a utopian direction. In contrast, Spanish lawyers strategically melded professional concerns into those of the sovereign nation. From a comparative perspective, the study of Barcelona advocates is particularly illuminating, because Spain's "liberal revolution" was, in fact, more representative of what took place throughout southern and western Europe. Continental revolutionaries and reformers found Spain's formula of constitutional monarchy more viable than the radical republican ideal of Jacobin France or the United States. It is often forgotten that the word "liberal" was coined in Spain during the Napoleonic Wars when delegates to the country's first constitutional assembly (1810–14) proudly took on the name *liberales* and promulgated a constitution that served as a blueprint elsewhere. The study of lawyers in Barcelona, then, offers an instructive vantage point to explore the links between lawyers, revolution, and liberalism in Europe as a whole.

This history, though, cannot be treated as an isolated case study. The outbreak of revolution in Spain was part of a continuum of events that began in Paris in 1789 and reverberated throughout the continent. Because the French Revolution was drawing to a close just as Spain's was dawning, lawyers — like other educated men and women — began to pick and choose which models were worth emulating and which should be discarded. Although the French Revolution taught that constitutional governance would open vast opportunities for advocates to ascend to the bench, to serve as public administrators, to run for elected office, to populate legislative assemblies, and to emerge as national leaders, it also demonstrated that popular sovereignty harbored the potential to turn against the bar itself. During the most radical phase of the Revolution, the Jacobins regarded French "colleges" and "orders" of lawyers as obstreperous corporations of the Old Regime and abolished them along with the guilds, so that any citizen could engage in legal representation. In 1793 university law schools were also suppressed. These reforms were rooted in the radical notion, based on street prejudices given philosophical currency through the writings of Voltaire, that advocates, armed with volumes of contradictory commentary, tended to prolong and exacerbate rather than resolve disputes.[5] As is well known, the judicial dimensions of the French revolutionary experiment went terribly wrong. Advocacy became dominated by individuals of varying expertise, many with elementary and instinctive conceptions of law and procedure; revolutionary tribunals, particularly penal ones, delivered an abominable brand of justice. In 1804 Napoleon reestablished an advocate's monopoly on pleading, although it was not until 1810 that he formally restored the Orders of Lawyers.

As the revolution descended on Spain, lawyers were conscious of the need to avoid such an agonic experience. The disastrous record of amateur justice in France worked to the advantage of advocates elsewhere. The assault on the bar became regarded as one in a string of dangerous and utopian measures that had ultimately led to the Terror and perverted the course of the revolution itself. In Spain, lawyers never faced deprofessionalization — the abolition of the monopoly on pleading. Nor did they have to confront calls to adopt the Prussian system, in which advocates and proctors would be fused into a single practitioner (the attorney), whose number would be limited. A version of this had been tried during the French Revolution, also without success. To lawyers everywhere, the implementation of either model threatened to transform radically the essence of their livelihood and, at the very least, was a recipe for massive unemployment. Neither proposal was mooted in Spain precisely because lawyers had assumed such a large role in framing liberal ideology. With one eye on the French Revolution and the other on their own, delegates to the constitutional convention in Cadiz in 1811 pledged to preserve an advocate's monopoly on pleading and to prohibit the use of *numerus clausus*. Incidentally, the proscription against numerical limitations was promulgated the same day as the abolition of torture.[6] In this way, open access to the profession was deemed synonymous with the triumph of justice and, in the words of one deputy, "enlightenment and public utility."[7]

The experience of lawyers in Barcelona can help shed light on what occurred in other places in Europe because the Spanish revolution was emulated elsewhere. In the early nineteenth century, the Constitution of 1812 served as model throughout the continent and was even implanted for a short time in Naples and Piedmont in the early 1820s. As far away as Russia, revolutionaries cited Spanish liberalism as an exemplar.[8] Designed as a middle road that would bury the Old Regime while avoiding the uncontrolled democracy of the French Revolution, liberalism was an elitist doctrine of government, which represented an alternative to both absolutism and democratic republicanism. Ultimately, the formula that gained acceptance among liberals everywhere was a constitutional monarchy with a limited franchise. This is what occurred in France where the July Revolution of 1830 ushered in a parliamentary monarchy where just over 3 percent of the population could vote. Similarly, the First Reform Bill (1832) set the British franchise at about 5 percent. Initially democratic, Spanish liberalism turned out to be the most conservative. The Constitution of 1812, also the law of the land during the Constitution Triennium (1820–23), proclaimed nearly universal manhood suffrage, but liberals, after witnessing decades of war and repression, lost faith in the masses. The Constitution of 1837 limited the franchise to 5 percent of the population, while the Constitution of 1845 reduced it to about 1 percent: approximately 100,000 adult men of property, commerce, and the professions in a population of some 10 million souls enjoyed the right to vote.[9] In the eyes of many, this was understandable given that Spain had a smaller middle class and lower levels of literacy than Britain or France. As we shall see, Barcelona lawyers were key actors who helped forge this elitist — though still revolutionary — path that abolished aristocratic privilege and the guilds, sold off the monasteries and church lands, instituted parliamentary governance, sanctioned free markets, and, in the process, bore the bar many professional fruits as well.

On balance, liberal revolution was as much a "lawyer's revolution" as it was a "bourgeois revolution."[10] If one observes each plank of the liberal platform, it is impossible to ignore the extent to which lawyers were able to advance their own interests. Men of commerce were certainly pleased by the abolition of the guilds, the coming of free markets, and the increased alienability of property, but lawyers also profited mightily. With the establishment of parliamentary governance, they filled posts as representatives in municipal, provincial, and national assemblies. Separation of powers favored the autonomy of the judiciary and the bar. The promise to eradicate the notorious corruption of the courts offered opportunities for qualified advocates to ascend to positions as judges, prosecutors, and court secretaries. An enumerated set of individual rights not only protected citizens against arbitrariness but also endowed lawyers with greater latitude in making their cases in public; critically, the right to counsel allowed advocates to represent clients in commercial and penal forums, where their actions had been restricted. Finally, the liberal crusade to expel the religious orders, to sell their properties, and to reduce drastically the power of the church meant that lawyers would definitively replace priests and monks as the most powerful profession within state and society. It has often been asserted that liberalism was the ideology of the "bourgeoisie," but this is surely only half of the story. It was infused by the concerns of lawyers to such an extent that it was articulated by them and conspicuously in their own interests. As Tocqueville had remarked with regard to the United States, "Lawyers ... form a power that is hardly feared, scarcely perceived, that has no banner of its own ... but it envelopes society as a whole, penetrates into each of the classes that compose it, works in secret, acts constantly on it without its knowing, and in the end models it to its desires."[11]

Of course, when Napoleonic troops crossed the Pyrenees in February 1808 and inaugurated the revolutionary era in Spain, neither lawyers nor anyone else for that matter had any idea what was in store. Nor did they act according to a studied plan on how to institute and profit from political change. They reacted to situations, debated ideas, changed strategies, made mistakes and adjustments, and blundered through by trial and error. The path from the democratic aspirations of 1812 to the elitist denouement of the early 1840s was paved with violence and alternating periods of revolution and repression; some lawyers were more adept at negotiating precarious situations than others. As a group, however, advocates emerged as valuable intermediaries able to reconcile conflicting demands of various groups. With heterogeneous backgrounds and an ample range of clients, they had a unique perspective on the fears and ambitions among men and women from society's diverse ranks who had much to gain and lose as the Old Regime disintegrated. It must be emphasized that the bar did not march to a single drumbeat; it comprised congenitally contrarian and skeptical practitioners of varied ages, backgrounds, ideas, and allegiances. The challenge, then, is to acknowledge this diversity while tracking broad trends, and to distinguish between lawyers who were dynamic political actors and those who steered clear of controversy. The rest of this chapter does just this. While recognizing the diversity of the bar, it discusses how lawyers participated in revolution; navigated a middle road between democracy and absolutism; and, by balancing political ideals with practical concerns, helped mold liberalism into an ethos of the elite and the educated.

The Spanish Revolution or the War of Independence (1808–1814)

In February 1808, French and Italian troops occupied Barcelona, Madrid, and other cities, and placed Joseph Bonaparte on the throne. Lawyers had plenty of reason to worry. Although Napoleon's record was better than that of the Jacobins, he had only reestablished an advocate's monopoly on pleading as a means to bring stability to a judicial system that had run amuck. Otherwise, he was suspicious of lawyers and did not hesitate to denigrate them in public. Unconvinced of the utility of judicial autonomy or the balance of powers, Napoleon considered the bar a necessary evil that needed to be closely monitored by the Ministry of Justice.[12] If anyone held any doubts over whether Joseph shared the philosophy of his brother, these were cleared up in October 1809 when the new king of Spain undertook a reorganization of consular courts. Modeled after French precedent, he barred lawyers and proctors from intervening in mercantile cases and also prohibited ordinary courts of justice from assuming jurisdiction over them. The stage had been set for this law at the constitutional convention held by Spanish partisans of the French in Bayonne in 1808 when delegates had complained that advocates were ceaselessly meddling in commercial affairs.[13] Whether lawyers could access these tribunals was no small matter. The mercantile law was a source of much business, and, what is more, represented an area of future growth and great lucre. To many, the prohibition was a harbinger of laws that would restrict an advocate's maneuverability and autonomy. In Barcelona, lawyers had another reason to be worried. The plan was to integrate Catalonia directly into France, subjecting its residents and lawyers to French law and codes.

The Spanish resistance to the occupation was initially known as the "War against the French," although it would be later labeled the "Spanish Revolution" and ultimately the "War of Independence."[14] It was a complicated conflict in which each side recruited men of varied ideological beliefs. Whether an enlightened lawyer became a collaborator or a patriot, for example, depended on whether he believed that Bonapartism or liberalism offered the best formula for progress. As many historians have emphasized, the political ideas of the *afrancesats*, the collaborators with the French, were not so different from those of Spanish patriotic liberals who rallied around the Constitution of 1812. Given that the British were in Iberia fighting what they called the "Peninsular War," allegiances often depended on whether one believed that Britain or France represented the exemplar or the enemy. With respect to those advocates sympathetic to absolutism, most gravitated to the resistance, viewing the war as a dynastic conflict between Bonapartes and Bourbons, although some collaborated with the French in order to stay in Barcelona and protect their families and property. Overall, the political map differed from international wars of the early modern period. Previously, the Catalan estates had allied themselves with the belligerents of Castile, but during the War of Independence, most politicized Catalans were Spanish patriots. Barcelona lawyers found themselves on both sides but, like the rest of the populace, tended to support the patriotic cause.

Among the *afrancesats* was a handful of enlightened lawyers in Barcelona, believing that the mission of the French was to rid the country of political despotism and religious superstition, the twin ills that had long plagued Spanish society. This was the case of Juan Madinaveytia, crown counsel (*fiscal*) at the Audiencia during the monarchy of Charles IV. Because of his rumored fanatical following of Voltaire and Montesquieu, he had run into problems with the Inquisition. In exchange for his collaboration with the French, he was appointed regent of the Bonapartist Audiencia in 1809. In contrast, Ramon Casanova was a lawyer-*afrancesat*, who had not been a distinguished jurist. Unconvinced of the virtues of private practice, he, like a few others, had used his legal education to forge a profitable career as a commercial agent to foreign merchants. Suspiciously described by one French official as "too enlightened to be an admirer of his imperial royal majesty,"[15] he nonetheless became a zealous collaborator. Appointed chief of police and Audiencia magistrate, Casanova maintained order with an iron fist, and if this was not enough to provoke the ire of his countrymen, he also ran a band of agents who pillaged the properties of those who had fled the city. A character seemingly scripted right out of the French Revolution, he was languishing in a Parisian jail when the war ended, having been convicted of murdering and stealing the fortune of a Milanese moneylender.[16]

Most enlightened lawyers, however, did not side with the French. Madinaveytia and Casanova — the hard core of the early occupation — were notorious for their authoritarian tendencies, relentless ambitions, and ostentatious life-styles. They were not the sort of men who persuaded others by the sophistication of their ideas, the cogency of their arguments, or the beauty of their oratory; instead, they were disposed to tender threats to dragoon obedience. Although other *afrancesat* lawyers were less opportunistic and had better reputations, most enlightened men of the law sided with patriotic liberals. Barcelona was not a theater of heroic resistance as were the besieged cities of Zaragoza or Girona; nor did its residents rise up in arms against the French as had occurred in Madrid in May 1808. In May 1809 Napoleonic authorities — headed by Madinaveytia and Casanova — brutally repressed a patriotic conspiracy. Thereafter, the Barcelonese remained intimidated and quiet. Although Barcelona was uneasily calm, Catalonia was one of the regions in Spain where the French had the most trouble establishing their hegemony. Imperial troops never pacified the Catalan countryside. They steadily expanded their control of major towns until a series of losses in other parts of Iberia to the British — combined with the heavy toll taken by their armies in Russia and eastern Europe — forced them to begin their retreat in the latter months of 1813. Barcelona remained occupied from February 1808 until the late date of May 1814.

Many lawyers who espoused enlightened — and even democratic — ideas emerged as leaders of the patriotic resistance. The outbreak of war instantly discredited judges and other royal officials, long thought to be corrupt, which left a vacuum of power for lawyers and other notables to occupy. Some advocates served on *juntas*, governing committees that sprouted up in free towns. The elder Manuel Barba, who had been one the leaders of the Enlightenment in the days of Charles III, departed his family estate in Vilafranca and headed to Lleida, where he was one of the founding deputies of the Junta Superior of Catalonia, the focal point of the patriotic resistance. With significant personal wealth, Barba was an example of a man who possessed the independent means to act on principle rather than out of necessity. Three Barcelona lawyers later joined the Junta Superior, which became known for its radical tendencies.[17] In the first year of the war, Lleida was the scene of violent antiseigneurial revolts reminiscent of the French Revolution. One Audiencia magistrate, Mariano Fortuny, left Barcelona for the provisional capital in September 1808 to help organize the administration of justice. His tragic fate demonstrated the risks that lawyers ran when striving to uphold the principles of law and procedure during convulsive scenarios while others were bent on exacting revenge. After refusing to appease a bloodthirsty crowd that clamored for the summary execution of a group of French prisoners, Fortuny, his wife, and his son were slaughtered along with the prisoners on New Year's Day 1809.[18]

As a general rule, lawyers on juntas worked to maintain the rule of law and to prevent the outbreak of mob violence. The course of events in a specific town, the proximity of French armies, and pressures coming from rival sources of power on the patriotic side affected the makeup of a junta and caused its composition to shift over time. A few juntas were quite conservative, seeking to preserve what was left of traditional authority in a town, but these were the exception. For the most part, the juntas nourished and fed off the liberal cause then being championed by the Junta Central in Cadiz, an Atlantic city a few kilometers east of Gibraltar, which along with Barcelona, was Spain's chief port to the Americas. One Barcelona lawyer, Joan de Balle, headed off to Cadiz to serve as deputy to the constitutional convention where his speeches echoed the liberal ethos then running rampant at the bar. Lauding the "valor and heroism of the oppressed people of Barcelona who for so long suffer under the most tyrannic slavery," he issued the clarion call that "everything that smells of feudalism should be buried once and for all." He pledged to "reestablish the just liberty and reasoned equality for all peoples of the Monarchy" as a means to bring about "general prosperity."[19] During the invasion, the liberal bug became so virulent that it was even caught by some unsuspecting hosts. The traditionalist law professor Ramon de Dou also served as a delegate in Cadiz. Although among the assembly's most conservative deputies, he put his signature to the Constitution of 1812, which proclaimed popular sovereignty, parliamentary governance, and separation of powers.

In addition to the juntas, the other institutional pillar of the patriotic resistance in Catalonia was the "Legitimate Audiencia," founded by the regent

Francisco Olea Carrasco, who had fled Barcelona in September 1808 after having declined a French "invitation" to form part of a municipal policing committee. Located in Tarragona, this body sought to maintain some semblance of administrative and judicial order in free territories. The realities of war, however, caused the Audiencia to abandon the city and go on the run. After suffering setbacks in the summer of 1808, the French accumulated one victory after another: Girona succumbed in December 1809 and Lleida fell in May 1810. In May 1811 the Audiencia abandoned Tarragona, escaping in two ships carrying ninety-three persons a few weeks before the city also surrendered in a sea of blood in June.[20] Under the protection of the Spanish army, the itinerant court later traveled from Vic to Manresa to Reus.[21] During its peripatetic existence, the few lawyers on its rolls were residents of the place in which it then happened to be located in addition to some other advocates from Barcelona and other occupied towns, seeking shelter or trying to contribute in some way, albeit symbolically, to the patriotic cause.[22] Otherwise, there was no reason to follow the court. It did not generate much legal work: civil litigation was all but nonexistent, although it did show a small increase toward the end of the war.[23]

Some lawyers joined the army, Catalan militias (*somatents* or *miquelets*), or "guerrilla" groups of resistance. One of the more intriguing stories was told by Miquel de Castells, who on the eve of the French invasion was peacefully practicing law in Barcelona, as he had been for the previous thirteen years. Convinced that occupying a judicial post or joining a junta was too commodious, he "took up arms in defense of Sovereignty and Country" and braved the grisly aspects of the war. Castells could have died as a consequence of his valor, as did many others, but he was one of the fortunate. Taken prisoner and sent to jail in France, whence he escaped before being caught, he returned to Barcelona pursuant to the armistice of 1814. In recognition of his heroism and acumen, royal officials rewarded him with an appointment to the Audiencia bench. A magistrate of moderate sensibilities who commanded immense respect, Castells was to become one of the most venerated legal minds in Catalonia. Others lived to tell similar stories from the battlefield. Miquel Gibert was an apprentice in Barcelona, who followed the Legitimate Audiencia to Tarragona, where he passed an exam and took the oath. During the siege of the city, he put down his quill pen in exchange for a bayonet and then spent the rest of the war "in various commissions of military service."[24]

Most lawyers who took up arms were not seasoned practitioners like Miquel de Castells, but students, apprentices, and novices like Miquel Gibert.

Because many young lawyers did not have to look after families, they could take greater risks. As is often the case, the youth was more idealistic. During the war, students who joined the resistance were promised course credit, a policy designed "to stimulate them to take up arms in defense of the mother country."[25] Some may have been conscious that volunteering could pay future dividends. After the expulsion of the French, veterans took advantage of their reputations as war heroes to open doors and further careers. Josep Ventosa, for example, was taken captive after Tarragona succumbed to siege in 1811. After spending more than two years in a French prison, he came home, moved on to study law, built a profitable commercial-law practice, won elections as dean of the College of Lawyers, and became the patriarch of an esteemed legal family.[26] Another solider during the war, Josep Bertran went on to occupy a series of distinguished positions, including army judge, Audiencia magistrate, mayor, and university rector. Leaving his mark for posterity, he sired a line of millionaire lawyer-financiers.[27] These individuals were no bit players. One would be hard pressed to find more prominent jurists in Barcelona than Castells in the 1820s, Bertran in the 1830s and 1840s, and Ventosa in the 1840s and 1850s. War of Independence veterans came to occupy the pinnacle of the profession.

It would be a mistake to assume that everyone associated with the resistance looked upon the constitutional project with favor. Although the bar became gradually identified with liberalism, a unanimous consensus never existed. As was the case with other Spaniards, some lawyers worked to expel the French in defense of the Old Regime and to preserve the union of throne and altar. To such men, this was a dynastic war between Bourbons and Bonapartes, and they volunteered their services to restore the former and expel the latter. For example, the absolutist Armengol Dalmau, a prosecutor in ecclesiastical courts and a friend of the Jesuits, took up arms as a captain in the *miquelets*. Similarly, Ramon Mirambella carried out various missions for the junta in Cervera, a town known for its absolutist sympathies. He served as a "judge for reprisals" on a committee of public safety created to ensure that antiseigneurial violence, which had taken place in nearby Lleida, did not spread. Accompanying troops on campaign, he presided as a magistrate on a military tribunal that cracked down on deserters and rebels. Boasting stellar credentials, both men were appointed *alcalde mayor* in Barcelona after the war, when Spain, like the rest of the continent, restored its absolute monarchy in concert with the spirit of the Congress of Vienna (1815).[28] Although the ideological proclivities of these two men were not out of the ordinary, they were on the wane. Most politicized lawyers would gravitate toward the liberal and not the absolutist cause.

The War of Independence opened opportunities for lawyers to occupy positions of authority on both sides, but the great majority of established litigators neither felt such an undying sense of patriotic duty compelling them to join the resistance nor sympathized with Napoleon and Joseph enough to collaborate. To be sure, most sought shelter as a way to protect themselves and their families. Disappearing was not a passive task: one could not simply stay at home and sit out the conflict in peace. Occupied cities and towns needed to be pacified, so expertise in law, administration, and policing was at a premium. Any lawyer remaining in Barcelona would be forcibly recruited into the Bonapartist bureaucracy. Consequently, the great majority fled. They were not alone, as the city's population may have shrunk by as much as two-thirds.[29] Many lawyers drifted out in the early months of the occupation, but those who remained were given another weighty reason to exit. In April 1809 General Duhesme, then the highest Napoleonic authority in Barcelona, opened the Audiencia, which had been closed for about a year, in an attempt to administer a modicum of formal justice. During these inaugural ceremonies, ten of the thirteen remaining magistrates refused to swear allegiance to Joseph Bonaparte. The magistrates suffered prison, house arrest, and finally the threat of death before they agreed to take the oath.[30] Upon witnessing the arrests in April, many lawyers abandoned the city, aware that they could face a similar ordeal. In January 1810 annual opening ceremonies were celebrated, but only three lawyers signed the rolls.[31]

For those who chose to remain in Barcelona, there was no tightrope to walk. Neutrality was not tolerated. The plight of Josep Riera, an elderly litigator who had practiced for some forty years, demonstrated what could happen to those who tested their fate. Remaining in Barcelona with his wife and family, Riera surmised that his advanced age would allow him to live in peace. He was wrong. In December 1809 he became victim of one of the many crackdowns supposedly directed against men suspected of conspiring with resistance armies. Pulled out of bed while asleep and transported along with fourteen individuals, first to a prison, next to a boat, and then to a warehouse at the pier, he was charged with treason. After a few days, authorities released him, and some time later offered him a judicial post. Upon refusing, he fled Barcelona rather than undergo what portended to be another round of humiliation. Recounting his saga after the war, he called a number of witnesses to confirm his story. One man imprisoned alongside him testified that on

"The Heroism of Barcelona Authorities on the 9th of April of 1809." A number of Audiencia magistrates refuse to swear allegiance to Joseph Bonaparte. In and around the benches, a few lawyers are dressed in togas. (Detail of an engraving by Francisco Fontanals of a drawing by Antonio Rodríguez, Institut de Cultura, Arxiu Històric de la Ciutat, Barcelona)

the night of their arrest, "he had seen Riera so unhinged, crying like a baby, a spectacle that moved one to the greatest compassion."[32]

Napoleonic authorities left only the sick in peace. This was the case of Jaume Tos, author of the guidebook on emphyteusis and advocate for the Duke of Medinaceli, the wealthiest aristocratic house in Catalonia. Upon the outbreak of war, Tos stayed behind in Barcelona because he suffered from a debilitating illness. The unfortunate advocate had "a large inflammation of the scrotum... the inflammation and gangrene of which became complicated and extended throughout the prostrate and urinary tract." During the war, a surgeon performed an "operation," most likely a castration, and saved his life. In a rare sign of empathy, the French never recruited him.[33] The good advocate, though, had an iron constitution. In 1826 he reedited his handbook on emphyteusis, and when he died, not too long thereafter, he was the bar's second-most senior member.[34]

For those lawyers who fled, most sought shelter in the free towns and waited for things to settle down. If Napoleon had emerged victorious, and Catalonia had been annexed to France as promised in an imperial order dated October 1810, many would have surely resurfaced as practitioners in Bonapartist courts. In the meantime, retiring to sleepy towns was the best way to dodge the belligerent sides. Many continued to practice by scrounging up whatever legal business they could. Only after Bonapartist troops had already begun their retreat did many such men declare their patriotic preferences. In opening ceremonies of the Legitimate Audiencia in January 1814, when a French defeat was imminent, fifty-two lawyers gathered in Reus to take the oath to Ferdinand VII, the son of Charles IV, the new king of Spain. By so doing, they documented that they had not been in Barcelona or other occupied cities where they would have been suspected of collaboration.[35]

At the end of the war, those who had not appeared in Reus were asked to account for their whereabouts. While a few bragged of having valiantly served the patriotic cause, the great majority gave the impression of having been lying low. The future inaugural dean of the Barcelona College of Lawyers, Miquel Llobet, dryly noted that he had been "expatriated during a span of six years." Lluís Franquesa remarked that "he never practiced law in the location of this superior tribunal in the years of the revolution." Pere Bassons left Barcelona once General Duhesme "declared them [lawyers] subject to his authority." Antoni Bonfill boasted that he had "never remained in occupied territories," as did Tomàs Lladó, who "always remained in free towns." Rafael Comes had been residing in Vic when the Audiencia arrived there; he gladly took on the role as examiner for new aspirants to the bar. Another typical story was that of Pasqual Clarís, who, after fleeing Barcelona, "continued practicing" in his hometown of Berga. Gaspar Regordosa resided in Igualada until the town fell to the French, after which he retreated to the village of Calaf, "where he dedicated himself to the practice of law." Francesc Pouplana sought shelter in the town of Arenys de Mar, Josep Abellà in the village of Sant Hipòlit de Voltregà, and so on. One curious story was that of Josep Grau, who gallantly pursued an appeal by chasing down the Royal Council, which was continually on the move. During the course of the war, he resided in Cervera, Seville, Cadiz, and finally Madrid, after it had been abandoned by the French.[36]

Those who accepted posts in Bonapartist administration were aware of being on dangerous ground. Although some certainly sympathized with the mission of the French, others collaborated as a means to protect their property and family. Irrespective of their motivations, most strove to build reputations as men of confidence who put the unshakable principles of justice above the expediencies of politics. Following the war, Bourbon officials allowed these individuals to return to practice. The Spanish accepted the excuse, offered by collaborators since time immemorial, that they had worked with an evil system to stem the arbitrariness of the occupier. Tomàs Florenza, judge of the court of first instance, claimed that "he solely dedicated himself to administering justice to the inhabitants of this capital who languished under the yoke of the tyrant." The elderly Vicenç Rovira, a court of appeals magistrate, explained that he always sought "to treat his compatriots as well as possible, always and ardently interested in the plight of those good Spaniards who had the misfortune to become caught up in judicial proceedings and face accusations." Josep Valentí, president of the court of first instance, called a number of witnesses to attest to his reputation as a "good Spaniard"; among his laudable deeds, he had secured the freedom of a group of men suspected of having poisoned the French wine supply in Mataró. Lluís Selva, another court of appeals magistrate, summoned one grateful soul who testified that he was "to be shot within twenty-four hours" before the judge rescued him. Joan Homs proved that he had liberated four citizens wrongfully accused of murdering a cadre of French soldiers in Esplugues.[37] In 1819 Bartolomé Revert, a high-profile collaborator, was even allowed to return to practice. To boost his reinstatement claim, he reminded officials that he was the magistrate who, while investigating the murder of Guiseppe Canton, arrested, adjudged guilty, and imprisoned the hated police chief Ramon Casanova.[38]

Joining the resistance or fleeing from Napoleonic troops nourished feelings of Spanish patriotism. As far as anything resembling nascent "regionalism" surfacing, it took place on the Bonapartist side and came at the insistence of a single individual. Tomàs Puig was an enlightened lawyer from the border town of Figueres, who enjoyed a brief spell of considerable influence under the short tenure of Marshall Augereau. In his writings, Puig envisioned the creation of a quasi-autonomous Catalonia within either France or the Iberian monarchy of Joseph Bonaparte.[39] In 1810 he convinced Augereau to emit a few decrees in both Catalan and Spanish and to oblige the court of appeals (the name of the reorganized Audiencia) to emit decisions and court orders in Catalan.[40] If the purpose was to try to stir up sympathies among the populace, the attempt failed for three reasons. First, although most everyone spoke Catalan, lettered men and women were accustomed to reading literature and official documents in Spanish, which, since the age of Cervantes, was a language held in higher esteem even among Catalans. In other words, most literate people regarded Catalan edicts as nothing more than puzzling. Second, the vast majority of the population was illiterate. Finally, amid the hardships of war, few could have cared about linguistic niceties. In 1811 Bonapartist authorities abandoned the experiment. Decrees and judicial decisions were exclusively published in Spanish, even though Puig had been appointed president of the court of appeals.[41]

Linguistic policy was briefly revisited in 1812 in the course of discussions about the most efficient means to carry out the annexation to France. It was decided to maintain Spanish as the official language; juridical Catalan had not been used for about a century and could not be revived overnight by imperial fiat. Similarly, a commission of *afrancesat* jurists in charge of implanting Napoleonic codes in Catalonia voted overwhelmingly in favor, nine to one, of translating them into Spanish.[42] In the end, a few tepid attempts to promote Catalan language were short-lived and unsuccessful.

This collection of short biographies — a prosopography of sorts — resembles a collage with recognizable patterns rather than a fixed portrait. The bulk of politicized lawyers espoused advanced opinions — mostly liberal and some *afrancesat* — although a few remained faithful to absolutism. While generally partial to the goals of the resistance, many practitioners kept a low profile and retreated to the free towns where they bided their time with an eye to coming to an understanding with whoever proved victorious. Throughout the conflict, Catalan lawyers and other individuals absorbed intense feelings of Spanish patriotism; nonetheless, it is possible that an isolated individual or two flirted with nascent regionalism in addition to Tomàs Puig. Another common strategy was to strive to maintain a reputation as a discriminating jurist dedicated to the equitable distribution of justice during trying times. Like many Spaniards, lawyers were in the process of formulating opinions, debating and digesting the mélange of ideas that were to dominate the new century and transform the continent. They did not harbor monolithic opinions but showed an uncanny skill at surviving, and even thriving, within delicate situations. Amid the diversity of the bar, liberalism was on the rise. As the Old Regime crumbled, lawyers were poised to become the brains of the constitutionalist state. They would have to wait, though, as the restoration of absolutism in 1813 suppressed the constitution and put aspirations on hold.

With the Revolution of 1820, however, they would pick up from where they left off and emerge as a political elite.

Revolution: The Constitutional Triennium (1820–1823) and the Revolutionary 1830s

In 1821 an anonymous author published a curious pamphlet entitled, *A True and Profitable Conversation between a Peasant Named Isidro and the Lawyer, Doctor Julià*. The subtitle promised to provide relevant information to "reactionaries and liberals, lukewarm or indifferent, and particularly to peasants who understand nothing of current events."[43] The "current events," to which the author referred, involved the establishment of a constitutional monarchy. The Revolution of 1820 — a military *pronunciamiento* — had forced the king of Spain, Ferdinand VII, to accept a parliament and to swear allegiance to the Constitution of 1812. The high watermark of the international influence of Spanish liberalism, the revolution had a domino effect, provoking parallel revolts in Latin America (against Spain), Portugal, Greece, Naples, and Piedmont. The latter two states even adopted the Spanish constitution as their own. There was a distinct possibility that the fervor would spread throughout Europe and bring down the absolutist consensus of the Congress of Vienna. This might have occurred had not the armies of the Holy Alliance invaded Piedmont and Naples in 1821 and Spain in 1823 and quashed the liberal regimes. At the time the pamphlet was published, the author was conscious that the constitutional regime was newly born, was on precarious ground, and needed to widen its appeal among the populace.

In the pamphlet, a fictitious lawyer didactically explains the virtues of the Constitution of 1812 to a fictitious peasant. The pamphlet is fascinating, for it highlights a professional rivalry underlying liberal-absolutist conflicts when lawyers and clergy vied for the souls of the people. Just as lawyers had everything to gain by liberalism, the clergy had much to lose, for liberals promised to dissolve the monasteries, to expel the monastic orders, to abolish the Inquisition, and to reduce the number of priests. The pamphlet tells of a conversation between a peasant who travels to a market town and a lawyer who resides there. In the course of friendly banter, the peasant repeats ideas that had been put into his head by a local friar. The lawyer, of course, is happy to clear up the confusion. He explains that the constitution did not prohibit the parish priest to attend to his flock, to preach the catechism, to say mass, or to administer the sacraments. The regime sought only to sell the monasteries and other church properties to defray "the enormous debt that the crown has acquired, particularly during this last cruel war against Bonaparte." The sale of church lands, the abolition of the tithe, and the vast reduction in the number of the clergy would reduce the financial burdens on the peasantry. The sovereignty of the parliament would guarantee that there would "be no paupers."[44]

As the parable continues, the lawyer outlines how the government planned to curb the power of the nobility, the judges, and the monarchy. Nobles would be allowed to maintain their titles and lands but would lose their "privileges as conquerors," including their exemption from taxation; they would no longer be considered "superior to other men." In the realm of justice, the lawyer promised that ordinary persons would no longer suffer at the hands of feckless judges or mayors, who, vested with the absolutist authority of the monarch, were said to have used one small infraction as a pretext to confiscate a home of a hardworking and otherwise honest family. Under the constitution, only persons who had committed "grave crimes" would suffer prison, and fines would be proportionate to the severity of the offense.[45] With respect to the relationship between the monarchy and the parliament, the lawyer explained:

> Yes, Isidro, by virtue of the constitution, we have a king, and we have the power to vote over his means of government, through our representatives to the parliament elected by ourselves, according to the respected public opinion of savants, liberals, and good-doers. These representatives work day and night to pave the roads by which the government will lead us all to happiness. There is no doubt, Isidro, that equity and justice will reign and the old arbitrary ways, the remains of barbarism and tyranny, will be buried forever.[46]

Obviously, the fact that a hypothetical lawyer was cast in the role as a teacher of liberalism does not evidence that every single lawyer would uncritically repeat this dogma upon request. As was the case during the War of Independence, the profession was large and disputatious enough to encompass men of diverse and adverse beliefs. But it does evidence that liberalism had become so firmly rooted at the bar that lawyers were portrayed, and identified, as its public face. The pamphlet is a clear summary of liberalism as it was then understood in Europe. Church and state would not be separated as had occurred as a result of the French and North American revolutions, but the monasteries would be dissolved, the orders expelled, the Inquisition abolished, and the number of clergy drastically reduced. The nobility would not be stripped of its titles and lands as had taken place in the French Revolution, but aristocrats would forfeit their legal privileges and hence would be treated as other citizens under the law. Although the king would not lose his throne and his head as in Paris in 1793, he would have to cede much of his sovereignty to a legislature elected by the people. Public opinion would not give way to mob violence, encouraged by evildoers such as Robespierre, but would be framed by "savants, liberals, and good-doers." In short, the model was Britain and not France. Of course, this was easier said than done. The question was how to implement this unquestionably revolutionary agenda without allowing the process to devolve into chaos and anarchy. At the end of the pamphlet, the peasant exclaims, "We should arm ourselves to defend the constitution." The lawyer, however, warns against peasant revolt: "This should be done with order, and this is now being carried out by the militias."[47]

The strong arm of the revolution in Spain, the militias counted many lawyers and students within their ranks. A lawyer dressed in uniform with bayonet in hand was not an uncommon sight in Iberia, just as it was not uncommon in the United States where a number of presidents, from Andrew Jackson to Abraham Lincoln, alternatively took up arms, law, and politics. In Spain, the mission of the militias was to dissolve the absolutist order, to replace its personnel, to implement revolutionary laws, and to double as a police force by controlling popular uprisings and cracking down on criminality. During the Constitutional Triennium, militias also left on campaign to fight alongside the army in the war against counterrevolutionary absolutist rebels, the "royalists," who had risen up in arms against the constitution. In the perfect world of Spanish liberals, revolutions were to be bloodless. They would consist of military *pronunciamientos*, which would give way to civilian juntas and ultimately constitutional assemblies, which would then promulgate laws that would dismantle the Old Regime. The world was far from perfect, though. *Pronunciamientos*, juntas, free speech, militias, assemblies, and revolutionary laws created a politically charged atmosphere, which sparked uprisings of the radical left and the reactionary right. The militias, then, sought to control and even channel popular violence when it furthered their objectives and to suppress it when it was deemed threatening.

With liberal blood pumping through their veins, students and young lawyers joined the militias. In an exhaustive study of the Madrid militias, the historian Juan Sisinio Pérez has found that the municipality sought to recruit 190 lawyers into the city's national militia of some 10,500 individuals.[48]

Because the Madrid bar could have numbered only a few hundred persons, it appears that all young lawyers were targeted.[49] Unfortunately, Barcelona militia lists do not contain occupational breakdowns, but it is safe to assume that many lawyers signed up. Catalonia accounted for one-third of militiamen in Spain. In Barcelona, some 15 percent of the population were members, half of whom were men between twenty and thirty years old. Initially, militias consisted of persons from propertied, professional, and merchant families, given that liberals were hesitant to arm poorer persons, theoretically inclined toward more radical and utopian beliefs. In need of manpower, organizers drafted many artisans as well, but they strove to keep ranks closed to the most desperate and hence most violent sectors of the populace.[50] As such, young lawyers and law students were prime candidates. Manuel Gibert, an army veteran from the War of Independence, was a law student when he was called up. Upon being given the opportunity to turn over arms after a promise of amnesty in 1823, he bravely deposited "ninety-one rifles with their corresponding bayonets, eighty-three scabbards, eighty-five cartridge belts with their bullet rings and knife holders, and twenty-six rifle carriers."[51]

Many militia commanders were men like Manuel Gibert, who had earned their stripes during the War of Independence. Lawyers with wartime experience were ideally suited for commands, which required technical knowledge of armaments and strategy in addition to the expertise to make on-the-spot decisions that executed revolutionary laws while theoretically respecting the rights and integrity of prejudiced people. Josep Elias, for example, was appointed head of the first regiment of the Barcelona militia. He was obviously qualified, because, aside from holding a law degree, he had amassed valuable military experience during the War of Independence. A hero of the siege of Girona, he had worked to supply the city by undertaking "many interesting and risky commissions" in "the free lands and those occupied by the Vandals" and had "been persecuted, identified, and threatened with death by the French barbarians."[52] Ramon Maria Sala, a former army judge during the war, was also a militia commander. Not only did he run one of the most profitable law offices in Barcelona, but he also headed the eighth battalion of which his son, his apprentice, was also a member.[53]

Just as the organizers of the patriotic resistance during the War of Independence had promised students who had taken up arms that they would receive course credit, liberal leaders took similar steps. Students who volunteered for militia duty would be able to receive course credit for their efforts (courses in practical jurisprudence would be waved), and they would also be exempted from being drafted into the army. This latter promise was quite enticing because a draftee's likely destination was Latin America where the Spanish army was bogged down in colonial wars of independence and where death was a distinct possibility. Years later, many militiamen, when asked by absolutist judges to explain their activities, strategically latched onto these inducements to try to excuse their actions. For example, Manuel Josep de Torres, later dean of the College of Lawyers, stated, "It is true that at a young age I followed the example of my friends, and with the hope of claiming an exemption, I enlisted in the so-called national voluntary militia."[54] Another lawyer, Josep Sol — a participant in a patriotic *tertulia* in the town of Reus — recounted that he had volunteered to avoid the draft and "so that they would give him course credit."[55] To be sure, these claims were disingenuous attempts to explain away actions when faced with inquiries that could lead to being banned from the bar. It is unlikely that anyone would have preferred potentially risky militia service to quiet study unless he believed in the cause. Even with respect to the draft, only one in five persons was selected, and, what is more, exemptions could be purchased. Like course credit, an exemption was a bonus or financial reward, but, for most, it could not have been the driving motivation. Even for the few who were cajoled into joining by peer pressure and attracted by the promise of a draft exemption, the esprit de corps had the effect of indoctrinating new recruits in the liberal creed.

The militias were not always the disciplined forces of order as their supporters claimed but, like similar citizen armies throughout history, faced periodic accusations of abuse of power. Extortion, kidnapping, robbery, and murder were common criminal acts committed by a rogue militia preying upon innocent persons deemed to be enemies of the cause because of associations, family backgrounds, professions, or religiosity. In some cases, students and lawyers were scandalized by what they saw. As Juan Martínez, an eminent liberal jurist later in life, asserted, "I enlisted in the so-called National Voluntary Militia believing that its sole function concerned the establishment of order and security in the towns, and I quit after having witnessing abuses committed by the commanders."[56] In some cases, however, lawyers and law students acted as a stabilizing element in the militias by using their influence and authority to secure fair treatment of persons facing life-threatening situations. Vicenç Rius, a future university professor and dean of the College of Lawyers, explained that he "extended many favors to the Royalists."[57] Antoni Vidal used his connections to save a group of Trinitarian monks threatened with death sentences. One of the victims thanked him: "He intervened in order to liberate us from those barbarians."[58] As a whole, the militias' reputations were not irretrievably stained by accusations of abuse of power. On the contrary, militiamen wore their service as a badge of honor. Upon applying to the bar in 1821, Antoni Carreny identified himself as a "Retired infantry lieutenant, constitutional town councilman of the city of Cervera, and lieutenant colonel in the local militia."[59] Another applicant, Manuel Josep Oños, proudly presented his credentials: "Bachelor in laws, and militia volunteer for this capital and for that of Zaragoza."[60]

In spite of scattered rumors of impropriety and criminality, leading members of the legal community supported the militias. Even such ordinarily peace-loving individuals as law professors did their share. During the Constitutional Triennium, a group of liberal professors from Cervera organized university studies in Barcelona and, by so doing, carried out a long-established goal voiced by enlightened reformers since the days of Charles III. Although this experiment was short-lived, it set the stage for the university to be permanently moved from Cervera to Barcelona during the 1830s. In any case, when French absolutist armies — under the banner of the Holy Alliance and led by the Duke of Angoulême — descended on Barcelona in 1823 and the status of the constitutional regime became precarious, law professors ordered students to enlist in a "Battalion of the Literary University." Fortunately for students, once the "One-Hundred Thousand Sons of St. Louis" crossed the Pyrenees, little fighting ensued. As it turned out, few had the stomach for another all-out war against the French. When asked about their participation, law students explained that their professors had forced them to enlist, but the battalion had been constituted at such a late date that it had never assembled.[61] Even so, many students had already joined. Antoni Vidal recalled that he "never served during the time that students were supposed to be at university," but he did "during the four months of vacation."[62]

Lawyers and students again enlisted in the militias in the 1830s, the final and most violent phase of the liberal revolution.[63] In 1833 the death of Ferdinand VII ignited a second civil war between liberals and absolutists. The latter were now called "Carlists," because they rallied behind the dynastic claims of Ferdinand's brother Carlos. For their part, liberals supported his daughter, Isabel II, about three-years old upon the war's outbreak. The "Carlist War" (1833–40) was the most brutal conflict that Spain had ever experienced. As much as 2.5 percent of the population may have perished. Because fighting was concentrated in the Basque Country and Catalonia, Barcelona lawyers and students were certainly among the some 175,000 government forces who died in battle or prison.⁶⁴ In opening ceremonies at the Audiencia in 1837, some lawyers could not attend because they were "indisposed," but five later appeared to take the oath; they had been engaged with the eleventh, twelfth, and fifteenth battalions.⁶⁵ Many law students later received university fee waivers in recognition of militia or army service. Antoni Benavent described himself in 1836 as "colonel in the national militias and fourth-year law student." Antoni Carrera, a successful midcentury advocate, was complemented for having performed with "obedience and valor" in the national artillery guard of Barcelona in Moià and Mataró in 1835 and 1836. Juan Baeza, arrived in Catalonia from Andalusia, a sergeant in the Cordoba battalion. He began his studies at Cervera, completed them in Barcelona, received his license in 1841, and then practiced for some twenty years. His degree was "conferred for free, because he was in the militias." A Barcelona native, Lluís Roquer, served as captain and then colonel, and "left on campaign in the years 1835, 36, 37, 38, 39, until mobilization was concluded." Joan de Gispert had his matriculation fees waived, after having suffered various tragedies. He was congratulated for his family's "adherence to the constitutional cause in the periods of 1822 and 1837."⁶⁶

In addition to the militias, the secret societies were also an engine of liberal ideas and strategies. They comprised educated men who helped shape public opinion and, if their detractors are to be believed, conspired to provoke popular uprisings. Populated by army and militia officers, merchants, educated artisans, and lay professionals, the societies consisted of members who underwent obscure initiation rites in which they vowed to form a network of brotherly love and mutual self-help. Given that societies were in fact secret, it is impossible to break their membership down into occupational categories. Because lawyers headed the lodges in Barcelona, however, it can be assumed that they populated the rank and file. The Freemasons, who had been established in Spain since the mid-eighteenth century, temporarily split into various groups during the Constitutional Triennium. Josep Elias led the "Anilleros," the society of the Moderate Party, while another advocate, Ramon Salvató, was rumored to have founded the "Comuneros," the lodge of the radical Exalted Party. Among its five hundred members, this latter group included at least one Audiencia magistrate.⁶⁷ In 1823, as the constitutional order was crumbling, the Carbonari — a society of republican proclivities — split from the Comuneros. The lawyer Francesc Pi i Margall, founder of the Federal-Republican Party in the mid-1850s, later emerged from Carbonari circles. In his memoirs, Conrad Roure gave an account of Mason meetings in the early 1860s. Although he does not name names, he implies that a few of his colleagues at the bar were members.[68] It is likely that during the heady days of revolution, in the early 1820s and the mid-1830s, affiliation had been more widespread.

The patriotic *tertulias* also broadcast the liberal message. Modeled after the clubs of the French Revolution, meetings took place in public — usually in cafés or shops — where militiamen, pamphleteers, students, secret-society members, and other politicized individuals discussed and debated the course of revolution. In the absence of documentation, novels provide a glimpse of participant profiles. Benito Pérez Galdós, in the *La Fontana de Oro* (1870), depicted the ambience of a club that met in a Madrid café during the Constitutional Triennium. Barcelona also had its own liberal cafés, such as Comercio, Constancia, Neptuno, and Titó. In the novel, Galdós cast his leading man as a student of the humanities, although he could just as easily have chosen a law student. In *Mendizábal* (an adaption of Dickens's *Great Expectations*), he did just this: a law school graduate arrives in Madrid from Zaragoza in 1836 to clerk for Juan Álvarez Mendizábal, prime minister during the most radical phase of the revolution. Gustave Flaubert's *Sentimental Education* (1869) is a famous portrait of a clique of young lawyers, students, shop owners, and artists during the Revolution of 1848 in Paris. In one amusing scene, a revolutionary lawyer drags his chum, the protagonist, a failed law student and a romantic vaguely contemplating political activism, to a meeting of the ironically titled "Club de l'Intelligence." Flaubert, who had studied law himself, satirically depicts the speech of a Spaniard, no doubt a veteran of the conflicts of the 1830s or early 1840s, and probably a student as well, whom he describes as a "patriot from Barcelona . . . a negroid ape, an extremely hairy creature."[69] The message of the Barcelona revolutionary reached Paris's young lawyers as well.

In order to appreciate the relationship between lawyers and revolution, it is crucial to stress that even those who joined secret societies, patriotic clubs, and voluntary militias did not carry out the most spectacular and ultimately consequential deeds. Early nineteenth-century "revolutionaries" did not usually join the crowd. Even France's most famous revolutionary lawyers — Robespierre, Danton, Lindet, Villeneuve — emerged in the wake of convulsive scenarios, seizing the reins of power while claiming that their political vision respected a just, incorruptible, and natural legal order. To repeat the observation of George Rudé, men of law and letters did not physically storm the Bastille.[70] In Barcelona, the situation was similar. To say that a lawyer was a revolutionary is not to imply that he personally burned down churches or carried out violent acts against persons and symbols of public authority. Even with respect to the militias, it was more common for lawyers to serve in those battalions entrusted with securing order in the towns rather than those which left on battlefield campaigns. This was particularly true during the 1830s, when the militias involved in combat tended to be recruited from society's lower levels, while those involved in policing were from the middling ranks.[71]

As far as lawyers were concerned, theirs was a revolution of order and not of violence. In tumultuous times, they saw themselves as a bastion of stability. Ramon Sala, an Exalted Liberal, emphasized this point when he became embroiled in a debacle during the Constitutional Triennium. At the time, Sala had taken on the role as counsel for Colonel Josep Costa, the former head of the Barcelona militia, the charismatic idol of the *descamisats* (the Barcelona version of the *sans-culottes*). Costa had been thrown in prison in 1822 during a typical revolutionary scenario in which one liberal faction, upon coming to power, carried out a purge against the previous one. The complicated details are not worth reviewing, but it is interesting to focus on one of the arguments made by Ramon Sala to rebut accusations leveled against Colonel Costa and his alleged co-conspirators. In a pamphlet, Sala considered that it was ludicrous that five persons who supported Costa could be accused of constituting a "faction," instigating a "riot and uproar," and of being "republicans." Sala insisted that because three of the five were "lawyers," their activities were, by definition, orderly, legal, liberal, and constitutional.[72] To him, it was absurd to assume that men of the law could be engaged in illegal, republican, or violent conspiracies. His arguments, though, did not convince everyone.

Although lawyers did not personally carry out violent acts, they did use their authority to stamp them with a mark of legality. This was made apparent in the summer of 1835, the high watermark of revolutionary violence in Barcelona. The Revolution of 1835 featured the burning of convents and the murder of clergy (25 July) and later the torching of the Bonaplata factory, the ransacking of police stations and government offices, the assassination of General Bassa, and the mutilation, cremation, and possible devouring of his body (5 August).[73] As was the case with similar convulsions throughout Europe, the protagonists and supporting casts of these dramas were artisans, small-time merchants and shopkeepers, seamen, and workers, although it is possible that an odd lawyer-militiaman or student-militiaman could have been involved at one time or another.[74] Similarly, in the countryside, it was peasants — and not their lawyers — who refused to pay tithes and feudal dues, occupied convents, physically exclaustrated regular clergy, pillaged churches, and destroyed relics. Lawyers did not personally commit these spectacular deeds but carried out the practical nuts and bolts of revolution. In the wake of popular violence, they and other notables drafted laws that abolished the tithe and other feudal dues and that disentailed and auctioned off monasteries and church lands. The judges, militias, and the army then executed these enactments in the name of legality.

By examining the decisions of the army judicial official Josep Bertran during the Revolution of 1835, some light can be shed on this phenomenon. During the burning of the convents on 25 July, the army and militias held their fire and many "respectable" people poured onto the streets to witness the burning of churches and the exclaustration, and even the murder of nuns, monks, and priests. After the dust had cleared, Josep Bertran refused to prosecute those responsible for these heinous acts. In his official report, he denounced "the excesses committed against public order and humanity," but he did not bring charges against a single person. In addition, he chose not to condemn soldiers and militiamen who, by refusing to stop the violence, had intentionally encouraged its escalation by conveying to the perpetrators that they could act with impunity. Bertran explained that members of the clergy had brought such a fate upon themselves because they supported the absolutist cause and "wanted to submerge us once again in that frightening chaos of despotism and ignorance."[75] The Revolution of 1835 set the stage for laws in all of Spain, first promulgated in 1836, that sold the convents and monasteries or converted them into municipal property. Incidentally, when Josep Bertran took on the role as a mayor of the city in the early 1840s, he carried out much of the legal work needed to dissolve the monasteries and convents. For example, his name appears throughout documents ordering the destruction of the Convent of Saint Joseph, of the Discalced Carmelites, which was replaced by the Boqueria market on the Ramblas.[76]

Josep Bertran had an exceptional career and was one of the most powerful men in Barcelona. The revolution, though, was filled with smaller Bertrans. Doubling as army and civilian judicial officials, mayors, junta members, and militiamen, lawyers, together with other liberal notables, piloted revolutionary violence by allowing it to be directed against the clergy, while preventing it from threatening private, and even seigneurial, property. What is also interesting about Josep Bertran is that, even though he played such a prominent role in the aftermath of the Revolution of 1835, he was a leading voice of the Moderates, the more conservative of the two liberal parties. Like so many others, he had witnessed the horrors of mob violence and had also seen thousands die in battle from the War of Independence to the Carlist War. Like liberals in France and Britain, he supported property qualifications on the right to vote and other laws designed to protect constitutional systems from devolving into chaos.[77] Once a constitutional order was established, he achieved a reputation as a conservative man of the establishment. Of course, not all lawyers were Moderates; some were Progressives. This was the new name of the old Exalted Liberals, the radical party of the Constitutional Triennium, which had also modulated its message by the 1830s. Although Progressives favored a larger franchise than the Moderates, they also recognized that a stake in property or commerce, or working as a fee-charging professional, should be a prerequisite for electoral participation.

As evidenced by Bertran's actions and statements, lawyers tended to support a strong hand against the church, a stance that grew out of professional rivalry in addition to political ideology. However, advocates were more compromising with respect to the seigneurs, who, after all, had always been a fine source for well-paying legal work. No lawyer could be found lobbying for the resurrection of feudal jurisdictions and baronial courts, which had been definitively abolished in the wake of the War of Independence. However, a good number of advocates defended seigneurial property interests. On one level, these opinions were a legacy of the eighteenth century when even enlightened thinkers had convincingly contended that emphyteusis was a more productive means of property exploitation than salaried labor. On another level, the seigneurs, who had been divided between liberalism and absolutism, were keenly aware of the direction in which winds were blowing and hired lawyers to defend their patrimonies. This was the strategy of the Duke of Medinaceli, the largest landowner in Catalonia aside from the church. In a dispute with the state over the ownership of a convent slated for public auction in the early 1840s, the duke hired Joan de Balle as counsel.[78] Although Balle had been deputy to the constitutional convention of Cadiz, like many men of his generation he had turned conservative after having witnessed decades of violence and repression. Having once vowed that "everything that smells of feudalism should be buried once and for all," he later became a spokesman for baronial interests.[79] For its part, the house of Medinaceli was smart enough to know on which horse to bet: the absolutist Jaume Tos had counseled it during the era of aristocratic reaction, while Joan de Balle, the distinguished deputy to Cadiz, was the perfect man for the liberal age. Top lawyers could be bought, and some barons did just this.

The case of Joan de Balle, although not out of the ordinary, was not typical either. After all, only a few advocates were on the payroll of the nobility. For every lawyer defending seigneurial interests, another argued, as did French revolutionaries, that lands should be put in the hands of those who worked them and that feudal remnants should give way to laws recognizing freeholds and alienable property. Such divisions were manifest within the Spanish legislature in the early 1820s when Ramon Salvató, a deputy for the Exalted Liberals, voted in favor of legislation that eliminated many seigneurial privileges and which contemplated the future abolition of emphyteusis. In contrast, his eminent colleague at the Barcelona bar and judge, the Moderate Joaquim Rey, inveighed against the law.[80] Outside the legislature, however, lawyers were probably not so divided. Advocates represented persons from different walks of life — men, women, bankers, merchants, artisans, peasants, and criminals — and, when the financial inducement of litigation was removed, were prone to compromise. With respect to emphyteusis, an agreement was reached. Following the Revolution of 1835, legislators — most likely on advice from Catalan and Valencian lawyers and parliamentarians — reformed civil emphyteusis in order to reduce its most onerous obligations and eliminate its most feudal components. Within this complicated negotiation, the barons lost out but not entirely. Revolutionary laws of 1837 left emphyteutic property divided into direct and usufructory ownership and hence preserved some obligations, which, though considerably less lucrative than before and harder to collect over time, were not worthless. This pact represented a new phase in the blending of bourgeois and baron, transforming the composition of the "gentry."[81] With respect to property as well as politics, Spain followed the path of Britain rather than France.

The composition of the juntas also illustrates that lawyers tended to gravitate toward centrist positions. Like those of the War of Independence, the juntas were revolutionary governing committees that sprouted up in the wake of urban unrest, endowed with the mission to diffuse volatile situations by redressing at least some of the demands of the crowd. It was common for an elite junta to be replaced by a more popular one, or vice versa, depending on the course of events. Lawyers tended to figure to a greater extent on elite ones. For example, during the Revolution of 1835, two juntas were constituted. The first was a typical gamut of urban notables who emerged to fill a vacuum of power; it counted at least seven lawyers or judges among its thirty members. In contrast, only one of ten individuals was a lawyer on the second, more radical, junta.[82] In another scenario in 1842, two juntas again appeared. The "Popular Junta" did not contain a single lawyer but comprised a newspaper editor, carpenter, clerk, can maker, confectioner, chocolatier, and other men of similar callings. In contrast, the more cautious "Consultive Junta" counted at least three lawyers or judges among its twenty-five members.[83] Following the Revolution of 1854, another "popular junta" was replaced by an "official junta," which had four lawyers among its sixteen members.[84] Elite juntas did not represent the proverbial specter of reaction. On the contrary, these committees were engines of change that usually espoused more progressive views than those of an overthrown regime. However, unlike popular juntas, they leaned toward compromise and gradualism.

In addition to participating in grand debates over property, the church, and the vote, lawyers took advantage of the opening of political space to augment their corporate power. On 10 October 1822, they launched a College of Lawyers, naming their most senior member, Miquel Llobet, as dean. In accordance with new Audiencia ordinances, they replaced the single court-appointed public defender with a corps of public defenders, which consisted of a rotating group of private practitioners who divided cases among themselves to provide a higher quality of justice to the poor.[85] Upon the return to absolutism in 1823, royal officials suppressed the College of Lawyers and its public defenders, but both reemerged during the revolutionary 1830s. Making clear to the government that it would not tolerate being used as a vehicle to cap numbers while ensuring members that it had no intention of acting as a guild, in 1833 the board of directors announced: "There is no necessity nor utility in limiting the number of lawyers in the realm." Enrollment in the college should be "free and frank for all who apply," so that lawyers "like all professionals, enjoy liberty and independence in their practices."[86]

Repression: The Ominous Decade (1823–1833)

Although by no means espousing unanimous opinions, Barcelona's lawyers migrated to liberalism. They looked favorably upon what it had to offer. Since the mid-eighteenth century, generations of lawyers had been fed up with judicial corruption and welcomed the coming of a regime that pledged to cleanse the atrocious state of royal courts by offering positions to qualified men who could aspire to judgeships and prosecutorships on merit. The promise to move the university from Cervera to Barcelona would extricate legal education from professors sympathetic with the Jesuits and steeped in the *ius commune* and place it in the hands of younger scholars cognizant of much-needed curricular reforms. A College of Lawyers with autonomous governing authority would endow the bar with a corporate presence and allow lawyers to provide a higher quality of legal representation to the poor. Liberals vowed to protect an advocate's monopoly on pleading, which had been threatened by republicans and absolutists throughout Europe. The enlightened reform of procedure would amplify the scope of a lawyer's maneuverability, raise his profile, and permit him to intervene in proceedings where his actions had been resented and resisted. All these factors contributed to making liberalism attractive even to the apolitical and the skeptical. Yet lawyers were not simply drawn to liberalism; they were also pushed there. During periods of absolutism, royal officials instituted repressive measures, leaving those members of the bar, who had been indifferent to politics or even torn between sides, with no logical alternative but to lean toward the liberal cause.

During the first restoration of absolutism, from 1814 to 1820, the captain generals persecuted high-profile liberals and *afrancesats* alike, and some lawyers got caught in the net. For example, Ramon Salvató — a vociferous supporter of the Constitution of 1812 — endured two years in jail in the town of Tortosa. Similarly, Josep Elias spent more than a month in a military jail in the fort of Canaletas in Barcelona.[87] Other lawyers also suffered prison terms or, like thousands of other Spaniards, fled into exile to escape such a fate. However, advocates were not targeted as a group, at least not in Spain. The same cannot be said for Latin America, where creole lawyers had also turned revolutionary. As leaders of independence movements, they continued their revolutionary activities even after peace had been established in Europe. If ever proof was needed to confirm the divorce between throne and bar, it tragically occurred in the kingdom of New Granada (later the three countries of Venezuela, Ecuador, and Colombia), where in the *annus horribilis* of 1816, the Spanish army executed twenty-eight lawyers, nearly one-quarter of those in the kingdom.[88] Back in the metropole, nothing like this occurred. Having been dispersed during the War of Independence, most Barcelona advocates returned to their homes, their practices, and their studies. Decisions executed by Napoleonic courts were given full faith and credit, and lawsuits commenced under the French were permitted to continue in their course.[89]

The second restoration of absolutism, 1823 to 1833, ushered in harsher policies. For good reason, this period was later labeled the "Ominous Decade." The captain generals dared not undertake such scandalously repressive measures with respect to lawyers as they had in Latin America, but they did brandish equally depraved tactics when dealing with persons of lesser status. In 1828 and 1829, the captain general of Catalonia, the Count of España, infamously known as the "Tiger," undertook a brutal persecution, which consisted of a familiar battery of roundups, imprisonments, interrogations, tortures, forced confessions, and military "trials." The accused were charged with having conspired with exiled liberal army officers who were planning a *pronunciamiento*. Many conspiracies had been taking place at the time, so such a threat was real, but officials had little clue as to who was involved. In the end, thirty-five men perished by firing squad, while an additional four hundred or so were sent to penal colonies in North Africa. Of those killed, the greatest number were army and former militia officers as well as artisans or persons of unknown occupations. Others included lower-rung professionals prone to radicalism: a painter, a tax collector, a mailman, a language teacher, a notary apprentice, and a currency dealer.[90] Although lawyers were spared from the wrath of the sword, many were scandalized by the barbarity of military justice. As the democratic lawyer Rafael Degollada lamented in 1842, "It is sad to say that the history of the liberal town of Barcelona, on the one hand has exhibited to us its love of work, respect of law, enthusiasm, patriotism, all kinds of sacrifices; on the other, prisons, persecutions, deportations, marshal law, and executions."[91]

Unlike the first restoration of absolutism, the Ominous Decade featured an explicit purge of lawyers. Beyond isolated cases of imprisonment, royal officials did not physically persecute members of the bar. In a worst-case scenario, an advocate could usually work his connections and organize a flight into exile. Instead of bare-knuckled intimidation, the monarchy promulgated a series of laws designed to endow the bar with an older and more docile personality. Although less ominous and arbitrary than executions and imprisonments, the strategy was assiduous and effective. For the most part, policies were directed against students and young lawyers. In 1826 Ferdinand VII raised the minimum age of practice from seventeen (the traditional age under Roman law) to twenty-five years old.[92] Given education requirements, this measure was essentially equivalent to raising the age from twenty-one to twenty-five. Even so, it reduced the number of applicants by eliminating candidates who were forced to wait years before being allowed to undergo examination. The rule may also have dissuaded a few young men from beginning study given the long wait. In 1830, following France's July Revolution, royal officials shut down all universities in Spain and did not open them until late 1832. The suspension of two academic years slowed down the supply of new lawyers.

Ferdinand also strove to reduce the size of the bar by reviving policies initiated by his father, Charles IV. In 1829 the Royal Council ordered the Audiencia to carry out a census of lawyers in Catalonia and to investigate in which towns their quantity could be reduced. Assembling a list of names and an order of seniority was to be the first step in deciding who was allowed to remain in practice and who was to be excluded. As part of his mandate, the crown counselor ordered Miquel Llobet, the most senior member of the bar and the inaugural dean of the college during the Triennium, to compile a list of advocates and to distinguish between those who were actively engaged in courtroom representation and those who were not. Llobet, however, refused to collaborate. A seasoned advocate who had avoided explicit political affiliations, he was not without liberal credentials. He had been a member of Manuel Barba's enlightened circle in the 1760s and may have been in broad agreement with the Constitution of 1812.[93] Faithful to the ethos of freedom of practice and protective of junior members, he played dumb and ill. His son and apprentice, Joaquim, answered the request. His father was sick, he explained, adding that "he has asked for me to reply that he does not know who and how many practice." In the end, the prosecutor repeated the advice of royal officials from the reign of Charles IV. He recommended that the Barcelona bar be capped at one hundred and places be determined by seniority.[94] Although a strict *numerus clausus* was never implemented, the bar did shrink in size as a result of the so-called purification proceedings.

Of all the measures designed to harness the revolutionary proclivities of the bar, the purification proceedings were the most repressive. Many graduates could not enroll because of the age limit, but those who were twenty-five or older had to overcome this additional hurdle. Lawyers on the rolls before 1820 were not required to be "purified," but those who had qualified during the Constitutional Triennium and all new candidates had to be cleared. Accordingly, it was young lawyers and law students who felt the brunt of the purge. Under these proceedings, a candidate had to satisfy authorities that he was fit to practice law by revealing his whereabouts, associations, and activities during the Triennium. During a proceeding, an *alcalde mayor* or similar royal official deposed at least three witnesses willing to confirm an applicant's account and to vouch for his moral integrity. Having volunteered for militia service was not automatic grounds for disqualification. In fact, volunteerism had been so widespread that in 1827 the Royal Council had no choice but to instruct officials and magistrates not to block lawyers, doctors, and surgeons from obtaining licenses if their sole blemish was having volunteered and served in the militias. The council, however, prohibited voluntary militiamen from the judiciary, professoriate, and royal administration.[95] In any case, militia members were suspected of having engaged in parallel activities, which would have been considered grounds for disqualification or disbarment, so absolutist judicial officials were eager to know who they were, what they had done, and what they knew about others. Those who had been drafted into the "official militias" had less explaining to do, but those who had joined the "voluntary militias" — constituted before the official ones had been formed — had to face tougher inquiries.

The standard line given by a candidate who, despite having volunteered or having been drafted, still believed he could pass included some combination of the following rehearsed denials: "Never fired arms against royal troops," "never dressed in uniform," "never was a member of the patriotic *tertulias* nor a member of a secret society," "never worked as a journalist or pamphleteer," "never took on a position in the revolutionary government," or "never was an Exalted constitutionalist."[96] Former militiamen could not always repeat all these utterances, as many had dressed in uniform, participated in *tertulias*, doubled as journalists, and had been Exalted Liberals. However, candidates strung together as many of these phrases as could be plausibly confirmed by witnesses. They then usually offered the excuse that they had joined to take advantage of various inducements offered by the liberal government, which had promised student militiamen that they would be exempted from being drafted into the army and could receive some course credit. No doubt, some made use of family reputation and connections to sway sympathetic judges. For example, one *alcalde mayor* recommended a candidate for purification even though he had been a militia member and had apparently dressed in uniform. In his report, the judge reasoned that the candidate's unfortunate decision was the result of the typical follies of youth: "Against the wishes of his mother, between his sixteenth and eighteenth birthday . . . he enlisted in the voluntary militias." Another witness added that the candidate "was not motivated by the exaltation produced by the perversity of an immoral heart."[97] In other instances mothers escorted their sons to the courthouse to use their feminine wiles to persuade a judge. One mother testified, "During the time of the political convulsions, he lived in my house without taking part in the so-called constitutional system. He was not a member of the voluntary militia or member of the Patriotic Club."[98]

To boost their applications, some aspirants presented purification certificates dispensed by university boards that screened students before they could be admitted to study. Linked to the Inquisition, these boards deposed applicants and witnesses and issued certificates attesting to "purity of blood."[99] Reading as if they had been drafted at the height of the Counter-Reformation, a typical certificate described an applicant's family by employing a number of astonishing descriptions: "good Christians," "Roman Apostle Catholics," "of clean blood," "without any mixture of Moors, Jews, Lutherans, or any other reprobate sect," "without either a stain or mark on its blood," "without a stain of heresy," or "without showing even a shadow of Saracen descent."[100] The Inquisition, restored during the Ominous Decade, was to be definitively abolished upon the death of Ferdinand in 1833. During the waning years of absolutism, however, liberalism was its new heresy.

It is impossible to ascertain the identities or count the number of the disqualified or disbarred. Because a candidate registered for a bar exam only once he had been "purified," there are no records for those unable to progress to this stage. Undergoing an inquiry was optional, so anyone doubting his chances was unlikely to appear before an *alcalde mayor* and risk arrest, imprisonment, or exile. After all, punishment for treason or heresy was still death, at least on the books. In short, only those convinced of being able to pass underwent a proceeding and hence generated documentation. The testimony of those admitted, however, reveals the profiles of those shut out. Those purged included Exalted Liberals; visible discussants in patriotic *tertulias*; known members of secret societies; journalists and pamphleteers; politicians, administrators, and judges in revolutionary towns; and militiamen seen in uniform executing revolutionary decrees, persecuting absolutist officials, leaving on campaign, or undertaking illicit acts. When the dust had cleared, the combined effect of the purifications, the age limit of twenty-five, and the parallel persecution of political elites had taken its toll. Out of 176 lawyers on Audiencia rolls in Barcelona in 1819, only 112 were still practicing in 1825 and the size of the bar had shrunk to 149.[101] This was an enormous reduction from the 245 lawyers enrolled on the eve of the War of Independence. Many dropped out because of attrition, as litigation was erratic during revolutionary times.[102] Some lawyers received posts because of the reshuffling of court and administrative personnel during frequent regime and governmental changes.

Yet ideology was one of the chief reasons why many lawyers and students were prevented from pursuing or resuming their professional activities.

Some overcame hardships and lived to tell romantic stories of prison, exile, and return. A few heroic men were able to make use of their reputations to obtain judgeships, run for parliament, and, in the case of Ramon Salvató, ascend to minister of justice of Spain in 1839.[103] Yet these individuals represented the few and the fortunate. Although a few triumphed in the face of persecution, many more were less headstrong or ambitious, or did not have the financial means or connections to overcome prison, exile, the loss of livelihood, or even year-long gaps in study or practice. Many a promising career was no doubt delayed or derailed as a result of the idealistic decisions of a liberal youth. Then there were those who died in battle or prison, disappeared after exile, or just gave up on law and pursued another career. In searching for reasons to explain why lawyers grew elitist during the 1830s, we should not pay attention only to periods of revolution but also to those of repression. The purge of students and lawyers during the Ominous Decade eliminated many radicals from education and practice. Even more important, the longevity of the purge sent a clear message to those contemplating future activism: Democratic or "Exalted" liberalism was treacherous territory, whereas softer versions represented a viable middle ground. Many lawyers migrated to centrist positions not only because they feared mob violence, had witnessed the horrors of civil war, or were sympathetic to competing claims but also because they preferred to pursue a path that left them less personally exposed to persecution.

We should be careful not to overstate the severity of the purge, which was aimed not at the entire bar but at its "Exalted" sector. During times of revolution and repression, many established advocates rode out storms, carried on litigating, complied with authorities, and did their best to dodge political associations, which could prejudice their chances of winning lawsuits when judicial personnel was reshuffled upon regime change. Moreover, it must be emphasized that the majority of young lawyers did not encounter problems during purification proceedings. Most candidates for the bar had spent the Constitutional Triennium in places where there was little militia recruitment. For individuals who grew up outside Barcelona or other revolutionary towns, it was easy to line up a battery of witnesses who could confirm that the applicant had not actively supported liberalism. A typical deposition usually included the following negative assertions: "I never enlisted in the national voluntary militias. I have never pertained to any of the reprobate society of the Masons and Comuneros. I have never been a member of or a participant in the so-called patriotic clubs."[104] Even a diehard liberal would keep his true beliefs silent in order to pass a proceeding and be admitted to the bar. These rote phrases were like the oaths reproduced in the epigraph of this chapter.[105] Many lawyers pledged their allegiance to the "political Constitution" during the Constitutional Triennium and then a few years later, upon the restoration of absolutism, swore that they never believed "in the absurd principal that people could be arbiters who could vary the form of established government." More than one hundred lawyers took both oaths, which were incompatible. In order to continue their livelihood, lawyers, like others, did not hesitate to lie under oath.

With incentives being as they were, it was quite common to testify to having loathed liberalism. The majority of such statements must be regarded with skepticism, because gratuitous claims of philo-absolutism during purification proceedings were as self-serving as those of students who claimed to have joined the militias because of peer pressure, to avoid the draft, or to receive course credit. Nonetheless, a few genuine absolutists were members of the bar. In 1825 Manuel Pinós enrolled after proving that he possessed "the most healthy ideas in favor of the legitimate government that reigns over us." In his purification proceedings, witnesses testified that he had "succeeded in avoiding all affiliations that implied adhesion to the revolutionary government."[106] In 1826 three Barcelona lawyers, Tomàs Lliurella, Pio Serra, and the aforementioned Manuel Pinós — all of sterling absolutist credentials — vouched for the Lorenç Puig who also testified to having despised liberalism.[107] Another applicant, Magí Mestre, was the child of an absolutist mayor. Overseeing his purification, the father testified that his son "manifested disaffection at all times toward the abominable constitutional system."[108] A few had even taken up arms and joined royalist rebels. An applicant to the bar in 1826, Francisco Marquéz de Aguado, had been a "captain of the Third Company of Royalist Volunteers in the city of Alcaraz." To confirm his story, two lawyers from outside Barcelona attested to the candidate's "limitless aversion" to the "revolutionary maxims of the so-called constitutionalist system."[109] Oriol de Gil, admitted to the bar in 1831, also testified to having "taken up arms in defense of Throne and Altar."[110] Jaume Panon, a priest from Palafrugell seeking admission to the bar, presented evidence of having narrowly escaped a band of militiamen who attempted to kidnap him to extort money from his family.[111]

These absolutist lawyers were the exceptions that proved the rule. A handful of such individuals, often associated with ecclesiastical and seigneurial circles, would stir up trouble periodically throughout the nineteenth century. However, they represented a fringe — albeit a bothersome and vocal — minority. In one study of absolutist militias in Madrid from 1823 to 1833, only eight lawyers were enrolled in a corps of more than five thousand.[112] In another study of more than seven hundred men suspected by the police of being Carlist absolutists in the 1830s in Catalonia, not a single individual was a lawyer — most were artisans, day workers, proto-industrial workers, and peasants.[113] Such minuscule numbers pale in comparison to previously mentioned figures that reveal dozens of lawyers in the liberal militias.

A Lawyers' Revolution?

In 1835 Tocqueville published the first volume of his *Democracy in America*. On the basis of his visit in the early 1830s, he had one eye on the United States and the other on his own "hemisphere." By observing the workings of the world's only existing democracy, he sought to "discern clearly its natural consequences, and to perceive, if possible, the means of rendering it profitable to men."[114] A lawyer himself, he paid careful attention to the bar. In so doing, he tried to solve the conundrum of why lawyers had become so radical during France's brief experience with democracy but were then exerting a steadying and conservative influence in democratic America. He explained that the actions of French advocates were out of the ordinary; their revolutionary proclivities were not reflective of their natural disposition but of specific historical circumstances. Having been excluded from political power, they turned against absolutism. "In a society in which lawyers occupy without dispute the elevated position that naturally belongs to them, their spirit will be eminently conservative and will show itself as antidemocratic." As he stated, "The American aristocracy is at the attorney's bar and on the judge's bench."[115]

When Tocqueville portrayed lawyers as antidemocratic, eminently conservative, and aristocratic, he was not being critical. To this most exemplary of continental liberals, these were words of praise. As a lawyer and an aristocrat himself, he felt it was healthier that democracy's aristocracy consisted of lawyers and not the landed nobility. As an enemy of the Old Regime and the French Revolution, he lauded elitist associations of conservative learned men who served to protect free governments from what he famously described as the "tyranny of the majority." As an admirer of American lawyers, he observed that, through the institution of the jury, "their spirit penetrates to the heart of legislatures, into administration, and in the end gives to the people themselves something of the instincts of magistrates."[116] At the time Tocqueville was writing, he was aware that continental advocates had seen better days. As had occurred in Barcelona, the number of French advocates had plummeted as a result of revolution, Bonapartism, and absolutist restoration and repression. However, the bar would not languish in this depleted state for very long. Tocqueville was correct, for what he had seen in America would also come into fruition in his own hemisphere. Over the course of the century, lawyers in France, Spain, and Europe would shed their revolutionary pasts, increase their numbers and influence spectacularly, and also become a conservative force in society.[117]

Despite Tocqueville's observations, not many historians have paid attention to this phenomenon. One of the few who has done so is C. A. Bayly, who has explained that, although lawyers suffered during the age of revolution, they rose as a consequence of the resurrection of the bureaucratic state. Unlike Tocqueville, however, Bayly does not specifically link this occurrence with either democracy or liberalism: "Lawyers and bureaucrats... thrived and prospered under *all forms of government*, because all governments needed to increase taxation." He also explains that "lawyers in turn became the double of the state, working within civil society to facilitate and legitimate its claims."[118] Bayly should be applauded for recognizing the key role of lawyers in legitimating the modern state, but his interpretation leaves out politics and strips lawyers of agency. To him, lawyers burgeon when states are stable and wither when they are not. But lawyers did not flourish under "all forms of governments," nor did they shudder at the sight of insurrection. Active within revolution, lawyers worked to institute liberal systems, which, among other things, were cast and calibrated with the interests of the bar in mind. As demonstrated in the case of Barcelona, lawyers were not passive actors who yearned for stability at all costs, but were integral in forging an elitist — though still revolutionary — road toward a constitutional order. Indeed, lawyers did not prosper under any tax-collecting state but faced hard times under absolutist ones and thrived under constitutional ones. Unlike Jacobinism, Bonapartism, or absolutism, liberalism was lawyer friendly.

To be clear, it is not meant to be asserted that Spanish liberalism was an unadulterated story of success. Anyone familiar with the general outlines the country's history knows this not to be the case. While Spanish liberals succeeded in avoiding the perils of absolutist despotism and the tyranny of the majority, many promises were left unfulfilled. The end of the revolutionary era ushered in a new rash of problems. The large role that lawyers played in forging an elitist consensus bred a distrust of the masses and arguably planted the seeds for oligarchy and corruption. Similarly, the importance of *pronunciamientos* and the militias — in addition to the fact that liberalism proved triumphant as a result of military victory over the Carlists — set the stage for the intervention of the army in politics. Amid these occurrences, though, Tocqueville's prophesy turned out to be correct. Once constitutional governance was firmly instituted on the continent, lawyers grew conservative. In Barcelona, liberal advocates would abandon their most idealistic goals, build powerful corporate associations, and become a pillar of order in society. What is more, the bar underwent an exercise in collective amnesia, as elder lawyers disremembered their youthful activism and idealism. It was rare for a midcentury practitioner to be found bragging about his days in the militias, secret societies, or patriotic clubs. Instead, advocates articulated an institutional memory that bridged over the difficult-to-interpret experiences of absolutism and revolution and stretched back to a golden age of advocacy during the constitutional splendor of medieval and early modern Catalonia. Although lawyerly conservatism was in many respects a consequence of industrialization, the pillars of the conservative profession were already firmly in place by the close of the liberal revolution.

4 The Conservative Profession
INSTITUTIONS, LEADERS, AND THE LAW

> LAWYER: Do you believe, Isidro, that a head of his household should be able to organize his possessions and dependents to better them and make them more happy?
> PEASANT: Yes, this is certain.
> LAWYER: Well, this is what is happening among us: the Spanish Nation is free and independent and in plain exercise of its natural rights, and for this reason should do what it is doing, and strive to do more.
> PEASANT: You have lost me, sir doctor. I have not understood a word you have said.
> ∾ *A True and Very Profitable Conversation between a Peasant Named Isidro and the Lawyer, Doctor Julià* (1821)

IN THE PRECEDING CHAPTER, we discussed a pamphlet, published in 1821, in which a fictional lawyer didactically explained the virtues of the constitution to a peasant, who, according to the author, belonged to a class of individuals who understood "nothing of current events."[1] As the liberal revolution wound to an end in the early 1840s and reached its elitist conclusion, it is a worthy exercise to explore the extent to which the lawyer made good on his promises.

On paper, at least, many were fulfilled. Spain was a parliamentary system in which the monarch and the legislature governed, according to the Constitution of 1845, in shared sovereignty. With the victory of liberalism, the Old Regime was buried — the guilds and the tithes were abolished, the nobility lost its privileges, and church and municipal lands were auctioned off. Expelled in 1836, the religious orders began trickling back in the 1840s, but they had lost their monasteries, convents, and lands, and their numbers had been decimated. Most legal impediments to capitalism evaporated, and, in theory, society became open to the idea that talent and enterprise begot merit. In politics, however, many baseline promises went unfulfilled. The frequent intervention of the army in politics perverted the principle of popular sovereignty. Restrictions on press and assembly undermined elementary freedoms. The franchise was small, growing from 1 percent of the population in 1845 to 2.7 percent in 1865 to 5 percent in 1875. Middle-income lawyers enjoyed the right to vote; however, the family farmer, the pamphlet's other protagonist, would have enjoyed this right only if his holdings were large enough.[2] Universal adult manhood suffrage, equivalent to roughly 25 percent of the population, was exercised from 1868 to 1874 and achieved in 1889. Even so, oligarchy and electoral fraud prevented the conduct of fair elections. Finally, high rates of illiteracy and poverty had the effect of excluding large sections of the populace from the public sphere. This summation constitutes a rough description of the balance sheet of liberalism in Spain and indeed much of southern Europe.

For our purposes, it is worth focusing on the promises made by the lawyer to the peasant in the realm of justice. In the pamphlet, the peasant complains that "it is bad that lawsuits will continue, because they are the source of my poverty."[3] The lawyer responds that the constitutional regime would provide more courts with speedier procedures to reduce the travails and expense of litigation. He also pledges to uproot corruption and eliminate arbitrariness by instituting procedural safeguards so that judges and mayors could no longer use minor incidences of illegality to prey upon hardworking families.

Did liberals provide more courts, smoother procedures, and a higher quality of justice? This was the goal, but results were modest. The Constitution of 1812, which was also the law of the land during the Constitutional Triennium (1820–23), set forth an initial blueprint for judicial reform, but absolutists also saw the need to extend the reach of royal justice. In 1828 the monarchy added more than twenty *alcaldes mayores* in Catalonia in order to fill the void created by the definitive abolition of seigneurial jurisdictions in 1814.[4] Thereafter, liberal governments actually decreased the number of court seats, probably because many were too remote and hence not busy enough to justify the expense of outfitting them with salaried personnel. In 1830 a census recorded the existence of forty-three *alcalde mayores* in Catalonia; in 1858, there were thirty-six district court seats; and by century's end, the number had climbed to only thirty-nine.[5] In Barcelona, the situation was similar. In 1769 Charles III had created five courts of first instance for Barcelona and its environs, and at the end of the nineteenth century, there were still only five district courts. Liberal reforms, though, improved things significantly: courts were staffed with more full-time personnel so that they could handle more lawsuits.

The consolidation of a liberal order did not usher in a drastic change to the organization of judicial power. Courts, procedures, professional roles, and even the law demonstrated remarkable resilience when so much of the Old Regime crumbled. Spain did not represent an exception but rather a middle road. Things did not continue as uninterrupted as in England where the crown courts, quarter sessions, and assize circuits suffered little alteration,[6] but they were not like France either, where the Jacobins and then Napoleon radically redrew the map of appellate and first-instance jurisdictions. In Spain, liberals purged and cleansed personnel and endowed courts with greater resources, but they did not significantly reconfigure jurisdictions to uproot traditional patronage networks. In 1835 the Progressive Party passed legislation reorganizing judicial power, but, as applied to Catalonia, this often consisted of switching names, persons, and titles rather than overhauling jurisdictions or procedures. The first level of professional justice, the district courts (*juzgados de partido*), were often found in the same towns and the same buildings as the previous courts. The district court judge, the *juez de partido*, possessed a law degree and adjudicated civil and penal cases using similar procedures as his predecessor, the *alcalde mayor*. The Audiencia of Barcelona maintained its organizational structure: one criminal and two civil chambers, each staffed with five magistrates, together presided by a regent. The Supreme Court in Madrid was the highest court of appeals in Spain, replacing the old "Chamber of One Thousand Five Hundred" at the Royal Council.[7]

One way to improve the quality of justice dispensed to ordinary men and women was to improve the situation of the towns. Of the two liberal parties, the left-wing Progressives and the right-wing Moderates, only the former came to consider this a priority. The legislation of 1835 maintained the system of the Old Regime whereby mayors or deputy mayors resolved minor civil disputes and prosecuted and adjudged petty crimes. The first major improvement occurred in 1855 when the Progressives created "justices of the peace." Like the mayors, the JPs were unprofessional men — the only formal requirement was to be able to read and write. Nonetheless, the same person could not serve as both mayor and JP, which, at least in theory, established a separation of powers in the towns.[8] In 1870 the Progressives passed the Organic Law of Judicial Power, a massive reform that created thousands of municipal courts in Spain, each equipped with a judge, prosecutor, and judicial secretary. Municipal judges, like their predecessors (the mayors and the JPs), heard minor disputes, prosecuted petty crimes, helped execute judgments, and undertook investigations, depositions, and interrogations under instructions from district court judges. In cities such as Barcelona, endowed with four such courts, municipal judges and prosecutors held law degrees, but outside major cities such credentials were less common. Lawyers rarely appeared in these courts.[9] Municipal judges were empowered to hear suits of higher quantity than the JPs in order to relieve pressure on the district courts. To litigants, however, this raised the monetary threshold needed to gain entrance to professional justice.[10]

Professional justice began at the district courts, but when small sums were in dispute, these tribunals employed an abbreviated procedure in which the parties were not required to hire counsel. According to the Code of Civil Procedure of 1855, full procedures were not set into motion unless a suitor claimed more than 3,000 reales, an amount greater than the yearly income of most artisans in Barcelona, which could be disputed only among persons with much to gain or lose.[11] Lawyers' fees for a given case usually exceeded 1,000 reales, and they commonly ran into the thousands.[12] In other words, most full-blown civil cases, in which lawyers took off their gloves, rolled up their sleeves, and got down to the adversarial business of lawyering, usually concerned quantities that could be contested only among persons with substantial incomes or patrimony, or claims to inheritances, property, or proceeds. It is not possible to compile statistics on litigant profiles for the nineteenth century, as one author has done for the eighteenth; nonetheless, it can be safely asserted that civil litigants consisted of gentry, merchants, professionals, wealthy artisans, property owners, rentiers, peasants, shopkeepers, and middlemen involved in commerce, agriculture, industry, renting, and conveyancing.[13] In the end, lawyers provided many of the same services, applied essentially the same body of civil laws, and often litigated in the same physical spaces as they had under the Old Regime.

The grand liberal promise — made by the lawyer to the peasant — remained unfulfilled. On balance, liberal justice was significantly better than Old Regime justice, but, despite improvements, lawsuits never became either swift or affordable. In 1890 one Audiencia magistrate stated what all had fatalistically come to regard as a truism: "The administration of justice is slow and expensive and does not provide the necessary guarantees to defend the rights of those it is supposed to protect."[14] District court procedures were cumbersome and remained vulnerable to manipulation by lawyers and proctors employing dilatory tactics. Backlogs caused delays in having appeals heard. Many of the same criticisms of absolutist justice were uttered in the liberal era. As one novelist lamented in 1915, "The lawsuits never ended. They were drawn out over years and appeals. Their death was the Supreme Court where it seemed that all lawsuits waited endlessly."[15] Complaints of naked venality and arbitrariness were heard with less frequency in the liberal era than they had been under the Old Regime, but accusations were periodically mooted. Municipal courts, in particular, had an atrocious reputation. This was no minor matter as these courts adjudicated the great majority of the country's legal disputes.[16] Usually without a law degree, municipal judges and prosecutors were said to be in the pockets of political bosses upon whom their appointment and continuity depended.[17]

The critique of penal justice followed a similar pattern. With the coming of a liberal order, torture was abolished and criminal law and procedure underwent piecemeal improvement. Still, the pace of reform was comparatively slow. Even after the modern criminal trial had been implemented in 1882, critics complained that innocent people were often thrown in jail on the basis of the slightest of suspicions and the thinnest of evidence.[18] The republican Left clamored for further safeguards that would prohibit the detention of persons who had not been accused of crimes, that would oblige authorities to bring the incarcerated quickly before a judge, and that would allow for persons facing misdemeanor charges to be released on bail. They also demanded that cruel punishments, such as execution or life in prison, be abolished.[19] Taken as a whole, calls to dispense a purer and more moral brand of penal justice and to streamline civil procedure became regarded as a lost dream. In the nineteenth century, civil justice and high-quality criminal defenses remained a commodity to be purchased rather than something that was distributed divinely, royally, or even all that liberally. Things never returned to the ways of the early modern period when an ample sector of the population could afford experienced counsel.[20] The shortcomings of the system were not unique to Spain but reflected the state of affairs in all of Europe. With regard to justice, the dreams of the Enlightenment were only partially realized.

Not surprisingly, the lawyer made out significantly better than the peasant. Courts became more fully staffed, which created jobs in the judiciary. In 1844 the Moderate Party passed legislation that outlined district court organization.[21] In addition to a judge, tribunals were equipped with a chief clerk or "secretary" (*secretario*) and a "prosecutor" (*promotor fiscal*), both of whom possessed law degrees, in addition to two bailiffs (*alguaciles*) and a jail keeper (*alcaide*). This hardly represented a grand innovation but adopted a structure that had been in place in the busiest courts since anyone could remember.[22] Nevertheless, the reform created more full-time jobs in the judiciary, all with a fixed salary, which could be filled by members from the bar. Beginning in 1851, the government began to institute "laws of incompatibility" that restricted lawyers from serving as judges in the locale where they were born. In theory, this reduced the ability of some Barcelona lawyers to ascend to the bench in the city. However, it appears that such laws were not enforced until the 1860s.[23] As a general rule, judicial appointments, dismissals, and promotions remained highly political. Liberals never succeeded in keeping appointment and promotion independent of ideology and disentangled from oligarchy, but this did not mean that the courts were staffed by incompetents. Well-qualified candidates, who knew how to create, nurture, and exploit networks, garnered coveted posts in the judiciary.[24]

Procedural reforms provided defendants and litigants with a greater basket of rights, which, in turn, granted lawyers a wider latitude to frame their cases and mount their defenses. Liberals did not immediately institute public "trials" — ongoing and uninterrupted spectacles on the English model. The criminal trial, in fact, did not come to Spain until the country's first full Code of Criminal Procedure appeared at the late date of 1882. The jury, although periodically used for press offenses and briefly making an appearance in the early 1870s, was not definitively instituted until 1888.[25] Until 1882, penal cases remained largely faithful to Old Regime procedures. They were divided into summary and plenary phases in which the investigating and adjudicating judge was one and the same person. The civil "trial" was never instituted in the nineteenth century. In fact, until 1882 there was not much difference between civil and criminal procedure. Civil lawsuits and criminal cases were colloquially called "matters" (*asuntos*) or "businesses" (*negocios*), for lack of a better word.

The introduction of public hearings, held whenever evidence was submitted or witnesses examined, was the chief liberal procedural reform. For criminal cases, the law of 1835 allowed defense lawyers to call and examine their own witnesses (material and expert), to cross-examine witnesses, and to present their own evidence. The Code of Civil Procedure (1855) did not provide for cross-examination, but it did permit parties to file counterinterrogatories so that a judge questioned witnesses in public, in the presence of lawyers and the parties, using interrogatories submitted from both sides. Lawyers were not permitted to examine and cross-examine witnesses in civil hearings until 1881. Even then, questioning had to follow preapproved interrogatories, except in cases in which a witness was patently hostile.[26] In addition to providing greater transparency, public hearings had the effect of obviating many antiquated motions and reducing reliance on paper communications, but things did not speed up significantly. Civil procedure still consisted of a battery of complaints, answers, motions, interrogatories, appeals, and supplications. Parties could be added and subtracted, cases could be remanded, new suits could arise during the execution of judgments, and so on. On balance, lawyers had the best of both worlds. Not only did they make their cases in public, but a normal civil case remained an ongoing affair that supplied work for months, and often years, on end.

While judicial procedures guaranteed steady business, Audiencia hearings raised the bar's visibility and prestige. The Barcelona Audiencia continued to hear criminal and civil appeals originating throughout Catalonia and held original jurisdiction in a few exceptional matters. With regard to appeals, lawyers filed briefs and argued cases in front of panels of magistrates in public. This represented a change from the eighteenth century when oral argument had not been given much purchase. In his writings on civil procedure completed in the 1790s, Ramon de Dou made only passing mention of oral argument, observing that lawyers had the opportunity "to explain orally whatever they deem convenient."[27] In 1805 the Royal Council decreed that all apprentices were required to attend hearings, a sign that oral argument was gaining importance.[28] It is likely that hearings became gradually endowed with greater pageantry, perhaps as English and French forensic practices spread into Spain.

In the nineteenth century, appellate procedural reforms elevated the importance of oral argument. For well-publicized criminal and civil cases, apprentices, students, and curious men and women from the public lined up to listen to celebrated advocates showcase their oratory and acumen. Audiencia hearings began shortly after noon, would run straight through the midday meal, and could last up to five or six hours. When an appearance was scheduled, an advocate spent much of the morning grooming himself and rehearsing; families nervously adjusted mealtimes and schedules. The purpose of these hearings was not only to decide the fate of parties but to uphold — or, better yet, to reinvent — the humanist heritage of the bar by exploring the mysteries and nuances of law.[29] This represented a significant change from the eighteenth century when the Englishman Joseph Townsend had observed that "the process is by written evidence, and the only parties visible in court are the judges and the pleaders."[30] During the Napoleonic occupation, the French had surmised that lawyers would "not become easily accustomed to pleading in public."[31] They were wrong. Lawyers welcomed procedural reforms and public hearings, which granted them a stage upon which they loved to perform.

The forensic orator who basked in the praise of his colleagues and packed the galleries became an iconic figure at the bar. In 1886 the college dean Manuel Duran eulogized many of the famous speakers whom he had observed during nearly a half century of practice. Manuel Josep de Torres, for example, "was distinguished among the public for his ease with words, for his contrasts of tone, for his facility with phrases and cultivated style, for the heat that his convictions generated . . . for his clarity and method of exposition, for the logic, novelty, and insinuations of his arguments, for his capacity to dismantle his adversary, for his strategic use of emotion to win over the gallery." Other lawyers achieved vaunted reputations for "ordinary vehemence," for "grand oratorical movements," or for their "attractive and insinuating . . . elegance." Forthrightness was another virtue. Josep Ventosa, a War of Independence veteran, was "clear in his speeches and writings, his style was simple and his pronouncements cold; but as an orator, he had the resplendent dignity of a good-faith polemicist." Romanticism also penetrated the courtroom. Francesc Permanyer translated his "youthful literary pursuits" into the "eloquent speech in his virile age." "His imagination, enhanced by his poetic sensibilities, put an abundance of felicitous phrases on his lips to express ideas. He possessed the rare ability to match his intelligence with words so that concepts blossomed as soon as he entered a debate, and he could rapidly transfigure them, never lax and always finding the perfect word."[32]

If procedural reforms raised a lawyer's profile, industry and commerce were the great generators of new business. Economy and population had stagnated during the first four decades of the century because of war and revolution, but by the mid-1850s the factory system was billowing away and the city's population had surpassed 180,000, more than double the size of a century earlier. By century's end, more than half million people lived in Barcelona. With demand for housing on the rise, one of the most significant sources of legal work was the property market. In 1854 the municipal government began to tear down the medieval walls and in 1860 commenced the development of the Eixample quarter, a large residential grid surrounding the old center. What made conveyancing so lucrative was that much of this land was governed by emphyteusis; moreover, because of centuries of subinfeudation, as many as three middling "seigneurs" could exist within an ownership chain. Complicating matters even further, dubious Supreme Court jurisprudence held that a major liberal reform of the 1830s limiting — or "defeudalizing" — emphyteutic obligations in Catalonia was not applicable in the city of Barcelona. When the tortured juridical reasoning was stripped way, these decisions simply had the effect of augmenting the amount of money needed to be spread among direct and middling parties, and their legal representatives, for any transfer to take place.[33] Transactions were intricate, a state of affairs that delighted notaries and lawyers as much as it frustrated some buyers and sellers, who resented having to pay off persons holding what were essentially feudal interests.

In addition to the property market, banking, industry, and commerce also generated much legal work. In 1844 the Bank of Barcelona opened its doors and thereafter became the chief financial backer of the textile industry and an early promoter of the railroads. Other investment, savings and mortgage, and agrarian-credit banks followed. At the stock market, brokers traded shares in banks, railroads, steamships, insurance companies, and other large business ventures. In 1876 the Hispano-Colonial Bank was founded with the chartered purpose to celebrate lucrative contracts with the government in the remaining colonies: Cuba, Puerto Rico, and the Philippines. This is not to say that the economy was a roaring success. It was victim to worldwide downturns in the 1860s and in the 1890s, which caused many banks and other firms to become insolvent. The textile industry was dominated by family firms and closed partnerships, characterized by tight capital arrangements between country and city, which hindered innovation. Catalan factories were smaller, and less efficient, than others in Europe, forcing manufacturers to rely on protected Spanish and colonial markets. These problems, though, did not visibly affect a steady law practice. Lawyers coordinated intricate ownership, governance, and successions mechanisms, whether companies were individually held, family-owned, partnerships, or joint-stock entities, or one of the various complicated hybrids. Payments, guarantees, and insurance remained a staple of the commercial law. Lawyers litigated cases, and convoked creditor and investor meetings, when ships went down, deals went wrong, banks went bust, or persons, companies, or partnerships could not meet their obligations or fought over profits.

The rise of mercantile lawyers to positions of power and prestige was the most visible sign of the effects of the industrial economy on the bar. This was no minor occurrence. Not until the Code of Commercial Procedure of 1830 were clients granted the unassailable right to be formally represented by counsel at the Commercial Consulate, the tribunal that held original jurisdiction over all significant cases among Catalan merchants on land or at sea. Lawyers had been active here for decades, but their maneuverability had been restricted and their presence, at times, resented. In 1846 Josep Ventosa, a War of Independence veteran and the quintessential mercantile lawyer of the early industrial era, won elections to the deanship of the College of Lawyers. As a young liberal, he had been a vigorous campaigner for revolutionary laws that had suppressed feudal impediments to commerce and industry but, like so many men of his generation, had become conservative with age. He served as college dean until 1850, a term longer than any of his predecessors. Another distinguished liberal notable was the civil- and mercantile-law professor Ramon Martí d'Eixalà, who, during the 1830s, had been one of the chief promoters of moving the University of Cervera to Barcelona. In 1848 he published the *Institutions of Mercantile Law in Spain*, a volume that went through various editions, was updated by his disciples, and was probably the most widely used textbook and guide of its kind in Spain.[34] Law professor, practicing lawyer, journalist, and Moderate Party politician, Ramon Martí was one of the city's most powerful men of the 1840s and early 1850s. During the deanship of Ventosa, he served as first deputy on the board of directors. Ventosa and Martí's stewardship of the College of Lawyers inaugurated the grand era of the mercantile advocate.[35]

Martí d'Eixalà would become regarded as the intellectual patriarch of the midcentury bar. His eldest disciple, Francesc Permanyer, a commercial lawyer and civil-law professor, was one of the most powerful men in Spain in the 1850s and early 1860s. In 1863 Permanyer was appointed the country's first overseas minister, a position that spoke volumes about the colonial business of his and his colleagues' clients.[36] He died in 1864, at the age of forty-seven, after which the baton passed to another disciple of Martí d'Eixalà, a man named Manuel Duran, who would become the most prominent figure at the Barcelona bar for the rest of the century. A professor of mercantile law, Duran — like Permanyer and Martí before him — frequently assumed the role as representative of Catalan industry while serving as a deputy or senator in Madrid. He was not alone, as various mercantile lawyers and parliamentarians — Joan Illas, Josep Leopold Feu, and others — together fulfilled this role. While in his mid-seventies, Duran capped off his career by serving a short spell as minister of justice in 1899.

Not all commercial lawyers were university professors or parliamentary deputies; some were content to litigate, negotiate, and simply make money. Manuel Josep de Torres, an ex-militiaman, was the longest-serving dean of the College of Lawyers of the century, his tenure running from 1864 to 1873.

With a diverse practice, he had become the bar's top earner in the 1840s when he had been adviser to the city's wealthiest banking house, the Fontanellas, the Barcelona agents for the Bank of San Fernando (later the Bank of Spain) who had made their fortune through Mediterranean and colonial commerce and by acquiring the concession of a number of royal monopolies.[37] The list could go on and on. Ventosa, Martí d'Eixalà, Permanyer, Torres, Illas, Feu, and Duran represented the elite of a puissant sector that ministered to the needs of trade, finance, and industry. They and their closest colleagues were only the most visible among a welter of mercantile-law specialists or, more commonly, advocates who combined commercial and civil work, the bedrock of a thriving practice. Of course, not all mercantilists represented big business and high finance; others serviced more modest clienteles. One example of a midlevel mercantilist was Ramon Cabañeras, who in the 1870s operated a busy practice out of a converted closet in his brothers' silk-lace shop.[38]

The ballooning number of commercial cases eventually overwhelmed the old Commercial Consulate. In the aftermath of the Revolution of 1868, the Progressive Party abolished all commercial tribunals in Spain, which, in spite of piecemeal reform, were now considered remnants of the Old Regime. Having existed since the Middle Ages, these courts functioned with antiquated procedures and were thought to be controlled by big business. Another problem was that the abolition of the guilds had made it difficult, if not impossible, to distinguish who was a merchant from who was not. As a result, artisans, shopkeepers, and small-time dealers had become caught up in proceedings designed for sophisticated traders, agents, brokers, wholesalers, and bankers. As ordinary people engaged in routine business dealings, civil and mercantile jurisdictions became hopelessly entangled.[39] By moving commercial cases to the courts of ordinary justice, jurisdictional quandaries evaporated. Judges and lawyers could apply the civil and mercantile law to a single case as need be.

Lawyers also expanded their reach into areas that had been previously reserved for ecclesiastical-law specialists. Under the Old Regime, only those persons with a degree in "canons" were permitted to appear in ecclesiastical courts. This changed in 1842 when the Progressive Party fused the two degrees of "laws" and "canons" into the single "licentiate in jurisprudence." In 1857 the degree was renamed the "licentiate in law."[40] With the 1842 reform, any lawyer could represent clients in ecclesiastical forums. Most who did were pious men, as liberals and freethinkers would do clients little good by appearing in such forums. The Law Unifying Jurisdictions (1868) did not

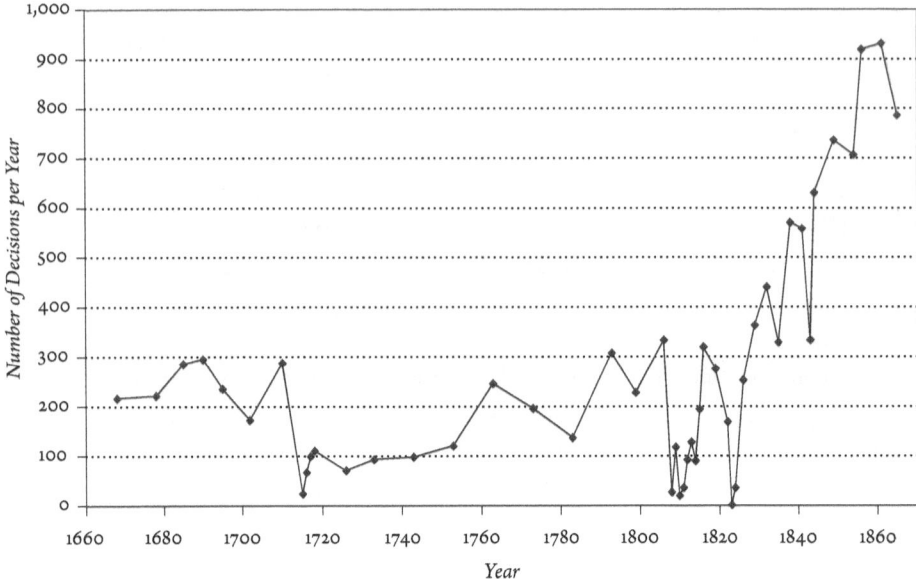

Figure 1. Civil Decisions Issued by the Barcelona Audiencia. *Source*: ACA, RA, Inventario de Libros de Conslusiones Civiles (1372–1844); ACA, RA, Registros de Sentencias y Autos; and ACA, RA, legs. 219–324 ("Dominación Francesa").

abolish ecclesiastical courts as it did with the commercial consulates, but it significantly narrowed their mandate, which became limited to "sacramental causes, benefices, and ecclesiastical crimes." The law annulled their jurisdiction over laypersons, except for cases concerning "separation and nullity of marriage."[41]

We can arrive at some idea of how much law was booming by examining litigation rates. They do not provide a measure of raw quantities of legal business but constitute a reliable barometer. Simply put, rising levels of litigation were good news for lawyers, while falling levels were bad. Figure 1, which tracks civil judgments at the Audiencia, illustrates many of the trends mentioned previously. The coming of absolutism in the early eighteenth century caused litigation rates to plummet, which paralleled a sharp decrease in the number of lawyers. Beginning in the second half of the eighteenth century, however, lawsuits recovered gradually. War and revolution caused acute and periodic crises in the early nineteenth century, but the consolidation of a liberal-constitutionalist order by 1840, paired with industrial takeoff, pushed the number of lawsuits steadily upward.

Figure 1 is a reliable indicator of general trends, but it must be read by taking two further factors into account. First, despite surging lines, it still understates the quantity of work that industry, commerce, property development, and finance generated, because few cases that began at the Commercial Consulate, which had its own internal system of appeals, ended up at the Audiencia. As such, the Audiencia can serve only as a barometer for civil cases coming from the ordinary courts of justice. In other words, it cannot account for commercial litigation, which was also booming. Second, the rise in the number of civil decisions in the late 1830s was not solely due to more lawsuits being filed but was also the consequence of a key legislative change. Beginning in the 1835, the Audiencia chambers almost exclusively heard appeals and did not get bogged down adjudicating cases in first instance, as it had under Old Regime procedures when one party was poor, a widow, a minor, an invalid, a rape or rapture victim, a royal or ecclesiastical entity, or some other person or institution with a privilege. Dedicated exclusively to appeals, the court was able to process more cases. As such, the increase in litigation beginning in the late 1830s also reflected this change. This caveat aside, it is clear that the district courts were hearing more cases, which were coming to the Audiencia on appeal.

Figure 1 does not measure litigiousness, in other words, lawsuits per population. Further statistics can shed light on this, although the previously mentioned changes in Audiencia jurisdiction, in addition to the fact that commercial cases are not accounted for, makes any calculation rough. From the census of Floridablanca in 1787 to the next completed census of 1857, the population in Catalonia almost doubled, increasing from some 875,000 to 1,650,000 persons, while the city of Barcelona grew from some 92,000 to 178,000. During the same period of time, Audiencia civil decisions increased from about 200 to 300 per year to around 900. On the basis of these figures, it appears that civil suits were multiplying at a greater rate than population.[42] During the same period of time, the number of lawyers in Barcelona rose from 197 to 462, increasing at a rate greater than population but less than the proliferation of lawsuits.[43] In concrete terms, the number of lawyers in society was on the rise, and the available lawsuits for each lawyer was also increasing. To be sure, advocates were awash in litigation and other matters. For a competent practitioner who had managed to emerge from the revolutionary era with his practice and health intact, the middling decades of the century were a boon.

If we bundle these observations together, the conclusion is evident. Lawyers were blessed by a booming property market, a growing economy, the availability of judicial posts in an expanding court system, the possibility of aspiring to elected or appointed office, and soaring numbers of lawsuits. In addition, procedural reforms allowed them a greater latitude in framing their cases, raised their profile, and gave them access to forums and proceedings where their presence had been resisted. It would not be accurate to state that they had recuperated their lost power of the early modern period when they had constituted a larger percentage of urban population, possessed a client base from a more ample swath of society, wrote treatises distributed throughout Europe, and wielded enviable political influence. What is indisputable, though, is that lawyers had achieved renewed prominence. Having overcome the deflation of litigation and a crisis of identity during the early to mid-eighteenth century, and the tumult of the revolutionary decades of the early nineteenth, they thrived in the liberal-industrial era. If the early modern period represented a golden age, then the nineteenth century was a silver age. The Barcelona bar, together with others throughout western Europe, embarked upon a renewed epoch of splendor.

Institutions and Leaders

Lawyers were liberal, but this was, of course, a vague description. By the mid-nineteenth century, liberalism was no longer a revolutionary ideology but a political culture shared by urban, educated men and women throughout Europe. It was defined by some baseline tenets — constitutional monarchy, elections, a free market, judicial and individual rights, an ethos of merit based on talent — but these were broad categories, subject to interpretation and dispute. Lawyers, like others, could disagree over the size of the franchise to such an extent that some thought the right to vote should remain limited to a small percentage, while a few democrats campaigned for universal manhood suffrage. With respect to religion, some favored keeping marriage a sacrament and allowing ecclesiastical courts to retain their jurisdiction over the family, while others wished to reduce marriage to a contract, to abolish ecclesiastical courts, and to put all family law under the exclusive purview of the tribunals of ordinary justice. With respect to judicial rights, most favored freedom of speech and assembly, but they disagreed on what kind of publications and meetings should be made illegal under press laws designed to protect the constitutional monarchy from treasonous threats from the absolutist right and the republican revolutionary left. These debates were like so many others, and each issue contained a middle ground. The respective powers of the legislature and the monarchy, the influence of the church and the reach of the ecclesiastical law, the limits of speech and assembly, the rights of criminal defendants, the ability of workers to organize collectively, and numerous other issues were the stuff of everyday politics. To say that a lawyer was liberal had become a truism, a broad description that included educated persons with a wide range of opinions.

Of course, some lawyers were not liberal, the proverbial exceptions that proved the rule. For the most part, absolutist advocates remained associated with ecclesiastical or old aristocratic circles. Felip Vergés, university professor of canon law, was the most outspoken representative of a small — but periodically vocal — absolutist wing of the midcentury bar. A father of ten who upon his wife's death took a vow of celibacy and joined the priesthood, he was both a lawyer and a cleric, a fire and brimstone preacher of charisma and emotional force. Affectionately described as a "buffoon"[44] in a eulogy by a colleague, he energetically opposed each and every modern political ideology, arguing rather unoriginally but adamantly that enlightenment, liberalism, freethinking, socialism, and anarchism were all permutations of the original sin and singular heresy of Protestantism.[45] In 1872 he was imprisoned for a few days. The police arrested him outside his office and charged him, along with a number of ecclesiastics, with supporting armed Carlist guerrilla bands active in nearby towns. These skirmishes were about to escalate into the Second Carlist War (1872–75), but as far as Vergés was concerned, he spent only a few days in jail. The judge summoned a few of his students who unanimously testified that their professor did not preach the Carlist gospel. Whether he supported armed rebellion was certainly debatable, but he was a vigorous defender of the union of throne and altar who regarded liberalism as nothing less than a sin. Later in life, he left the university to serve as vicar general of Barcelona, the highest judicial office in the diocese.[46]

The Vergés family remained a thorn in the side of the municipality for much of the remainder of the century. At the time of the arrest of Felip Vergés in 1872, one of his sons had just launched a massive civil lawsuit against the city. The case generated vast publicity not only because the suitor claimed an astronomical amount of money but also because of what was at stake. In dispute were the lands upon which the Citadel fortress had sat. Upon the conclusion of the War of Spanish Succession (1702–14), Philip V had built the fortress to prevent the rebellious city from again raising arms. Its construction had involved egregious acts of cruelty that had become etched into collective memory: some one thousand houses, 17 percent of those in the city, had been razed to clear space for the fortress and its esplanade.[47] In the nineteenth century, terrible executions of patriots and liberals had taken place behind its walls. In the aftermath of the Revolution of 1868, the municipality tore it down, a grand symbolic gesture, the Barcelona equivalent to the storming of the Bastille. The lands were converted into a public park, which served as the scene for the World Fair of 1888. The lawsuit, in the meanwhile, dragged on for more than two decades and turned into a cause célèbre.

In the lawsuit, Francesc Vergés i Mas represented the Marquis of Ayerbe, then a minor, whose widowed mother claimed that her son was the rightful owner of the lands. This lawsuit resembled usurpation cases that would become quite common in the late twentieth century, as descendants of persons deprived of property under communist or fascist regimes sued to gain compensation or reclaim possession. In the 1870s, however, there was obviously no such precedent. The argument was novel. Given that the usurpation had taken place more than a century and a half before the suit was filed, few thought that Ayerbe could prevail. They were wrong, though, as the suitor had a strong case in law. Francesc Vergés i Mas contended that because the revolutionary decree of 1868 had declared Philip V's confiscation in 1716 to be illegal, the lands should return to their rightful owner.[48] Because nobles had never been dispossessed of their lands, there was no legal basis for assigning ownership to the municipality. In the end, Vergés i Mas won the case: the Audiencia ruled that Ayerbe should be compensated more than 3 million pesetas; the city, for its part, successfully petitioned the central government for relief.[49] The collegial nature of legal practice meant that the Vergés family was held in high esteem because of its forensic talent, but few shared the family's political convictions. Indeed, the legal community rallied around the municipality. At one point, a coterie of the bar's top advocates from diverse political parties drafted a legal opinion siding with the municipality.[50]

During the middle decades of the nineteenth century, this liberal bar grew increasingly conservative. This is not to say that lawyers became sympathetic to absolutism. Rather, they slowly abandoned the promise to provide a better version of justice to the common man and settled into legal practice that looked much like it had in the eighteenth century. Despite the previously mentioned changes — despite the rising prestige, visibility, reputation, power, and wealth of elite lawyers — a practitioner continued to work in the same rhythms as the past. A law office was usually in or adjacent to a lawyer's home; it consisted of a practitioner and sometimes an apprentice or two, who were visited by clients and proctors. Advocates remained flooded with paperwork, continued to carry out many of the same tasks as they had previously, and were subsumed in claims, counterclaims, answers, responses, motions, appeals, interrogatories, counterinterrogatories, and procedural and substantive legal questions. Lawyers went about their work with a skeptical but practical dignity, participated in associational life, and subscribed to an ethos of disinterestedness, independence, and probity. Comfortable within the established constitutional order, veterans of the army, the militias, the secret societies, and the patriotic clubs disremembered their youthful activism.

The leadership was more conservative than the rank and file. The deans of the College of Lawyers, elected each year at a plenary meeting, were high-profile lawyers and university professors who, for the most part, represented rich clients: factory owners; agrarian gentry; the wine and liqueur export industry; large shareholders in banks, maritime insurance companies, railroads, and steamship lines; urban property owners, developers, and rentiers; and commercial houses immersed in Mediterranean and colonial commerce. They were the type of heavyweights who could competently represent the interest of the bar in the proverbial backrooms of the oligarchic state. The college's board of directors was usually more plural, but, for the most part, it also comprised high earners, longtime practitioners, well-connected individuals, and respected intellects. In 1864 the college established a physical headquarters on the Carrer Lleona, a street near the Plaça Reial. It remained there until 1895 when the municipality loaned it the stately Archdeacon's Palace, a building that faced the cathedral. The college's improved headquarters reflected its rising power. The college constituted a strong corporate presence in the city alongside associations such as the Catalan Agrarian Institute, the Industrial Institute, and the Atheneum. Many elite lawyers sat on the boards of these organizations, in addition to those of banks, companies, charitable foundations, and royal academies, creating much directorship overlap and interlock. Advocates formed an identified locus of institutional power in conjunction with industrialists and financiers, property holders, rentiers, and intellectuals.[51]

On one level, conservatism was a logical consequence of institutional consolidation. Revolution had been a time of youth, but when the bar settled down during the industrial era, seasoned and successful practitioners, content with the status quo and familiar with the inner workings of the city's economy and political culture, emerged to the fore. Still, this conservatism must be qualified in various ways. To begin, the college was officially neutral when it came to politics. According to uniform bylaws, promulgated by the government in 1838, applicable to all colleges in Spain, membership was obligatory for any lawyer wishing to appear before courts in the city. The Progressives briefly changed the law in 1841 by allowing any lawyer to practice "without the necessity of registering in any corporation or specific college," but in 1844 the Moderates reversed this, so that enrolment was definitively made obligatory.[52] Unlike other associations, the College had to refrain from emitting partisan viewpoints, because it had to represent the interests of all lawyers regardless of political affiliation. One of the unofficial but frequent jobs of the dean was to smooth out conflicts when a lawyer ran into problems with a judge and prosecutor; for this reason, the college needed to maintain an air of independence and avoid needless conflicts with the judiciary, which could prejudice its capacity to come to the aid of members in an evenhanded fashion.

The ethos of neutrality took time to calcify. Upon its foundation, the college was embroiled in the upheavals of the revolutionary 1830s. As a liberal institution, it resolutely declared in favor of the dynastic claims of Isabel II during the First Carlist War, sent delegates to meetings to discuss how to finance the war effort, and dispatched a congratulatory message to a controversial Moderate captain general, the Baron de Meer, notorious for his frequent recourse to repressive measures.[53] Following the volatile days of the 1830s, however, the board sensed the risks of this behavior and avoided explicit affiliations. If the college was identified with a specific government or even regime, it could suffer a backlash upon political change. The turning point occurred in 1843 when the municipality asked the college to render a legal opinion on whether the central government should indemnify the city the gargantuan sum of 10 million reales for having raised a militia the previous year. This was a loaded question, as the militias had become radicalized in 1842. They had manned the barricades for the first time and had opened fire on the Spanish army. This poisoned request caused a nervous, and probably divided, board to convoke an extraordinary plenary session to debate how it should respond: many members argued that intervening directly in politics — issuing legal opinions on matters that did not impinge on the practice of law or the organization of the college itself — was beyond its mandate. The board dragged its feet, set up a commission, but, as was often the case, did not act.[54]

In the end, politicians resolved the impasse. In 1844 the Moderates banned colleges of lawyers from publishing opinions that did not concern the exercise of legal practice or the rules of collegial organization.⁵⁵ All indications suggest that the prohibition was welcomed, as it protected the college from having meetings hijacked by those wishing to convert them into a sounding board for ulterior concerns. From then on, the board balked when requested to emit opinions that could cause it to be entangled in a political controversy. This ethos of neutrality was evident during the next major Carlist War (1872–75). In 1874 the board reluctantly agreed to take up a monetary collection when asked by the Ministry of Justice. Unlike the previous Carlist War, however, it did not emit a single statement in favor of the constitutional regime and, by the measured tone of its pronouncement, implied that its contribution should not be used to purchase arms or outfit battalions but only to provide "aid to the sick and the injured."⁵⁶ At the end of the war, the board discussed the status of a few applicants and members who had enlisted in Carlist militias. It opted to ignore the matter, contending that the college was a "corporation completely alien from political acts and opinions" and "has never excluded any member from its registry or lists for said acts or political opinions."⁵⁷ Later, it refused to issue a legal opinion on the conditions of the working class (1887) or even on the creation of a chair of Catalan law at the University of Barcelona (1891). In the first instance, it replied that it had no useful information, and in the second, it cited reasons of "delicacy" for staying out of the fray.⁵⁸

The college only issued confrontational statements when a law, or proposed law, threatened its autonomy or restricted a lawyer's "freedom to practice." In such cases, its modus operandi was to set up a committee to draft a written complaint to the parliament or the Ministry of Justice. It would usually team up with other colleges in Spain in order to deluge the government with complaints coming from all corners of the peninsula. The first major dispute occurred in 1844, when the Moderate government ordered that a public prosecutor be present at annual meetings to ensure that elections were being carried out according to uniform bylaws and to audit the list of public defenders. In response, the college protested this assault "against the decorum and independence of the profession."⁵⁹ When the Progressives took their next turn in power, they removed judicial oversight in 1855.⁶⁰ Other conflicts unfolded in a similar manner. It was impossible to convince a government to reverse a decision, but protests could put a complaint on the table so that when a different party came to power, the issue could be redressed. Throughout the century, the college entered into a clutch of reoccurring disputes over taxation, procedure, and the number of public defenders. A lawyer's "freedom of practice" anywhere in the country was another source of tension: the college protested against fees or restrictions placed upon advocates who sought to appear outside the jurisdictions of their residences. In some cases, the vehemence of the protest was disproportionate to the grievance. In other cases, it was not. These conflicts served as symbolic contests in which the Ministry of Justice and the bar jostled over the scope of professional autonomy.

Nevertheless, political neutrality was a myth, or, to be more precise, a legal fiction. The bar's political arm — the Academy of Jurisprudence and Legislation — was not subject to regulation and hence could publish opinions without fear of censure. Under the letter of the law, the academy was a separate entity with its own elected president and board, in which membership was voluntary; in reality, however, the academy was housed within the college, and many college deans and board members served at one time or another as academy presidents and board members. The college financially sponsored the academy and eventually dedicated the largest portion of its discretionary budget to a voluminous library, one of the largest of the city, one of the purposes of which was to outfit academy members with the scholarly tools needed to articulate conservative opinions.[61] In concrete terms, separate institutional presence was a thin veil. Officially, the Academy of Jurisprudence liked to date its origins to the Enlightenment. However, unlike its previous incarnation during the times of Charles III, it was not designed as a place to train apprentices in practical jurisprudence. Nor was the academy, as it would become in the twentieth century, a hallowed institution where membership was an honor bestowed on the eminent. In the nineteenth century, it was an association, in theory an open forum for fruitful debate and discussion. Any lawyer or notary holding a law degree, young or old, active or inactive, with a passable reputation, who underwent routine admissions procedures, could join. In practice, however, majority opinions and publications echoed the conservative predisposition of university professors, leading practitioners, and experienced notaries. Dissenters would participate in a few sessions, but their interest would inevitably wane. There were plenty of other associations, clubs, and newspapers where advocates of more progressive ideas could find a more receptive audience and like-minded colleagues.

The academy's early history was bumpy. Founded in 1840, it ceased to meet in 1842 and was not reinvigorated until 1857 when the college began to have funds at its disposal to bankroll its activities.[62] The academy was more active in some years than others; it usually convened between one and two dozen times, although there were some slow years when it met less frequently. During its sessions, members — called *académicos* — debated legal technicalities outside the comprehension of the layperson but by no means inconsequential to the lives and futures of the populace. It sponsored prizes and set up committees to dispatch reports to the Spanish Cortes or the Ministry of Justice. It was at times ridiculed for its meager publication record, for convoking competitions without awarding prizes, for organizing committees that never wrote reports, and for failing to meet other lofty goals set by overoptimistic presidents at the start of each academic year.[63] Unfulfilled expectations, however, were part and parcel of associational life. In spite of criticism, it was a vibrant forum. Its leading members published books and articles, were active in other economic and intellectual corporations, and doubled as politicians and journalists. The academy forged an enduring consensus of conservative juridical opinion on sensitive topics.

The image of a conservative bar also needs to be qualified by recognizing diversity, dissent, and division. Conservatives captured the college leadership, but this was not done without conflict or contestation. Indeed, at one point, it looked as if lawyers loosely associated with the Progressive Party, or who at least shared a more pluralistic vision of the bar, were destined to govern the college. The key point of inflection came in the late 1850s and early 1860s when record numbers appeared at annual meetings to contest elections to the deanship and board.[64] On one occasion, critiques of the board even spilled into the press, something that was rare, given that members assiduously strove to keep internal disputes out of the public eye.[65] The reason behind the sudden politicization was that the college had come into possession of serious amounts of money and hence could sponsor more ambitious projects. In 1855 the Ministry of Justice allowed the college to charge a tax of 10 reales every time a lawyer registered as a representative of a client, a system that had been instituted in Madrid a few years earlier.[66] As a result, coffers swelled. Before its implementation, the college operated on a modest annual budget of some 10,000 reales, consisting of induction fees and yearly dues. With the tax, the college could afford to waive practicing lawyer dues entirely. Its budget increased tenfold and, by the mid-1860s, regularly exceeded 100,000 reales.[67] Disagreements over how to spend treasury funds were equivalent to nothing less than how the bar saw its mission and future.

Members of the bar's conservative wing favored raising the bar's profile by establishing a permanent headquarters to convey majesty and erudition. They cast their gaze toward the Order of Lawyers in Paris and other French cities, where, since the eighteenth century, the library had been the centerpiece of the corporate home.[68] With time, this plan would prevail, but its proponents first had to fend off an alternative proposal. A rival faction sought to revive and sponsor a Mutual Aid Society for Catalan Lawyers, a fledgling pension fund, founded in the late eighteenth century, resuscitated in 1840, and continually on the verge of bankruptcy.[69] The fund provided assistance to sick, struggling, and elderly lawyers, and to widows and children of deceased members. In 1859 the Ministry of Justice approved a compromise board request whereby the money from the representation tax, not needed for day-to-day expenses, was to be divided into four parts: two parts would go to the Mutual Aid Society, one part to the Academy of Jurisprudence, and one part to the library.[70] In 1860 university professor Vicenç Rius, the president of the Mutual Aid Society, won elections to the deanship and prioritized the needs of the pension fund. Despite this brief spurt of support, the fund suffered from crippling financial problems and was never able to stay buoyant for very long.[71] In 1871 the college withdrew sponsorship, and in 1876 the Mutual Aid Society declared itself insolvent.[72]

The progressive wing's other major initiative was a juridical periodical, designed to act as a counterweight to the monolithically conservative opinions of the Academy of Jurisprudence and its obsessive preoccupation with civil law. In April 1859 a group of progressive lawyers launched *La Gaceta Jurídica*, which hit the streets twice a week; in January, it changed its name to *El Foro* (The Bar) and reduced distribution to once a week. For the most part, the paper was a forum for doctrinaire left-wing opinions, many of which would become reflected in major legislative initiatives during the revolutionary period in Spain, known as the Democratic Sexennium (1868–74). The editors published articles that called attention to the need to lighten criminal punishments, to increase rights of criminal defendants, to deploy the administrative law to prosecute electoral fraud, to erect a modern civil service on the basis of competitive examination, to ensure greater religious freedoms for Protestants, to improve the quality of municipal justice, and even to legalize and to regulate prostitution.[73] For entertainment, *El Foro* chronicled a number of causes célèbres taking place throughout Europe that often read like serialized novels, chock-full of tales of fraud, arson, rape, betrayal, kidnapping, counterfeiting, murder, paid assassination, husbands brutally murdering wives, and wives cleverly poisoning husbands. Ultimately, the periodical did not prove any more successful than the Mutual Aid Society. It ceased publication in July 1864. In 1866 Josep Maluquer, a Progressive lawyer started up a new organ, *El Derecho* (The Law). Appearing every fortnight, this periodical featured a wider variety of opinion than its predecessor but did not run for very long.[74]

In the end, conservative lawyers captured the leadership of the college and, once in power, remained there. The key election occurred in 1864 when Manuel Josep de Torres defeated Vicenç Rius as dean and, upon taking control, used funds to give the college its first home on the Carrer Lleona. The board ceased to sponsor the periodical and withdrew support for the Mutual Aid Society. Instead, the headquarters, the library, and the Academy of Jurisprudence absorbed most of the budget. Torres's decade-long tenure endowed the college with stability. This became evident during the Democratic Sexennium, a revolutionary period in which the country experienced four regime changes, countless governments, multiple episodes of urban unrest, and a renewed civil war. Previous epochs of revolution had triggered endless directorial shakeups. For example, during the Regency of Espartero (1840–43), the city experienced an outbreak of cholera in 1841, militias fought the Spanish army in the streets in 1842, and a democratic revolt in 1843 prompted the army to lay siege and bombard the city from the mountain of Montjuïc. Amid the turmoil, the college had three deans in the space of three years. During the Progressive Biennium (1854–56) — a period that featured multiple uprisings, a general strike, and another outbreak of cholera — the deanship underwent four changes in two years.[75] In light of this track record, a similar spate of instability could have been expected during the Democratic Sexennium, but nothing of this sort occurred. Following the Revolution of 1868, the College of Lawyers did not seek to mirror the ideological outlook of the country and calmly reelected Torres. In 1873 the elderly Torres ceded the deanship to his law office partner and disciple Melcior Ferrer. The college had successfully established a conservative personality, portraying itself as a beacon of order in a sea of revolution and instability.

The brains behind the conservative takeover was Manuel Duran, a commercial lawyer and university professor well connected in Barcelona industry and Madrid politics. A man of tremendous energy, Duran came to embody and represent Barcelona lawyers in all of Spain. His charisma, erudition, and organizational and motivational skills meant that whatever institution received his attention quickly sprang into action. During the Democratic Sexennium, he became president of the Academy of Jurisprudence. Until his tenure, the bar had functioned without any pageantry whatsoever. Under his leadership, however, academy opening ceremonies were endowed with pomp and circumstance. Municipal dignitaries — mayors, magistrates, bishops, vicars, provincial governors, university rectors — and other notables occupied front-row seats as invited guests. The secretary opened proceedings by summarizing the previous year's activities, and the president delivered a keynote address covered by the press. This event could be used to a greater symbolic effect than the college's annual meeting, a closed-door and sometimes divisive session in which internal debates, decisions, elections, and protests were not meant for public consumption and, following the removal of prosecutorial oversight in 1855, were out of earshot of the Ministry of Justice and the judiciary.

Manual Duran converted the academy from a dull forum capable of boring the most supple of minds to a locus of dissent that expressed visceral dissatisfaction with the cascade of legislative initiatives of the Democratic Sexennium. Just as progressive members had launched legal periodicals to promote juridical reforms, conservatives at the Academy of Jurisprudence criticized those pieces of legislation that they considered repugnant. The academy inveighed against laws proclaiming freedom of religion, requiring civil marriages, softening jail sentences, instituting trial by jury, reorganizing the judiciary, and reforming the agrarian law.[76] The one issue it ignored is also telling. Missing from the academy's agenda is any debate over the merits of the Moret Law (1870), the first step toward the abolition of slavery in Cuba, one of the most emblematic enactments of the period. At first blush, this was surprising because the academy president Manuel Duran and the soon-to-be college dean Melcior Ferrer were leading members of the Hispanic Overseas Circle, a powerful lobby of industrial and commercial interests, which vigorously opposed the Moret Law. Nonetheless, Duran and Ferrer kept slavery off the agenda. Strategic silence prevented the academy's reputation from being irretrievably tarnished and safeguarded the bar from being ripped apart along pro- and antiabolitionist lines. Cuban slavery was not definitively abolished until 1886, but lawyers conspired to keep this indefensible institution outside the scope of mainstream debate.[77]

The divergent opinions expressed within the legal periodicals, on the one hand, and by the Academy of Jurisprudence, on the other, evidenced that lawyers disagreed on a plethora of issues dividing Left and Right in Europe, including religious freedoms, criminal procedures and punishments, and suffrage. Conservative lawyers preferred a Catholic state, religious to civil marriages, fewer rights for defendants, stiffer punishments for criminals, and a small franchise; in contrast, progressive lawyers favored reforms that would

The conservative profession: portrait of Manuel Duran i Bas (Oil painting by Antoni Caba displayed at the College of Lawyers of Barcelona)

support a greater degree of religious freedoms, augment the franchise, grant the accused a larger basket of judicial rights, and institute lighter punishments. Yet, with time, conservatives wrestled control of the college away from their rivals. Upon assuming power, they ceased to sponsor the Mutual Aid Society and a legal periodical, built a stately headquarters with a voluminous library, and converted the Academy of Jurisprudence into an articulate voice of conservative opinion. The question is why? Why did conservatives successfully conquer the leadership? On one level, success was due to the efforts of individuals who mounted vigorous protests at annual meetings, campaigned hard, and contested elections. This should not be overlooked, and, in fact, it accounted for short-term victories. However, the Barcelona bar remained conservative throughout the century, indicating that structural factors were also at play.

To begin, the professoriate was the intellectual source of conservatism. Professors molded the personality of the bar by shaping minds of young men who passed through their classrooms. In one sense, professorial conservatism was common throughout Spain. Ten uninterrupted years of Moderate Party governance from 1844 to 1854 resulted in the permanent appointment of conservative professors and judges, who set the tone of the university and the judiciary for decades thereafter. However, Barcelona professors were particularly conservative even by Spanish standards. This is because many mid-century professors had been trained at the University of Cervera, where young men groomed for academic pursuits had excelled under lecturers known for traditionalist preferences and, in particular, their mastery of and firm belief in the virtue, beauty, and scientific perfectibility of Roman law, "written reason" to its votaries. Although the founders of the University of Barcelona broke with their mentors by embracing liberalism, they remained faithful to Roman law. Ramon Martí d'Eixalà, the intellectual guru of the university in the 1840s and early 1850s, forged a jurisprudential and philosophical path that reconciled tradition and reform, Roman law and liberalism.[78]

Professors did not confine themselves to the ivory tower but ran private offices, published in the press, ran for elected office, and vigorously participated in associational life. One of the chief reasons for moving the university out of Cervera was to uproot it from its placid, bucolic surroundings, ideal for meditative scholarly contemplation but far from removed from the pulse of economic, judicial, and political life. With the university in Barcelona, law professors could reap the rewards of big-city practice.

Professors who doubled as commercial lawyers and parliamentary deputies formed the nucleus of the "Catalan school" or the "Catalan conservative school."[79] This group comprised academics, prestigious lawyers, and other professionals, property owners, journalists, politicians, and assorted literati. Such men were redoubtably constitutionalist, but they did not believe in universal suffrage or unlimited religious freedom. They were liberal advocates: headstrong, independent, critically minded, self-styled, and in many cases self-made men who believed that success belonged to those who worked to achieve it. They were scholars of the Roman-canonic tradition and espousers of Thomist ethics and the virtues of a Catholic society. They were critics of Rousseau and the radical-democratic tradition of the Enlightenment, and they were followers of post-Enlightenment conservative philosophies, such as the Scottish school of common sense, Halmitonian pragmatism, French eclecticism, and German historicism. At times, professors encountered difficulties winning elections to the college deanship and board.[80] Many lawyers were hesitant to place too much authority in the hands of scholar-politicians whose first priority seemed to rest firmly with the concerns of big business rather than with the daily stresses of the average practitioner. Nonetheless, professors were far and away the most dynamic force at the midcentury bar.

Another reason why the bar's leadership grew so conservative had to do with the political allegiances of well-paying clienteles. The key economic position dividing a Progressive from a Moderate, in other words a left-liberal from a right-liberal, was trade protectionism. Moderates favored high protectionist walls to protect Catalan textiles and other industries, whereas Progressives, with some notable exceptions in Barcelona, favored low tariffs in order to provide cheaper goods to consumers and, in fact, to pressure industrialists to modernize their factories and to improve their international competitiveness. There were some distinguished lawyers of this latter opinion, the most prominent of whom was Laureà Figuerola. A onetime junta member and professor of political economy, he moved from the University of Barcelona to that of Madrid in the 1850s, where he ran a thriving administrative-law practice and launched a brilliant political career.[81] Minister of the Treasury in the 1870s, he was the architect of free-trade measures that incensed his conservative colleagues back home. It is no coincidence that Figuerola chose to settle in Madrid. In Barcelona, most prestigious lawyers were protectionist and, if they harbored dissenting opinions, did not broadcast them among clients. Once a lawyer became embedded in the world of industry, finance, banking, and commerce, he intermixed with protectionist associations linked to conservative political parties.

Well-paying agrarian clients also backed conservative parties. The rural gentry was intent on maintaining compromises reached on agrarian property in the 1830s and sought to prevent lands from undergoing another round of reform and disentailment. What is more, liberal legislation had not resolved ownership contests in a few regions. In particular, the Penedés Valley, a fertile wine-producing region some fifty kilometers outside Barcelona, was the source of ongoing conflict. The chief problem here, and in other viticultural zones as well, revolved around a customary landholding mechanism known as the *rabassa morta*. This was a "temporary" rather than a "permanent" emphyteutic establishment, which, according to custom, ran for the duration of the vine. The peasants working these lands — the *rabassaires* — wished to be treated as other emphyteutic peasants and have their leases declared permanent, the next best thing to outright (alodial) ownership. Instead, they saw their legal rights progressively deteriorate as a series of controversial Audiencia and Supreme Court decisions essentially downgraded their status from usufructuary owners to sharecroppers with heritable leases, arbitrarily set at a maximum of fifty years (presumably the average duration of a vine).[82] Only a few lawyers took up their cudgels.[83] Most supported the direct owners and the economic interests of those who profited from the fruits of peasant labor, the wine and liqueur industry, the largest export business in Catalonia.

The Conservative Profession: The Law

The rise of conservatism has thus far been presented as a story in which leading lawyers slowly abandoned the idealistic promises of the revolutionary era, and in which a powerful coterie of men — associated with wealthy urban and agrarian clienteles, the university, and political parties — came to direct the College of Lawyers and the Academy of Jurisprudence. Another dimension to this conservatism involved the legal tradition itself. Disagreements over multiple political issues surfaced at associations and appeared within publications. These debates, however, did not affect everyday legal practice. Indeed, there was much greater consensus concerning fundamental civil legal rules that should govern society. Barcelona advocates were no different from their colleagues elsewhere: The legal tradition acted as a conservative weight in all of Europe. Lawyers in Barcelona, Paris, London, or wherever — irrespective of their ideological inclinations — shared a mutual respect for the foundations of their calling. Just as London barristers agreed that the English common law was the best of all legal systems, and French lawyers grew fond of the French Civil Code and its volumes of commentary, Barcelona lawyers were convinced that Catalan law was well suited for the industrial age.

The antiquity, durability, and peculiarity of legal traditions are among the chief reasons why theories that have stressed the tight fit between law and capitalism can be misleading. By reading authors from Max Weber to E. P. Thompson, one could get the impression that the law provided an intelligible set of rules, rationally suited to the smooth functioning of capitalism (Weber) and the hegemony of an agrarian and mercantile bourgeoisie (Thompson). Yet law was not always so functional.[84] While it is indisputable that "Western" — and much "non-Western" — law secured property rights, a necessary prerequisite for capitalism, the law was a messy and idiosyncratic body of knowledge that often delivered bewildering results, sometimes incomprehensible to the average capitalist on the street. What is more, there was not a single formula that jurists agreed was best suited to promoting commerce, industry, or "bourgeois" domesticity. Nowhere were these anomalies so evident as in Spain where lawyers in Barcelona and Madrid endlessly argued over the content and structure of a civil code. Debates revolved around which laws were more liberal or more equitable, which were more favorable to creating prosperity and happiness, and which endowed society with a firmer ethical foundation. In a broad sense, both bars were conservative: each championed the juridical tradition into which its members had been indoctrinated, and each resisted change. The intensity of the debates ignited a prolonged conflict that would contribute to the rise of political Catalanism.

Examining the legal tradition, then, not only helps explore conservatism but also leads into a discussion of the genesis of Catalan nationalism. According to the juridical terminology of the time, Catalonia housed its own "foral law," which differed from the "common law" of Spain. The Catalan law had its roots in the laws of the medieval principality, preserved in complicated union agreements, periodically modified through the centuries. The common law, in contrast, was rooted in the historic texts of the Crown of Castile. The status of Catalonia was not unique but present throughout the Spanish periphery: the Balearic Islands, Aragon, Navarre, Viscaya, and Galicia also possessed foral-law regimes. The common law was relatively uniform, whereas the foral law not only differed from one region to the next but also exhibited significant internal variation in each region. The complicated relationship was further confused by the fact that many common laws were applicable within foral regions because they either overlapped with similar foral laws or had been imposed by legislative fiat or Supreme Court jurisprudence.[85] The precise relationship between these bodies of law was subject to intricate choice-of-law rules. The vexed question of whether a common or a foral rule applied in a specific instance often needed to be resolved on a case-by-case basis. Nevertheless, such conundrums were not out of the ordinary. In all of continental Europe, it was common for multiple systems of private law to exist within a single country or region. The purpose of codification, then, was to obviate differences in favor of uniform laws for all citizens. The question that was to plague Spain for decades was what laws should constitute the baseline of a civil code?

Catalan lawyers colloquially referred to their foral law as "Catalan law" and labeled the common law "Castilian law." Despite the presence of much overlap, family and inheritance were the major areas where the two systems diverged. Most Catalans were governed by what they called a "Roman" family organization in which a husband and wife maintained individual property and were relatively free to transfer their assets during life or by testament. This differed from a "Germanic" family organization in which family assets were considered "community property" of both husband and wife and were divided evenly among legitimate children by intestate succession. The Castilian law, for its part, contained family-law institutions, which, though containing many Roman-law institutions, were considered more Germanic. Only assets that a spouse owned before marriage were deemed individual property, whereas those acquired after marriage were community property. With respect to inheritance, a testator was required to spread his or her assets out relatively evenly among legitimate children, although he or she was allowed to endow a preferred child with a larger portion, the size of which depended on the number of children. The two legal systems have been said to reflect the organization of "stem" (Roman) and "nuclear" (Germanic) families.[86] To be clear, the difference between Catalan and Castilian law, between stem and nuclear families, had nothing to do with the influence of Roman or Germanic peoples on the soil of the respective regions. It was rooted in the evolution of medieval society within the various Iberian kingdoms when Roman and Visigothic compilations became received, rejected, mixed, and modified because of historical circumstances.[87]

In the minds of many, the Roman-Germanic dichotomy paralleled the ideological divide between Right and Left. Roman family law was considered more conservative because it fortified paternal authority and favored the continuity of large estates. A husband often brought more assets to a marriage than a wife, and, even when this was not the case, he invariably earned more during married life. Under the Roman law, then, he controlled the lion's share of family assets and hence could distribute them, during life or by testament, more or less as he pleased among his wife, children (legitimate or illegitimate), other family members, or outsiders. His power was so absolute that he could disinherit, for all intents and purposes, his wife and children. With respect to the persistence of large estates, the Roman-law inheritance regime permitted a "liberal" version of primogeniture. Revolutionary legislation of the 1830s had abolished "aristocratic primogeniture," known as *mayorazgo* in Spain, in which a noble title and estate automatically descended to a firstborn even when a testator was hopelessly indebted. However, in Catalonia and many other foral-law regions, testators were free to pass an estate voluntarily to a firstborn or any other person for that matter (after satisfying creditors and some limited obligations to other children), a practice that gave rise to "elective primogeniture." In other words, a solvent male testator in Catalonia — as in England and most places in the United States — was usually at liberty to leave an entire estate to a single, male heir.

In contrast, Germanic family law was considered more equitable, because it discouraged primogeniture, spread out assets more evenly among siblings, and gave a widowed mother greater authority. Because a wife jointly owned family assets, she could not be disinherited; moreover, she had greater say in distributing them to children especially when she outlived her husband. Younger children were guaranteed a greater minimum inheritance, given that a considerable portion of a family's patrimony was distributed through intestate succession. In Spain, a testator from a common-law region with a large family could pass only somewhere between a third and a half of an estate to a preferred child.[88]

Catalan law did not consist of a cold application of legal rules derived from Roman law contained in the Corpus Iuris Civilis. A plethora of customary juridical institutions — contained within compilations and glossed by jurists over centuries — governed marriage contracts, dowries, widowhood, various species of emphyteutic establishments, and a welter of other matters. The entire legal regime undergirded the structure of the customary family organization of the agrarian gentry. The head of the family, known as the *hereu*, was the firstborn male. He inherited an agrarian estate and was endowed with the legal tools (upon marriage and by testament) to provide for the widowed mother and his younger brothers and sisters; younger brothers, the *fadristerns*, were given a education in lieu of an inheritance, after which they would enter commerce or the professions and head out on their own; sisters were provided with dowries upon marriage or sent into convents. When there was no male offspring or competent male offspring available, the firstborn female, called a *pubilla*, could inherit the estate. Under Catalan law, women with assets were legally free to contract, mortgage, or distribute them as they saw fit. In the industrial age, this ideal family organization was breaking down, but broad testamentary authority allowed large properties to remain whole, and many patriarchs continued to structure successions using traditional laws, conventions, and labels.

This family organization also gave rise to a romantic portrait of agrarian life, later known as *pairalisme* (patriarchism). As we shall later see, *pairalisme* was not only present in juridical literature but penetrated history, poetry, theater, and fiction. It featured an idealized cast of characters — paternalistic *hereus*, enterprising younger brothers, loving mothers, and hardworking sharecroppers — who, bound together by the fabric of Catalan law, augmented the wealth and upheld the moral integrity of society by the sweat of their brows and through respect for tradition. The expression derived from the *casa pairal*, also known as the *mas*, the customary house of the *hereu* and his family, a structure that served the function of a small manor house. The owners of the *cases pairales* — the *hereus* or patriarchs — were the gentry. Although many were known as "seigneurs" or "barons," only a few held aristocratic titles. Many governed properties by emphyteusis and were direct owners, but many were usufructuary owners, especially in northern or "Old Catalonia" where they were called "usufructuary seigneurs." The gentry exploited large estates by infeudating, subinfeudating, or leasing them to sharecroppers, who lived in small houses, called *masoveries*, which surrounded the *casa pairal*. In this way, inheritance law intersected with the property law of emphyteusis. Anyone glancing at a landscape in which the *mas* of the patriarch, was surrounded by the *masoveries* of the sharecroppers, could not ignore feudalism's legacy.[89]

Controversy between Barcelona and Madrid first exploded in 1851 when the Moderate government proposed to promulgate a draft civil code, largely based on the Napoleonic Code and many of its siblings. Written by Florencio García Goyena, the draft code's provisions on family and inheritance showed astonishingly little respect for Catalan law. The author considered the region's flagship institutions — elective primogeniture and emphyteusis — retrograde and expendable. Sparking the ire of Barcelona lawyers, he contended that Catalan family law encouraged "paternal despotism."[90] The draft code contained an inheritance system based on a mixture of French and Spanish common law in which family assets would be distributed relatively evenly among children, although testators were given authority to favor a preferred child. The draft code abolished emphyteusis. If it had been implemented, the draft code would have entailed drastic consequences within Catalonia: many large estates would have been divided into smaller parcels by inheritance; and the relationships between the gentry and their sharecroppers would have been thrown into such disarray that nobody knew for sure what the agrarian landscape would look like.[91] In the end, the draft code never became law. It met trenchant opposition in Catalonia and other foral regions but remained on the table as the primary reference for future civil-law reform.[92] Debates swirled around whether it should be implemented, and if so, what changes were needed to make it acceptable.

It is not difficult to understand why Catalan lawyers were angered by the appearance of the draft code. Although it was based on the French Civil Code, which had immense international prestige, Catalans found it difficult to fathom the decision to use the historic laws of some of the country's poorest regions as a baseline for a future code, while assigning those of some of the richest into posterity. Barcelona's leading jurists did not possess an innate, burning love of tradition, but they were logically hesitant to tinker with the legal structure of the most productive regional economy in Spain. In protest to the appearance of the draft, various lawyers wrote articles in the press, while some headed and collaborated with lobbies of property owners and rentiers, which dispatched a series of petitions to Madrid.[93] Urban property owners also formed associations to launch a protest, given that lands laying outside Barcelona's walls were destined for redevelopment, and holders of emphyteutic interests were determined to conserve their considerable monetary value.[94] No Catalan lawyer, even those from the then-governing Moderate Party, came out publicly in favor of the government's project.

Above all, the threat to the inheritance regime was the chief source of discontent. Of the many who wrote on the subject, Joaquim Cadafalch, a practicing lawyer from the gentry, successfully set the terms of the debate. In the immediate aftermath of the draft code, he published a long pamphlet, *The Inconveniences of Forced Successions Established in the Draft Civil Code* (1852). He then popularized his theories at the Academy of Jurisprudence and published a number of articles, later combined in a prize-winning book:

Is it Convenient to Make the Legislation of the Diverse Provinces Uniform for All of Spain concerning Hereditary Succession and the Rights of the Surviving Spouse? (1862).[95] While being careful to cloak his arguments in polite language and avoid gratuitous insult, Cadafalch insinuated that the two different systems of successions bred two types of children and people — obedient and hardworking Catalans and lazy and rebellious Castilians. Armed with the power to increase and decrease inheritances, a Catalan father nurtured obedience and taught the value of hard work to his sons; in contrast, Castilian children, guaranteed of a minimum inheritance, had no incentive to obey their parents but went about life convinced that they would come into money once their parents had died. "Not only do children from wealthy families distinguish themselves by their indifference and slothfulness," he wrote, "they distinguish themselves for their lack of respect and obedience toward their parents and, later, toward public authority."[96] At the time that Cadafalch articulated this argument, it was already relatively well known. His most original contribution, however, was to couch the defense of Catalan law in the language of liberalism. To Cadafalch, the towering principle of "liberty" — and, in particular, liberty to testate and to contract — constituted the moral vertebrae of Catalan law. To make the case, he dispelled the belief that Catalan law was a legacy of feudalism, ill suited to the modern world. "It is not true that the Catalan family is governed by the principles of feudalism," he wrote. "Its fundament and guide is the pure, noble, and generous principle that echoes in every heart and embodies the world's desires: liberty."[97] Not only did he recast Catalan law as liberal; he also denigrated the Castilian law. It was not based on "liberty" but on the dangerous notion of "equality," which was "socialist and communist." Castilian and French law "attacked the family and negated the individual the right to transfer and distribute his own assets." Equal distribution of inheritances favored "dictatorship" and was the fruit of the despotic ideas of Robespierre, Saint-Just, Marat, Babeuf, Saint-Simon, and Napoleon.[98]

The debate between testate and intestate successions, impartible and partible inheritances, individual and community property, Roman and Germanic law, liberty and equality was nothing new. Across the border in France, the conservative thinker Frédéric Le Play was also carrying on a campaign to broaden testamentary liberty and hence rid France of partible inheritances. In an influential article entitled the "English Family" (1858), Le Play had argued that England's superior moral values and material welfare derived from its family and testamentary law.[99] According to Le Play and

Cadafalch, not only did testamentary liberty strengthen parental authority and hence family harmony, but it also spurred economic development. It allowed productive farms to remain whole, which facilitated intergenerational economic planning, predictability in the market for credit, and long-term productivity. Forced successions, in contrast, divided bountiful estates into small unproductive parcels, whose owners lacked the capital and access to credit for technological improvements. For his part, Joaquim Cadafalch substituted Le Play's English-French dichotomy with that of Catalonia-Castile. Just as England's economic record compared to that of France demonstrated the irrefutable benefits of testamentary liberty, Cadafalch reasoned that the superior economic record of Catalonia compared to that of Castile proved precisely the same point. He not only suggested that Catalan law be preserved but recommended that its family and testamentary law be incorporated into a Spanish civil code so that Castile could pull itself out of its lethargy. If Catalan testamentary laws were applicable throughout Spain, "Castile would be free, and its children's hearts would beat in unison. Its wealth would no longer stagnate, because experience and economic principles clearly demonstrate that no country stagnates when there is liberty."[100]

The argument that the proposed codification of the civil law in Spain threatened Catalonia's innate spirit of liberty and patriarchy proved quite cogent. It was not only the traditional families of the agrarian world who would be forced to change their practices; rather, persons who never felt particularly bound by the pull of custom would be affected if Catalan law on family and property was to disappear. Contrary to idealized depictions, it was not uncommon for an agrarian family to pass by the firstborn in favor a younger child, a son-in-law, or anyone deemed best fit to direct an estate or business.[101] Moreover, urban middle classes, who tended to spread inheritances more evenly, would lose flexibility in estate planning if testamentary liberty was abolished.[102] Wealthy owners of family businesses, accustomed to cold economic calculation, also recognized the virtues of Catalan law. Toward the end of the century, it became common for owners of large agrarian or industrial estates and enterprises to organize successions through the creation of joint-stock companies, in which fathers, sons, uncles, cousins, and even some outsiders were given shares. Easier to set up when testamentary authority has few restrictions and property was individually owned, companies were often viewed as better succession vehicles than wills, trusts, and marriage contracts, cumbersome institutions ill suited to the commercial world. In this way, the civil law complemented the mercantile law. Even those lawyers who encouraged clients to shun antiquated practices in favor of more modern and flexible inheritance mechanisms defended what was deemed "Catalan law," which, for the practically inclined, was simply synonymous with individual property and testamentary liberty.

It would not take an expert semiotician to expose the fallacies behind or "deconstruct" Cadafalch's dichotomies (Roman-Germanic; Catalan-Castilian; England-France; liberty-equality; obedience-rebelliousness). They were subjective, simplistic, contradictory, and, when submitted to historical scrutiny, utterly false. Most absurdly, if this logic was followed, the greatest example of Roman family institutions would have been England, which was the place where Roman law had the least influence in all of Europe. Intellectual anomalies aside, these dichotomies were consistent with continental juridical discourse, adjusted to the Spanish case and repeated throughout the Barcelona legal community. Liberty was heralded as the loadstone of the Catalan law and, as elsewhere, interpreted to be compatible with patriarchy. In a lecture delivered at the Atheneum in 1870, the notary Felix Falguera declared, "Roman and Catalan law are two interlocking gears that intermesh perfectly." He then went on to explain that the "three characteristics of Catalan law" were "the consecration of the father as the head of the family, the greatest liberty for all of its individuals . . . and the independence of the family from judicial power." Together, these constituted what he labeled "family liberty."[103] The awkward term "family liberty" never caught on; instead, "civil liberty" gained credence. In 1884 Manuel Duran wrote, "Civil Liberty is the true condition of free peoples. . . . The more free a commonwealth, the more free its property. Testamentary liberty is present today in the two freest nations in the world, England . . . and the United States."[104] Catalan law was characterized by "respect for paternal authority, the concept of family unity . . . dignity of the widowed mother . . . personal responsibility . . . liberty of action."[105]

It must be noted that ideological labels were extremely malleable when it came to the civil law. Most lawyers in Catalonia were satisfied, or at least unperturbed, with the generalization that Catalan law was more conservative and Castilian and French law more radical. However, some lawyers from the Left rejected this dichotomy. For example, Catalan Federal-Republicans also supported the region's family and inheritance laws. Their leader Josep Maria Vallès de Ribot praised the "indivisibility of patrimonies," the "inequality" of inheritances," and claimed that all of Catalan law was based on "property as a reward for work and family."[106] This type of language might seem surprising coming from a leftist, but this was not the case. The model for Federal-Republicans was not France but the United States where most states followed the English system of individual property and free testamentary donation. In Barcelona, Federal-Republicans represented artisans and shopkeepers, many of whom preferred to maintain the assets of husband and wife separate and pass down a family shop to a single heir.[107] It was in this spirit that one eminent jurist called upon "chemists, carpenters, locksmiths, dyers, carriage drivers, lace makers, and manufacturers of all kinds" to join the protest against the testamentary provisions of the draft code.[108] Republicans devised arguments with their own preferred ring. Amadeu Hurtado, for example, reasoned that Catalan prosperity was principally due not to the indivisibility of rural estates but to the deeds of entrepreneurial younger sons, who, deprived of an inheritance, sought out their own fortunes, enriching the region: "The creation of Catalan wealth was primarily due to younger brothers who were the secret motor force. They increased the country's wealth while the elder brother carried out the obscure work of harvesting the land."[109]

At the Barcelona bar, there was widespread agreement that the juridical organization of family and property in Catalonia was superior to that of Castile and, for this reason, should form the vertebrae of a civil code for all Spaniards. Because of the contrarian nature of legal practice, however, it could hardly be expected that opinions would be unanimous. A handful of Barcelona lawyers, influenced by French republicanism, swam against the current of opinion and argued that the French Civil Code represented the future path for legal reform everywhere. The Federal-Republican Party leader in Barcelona, Valentí Almirall, who later became the founder of political Catalanism, published a polemical pamphlet entitled *The Foral Law and Carlism in Catalonia* (1868), in which he asserted that "the organization of the Catalan family . . . does not correspond to the necessities of modern life."[110] He depicted the *hereus* as pillars of absolutism in the countryside. Later, another republican lawyer portrayed Catalan law as an obscurantist legal regime promoting "paternal tyranny, the subjugation of women, feudal dominions, and religious intolerance."[111] Over time, such denigratory characterizations were heard less frequently in Catalonia. Valentí Almirall, for his part, became swayed by the arguments of his adversaries. In 1881 he praised the "institution of the *hereu*" and agreed that Catalan law was imbued with "the principle of liberty."[112]

Catalan jurists went to great lengths to persuade colleagues throughout Spain of the advantages of their system. In the 1830s, Ramon Martí d'Eixalà proposed that the entire country could share testamentary liberty and emphyteusis if Spanish common law was returned to its Roman legal roots and disabused of subsequent, prejudicial Germanic influences.[113] Later, a more practical plan was put forward. Joaquim Cadafalch suggested that the draft code of 1851 would be acceptable if a mere *five* articles were changed in order to guarantee relatively unfettered testamentary donation and the continuity of emphyteusis.[114] The Catalans were not alone. In addition to jurists from other foral-law regions, there were some influential legal minds from common-law regions who agreed. In 1863 Segismundo Moret and Luis Silvela, two eminent lawyer-politicians, published *The Foral Family and the Castilian Family* in which they echoed Le Play's famous distinction between the English family and the French family. The superior economic development of the foral regions, they also argued, was proof that uniform laws guarantying testamentary liberty would be of benefit to Spaniards everywhere.[115] Similarly, an influential group of left-wing jurists, most of whom resided in Madrid, known as "Krausists," espoused compatible ideas. Votaries of the natural-law philosophy of the German Karl Krause and of the jurisprudence of the Belgian Henri Ahrens, they detested Roman law but favored laws that would guarantee ample contractual and testamentary freedoms.[116] Given this array of diverse but overlapping opinion, it was not completely out of the question that Catalan and other foral traditions could be blended with Castilian texts and laws to form a uniform code.

In spite of this scattered support, however, Catalan jurists never won the debate. Most common-law jurists did not look on Catalan legal institutions so favorably. In 1885 one Supreme Court magistrate rhetorically asked "Can this legislation that descends from the times of Wifred the Hairy be liberal?" He claimed that the *hereu* governed his mother and his brothers "with the despotism of a feudal lord." To him, Catalan families lived in a perpetual juridical war" because they were subject to an anachronistic legal regime of little purpose other than to line the "wallet of the lawyer."[117]

At the Conference of Spanish Jurisconsults, held at the University of Madrid in 1863, more than one hundred elite lawyers, many of whom were parliamentary deputies, gathered to discuss the reform of the 1851 draft code and other pending juridical matters. The draft code had generated such controversy that it never reached the parliament floor, so the conference represented the first public debate. Interestingly, emphyteusis was no longer a matter of dispute, as Catalan jurists had convinced politicians that it was best to leave this institution alone, given that legislative interference risked sparking agrarian violence.[118] The only major point dividing common-law from foral-law jurists was inheritance. Here, a compromise solution was reached. Practically all common-law jurists rejected the proposal that Catalan (and some other foral) laws should form the baseline rules governing family and property in Spain; instead, they preferred to structure a code around the central institutions of Spanish common law. However, delegates also voted that a future code should contain certain "special laws" for the foral regions.[119] The proposal was not new but had been floating around Barcelona for decades. In 1843 Francesc Permanyer and Ignasi Sanponts had published an abbreviated version of a Spanish civil code, in which they inserted a number of exceptional Catalan laws in the back as an "appendix."[120] In 1862 the leading commentator on Catalan law, Pere Vives, had called for "the modification of some specific articles" of the draft code "in order to satisfy all Spaniards." He also recommended that a future code should include "some exceptions."[121]

Following the conference of 1863, the way forward seemed clear. The Spanish civil code would consist of a set of laws for the entire country but would also contain an appendix with a list of "special" or "exceptional" laws for the foral regions. This solution guaranteed that the status quo would not be threatened: codification would not entail radical changes to the organization of property and family anywhere. At the time, nobody imagined that this dispute would later contribute to the rise of Catalan nationalism. In the 1860s, political Catalanism was not even a dot on the political landscape. In retrospect, however, it is easy to observe the dissemination of stereotypes that could threaten the spirit of compromise. The civil-law disputes had propagated conflicting images of family, which struck at the heart of what it meant to be Castilian or Catalan. In Barcelona, the Catalan family was portrayed as patriarchal, industrious, obedient, and liberty loving, whereas the Castilian family was said to be slothful, rebellious, and condemned to remain impoverished. In Madrid, the Castilian family was depicted as harmonious, communal, and sharing, while Catalan patriarchs were deemed despotic, feudal, and avaricious. Following the Conference of Spanish Jurisconsults, codification was again put on hold, but, as we shall see, these stereotypes remained and festered.

The Conservative Profession

In 1885 Manuel Duran became the dean of the College of Lawyers and put the finishing touches on its conservative image. To endow the college with some ritual, he recuperated an old custom — first instituted in the seventeenth century but which had fallen into desuetude — whereby lawyers celebrated their patron saint day by attending a mass in which they mourned colleagues who had died over the course of the year.[122] The bar's patron saint was Ramon de Penyafort (d. 1275), one of Europe's great legal minds and a local hero. Educated in Bologna where he earned a chair of canon law, Penyafort had divided his career between Catalonia and Italy. Even secular lawyers had to admire his accomplishments: counselor to the Catalan crusading king James I, confessor to Pope Gregory IX, sponsor of Thomas Aquinas, and compiler of the *Decretals*. Penyafort had spent his last years and died in the Convent of Santa Caterina in Barcelona. When the convent was burned during the Revolution of 1835, his tomb was salvaged and later brought to the cathedral. Reviving the cult of Saint Penyafort helped recuperate and celebrate the bar's medieval past.

In 1887 Manuel Duran christened a "Portrait Gallery of Catalan Jurisconsults" in the great hall of the college. The plan was to commission or find portraits of distinguished university professors and those deans whose tenure had lasted at least three years. In an inaugural ceremony, he delivered short biographies of the honored. His words echoed his speech at the Academy of Jurisprudence in 1883, "The Catalan Juridical School."[123] In his addresses, Duran portrayed an everlasting image of conservatism, continuity, and consensus. Distinguished jurists from the mid-nineteenth century, such as Ramon Martí d'Eixalà, Francesc Permanyer, Manuel Josep de Torres, and Pere Vives were said to be the heirs of the great minds of the early modern period — Joan Pere Fontanella, Lluís Peguera, Jaume Càncer, Tomàs Mieres, and Acacia Ripoll. Who was left out of this narrative was as revealing as who was included. Forgotten were enlightened lawyers such as Francesc Romà, Manuel Barba, Tomàs Puig, and even the inaugural dean Miquel Llobet. No efforts were made to find their portraits or tell their stories. Nor did Duran choose to remind his audience of the bar's revolutionary past, despite the fact that some of the honored had served in the army or the militias. Ramon Salvató, who overcame prison and exile to become the first minister of justice from Catalonia, was never mentioned. Manuel Duran also left out absolutists such as Miquel de Castells, Jaume Tos, and Ramon de Dou, even though Dou was among the most accomplished legal scholars in Catalan history. The bar was deemed constitutionalist, conservative, and Catholic, and remembered as if it had always been that way. Its foundations were traced to the Middle Ages and the Renaissance, while the pivotal and conflictive periods of absolutism, enlightenment, and revolution were obliterated.

The conservative nature of the legal tradition reinforced the image of the conservative bar. Despite changing times and the needs of industrial society, the law moved slowly in the hands of lawyers, who, unlike politicians, could guide legal evolution only through interpretation rather than through legislation. In the eyes of social reformers, jurists probably appeared to spin their wheels by discussing the intricacies of the land law and publishing exhaustive treatises on dying institutions. Indeed, if judged on publications alone, it was hardly perceptible that Barcelona lawyers practiced within an industrial city. The legal rights of workers were ignored, and, when they were finally addressed, solutions were out of step with the times. In 1895 Enric Prat de la Riba, a juridical writer and burgeoning nationalist ideologue, made the ludicrous recommendation that the organization of the *casa pairal* could be re-created in the factory, converting it into a *casa industrial*; the relationship between fathers and sons would be replicated by bosses and workers.[124] Despite all the professed virtues of the legal tradition, despite all the claims that ancient laws fostered harmonious relations and were suited to the modern world, the Catalan law failed to enter the factory. In the absence of legislation, strict contractual or "Manchesterian" principles governed industrial relations. A few republican advocates upheld the revolutionary and democratic heritage of the bar, and some represented trade unions, but, for the most part, the lawyer did not mix with the syndicalist or the worker.

The hard realities of legal practice starkly contrasted with image. While jurists were busy propagating the myth of *pairalisme* — with its harmonious cast of *hereus* and sharecroppers, fathers and sons, and even owners and workers — daily experience taught other lessons. Law offices buzzed with stories of deception and graft. Advocates who picked up legal work generated by the disentailing of church and municipal properties, not to mention those who undertook everyday evictions, were aware of the presence of massive social dislocation in a countryside characterized by poverty and migration. When taking on criminal defenses, lawyers represented persons driven to desperate acts to palliate inequality and blight. Upon visiting factories, they witnessed bleak and unsafe working conditions, miserable pay, and child labor. When counseling financial enterprises involved in Cuba or Puerto Rico, they navigated the legal niceties of a slave economy. When representing debtors and creditors in bankruptcy, they saw the human consequences of the cruelty of the market. When taking on inheritance disputes, they witnessed families torn apart by greed. To working-class leaders and Catholics traditionalists alike, this divorce between image and reality was probably seen as nothing more than the timeless hypocrisy of the rich. It has, however, a more sociological if not psychological explanation. After nearly four decades of intermittent but devastating civil war and revolutionary violence, jurists sought to overcome deep social schisms by disseminating intoxicating images of laws promoting social peace and harmony. The obvious fact that these same laws caused evictions, inequality, and poverty found little voice. Although sometimes contrary to reality, traditionalist conceptions of law soothed minds and acted as a spiritual tonic.[125]

The conservatism of the Barcelona bar — and other bars throughout Europe — was not a simple reflection of the antiquity of the legal tradition. Conservatism was a modern phenomenon, as leaders of the bar sought to anchor newly formed, or recently recuperated, associations in tradition to endow them with legitimacy. Something similar was afoot in France where the Orders had been stripped of their privileges during the Revolution and had been heavily regulated during the First and Second Empires. As they gradually reestablished customs and rituals in the nineteenth century, nobody sought to revive memories of the Revolution.[126] And this must have taken place throughout all of Europe. Lawyers enjoyed a boom in business and augmented their prestige and power as a result of commerce, industry, constitutionalism, judicial reorganization, and procedural reform. They projected their success back in time to the Middle Ages and to Rome, portraying the bar as an immovable pillar of society. It is an egregious error to assume that because lawyers practiced in what they perceived, and what many contemporary observers still think, to be the ways of the past, that this establishes a genuine continuum. Many traditions, methods of organization, and interpretations of the law had been preserved, but others were resuscitated and reworked to establish fictive, or at least impressionistic, links with tradition and to erase the difficult-to-interpret experiences of absolutism and revolution. Elaborating a monolithic historical memory strengthened corporate solidarity.

In Barcelona and much of Europe, then, conservatism was an outgrowth rather than a challenge to liberalism. In Barcelona, conservative jurists even came to argue that "civil liberty" — which according to the language of the day meant the freedom to testate and contract — was the constitutive principle underlying Catalan and Roman law. This assertion demonstrates just how far the language of liberalism had penetrated juridical discourse, especially given that critics claimed that Catalan and Roman law were associated with feudalism and absolutism, respectively. Liberal lawyers also praised many institutions that were normatively illiberal. Many advocates, from the Left and the Right, trumpeted the benefits of emphyteusis, which, no matter how it was construed, could never be considered a liberal institution.[127] Mercantilists engrossed in colonial commerce kept silent about the heinous institution of slavery, knowing that if called upon to defend it, they simply could not. Some advocates who entered politics orchestrated oligarchic networks, and collaborated with rivals to rig elections, to divide spoils, and to allocate jobs and, by so doing, undermined the same maxims that they publicly espoused. Such individuals were not necessarily held in high esteem at the bar, but they were not particularly reviled either. To be sure, feudal-law remnants, oligarchy, corruption, and slavery were not blots on an otherwise impeccable canvas but very much part of an abstract picture.[128]

With this in mind, it is worth recalling the image of the fictitious lawyer from the pamphlet *A True and Profitable Conversation between a Peasant Named Isidro and the Lawyer, Doctor Julià* (1821), published more than a decade before steam power arrived in Barcelona. A few decades later, the reputation of leading advocates would have made this depiction implausible if not risible. It no longer made sense to cast a typical lawyer as a spokesperson for the family farmer. Although the family farmer remained omnipresent in the countryside, he had disappeared from the concerns of legal writers, immersed in the economic interests of large estates and the mystique of the *casa pairal*. Advocates with high public profiles resembled not the fictional "Dr. Julià," who patiently chatted with peasants in market towns about the coming of a better world, but conservative men who stood shoulder to shoulder with clients from banking, textiles, railroads, insurance, steamship lines, colonial commerce, Cuban sugar and slaves, large agricultural estates, the wine and liqueur industry, and urban property development.

If one was on a mission to prove that Marxist-Gramscian theories were correct, one might be to tempted to end the narrative here. After all, the leaders of the midcentury bar faithfully defended the interests of the rich and powerful in industry and agriculture and had succeeded in wrestling the control of associations away from practitioners with more diverse clienteles and pluralistic ideas. Anyone unconvinced that industrial capitalism did not reconfigure the bar would only have to cast his or her gaze to midcentury Barcelona where the political opinions and the actions of eminent lawyers reflected the priorities of industry, high finance, and commercial agriculture. Mercantile lawyers, who hardly existed a century before, were among the most powerful men in the city.

All the same, there are good reasons not to accept such theories or to end the narrative here. In the first place, the legal boom of the era of industrial takeoff would not last forever and cannot be considered exemplary. A snapshot of the bar during middle decades of the century, when its interests were closely aligned with those of big business and agriculture, cannot be depicted as an everlasting status quo. Second, even when interests were aligned, client did not govern practitioner as a dog wags a tail. Although lawyers often deferred to their clients on matters of economic import, such as trade protection, when it came to politics, it was often the other way around. Then, urban and agrarian elites often deferred to lawyers, experts in legislation and matters of state. This had occurred in the age of revolution, when the implementation of a liberal order was overseen by lawyers who were careful to ensure that legislative reforms were calibrated with their professional interests in mind. As we shall see, it would again occur when lawyers, together with other professionals, would pull the middle classes toward Catalanism. To be sure, if Barcelona advocates had been concerned solely with their clients' economic interests, the narrative would have ended here. The bar would have been satisfied with the compromise reached at the Conference of Spanish Jurisconsults of 1863, which guaranteed the maintenance of the organization of property and family in the region. But lawyers would later abandon this compromise in favor of a more trenchant defense of Catalan law. While so doing, they would slowly embrace, plank by plank, the platform of the home-rule movement. Despite the fact that Catalanism offered few tangible benefits to high finance and big business, lawyers and other professionals succeeded in swaying industrial and commercial elites to follow their lead.[129]

The rest of this book, then, explores how lawyers slowly came to embrace Catalanism. It examines how the shared experiences of education, training, apprenticeship, and practice served to forge a common legal culture and a strong corporate identity, which would endow the bar with different concerns, interests, and stresses than those of men of commerce, agriculture, and industry. Lawyers who began practice during the latter third of the nineteenth century had no memories of past divisions of the revolutionary and reactionary era and grew up in an ambience where the historical memory of the bar, reinforced by the college and academy, was one of consensus and continuity. Later generations, however, would not reap the fruits of the midcentury legal boom. Instead, they would face intense competition as the path to success became overcrowded. How the bar became increasingly corporatist, and ultimately nationalist, is the subject of the ensuing chapters.

5 The Corporate Profession
BACKGROUNDS, TRAINING, AND PRACTICE

Do you know, my dear boy... that in our society there are three men, the priest, the doctor, and the lawyer, who cannot appreciate the world? They wear black robes perhaps because they are in mourning for all virtue and hope. The unhappiest of the three is the lawyer. When a man seeks out the priest, he is moved by repentance, by remorse, by passionate beliefs that elevate him... But when he comes to us, the lawyers, we see the same ill feelings repeated again and again, never corrected. Our offices are gutters that cannot be cleansed.
∾ Honoré de Balzac, *Colonel Chabert* (1832)

In a society that every day runs further afield from the end to which it has been destined by our Father, among the rumblings of a corrupt generation that claims to exercise rights that do not belong to it, between a reckless adventurer that tramples over a weak-spirited soul, between the power of gold that threatens to buy justice to be used against a poor sot without resources unable to assert his rights, rises the figure of the lawyer. Face to face with the image of justice, with one hand he points to the law and with the other he draws a circle upon which the sword of the magistrate falls.
∾ Manuel Angelon, *The Defense Lawyer* (1853)

The most important and terrible plague of Spain is the proliferation of a massive gang of young lawyers, who can be supported only by a fantastic quantity of lawsuits. Questions multiply in proportion to demand. Even so, many still cannot find work. Given that a gentlemanly jurist cannot dedicate himself to plowing fields or be bothered to sit down and weave, we are left with a brilliant squadron of loafers, full of pretensions, who inflate the demand for state jobs, shake up politics, and engender

> revolutions. They must earn their daily bread somewhere. It would be even worse if there were lawsuits for them all.
> — Benito Pérez Galdos, *Doña Perfecta* (1876)

LAWYERS FACED FREQUENT CRITICISM as a result of their enviable success. A conspicuous number of adages reflected popular wisdom and prejudice. Some are innocuous, offering practical advice or poking innocent fun: "To the lawyer, one tells the truth." "If you think you have fooled the doctor, the confessor, or the lawyer, you are fooling yourself." "The lawyer of the peasant gets paid beans." "With lawyers and patience, one wins the sentence." "The three most untidy things: the theologian's conscience, the doctor's table, the lawyer's testament." "The lawyer and the comic actor will play the devil as often as the saint."[1] Others are predictably scathing: "To speak much without saying anything is the genius of the lawyer." "Lawsuit finished, only the lawyer has won." "The doctor, a Christian; the lawyer, a pagan." "The doctor to prescribe, the barber to cure, and the lawyer to cheat." "Good lawyer, bad neighbor." Not to be forgotten is the one most often repeated today: "Lawyers and proctors, hand in hand, straight to hell."[2] It is difficult to trace the origins of an oral tradition, but, by their tone and content, many of these appear to have come down from the nineteenth century or even earlier.

Novelists also tapped into public outrage over the comportment of a profession sworn to uphold the principles of justice and to defend the poor for free but who often seemed bent on the naked pursuit of profit. No Catalan, or any continental author for that matter, wrote an equivalent of Charles Dickens's *Bleak House* (1852–53), a punishing attack on the atrocious state of English justice, but Benito Pérez Galdós — often referred to as the "Spanish Dickens" — did take aim at lawyers in one novel. In *Doña Perfecta* (1876), a young civil engineer with progressive ideas returns from university to his rural hometown in Castile with ambitious plans for dams, bridges, and irrigation canals only to find the town plagued by priests, lawyers, and lawsuits. In a Manichaean contest, he vies for the hand of an heiress to an agrarian estate against a reactionary lawyer who apprentices in the town's most prestigious office. In the final scene, the heiress's mother sees to it that the engineer is killed, which predictably sends her daughter to a sanatorium rather than to the lawyer's arms. The allegory is not hard to interpret: priests and lawyers lamentably dominated Spanish public and private life, while men of science were considered threatening. Barcelona had no shortage of engineers, but many Catalan readers no doubt agreed with his depiction of lawyers as a "brilliant squadron of loafers,"[3] who drummed up lawsuits, searched out state jobs, and fomented revolutions.[4]

Magistrates and judges joined the chorus of criticism. During keynote speeches at annual opening ceremonies, held at the outset of each year at the Audiencia, they took time out to warn lawyers against sharp practice. In 1839, the regent lectured, "Never use the prohibited arm of lying, satirizing, and ranting."[5] A year later, one magistrate instructed, "Make use of all necessary materials so that your work is solid and aims toward perfection, but at the same time avoid all useless and superfluous material that deforms the judicial process."[6] In 1844, another regent warned, "Limit your writings and speeches to reasons and reflections necessary to further your cause, and omit all those that do not lead toward this end and that simply serve to inflate your clients' vanity or to keep them mired in erroneous opinions."[7] Some were less censorious and tried a softer touch. Another regent stated, "Lawyers, you belong to a profession that I will always honor. You are the practitioners who from the high seas guide the ship safely to port amid the rocks and the sandbanks. Direct your cases with truth, clarify the illusions of the misguided, and triumph will be yours."[8] Most were not keen on listening to such "advice." In addition to being condescending, it implied that advocates, when left to their own devices, were prone to rant, lie, satirize, confuse, employ dilatory tactics, pad briefs, and deviously raise client expectations in order to encourage spurious claims with no purpose other than lining their own wallets. In 1839 only those who had matriculated in the College of Lawyers during the previous year were required to attend opening ceremonies and take the oath. Given the option, few veteran advocates appeared to swear fidelity to Queen Isabel II and the constitution.[9]

In response to criticism, lawyers upheld the honor of their calling. Manuel Angelon considered the contention that lawyers were to blame for the frequent perversion of justice to be absurd. In *The Defense Lawyer* (1843), he charted a chronicle, beginning in Rome, of valiant advocates who put their reputations and lives at risk to defend the innocent in the face of tyranny. When it came to grand abominations, the shoes of blame were on the feet of the magistrates. Paying homage to Louis XVI's defense lawyers, Deseze, Tronchet, and Malesherbes, he proclaimed, "The head of Louis XVI fell rolling from the guillotine, but we still preserve the brief of the defender Deseze, and this document is perhaps the only public proof that in the year 1793 the principles of justice and charity had not been completely abandoned. Civilization wishes to forget the names of the judges who became the executioners of Louis XVI, but it has inscribed in gold letters the illustrious names of the three advocates who defended him."[10] Lluís Ricard de Fors understood that a lawyer's mission was to honor the "empire of reason," but, in consonance with the sentimental spirit of the times, he counseled his colleagues to empathize with the client: "If the lawyer does not suffer what he suffers, if he cannot cry when he cries, and if he does not feel a mysterious affinity with the pain afflicting his client, then he cannot defend with fire and conviction the causes of those who deposit their confidence in him."[11]

Not all literary portrayals were denigrating. Across the border in France, the novelist Balzac, in *La comédie humaine*, frequently called upon his fictional advocate Derville to defend honorable but down-on-their-luck Parisians. The novelist depicted the righteous lawyer awash in the schemes of an immoral society. In one novel published in 1832, Derville cries out, "I have learned so much practicing my profession! I have seen a father die in a garret without a sou or a stitch of clothing, abandoned by two daughters to whom he'd given 40,000 pounds income! I have seen wills burned. I have seen mothers rob their children; husbands steal from their wives; wives use love to kill their husbands or drive them mad.... I cannot tell you everything I have seen because I have seen crimes that justice is powerless to rectify."[12] Many educated Catalans read French, and some read Balzac, and there is evidence that a version of this character was known in Catalonia. In a French theatrical comedy entitled *The Lawyer*, translated into Spanish and published in Barcelona in 1841, a flattering depiction appears. In this hopelessly sentimental drama, the protagonist Rambert is seemingly based upon Derville. As the plot unfolds, he warns his client: "Before I decide to take a case, it is necessary that I believe it to be a good and just cause." Gesturing to his apprentices, he declares, "Look at these young men whose parents have deposited their confidence in me and sent them to learn this honorable career by my side ... My example will make an indelible imprint on their lives."[13]

Antoni Altadill was the closest equivalent that Barcelona had to a Balzac, Dickens, or Galdós. If judged on talent alone he was a poor imitation, but his popular novels entertained many. *Mysteries of Barcelona* (1860), a best seller for more than twenty years, followed a formula set by Eugène Sue's wildly influential *Mysteries of Paris* (1842–43), which enjoyed such success that it spawned a series of imitators in many major European cities. Altadill's version was chock-full of stereotypical Barcelonese from the boulevards and back alleys: avaricious bankers and textile merchants, corrupt police, shady jail keepers, small-time crooks and con artists, hooked-nosed usurers, slave-trading ship captains, Freemasons, and, not to be forgotten, humble men and women who become wealthy through good looks, marriage, hard work, charm, or the charity of a secret benefactor. The action transpires in the official and unofficial places of elite sociability: the Liceu opera house, the stock exchange at the Llotja Palace, and the Passeig de Gràcia, in addition to the gambling parlors, warehouses, silversmith shops, and the sexually laden salons of high bourgeois women. Among this motley cast, one of the villains is a double-dealing lawyer who fraudulently administers the estate of a widowed baroness by falsifying accounts, meddling in her daughter's amorous future, and using privileged information for personal gain. His machinations, however, do not deprive him of the "unlimited confidence from all of Barcelona" who mistakenly trust his "supreme intelligence, zeal, and probity."[14] Antoni Altadill, however, also depicted honorable lawyers. In *The Ambition of a Woman* (1865), a young advocate is the hero. Shortly after graduating from university, he wins an innocent verdict in a well-publicized criminal case and earns a "great forensic reputation." Catapulted into the bar's highest ranks, he becomes an "eminent and distinguished gentleman."[15]

It is always tempting to highlight instances in which lawyers, like priests and doctors, were targets of satire, but the bar also commanded immense respect.[16] Ridicule was an annoying and omnipresent occupational hazard, but it was not strong enough to dissuade ambitious young men wishing to ply their acumen in an attempt to better their station in life. And once members, few expressed regret and self-doubt. Convinced of the utility of their calling, they defended it tooth and nail. The nineteenth century was many things, but it was not an age of ironic self-deprecation. A legal career had broad appeal to persons from multiple walks of life. However, getting there was not easy.

Family Origins, Religiosity, and Language

During the second half of the century, new generations gradually altered the bar's serious image. Young lawyers entered a profession led by men who had witnessed and participated in the horrors of war and revolution of the 1830s, who had grown conservative with time, and who had been instrumental in forging key political compromises, which had resolved deep political cleavages and allowed society to mend and the economy to flourish. New generations, though, faced different horizons. The risks of the era of war and revolution faded into the past, and the path to success was more clearly mapped out than before. An aspirant seeking to enter the bar during the second half of the century would no longer be inclined to grab a bayonet and heroically defend the patriotic cause; instead, he would prefer to compose poetry and satire, chat about politics in a café, or sit down at a piano with his friends. The image of manliness changed from the lawyer-militiaman to the lawyer-gentleman. To many seasoned lawyers, the youth probably never had it so good. On the other hand, despite the outward appearance of young lawyers as dandies, sampling the joys of Barcelona while pursuing their careers, things were not so rosy. Developing a legal practice became increasingly difficult. The path to success became crowded, creating stiff competition and putting intense pressure on lawyers at early stages in their careers. By century's end, new generations would transform the bar, tilting it toward Catalanism, an ideology cast within the corporate interests of legal and other professionals. Catalanism called for home rule, which promised to create an autonomous bureaucracy centered around Barcelona and to provide more jobs for university graduates with troubles breaking into private practice.

Before returning to overcrowding and the rise of Catalanism at the end of the chapter, we must first discuss the formation of a cohesive corporate identity. In other words, if corporatism lent strength to Catalanism, it is imperative to explain the former to comprehend the latter. In order to understand corporatism, moreover, we should underscore not only what it was but also what it was not. For it would be a mistake to believe that corporatism was a *social* phenomenon that reflected the common material interests of lawyers with similar family backgrounds, religious practices, and political preferences. This would not be an accurate description of the bar. Rather, corporatism was a *professional* phenomenon, in which young men with diverse and adverse opinions about God and politics, born into families of differing levels of wealth, raised in urban and rural milieus, came to embrace a common professional culture inculcated through education, training, practice, and associational life. The leaders of the College of Lawyers and the Academy of Jurisprudence constituted the public face of the bar, but the rank and file was its heart and soul.

That corporate interests came to coexist with, and prevail over, class interests is one of the chief reasons why Marxist-Gramscian theories that have melded the professions into the "bourgeoisie" can be misleading. Lawyers shared styles, manners, associational life, and leisure activities with other middle-class individuals, from small shopkeepers to merchant bankers, but their material interests revolved around courts, fees, and clients rather than markets, prices, and tariffs. Similarly, it is not helpful to depict the bar simply as "liberal," as some scholars have been so inclined. To hold oneself out as liberal in the early nineteenth century was a firm declaration of revolutionary intentions, but by the second half of the century, liberalism was a broad political culture, which enveloped educated society and included persons with diverse beliefs from democrats to conservatives. In short, the blanket description of lawyers as bourgeois liberals is too vague and, to be sure, obscures both the diversity and the cohesiveness of the bar. Ultimately, corporatism was a response to diversity. Although lawyers came from heterogeneous family backgrounds and possessed different pedagogical experiences, they were bonded by having passed through, and survived, the competitive path from university student to established practitioner. The few hundred members of the bar were tied together by friendships, marriages, associational life, and years of classroom and courtroom alliances and rivalries. Youthful camaraderie evolved into adult collegiality, the glue that held the profession together.

It is best, then, to start by analyzing this diversity. In the first place, geographic origins were a major source. Throughout the century, less than half of the bar consisted of persons who had been born in Barcelona. The majority of practitioners came from cities, towns, and villages scattered throughout Catalonia. At first blush, such origins may not appear so diverse. After all, only 10 to 20 percent of the bar came from outside Catalonia, and many such individuals hailed from the bordering regions of Valencia and Aragon.[17] But Catalonia was, in and of itself, a geographically complex place, stretching from the mountains to the sea, wracked by civil war throughout the century. There were few places in Europe where such stunning differences between modernity and antiquity could be found by traveling only a few kilometers. The city and its industrial belt quickly gave way to the foothills of the Pyrenees where local customs and economies persisted. Some towns were politically liberal, but others were refuges for absolutists. Barcelona was also rife with inequality, as stark contrasts existed between rich and poor, and between established families and newcomers. Although lawyers were largely recruited from the "middle classes," this category could encompass a plethora of people who spent their childhoods in different places and among all sorts of people. It could include a lawyer from the landed gentry who had grown up in a remote rural area and who had been schooled at the seminary of the diocese where he developed pious Catholic beliefs. But it could also include an entrepreneurial artisan's son who had attended a public secondary school in Barcelona where he had been taught by laymen and had been exposed to varied political opinions. The members of the bar ranged from rich city lawyer's children with their future laid out before them to self-made men who used charitable scholarships, friendships, and sheer hard work to acquire an education and develop a career in a competitive world that favored the privileged.

Heterogeneity had been characteristic of the bar at least since the mid-eighteenth century when elite lawyers had complained that the profession had become a place where the "poor" (meaning those who were not wealthy) could carve out a career. Previously, we were able to gain a general idea of the composition of the preindustrial bar by analyzing data compiled on law school graduates who registered for bar exams during the 1820s. For the second half of the nineteenth century, we have also been able to compile statistics. Information in table 3, drawn from baptismal certificates of members of the bar deposited at the University of Barcelona,[18] reveals that social composition during the industrial era was quite like that of the preindustrial one. Although most lawyers came from propertied, commercial, and professional families, a sizable sector from popular origins was also present. As was the case with table 2 (in chapter 2), some of the descriptions were vague, but the overall portrait is telling.

The existence of similar studies allows us to situate these data within a comparative context. Like their counterparts on the continent, the bulk of Barcelona advocates, such as those from France and Germany, came from middle-class families involved in commerce, law, and other learned professions. In some places, such as Naples and Florence, cities that were not so industrialized, lawyers were recruited to a much greater extent from traditional sectors of urban and agrarian wealth, the gentry and the nobility. This was also true of English barristers during the first half of the nineteenth century, as the Inns of the Courts remained a repository for children of the gentry; with time, however, the Inns would open their chambers to a wider section of society. When analyzed in conjunction with other studies, the combined weight of the data confirms the sociological maxim that education and professionalization was a mode of social reproduction. Barcelona lawyers, however, were exceptional in one key regard: the bar contained a comparatively high percentage of lawyers from popular origins and a low percentage from the gentry. Only German studies reveal the presence of a similarly low percentage from propertied or rentier families, and no studies, including those of Germany, reveal such an appreciable component of persons from "popular"

Table 3. Social Origins of the Barcelona Bar, 1857 and 1897

	Number of Lawyers (%)	
Occupation of Father	1857	1897
Noble	7 (5.6)	7 (1.9)
Propertied (peasant, rentier, and *hacendista*)	18 (14.4)	55 (15.0)
Lawyer, judge, or notary	28 (22.4)	88 (23.9)
Proctor	2 (1.6)	13 (3.5)
Other learned professions	31 (24.8)	52 (14.2)
Commercial-financial-industrial occupations	22 (17.6)	77 (21.0)
Artisans, seamen, employees, and workers	17 (13.6)	75 (20.4)
Size of sample	125	367

Source: AGHUB, exps. (student university files).

(artisan and worker) origins. Compared to others, the Barcelona bar was remarkably open to entrance from below.[19]

This heterogeneous composition may seem surprising. The comparatively large number of lawyers from popular classes may have to do with the nature of the data sample, given that Barcelona was a more purely industrial city and hence housed a theoretically more mobile populace than other places for which we have data.[20] Whatever the case, it is evident that a good number of ambitious young men from popular origins used the law to break into the ranks of the privileged. A select few could even brag to have climbed the rungs of the social latter from bottom to top. Maurici Serrahima boasted the most famous "rags to riches" biography at the bar. Son of a poor artisan, he abandoned a career as a barber in his youth and began his long journey into the law by walking from his hometown of Manresa to Barcelona to attend university in the 1850s. There, he nurtured strategic friendships among classmates to enter high society. Following the Revolution of 1868, he accepted an appointment as counsel to the municipality, and his law office grew into one of the city's more bountiful. Friendly with persons of diverse beliefs, he earned the reputation as a no-nonsense advocate who remained ferociously independent of political and oligarchic networks. He capped off a spectacular career by being elected college dean in the 1890s.[21] Serrahima's accomplishments were atypical but not altogether out of the ordinary. Many successful, as well as modest and struggling advocates, came from humble origins. In one

Portrait of a self-made lawyer as a middle-aged man: Maurici Serrahima at thirty-five (Photograph from Serrahima, *Un advocat del segle XIX*, 33; image courtesy of Biblioteca de Catalunya, Barcelona)

of Altadill's novels, a young man identifies himself as a final-year law student: "I have no parents, nor personal fortune, but I am young and honorable."[22]

The extent of this heterogeneity should not be exaggerated. Cases of single-generation social climbing, like that of Serrahima, were rare. In most cases, lawyers from artisan backgrounds were sons of upwardly mobile fathers, entrepreneurs on their way to becoming successful businessmen, who could afford to pay for the education of their children. Take the case of Narcís Verdaguer, one of the founders of Catalan nationalism, who went to Barcelona to study law in the 1870s and became a respected midlevel practitioner. His baptismal certificate reads that his father was a "carpenter," although, according to a biographer, the father was an educated "master builder" who employed a crew of carpenters. Narcís Verdaguer's son remembered the grandfather as "a building entrepreneur."[23] Another similar case was that of Francesc Rius i Taulet, the mayor of Barcelona during the World Fair of 1888, who first entered the bar in 1858 and practiced for a decade before turning to politics. His baptismal certificate read that his father and godfather were "tailors," although his biographer recounts that his family ran a profitable business in distributing ecclesiastical clothing.[24] These men represented the rule and not the exception: a rich or upwardly mobile artisan could afford to provide his children, often with the help of an uncle or other family member, with a higher education. But most artisans could not. For most children of artisans, the threat of downward mobility was significantly greater than the prospect of upward mobility. For every one lawyer from an artisan family, there were obviously hundreds of industrial workers with such backgrounds.[25]

The cost of education was the principal reason why most Spaniards had no possibility of accessing the professions. Until the mid-nineteenth century, there was not much in the way of public schooling. The Moyano Law of 1857 established free primary schools in Spain, but many of these were of poor quality. Moreover, even if a student showed promise, parents still had to pay for secondary and university education or hope that their child was fortunate enough to receive a charitable scholarship. At the time, matriculation fees for a public secondary school, an *instituto*, ran about 120 reales a year. University was more expensive, as law school cost 280 reales.[26] These sums were not unattainable, given that average artisan earnings in Barcelona oscillated between 2,000 and 4,000 reales per year.[27] But even if an artisan earned more than the average amount, such fees were not usually affordable, considering that families often had numerous children to care for. Moreover, after completing coursework and exams, a onetime fee for a law degree was an astronomical sum, often many times the price of the combined total of matriculation and exam fees. During the second half of the nineteenth century, students who successfully completed a law degree paid a total of around 1,200 pesetas (4,800 reales) for their fees, exams, and degree, and probably at least half as much for a secondary-school education.[28] This represented a hefty amount that only the most prosperous artisan families could afford. In one of Altadill's novels, the author depicts a family of shoemakers with a life savings of 6,000 reales, which incidentally was not destined to provide their single son with an education but to purchase him an exemption from the draft.[29] Education was not always a priority.

Sons of artisans did not leave a clear ideological imprint on the bar. This observation confirms sociological generalizations that have stressed that newcomers do not necessarily use their privileged positions to defend the material interests of the classes from which they came but instead accept, and come to espouse, the dominant ethos of the elite. Surely, some children of artisans provided legal advice to artisans families, but it would be a mistake to assume that sons of artisans had artisan clients, defended artisan interests, and championed the plight of the lower middle classes. Children from nonprivileged backgrounds, who were hardworking and intelligent enough to break into the bar, were a diverse group whose ambitions often betrayed their origins. For example, university professors and first cousins Felip Vergés and Francesc Permanyer were sons of a bottle maker and a soap maker respectively; but these conservative and piously Catholic men loathed the democratic and anticlerical convictions common among many Barcelonese with similar occupations as their parents.[30] It was an iron rule that most lawyers, regardless of their origins, sought to court the wealthiest clients possible. For this, it was not always helpful to advertise one's past. If one was not a character in a romantic novel, humble origins were not usually worth bragging about.

On the other end of the scale, the gentry exerted an influence that exceeded its numerical weight. According to Catalan tradition, the firstborn son, the *hereu*, inherited an estate, while the younger sons, the *fadristerns*, received an education in lieu of a inheritance. It was common for large agrarian property owners to train younger sons in the law as a strategic mechanism to maintain privilege and patrimony.[31] Theoretically deprived of a guaranteed source of income and forced to forge their own way through life, younger sons were expected to enter the professions, commerce, or the church. Many read law. As the Catalan adage stated, "First son, the *hereu*, the second, a priest, and the third, a lawyer."[32] Still, as table 3 indicates, only a small percentage of the Barcelona bar comprised second sons of the gentry. It appears that many such individuals returned to their home counties after graduating from university, where their family connections were stronger, rather than trying to make their mark in the rough-and-tumble legal world of Barcelona. Of course, things were never so rigid, and the organization of the ideal family, as far as it ever existed at all, was disintegrating in the industrial era. In many instances, the *hereu* studied law, either to manage the family patrimony or to enter private practice; for large estates, families often hired a proctor or a lawyer as an administrator.[33] Unlike artisans, children of the gentry faithfully defended the interests of the circles into which they were born. To cite two well-known examples, leading midcentury defenders of emphyteusis at the Academy of Jurisprudence, Josep Bertran and Joaquim Cadafalch, came from families with large estates.[34] Others with such backgrounds could be counted on to support their origins, the hand that fed them and a number of others.

As can be expected, many lawyers were sons of various species of legal professionals. Nearly one-quarter of the bar consisted of individuals raised within a household of a lawyer, judge, notary, or proctor. Corporate self-recruitment was even more common than table 3 suggests, for uncle-nephew relationships were omnipresent. These cannot be measured (because baptismal certificates only rarely reveal an uncle's profession), but it was evident that many advocates got their start under, and owed their success to, the tutelage of a collateral family member. Here the previously mentioned case of Josep Bertran is illustrative. His bar exam application reveals that he trained in the office of Tomàs Ros, a longtime practitioner who was most likely an uncle or his mother's cousin.[35] Also informative is the story of Francesc Rius i Taulet, the son of an ecclesiastical clothing merchant who became a practicing lawyer and later mayor. He was the nephew of Vicenç Rius, law professor and dean of the College of the Lawyers. Interestingly, the uncle, a dead-serious Romanist, was also the son of a tailor, a former militia member, and possibly a self-made man.[36] Lawyers who apprenticed in offices under mentors with whom they shared a paternal or maternal surname clutter university files and college lists.

Distinguished lawyers did not emulate the rituals and practices of agrarian dynasties as did the heads of industrial, banking, or even artisan families. Prestigious legal families added stability and continuity to the bar, strengthening corporate solidarity. Although some would become "dynasties" in the twentieth century, it would be too early to christen any of them as such in the nineteenth. Not one prominent lawyer publicly claimed to be a descendant of a famous jurist from the early modern period and only very few could boast direct-line ancestors practicing law in the eighteenth century. Some lawyers from rural areas came from families of generations of property owners, notaries, clergy, and lawyers. Yet there were no well-known descendants of Fontanella, Càncer, Ripoll, Peguera, Xammar, Magarola, or other distinguished seventeenth-century jurists at the bar. The powerful families of the modern era — Ferrer, Ventosa, Maluquer, Permanyer, Bertran, Duran, Borrell, Vilaseca, Castellar, Font del Sol, and Vergés — were newcomers to the Barcelona elite, featuring patriarchs of diverse backgrounds who rose into prominence alongside an industrial bourgeoisie.

For the most part, professional families did not adopt the inheritance practices, or shroud themselves in the mystique, of the *casa pairal*. There was the ordinary pressure for at least one son (or nephew) to take up the reigns of a practice, but a father often encouraged two or more to do the same. Moreover, even in the case of single son, maintaining a successful legal practice from one generation to the next was challenging. Legal patrimony was evanescent, consisting of goodwill and networks that could not simply be handed down, like a shop, from one generation to the next. Despite high levels of endogeny, examples abound of sons who studied law and apprenticed for a few years but then vanished from the bar. A thriving practice could be built up in one generation, but it could be undone quicker. An incompetent or frivolous son of a banking family might take decades to dissipate a family's wealth through risky ventures; during his lifetime, he would be surrounded by sycophantic men and women proffering endless investment and amorous opportunities. But a slothful or mediocre lawyer would find his father's clients abandoning him like rats from a sinking ship. Although it was not uncommon for paternal love to blind sound judgment, a veteran advocate might look to place an underachieving or unambitious son in a less-demanding profession. Take the case of Pere Vives, a dean of the College, a top midcentury practitioner, and an eminent legal scholar. His son Felix struggled in his studies, so was encouraged to become a notary. In the meanwhile, Vives passed on his practice to his son's live-in tutor and boyhood chum Maurici Serrahima, who, faithful to his mentor's legacy, continued to run one of the city's most highly regarded offices.[37]

Merchants, professionals, and men of commerce and industry often chose to educate some of their children in the law. Manuel Duran, the most powerful advocate of the second half of the nineteenth century, was the son of a prestigious medical doctor, and his children became doctors and lawyers.[38] Other lawyers were children of wholesalers, currency dealers, pharmacists, engineers, or textile, paper, and chemical manufacturers, to list some of the diverse callings that appeared on baptismal certificates.

The bar was not a desired destination for the ostentatiously wealthy. Few nobility opted to read law, which is not surprising because there were simply few titled nobility around. Nor did children of the high bourgeoisie choose to embark on a competitive legal career. Some men of the Bacardí and the Milà de la Roca clans — components of what could be called a mercantile oligarchy — were enrolled in the College of Lawyers. They dedicated themselves to intellectual and associational life, business, banking, investments, and colonial affairs, but were not high-powered litigators or institutional leaders.[39] Furthermore, if we focus on the grand or "good families" of the industrial era — Fontanellas, Girona, Güell, López, Vidal-Quadras, Ferrer Vidal, Arnús, Estruch, among others — none of their children sought to develop a law practice. A legal career was hard work and tedious; success was slow and by no means guaranteed; remuneration was modest, especially at first. Lawyering had little appeal to someone born into the lap of luxury. Consumed with affairs of a family business, sons of high bourgeoisie were encouraged to pursue careers in finance and industry, for better or for worse, to the advantage of some families and to the detriment of others. Law, like medicine, architecture, or religion, was a step down, just as the world of finance was a step up for scions of professional families.[40] Not even the most successful law practice could yield the riches of the banker or industrialist. No top mercantile lawyer ever entered the high bourgeoisie through practice alone. The best way in was marriage, and some legal families — such as the Bertran[41] and the Ferrer[42] — took this route.

Social origins did not determine future ideological disposition. Young men's minds were also molded by teachers and friends. In theory, parents were at liberty to send their children to either public or private, lay or religious schools where headmasters and their teachers enjoyed a wide latitude to interpret a state-set curriculum and to teach the values they pleased.[43] In midcentury Barcelona, religiously inclined parents could send children to the seminary, which imparted classes to young men destined for the priesthood as well as other occupations, or to the Piarist School. Families who preferred lay education could choose between the public *instituto* or one of the various private boys' schools in and around the city. Outside Barcelona, however, choices were more limited. In the provincial capitals (Girona, Tarragona, and

Lleida), the choice between lay and religious education was usually between the *instituto* and the seminary. In other towns, there was often no choice. In bishoprics that were not provincial capitals (Vic, Solsona, La Seu d'Urgell), the seminary was the only school for kilometers. In some towns (Igualada, Mataró, Vilanova, and Sabadell), the Piarists held a monopoly on education; in others, local authorities sponsored a public *instituto* or a semipublic municipal school. Schools opened and closed, complicating this rough sketch. One tendency, however, was clear: lawyers were increasingly educated by laymen. Evidence suggests that around 40 to 45 percent of members of the College in 1857 had attended religious schools during the majority of their secondary-school years; by 1897, this figure dipped to around 25 percent. These calculations are rough, given that many students transferred between clerical and lay schools, picking up courses here and there, in order to round out a curriculum.[44] To be sure, a sizable chunk of the bar received a mixed education from laymen and monks.

In the absence of data, it remains an open question whether the trend toward pedagogical laicization carried into the twentieth century. An educated guess is that it did not. By the latter decades of the nineteenth century, the Jesuits staged a brilliant comeback and began to educate many children from the Barcelona elite. Before their first expulsion in 1767, the Jesuits had dominated education in the city. In the nineteenth century, they slowly made their presence felt, despite suffering periodic expulsions during revolutionary interludes. In 1847, the Jesuits established a foothold in the town of Manresa where they ran a school that attracted a handful of future lawyers. In the last quarter of the century, Spain underwent a veritable religious revival as the number of regular clergy soared.[45] In Catalonia, Piarists and Jesuits opened new schools, bought some existing private schools, and staffed them with monks. By century's end, Barcelona's Jesuit Sacred Heart School, founded in 1881, was the largest private school in Catalonia, boasting a secondary-school student body of more than 250 boys. It was the fashionable destination for the wealthy. The second largest was the Jesuit school of Manresa, while the Barcelona Piarists were a close third.[46] It would take some time, however, for children educated in these schools to alter the composition of the bar. The effects of this revival would not be felt until the twentieth century.[47]

The diversity of geographic, social, and pedagogical experiences meant that law students entered university with diverse beliefs. A boy born and raised in Reus (the second largest city in Catalonia), who had attended the local *instituto*, was likely to possess more secular values than one from Vic where the seminary had a vaunted reputation for churning out pious young men of fiery absolutist beliefs.[48] A son of a Barcelona artisan who received an ecclesiastical scholarship at a seminary or Piarist school was likely to mature with a more favorable concept of religion than one of a similar social standing who attended a public *instituto*. A privileged child who boarded at an elite private boys school in a bucolic setting, where he spent recreational time on horseback, had an experience distinct from a boy who attended day classes at a local school where he made friends with students from diverse walks of life. Even private schools differed from one another. According to the state curriculum, all were required to impart religious education, but some were more committed than others. In his memoirs, Conrad Roure recounts that he boarded at the Figueras School, probably a relatively secular place, where he forged lifelong friendships with future law school classmates, fellow republicans, and Freemasons.[49] The conservative law professors Manuel Duran, Francesc Permanyer, and Felip Vergés, in contrast, sent their children, many of whom became lawyers, to the Antiga School, which instilled conservative and Catholic values into disciplined and ambitious young men.[50]

Finally, lawyers came from families with diverse linguistic orientations. At first glance, this may not seem evident. Most members of the bar had attended the University of Barcelona, which was the assigned place of education for boys who came from one of the four provinces of Catalonia (Barcelona, Girona, Lleida, Tarragona) or from one of the Balearic Islands of Mallorca, Minorca, and Ibiza. Persons who grew up in these places lived within what is called a "diglossia": everyday conversation among natives took place in Catalan, while Spanish was used for writing, formal oratory, and within all levels of education.[51] Yet, geographic and social origins left linguistic markers. Whether a young man was fully comfortable in Spanish was dependent upon where he was from, who his parents were, and what school he attended. In general, the urban and the wealthy spoke and wrote better Spanish than those from rural areas. However, even privileged individuals were not always comfortable in the language of the monarchy. The Barcelonese were not know for speaking either language that well. Writing in the 1880s, an urban guidebook author observed that, although all city dwellers could converse in Spanish, the unlettered were hesitant to do so for fear of "speaking badly," while the cultivated also clung to "their habit of speaking Catalan at all hours." Nor was their Catalan more mellifluous. It was a far cry from that of the "famous codes, solemn treatises, and magnificent chronicles of the Middle Ages." In rural and mountainous areas, spoken Catalan was said to be of high quality, but in Barcelona, the language had become "plagued with innumerable Spanish expressions."[52]

Also contributing to linguistic diversity was the fact that many students and lawyers did not speak Catalan, so daily conversations often shifted between languages. In his memoirs, Joan Maluquer, who commenced university in the late 1860s, indicated that he usually chatted in Catalan, but he often switched to Spanish when addressing various colleagues.[53] Many members of the bar came from families who had moved to Barcelona from other regions in Spain or from the colonies. A few lawyers arrived after graduating from university elsewhere.[54] First- and even second-generation immigrants had no reason to learn Catalan, for it was thought to be a dying language used only for informal or private matters or for literary genres such as poetry or theater. Even among Catalans, some families spoke Spanish at home for one reason or another. Here the case of Luis María Camino, a successful mercantile lawyer, is instructive. He always spoke in Spanish even though he had been born in the Catalan town of Lleida to parents from Catalonia. The reason was that his paternal grandfather had come from Galicia, and hence Spanish had always been the language of his family home.[55]

For a young man who aspired to become a lawyer or other educated professional, the quality of his spoken Catalan was not a concern. In contrast, it was absolutely imperative to learn to write and to speak Spanish at an early age. In order to aid the region's youth, two eminent lawyers, Joan Illas and Laureà Figuerola, took time out of their practices, and numerous other activities, to publish a primer on Spanish grammar in 1853.[56] Similarly, an advertising pamphlet of an elite boarding school from 1887 promised to produce pupils who spoke as if they had been raised in the "kidney of Castile."[57] Law students with good Spanish had a head start on those who struggled. The better a future lawyer could hone his Spanish oratory, the more elegant his powers of written expression, the better a chance he had of winning lawsuits. As was logical, lawyers spoke significantly better Spanish than most other Catalans, and some distinguished litigators were among the most acclaimed orators in Spain. When students arrived at university, however, they constituted a cacophony of voices.

University and Early Years of Practice

Students arrived at university possessing heterogeneous social and pedagogical backgrounds. Yet whether a young man was a native of the city or came to

Barcelona by ship, by carriage, by train, or by foot; whether he was a first or a second son; whether he had been educated by monks or laymen; whether he was rich or poor; whether he struggled in Spanish or spoke as if he was from the "kidney of Castile"; whether he lived at home, with an uncle or family friend, or in a lay or religious boardinghouse, university and early years of practice were a leveling experience. Young men, of diverse backgrounds but similar ambitions, became acquainted with their future colleagues and role models and eyed similar opportunities. The weight of bourgeois culture paired with the lure of the bar exerted a binding influence. A motley group of adolescents cohered into the basis of a future legal profession. Upon entering law school, a distinct and everlasting corporate identity began to take hold.

In 1835 the university law school opened in Barcelona and in 1841, the University of Cervera, which had disintegrated over the course of the Carlist War (1833–39), was definitively closed. The experience of lawyers who attended university in Barcelona was different from that of their predecessors. Middle-aged and elderly advocates of the 1840s and 1850s had spent their university years in Cervera, Barcelona, or Valencia, and had managed to patch together a legal career amid war, revolution, and repression. Indeed, education had broken down to such an extent in the revolutionary 1830s that students were permitted to study under the tutelage of a lawyer and then show up at university to sit for exams.[58] It was also common for students to study outside Catalonia, in places where the war was less intense.[59] These young men had arrived in Barcelona where they had slowly familiarized themselves with legal culture and grown to know one another while adults. Later generations, however, attended law school together in Barcelona, observed their future mentors while students, and forged strong bonds at an early age. In short, professional indoctrination became a more intense experience than it had been earlier in the century. Conrad Roure, who attended law school in the late 1850s and early 1860s, recounted that he spent his mornings at university, then went to the café with his friends, and then apprenticed for a lawyer in the afternoons. As an adult practitioner, he continued to associate with classmates whom he had met in law school or even earlier.[60]

The law school was small, so all students came to know one another. From the 1850s to the late 1880s, it averaged fewer than one hundred students for every year of study; because of attrition, the number in a cohort would decrease from one year to the next.[61] From the 1840s to the late 1880s, the university usually awarded anywhere from thirty to eighty law licentiates a year, but there was enormous variation from one year to the next.[62] A few graduating classes were tiny, as was Conrad Roure's of 1863, in which a mere sixteen souls received their degrees at the close of the academic year. To celebrate, he and his fellow graduates rented out the restaurant Justin on the Plaça Real, inviting family and friends. In a demonstration of fraternal benevolence, a rich classmate footed the bill. As Roure writes, "There were toasts, speeches, more toasts ... and a few became honest victims to a little oratory furor. ... But isn't youth something that goes so easily to one's head!"[63] Needless to say, youthful camaraderie forged lasting relationships and allegiances that were carried into adult life.

The minimum number of years required to achieve the licentiate, the degree needed to practice, diminished from the high of ten in 1807 under the monarchy of Charles IV, to a low of five by 1884 where it remained through the twentieth century.[64] This gradual reduction did not mean that students spent fewer years in the classroom or finished at a younger age. According to the Moyano Law of 1857, a boy needed to be at least nine years old to begin secondary school, which meant that he could not start law school until he was at least fifteen. Given that law school took seven years to complete, even the most prodigious talent could not graduate until he was at least twenty-one or twenty-two. This, in fact, was the roughly same age of the youngest members of the bar earlier in the century. Liberal reforms did not change the raw quantity of education a student received but shifted the emphasis. As the amount of time spent at university became shorter, primary and secondary education became longer and broader. This transformed the image of the lawyer: a university graduate was no longer a "professor of law," steeped in the Roman-ecclesiastical tradition from an early age. This antiquated term fell out of use in the early nineteenth century. Instead, he was considered a well-rounded "gentleman" (*señor*), educated in arts, sciences, and law.

The midcentury law student was a docile creature, loaded with ambition but awed and intimidated by the majesty of the professoriate. The reputation, success, and influence of professors meant that students wisely courted their favor. If a student performed well, a professor could help him secure an apprenticeship. In contrast, a troublemaker or a slouch could have trouble living down a reputation. In the 1840s, the student body was inundated with liberal veterans of various ages from the Carlist War; the triumphant spirit of liberalism reigned, although it perhaps coexisted with war weariness. By midcentury, the student-militiaman disappeared, replaced by the student-gentleman with more cultivated tastes. Son of a militia captain and a wholesaler, Conrad Roure began attending law school in the late 1850s, during which time he and some of his classmates developed critical opinions of the elitist and undemocratic orientation of liberal parties. In theory, this leftist coterie could have been prone to activism, but their days were disciplined, uneventful, and serious; they attended university "without missing a single day" and even complained of boredom during the hour recess between each class. Roure wrote, "The professors were savants of legislative science and imbued us with unsurpassable qualifications." He admitted, "Student life in those years did not involve many events in which students became active as students."[65] Students had been politically active during the era of liberal revolution and would later rally around Catalanism. The middle decades, however, was a period in which they were practical, peaceful, and career oriented.

The teaching of Catalan law — as well as all law for that matter — also fortified cohesiveness. The law curriculum was the same for all universities in Spain. To the chagrin of many professors and students, no provisions were made to sponsor a specific course dedicated to Catalan law or even foral law. Rather, the various laws of the foral regions were taught within courses on Spanish civil law. Just the same, it was only logical that professors went into depth on Catalan law, given that students needed to be familiar with its general features, as well as its particularities and peculiarities, in order to practice. More important than lecture content was atmosphere. Buzzing through university halls, offices, and classrooms, were debates and discussions about the future of Catalan law during the age of codification. Generations of professors worked to preserve Catalan law through scholarship and associational activities. This intoxicated the minds of youths exposed to the material for the first time. Enric Prat de la Riba, the father of the nationalist movement, attributed his awakening to his years as a student in the 1880s. He recalled that professors "spoke to us of law as a living thing produced spontaneously from nothing less than national spirit.... Catalonia had its own law; Catalonia had its own language; hence, Catalonia had this mysterious national spirit that through the years gave birth to and renovated law and language."[66] Prat de la Riba was an ideologue who interpreted his lectures creatively, but even those who were more practical grew fond of their native legal regime.

After leaving university, lawyers did not always continue to show such deference to authority. A few carried forth the flame of revolutionary heritage that had burned so bright earlier in the century. A handful of lawyers were active in republican organizations, counseled and advised workers and trade-union organizers, and dedicated some of their time to defending persons accused of political and press crimes. This was risky behavior. It is not difficult to compile a list, which is by no means exhaustive, of leftist advocates who faced charges of treason during periods of martial law, were brought before military tribunals, and suffered imprisonment or exile. In 1855 Joan Nogués, a liberal veteran of the Carlist War, was exiled to France after counseling workers during the city's first general strike.[67] In 1869 Gonçal Serraclara was caught in a barricade during a failed republican uprising; after being found guilty at trial, he was allowed to flee across the border.[68] Around the same time, Ròmul Mascaró was sent to a penal colony in North Africa.[69] Two lawyers faced military justice during the Montjuïc Trials of 1897, an infamous episode in which the Spanish army imprisoned, tortured, and convicted a number of anarchists, four of whom were executed. The Federal-Republican Party leader Josep Maria Vallès de Ribot suffered a brief spell in jail, while the young Pere Corominas faced a terrifying ordeal before being allowed to flee abroad.[70] After the danger had subsided, all of these men were able to return to Barcelona and resume their practices. Nonetheless, their frightening experiences had a chilling effect on those contemplating similar activities.

In the case when an advocate faced the grim prospect of a military trial, family and friends would search out influential persons who could obtain private audiences with civil or military authorities to see whether a deal could be arranged. The bar was an effective network for such purposes, because leaders of the college and the academy were among the most influential men in the country. None of the previously mentioned individuals admitted to having provoked or participated in armed uprising, and, by the looks of it, their claims appear to have been genuine. Given that it was the content of their speech and the nature of their associations that got them into trouble, even conservative advocates would be sympathetic with their plight. Wary of creating an open rift with the army, the College of Lawyers never publicly criticized the savagery of military justice, but its leaders did intervene behind the scenes on behalf of fellow members. During the Montjuïc trials, for example, Pere Corominas's friends from law school — including the father of the surrealist painter Salvador Dalí — convinced the dean of the college and senator to the Spanish Corts, Josep Vilaseca, to lobby the prime minister in Madrid. The strategy proved successful, and Corominas was released. A Conservative Party senator, Vilaseca loathed the ideas of Corominas, a republican who flirted with anarchism. In this case and others, however, corporate solidarity prevailed over political ideology. The college would defend members, provided they had not committed serious crimes, whether their troubles arose from a small run-in with a judge to a life-threatening scenario with the army.[71]

For the most part, however, the extracurricular activities of young lawyers were innocuous. They were not unlike those described by Gustave Flaubert in his *Sentimental Education* (1869). Like Flaubert's clique, students and young lawyers engaged in journalism, theater, and politics. In Barcelona as in Paris, it was common for the rich to bankroll their poorer friends. Roure recounted that he and his mates rented a flat, colloquially referred to as a *taller* (shop), which they decorated with paintings and furnished with a piano. Here, they sponsored parties, held poetry readings, parodied the pretentious gatherings of their elders, and wrote and performed theater, *zarzuela*, and short opera. In the early years of practice, he and many young lawyers met at cafés, such as Suizo or Siete Puertas, frequented the bullfights, and held *tertulias* in the shops of their friends where they would discuss politics, theater, literature, and bullfighting. Maurici Serrahima joined a more conventional crowd but took part in similar recreational activities. He and his friends went by the name "the nocturnals," because, like many youth, they liked going out at night. They played billiards, performed Chinese shadow-puppet plays, wrote poetry and verse, dabbled in journalism and satire, and took off on swimming and hiking excursions.[72] In the popular novel, *Mysteries of Barcelona* (1865), a pair of law students, one poor and one rich, share a flat and frequent illegal gambling parlors and the salons of bourgeois and aristocratic women, where they engage in the follies of youth and pursue romantic adventures.

Not all midcentury students were dandies, but the odd bohemian was present. Josep Coroleu, the grandson of a prominent advocate from the War of Independence, entered law school in the late 1850s but ran into trouble with his conservative law professors. Interrupting his studies to shuttle between Paris, Barcelona, and possibly Rome, he dabbled in political, journalistic, and literary activities typical of young republican romantics. While in Paris, he served as a point of contact for exiles from Catalonia. Following the Revolution of 1868, he returned to Barcelona and finished his law studies but left practice after a few years. Instead, he earned a living as a journalist, translator, and historian.[73] Joaquín Costa, a law student in Madrid in the 1870s, came from a family of struggling Aragonese property owners. He tells of shifting from one boardinghouse to another, wearing the same shirt and trousers for days on end. He owned only two nonmatching shoes, both incidentally meant for the same foot. He spent nights soaking one of them, so walking would be less painful the next day.[74]

Making friends among classmates was a fine way to advance a career. To those who did not come from well-connected families, strategic friendships could provide an entree into the elite. Associational life was another route. Opportunities were abundant. Conrad Roure pledged the Freemasons. He claimed that his republican affiliations caused him to be boycotted by high society, which considered "honor and democracy two incompatible concepts." Although his political beliefs made him and his friends prime targets for recruitment, he also admitted to having joined out of "self-interest" so that he would not "die of hunger." The Masons strove to better their brethren's prospects by inserting them within networks of middle-class freethinkers who could ferry work their way and provide valuable connections. Roure confessed that the "Freemasonry, because of its protectionist character, offered a safe haven to those of us that had no other means by which to earn a living other than the practice of our career."[75] Other options were available. Young lawyers wrote for the press and frequented associations, including the Academy of Jurisprudence, the Atheneum, and other intellectual, religious, and economic groups. Attending sessions, studiously preparing for debates, performing secretarial tasks, flattering elders, delivering speeches, and publishing reports allowed an aspiring advocate to make a name. Preferring not be bothered by petty organizational tasks, associational leaders would grant opportunities to young men who shouldered the burden.

Above all, the primary goal for an aspiring lawyer was to find a mentor. The legal obligation that candidates undergo a specified period of formal apprenticeship was abolished in 1807, but as different governments alternated in and out of power, and politicians endlessly tinkered with degree requirements, it reappeared periodically. It was definitively eliminated in 1866.[76] Regardless of whether required by law or not, aspirants wishing to learn their trade, or to test the waters, apprenticed in law offices. A diligent student had a relatively easy time finding a place, because few established lawyers would pass up the chance to have a bright young man carry out tedious tasks for free or nominal wages. But those in the proverbial middle of the pack may have had a harder time finding somewhere to train. Where one apprenticed was a key choice, as some advocates were better mentors than others. It does not appear that families paid practitioners to mentor their sons, although this may have taken place privately or just have been part of the normal exchange of favors. An apprentice either worked for free, nominal wages or a stipend. At first, he would spend long hours copying documents, but, as his competence increased, he would be given more serious tasks, such as researching and drafting opinions. After receiving a law degree, he could begin to appear in court.

Successful advocates would look back on their apprenticeship years with nostalgia. Joan Maluquer learned his craft from men at the center of political influence. In the late 1870s, he moved to Madrid to pursue a doctorate. According to the Moyano Law of 1857, the University of Madrid was the only place in the country permitted to award this degree.[77] Unless one had professorial or magisterial ambitions, it was not necessary — a forensic reputation would be earned in the courtroom. Nonetheless, a good number of graduates headed off to the state capital in order to adorn their resumes. Incidentally, Joan Maluquer never completed his doctorate, but he did take advantage of his time. He apprenticed for the law office partners and powerful Liberal Party politicians Manuel Alonso Martínez and Germán Gamazo. One of his more intriguing projects consisted of preparing a legal opinion for the British ambassador on laws governing the discriminatory treatment of Protestants. After a one-year stint, he received a generous stipend and then returned to Barcelona, where he apprenticed for one of his father's younger cousins, Eduard Maluquer, who happened to be the leader of the "Gamacista" (centrist) wing of the Liberal Party in Barcelona. Later in life, Maluquer made use of his political contacts to garner an appointment as chief prosecutor to the Supreme Court in Madrid.[78] The connections of the Maluquer family, stretching from Barcelona to Madrid, intertwined within the oligarchic networks of the Liberal Party, were exceptional. They were, however, indicative of parallel networks, most of which existed on a smaller and local scale.

Some apprentices had more memorable experiences than others. It was common for a protégée to spend hours watching his mentor work, humoring him with gossip and youthful conversation while listening to him reminisce and counsel on law and life. This could be dull. Looking back on his time with Narcís Verdaguer in the 1890s, Francesc Cambó complained, "I did not learn much that would later serve me for the career of lawyer. Verdaguer's office was not of great importance and he wanted things to be so perfect that he himself did all the work."[79] More thriving offices were not always more exciting. The numerous apprentices of the prestigious commercial lawyer, Luis María Camino, were said to spend endless hours copying documents.[80] Still, Verdaguer tutored Cambó in emerging nationalism, while Camino's apprentices witnessed the workings of one of the top mercantile office of the 1880s. The mere presence in a law office enabled an aspirant to establish connections, to mull over prospects in law and related activities, and to contemplate the life awaiting him.

Just as students complained of spending hours copying documents or being left to gaze over their mentor's shoulder, an advocate was not always pleased with his devil. Writing in 1920, a Madrid lawyer, Ángel Ossorio, claimed that his apprentices spent their days reading newspapers, rolling cigarettes, gossiping about actresses and singers, drinking beer and devouring potato chips, sipping vermouth and sampling pastries, and boisterously arguing about politics, bullfighting, and well-publicized crimes. This caused them to "become distracted when reading the paperwork involved in a case, and consistently overlooking the fundamentals of law in all their writings."[81] His imperious tone conveyed the impression that when he was an apprentice in the 1890s such vices did not exist. To a certain extent, he was correct: a consumer society and the entertainment industry had grown significantly during the early twentieth century; in the 1890s, beer and chips had not yet made their way into the Mediterranean world. Nonetheless, nineteenth-century Barcelona, like Madrid, was full of cafés, theaters, and bullrings, where apprentices shot the breeze, whittled away the hours, and, if not careful, misspent their youth. The memoirs of Conrad Roure contain vivid descriptions, and even drawings, of famous bullfighters, actresses, causes célèbres, victorious generals, and politicians of the 1850s and 1860s.

If one did not have a father, uncle, or family friend in the market for an apprentice, other types of relationships could be tapped. Conrad Roure recounted that he owed his success to Josep Antoni Canals, a midlevel earner, who took him under his wing as an apprentice. The longtime family advocate, Canals was perhaps his mother's lover; at the very least, he acted as a surrogate parent after Roure's own father had died. Even after Roure had opened his own office, Canals still ferried a steady trickle of clients his way.[82] Another interesting, though atypical, story was that of Maurici Serrahima, who took advantage of a once-in-a-lifetime opportunity to enter the household of Pere Vives, a top civil practitioner. In the 1850s, Vives was in the market for a live-in tutor and companion for his son Félix, and the penniless Serrahima was a bright student in need of room and board. Once in the household, Serrahima converted his role from son's tutor to father's apprentice. He later married the sister of a law school classmate, from a family of wealthy pharmacists, who also came to be an eminent lawyer.[83] Manuel Duran apprenticed for the mercantile lawyer Josep Ventosa and then followed the age-old custom of wedding the daughter of his mentor.[84] Advocates frequently married their mentors' daughters and friends' sisters, persons within their social circles. Sentiments aside, young lawyers deployed numerous strategies to wiggle their way into favor with patriarchs of prestigious law offices and distinguished families. Love was not incompatible with professional advancement.

Connections were invaluable to get a foot in the door, but long-term success was dependent on talent and hard work. Law was a competitive profession. The bar was small enough so that a client, interested in hiring competent counsel, could easily make the needed inquiries to buy good representation. A young man, no matter how well connected, no matter how much he participated in associational life, no matter who his father or uncle was, or whom he married, or what office he apprenticed in, could not talk his way into even the middling ranks of the profession without diligence, acumen, and skill. When all was said and done, a reputation was earned by the ability to win winnable lawsuits. For every lawyer whose strategy was to milk his extrajudicial activities and friends, two or three others began as faceless devils but patiently rose through the ranks by earning a reputation, first of competence and perhaps later of brilliance, combativeness, style, and flare. This is how one of Balzac's scheming characters saw the long, hard road in 1834: "He must slave for ten years, live at the rate of a thousand francs a month, have a library and chambers, go into society, go down on his knees before a solicitor for briefs, sweep the floor of the Palais de Justice with his tongue. If this led to anything good, I should say no; but show me five advocates in Paris who earn more than fifty thousand francs a year at fifty!"[85] Barcelona's legal culture was somewhat different: lawyers did not have chambers but ordinary offices, and did not rely on proctors for briefs, but had to drum up business for themselves. However, as in Paris, law in Barcelona was a calling for the ambitious, patient, and hardworking. It did not promise instantaneous or vast riches. It was neither a place for dilettantes nor a comfy sinecure in which dedication could be halfhearted.

During the second half of the nineteenth century, the Barcelona bar grew from 363 to 861 lawyers. Of these, 260 and 433 were private practitioners, while many of the others worked as judges, prosecutors, judicial secretaries, court reporters, secretaries to banks and business, or estate administrators or were engaged in politics or business. Some lawyers did not practice but used their knowledge to administer family patrimonies or simply held a degree for show. Others retired or moved into something else because of old age, ill health, or lack of success. Despite rising numbers, lawyers were connected by a web of relationships. Education, friendships, apprenticeships, marriages, and associations bound them tightly together. While in practice, advocates became familiar with younger and older members as adversaries or allies in court or as colleagues at the college and the academy. The bar was not always a harmonious place, for it was rife with rivalries, alliances, and clans. But these were shifting rather than fixed in stone. They paradoxically led to cohesion, as the presence of rumor and gossip, conspiracy and strategy, formed a discursive labyrinth only intelligible among members of the club. Not to be overlooked, the shared experience of having survived the stresses of developing a legal practice in a competitive environment endowed lawyers with a strong esprit de corps.

Legal Practice: The Road to Success

During the second half of the nineteenth century, the bar underwent noticeable changes. Opportunities grew. While the elite of the midcentury bar had tended to develop civil-mercantile practices, later generations branched out, pursued complementary activities, explored multiple offerings, and pursued profits in the industrial city. However, much stayed the same. "Specialization" would not be a characteristic of the bar until the twentieth century when many law offices would develop specific areas of expertise (penal law, family law, labor law, estate management, administrative law, etc.). In the nineteenth century, the law firm had not yet come into being, and offices still consisted of a single lawyer or, at most, a partnership. Some advocates achieved reputations as "civilists," "mercantilists," and "penalists," but such individuals usually took on a variety of cases. They worked out of offices located in, or adjacent to, their homes, ambled about the same streets as they had for centuries, and received visits from clients, notaries, and proctors. A young advocate might have different goals from those of his mentor: he might choose to be more or less ambitious, pursue new frontiers, or abandon some lines of work. Still, he assumed that his daily rhythms would echo those he had observed as a young man. After all, an answer was an answer, a complaint a complaint, a witness interrogatory a witness interrogatory. Continuity in work practices from one generation to the next endowed the bar with a commonality of experience in an age of widening opportunity.

A successful lawyer would develop his own reputation and style, but, before so doing, he set off down an arduous road from neophyte to veteran. Professional development underwent one fundamental change during the liberal era. By midcentury, it had become common for a young lawyer to receive courtroom training by working for a few years as a public defender. Upon the foundation of the college in 1833, the bar appointed a corps of public defenders, literally called "lawyers for the poor" (*abogados de pobres*). For the most part, they consisted of recent university graduates, who, in exchange for their services, were absolved of the obligation to contribute to the profession's annual tax obligation. What was later called the "turn-in-office" (*turno de oficio*) became a standard phase of the professionalization process and, like university and apprenticeship, helped forge corporate solidarity. Lawyers also looked back on their days as public defenders with nostalgia.

The turn-in-office was yet another hurdle on the road to success. During law school, the intelligent and diligent would survive, but many dropped out or switched studies because of a lack of acumen or interest. A large number of students who started law, somewhere around 50 percent, did not finish the degree. Upon graduation, another 50 percent stayed in Barcelona, while the other half returned to their home counties.[86] Even among those who remained in the city, not all sought to enter private practice. As Manuel Angelon remarked, "Many young men study with the sole object of saying that they have a degree."[87] When a young man began the stint as a public defender, then, he realized that his university cohort, and those immediately above and below him, had been whittled down to a few dozen men who aspired to nutrify the ranks of the Barcelona bar. Lawyers later remembered their turn-in-office as a time in which they learned the tools of the trade. Not all succeeded, of course, as there was a large divide between theory and practice — a good student was not necessarily a good litigator and vice versa. The college lists are filled with persons who, after serving as public defenders and even practicing for a few years, encountered difficulties and never came into their own.

A stint as a public defender was considered a public service, part of training, an extension of university life, a rite of passage. It was not a period of time when a young man was expected to earn. In theory, a public defender represented the poor in penal as well as civil cases, but just about all of this work consisted of criminal defenses. An individual was considered "poor" if he or she earned less per day than two day laborers, a classification that covered men and women more likely to be indicted on criminal charges than to be parties to civil lawsuits.[88] In theory, public defenders were not compensated, although there was some controversy over whether they were permitted to charge small sums.[89] For most of the century, criminal work was good training for civil work. The modern criminal trial did not come to Spain until 1882, and until this occurred, criminal procedure was similar to civil procedure, and criminal appellate argument similar to civil appellate argument. Although an advocate was under no obligation to serve as a public defender, most relished the opportunity. Even those with cozy relationships with their mentors were advised to pass through the stage. After all, it was better to cut one's teeth and make novice mistakes on poor sots with no voice in society rather than on paying clients who, if dissatisfied, could tarnish one's reputation.

The College of Lawyers appointed a list of public defenders at the annual meeting, and the board of directors approved replacements. Absences occurred when a young man had to return to a family home to look after ill parents, or during summer, when many spent time enjoying the sea or mountains. By midcentury, the college established the unwritten rule in which a public defender was allowed to remain in the post for a maximum of four years, although most would look to relinquish the position earlier.[90] It is likely that there was some peer pressure to do this, given that others anxiously awaited a turn; upon graduation, a candidate sometimes had to wait a year or more before a slot opened. Subject to tedious negotiations between the college and the Ministry of Finance, the number of public defenders rose and fell but usually hovered around 20 percent of the practicing bar. In 1833 the first list numbered twenty; at midcentury, the corps grew to forty; and by century's end, it stood at eighty.[91] A public defender who performed well, especially in front of a gallery, could boost his reputation. Defendants felt less fortunate. Facing punishments from death to extended terms in a North African prison colony or a peninsular prison, they found themselves in the hands of neophytes and sycophants eager to make favorable impressions upon judges and prosecutors. Having worked as a public defender in the 1890s, the Madrid lawyer Ángel Ossorio confessed, "It was not just. Novices represented the poor, who were abandoned by those lawyers with more experience."[92]

As a public defender, a young advocate became familiar with a battery of routine offenses. Vagrancy, assault, rape, rapture, sodomy, murder, robbery, illegal possession of firearms, arson, fraud, forgery, conspiracy, and prison escape were standard fare. Crimes involving the judicial process itself, such as bribery, perjury, intimidation of witnesses, and falsification of evidence, were also commonplace.[93] After finishing his stint, a young lawyer usually continued to represent criminal defendants for some time. Although some persons accused of crimes earned slightly more than the minimum amount to qualify as "poor," many could come up with only small amounts of money and hence had no choice but to hire novices. Joan Maluquer claimed to have taken on fifty-two criminal cases in a year, an average of one per week, while literally burning the midnight oil, toiling in a small flat with a gas-lit lantern. He recalls experiencing a deep sense of guilt after winning an innocent verdict for a murderer. He did not charge much: "The earnings were small, as criminals have never been predisposed to enrich lawyers. We charged what they would give us."[94] As the Catalan adage stated, "For the new lawyer, poor, prostitutes, and relatives." Clients were equally dissatisfied: "Young lawyer, lawsuit lost."[95] Under these conditions, a lawyer slogged through the lean years immersed in criminal defenses until he could develop a more remunerative practice by capturing civil and commercial work. Ángel Ossorio recounted that when he began his career, his clients consisted of "petty thieves, brawlers, whores, schemers, vandals, abusers." At his zenith, the good advocate had moved up to "dukes, millionaires, and people of the upmost elegance."[96]

The goal was to transform a criminal-law practice into a civil-commercial one, but it would be a mistake to believe that well-earning lawyers abandoned the penal law entirely. When the money was right or when publicity promised packed galleries, there would be no want of takers for an interesting case. Although most defendants were poor, a good number were not. Highway robbers, fraudsters, counterfeiters, smugglers, forgers, arsonists, assassins, and embezzlers could afford to compensate counsel, often handsomely. For example, in 1861 *El Foro* reported that Pau Valls, a pious Catholic and conservative civil advocate, was to appear on behalf of a coterie of (no doubt well-paying) defendants accused of forgery. The case would "allow his vast talent and gentle oratory to shine" and "demonstrate his profound knowledge of penal law."[97] Other attractive work involved electioneering, political or print offenses, white-collar crime, or causes célèbres. Moreover, criminal cases were not always defenses. Procedures allowed the victim, or his or her family, to initiate or to join a case on the accusatory side. Although not terribly common, moneyed families seeking emotional retribution could recruit counsel to drive a case forward rather than sitting back and waiting for the wheels of justice to churn forth and deliver justice.[98] Some lawyers just loved the stage. Manuel Josep de Torres, a successful mercantilist, had an insatiable thirst for causes célèbres. He obtained renowned victories, or partial victories, for some well-heeled defendants. His brilliant oratory shone in "criminal cases … where human passions are in play and the facts have a dramatic quality." His friend Manuel Duran chastised those who "erroneously believe that these types of cases are always vulgar."[99]

Since the early eighteenth century, a lawyer had been free to charge whatever the market would yield. Beginning in the 1830s, this laissez-faire regime underwent one modification: a client was allowed to contest an "honorarium" (without having to sue) by requesting a presiding judge to examine and reduce it for a case. If a lawyer suffered a reduction, he was, in return, granted the right to have his bill and the judge's audit reviewed by the board of directors at the College of Lawyers, who could either uphold the decision, overturn it, or, as frequently occurred, find an intermediate level. A client was not likely to contest fees unless they were egregiously inflated, given that any request had to pass through two levels of scrutiny. Because the College of Lawyers had the last word, fees would never be reduced by very much. Nonetheless, the standing threat deterred some unscrupulous behavior. The understanding was that fees were not uniform but varied depending on the reputation of the advocate, the nature of the dispute, and the agreement with the client. This dual audit scheme proved to be an acceptable balance: it protected clients against creative billing, ensured lawyers decent earnings, and respected the rules of the market. One might surmise that it was not failsafe: some clients were bilked, and some lawyers were left holding the bill.[100]

Having established a reputation as a promising litigator, a young lawyer still had some ways to go before he could convert a practice representing "poor, prostitutes, and family members" to one that catered to "people of the upmost elegance." This could take decades. At first, compensation was modest. The Madrid lawyer Ángel Ossorio recounted that his first job was working as an editor of a weekly legal periodical, which paid a salary of 125 pesetas (equivalent to 600 reales) a month in the 1890s.[101] Joan Maluquer became a municipal judge in the 1880s, which brought him around 200 pesetas (800 reales) a month, an income he defined as "very small."[102] To be fair, young lawyers envied persons who could garner one of the few municipal judgeships in the city, positions acquired through political connections of which the Maluquer family had many. Although such emoluments were small, they were not starvation wages. Even if a struggling young advocate earned half the amount as Maluquer and less than Ossorio, say around 100 pesetas a month, and could eke out only a tough living from penal work and menial tasks, this figure was well above the average salary for an artisan. By the latter decades of the century, lawyers in the bar's lowest tax bracket ordinarily paid more than double the amount charged to the average artisan.[103] What is more, the bulk of lawyers earning small quantities were young. The expectation was that they would later earn more.

A rough idea of comparative salaries can be ascertained by examining tax records. These documents do not reveal how much money a lawyer earned but provide a comparative assessment based on the axiom that the more the government taxed an occupation per head, the more its average practitioner tended to make. In the first major tax law of 1845, the Moderates taxed the average lawyer — like the doctor, architect, and notary, and other educated professionals — more than twice the amount of the average carpenter, proctor, and midwife. This evidences a large divide between the incomes of the "learned professions" and those of the "manual arts."[104] In 1870 a democratic reform, devised by Laureà Figuerola, changed things dramatically. The average lawyer paid about five times the tax of an average carpenter or plumber. Even if this tax was intended to be progressive, it suggests that lawyers' salaries towered above those of artisans.[105] Given that artisan and worker salaries ranged between 2,000 and 4,000 reales per year in the 1860s, the figures imply that incomes for successful lawyers were at least, and probably well above, 10,000 reales per year.

State salaries confirm these estimations. The Moyano Law of 1857 set annual wages of law professors between 12,000 and 18,000 reales, and by century's end, they had climbed to between 3,500 and 10,000 pesetas (equivalent to 14,000 and 40,000 reales).[106] Teaching was not a full-time calling: professors were free to run law offices, so they could augment their incomes substantially. Further insight into what was considered a dignified salary can be ascertained by reviewing a conflict over district court prosecutor wages. In 1860 prosecutors earned between 7,000 and 11,000 reales per year. To practicing lawyers, this was considered unconscionably low, given that district court judges made between 12,000 and 18,000 reales. The rationale for the difference was that prosecutors — unlike judges but like university professors — were permitted to supplement their incomes through private practice. The editors of a legal periodical, however, considered this ludicrous, given that prosecutors in the city, where crime was rampant, did not have the time to tend to private clients. The salary was not enough for a man to live "like a career professional with a family"; it was "less than the doorman to many offices, and not as much as the jailer in some prisons, and could hardly be considered equal to that of a third or fourth provincial official."[107] The expectation was that prosecutors should be paid as much as judges and more than low-level bureaucrats. An accomplished lawyer also expected to make more than 10,000 reales per year in order to raise a family with multiple children.

With a solid reputation and a steady clientele, a hardworking advocate who delivered results could earn significantly more. Rafael Degollada claimed to have earned 35,000 reales per year as a young man in the mid-1830s.[108] The best trousered enviable sums. Maurici Serrahima's grandson boasted that his grandfather grossed as much as 100,000 pesetas (400,000 reales) per year at the pinnacle of his career. This figure might be an exaggeration, but it was not out of the range of possibilities.[109] If true, it represented a good year. Serrahima's own records indicate that he billed around half of this amount in the 1880s and 1890s. Nonetheless, the grandson's claims should not be dismissed. Serrahima may have had additional income from investments in business or real estate that would not have appeared on his law office books. His clients were a smattering of men, women, companies, partnerships, and municipalities.[110] To be sure, Serrahima's earnings represented those of a top office, aided by apprentices and operating at full tilt, of which only a handful existed at any time. Records reveal that a lawyer charged five to ten pesetas for short office visits, and twenty to fifty for more lengthy meetings and negotiations. A client often had to pay more than one hundred pesetas for the drafting of a document or a courtroom appearance. A lawyer usually charged a few hundred or a few thousand pesetas for a lawsuit, depending on its length and complexity.[111]

Needless to say, the gap between struggling lawyers, who made a thousand pesetas a year, and rich advocates, who earned more than a hundred times this amount, was gargantuan. Among the bulk of working practitioners, however, differences were not nearly as great. Corporate cohesiveness was strengthened by a similarity of earnings among practitioners at similar stages in their careers. As far as taxes were concerned, the highest earners paid some ten times the taxes of the lowest, indicative of a substantial but not an astronomical gap in earning differentials. Income inequality was significantly less than that which existed among men of commerce. In law, there was a ceiling on the amount of money one could earn through private practice; after all, there were only so many billable hours in a day. In contrast, the sky was the limit in business, banking, and real estate. If investments can be taken as an indicator of incomes and inheritances, top lawyers were not nearly as wealthy as successful bankers and industrialists, or wealthy rentiers and large property owners. Some advocates sank serious sums into factories, railroads, gas, mines, steamships, investment banks, mortgage banks, agrarian-credit banks, and real estate. But they did not figure on shareholders lists to the extent of men of commerce, rentiers, or property owners nor did they invest as heavily. In the 1850s and 1860s, the richest advocates might invest hundreds of thousands of reales in a single company, which paled in comparison to the millions of leading bankers. On average, lawyers invested less than men of commerce and slightly more than doctors.[112]

Private practice was not the sole route to success, as some used their legal knowledge to pursue complementary activities. "Secretaries" (administrators) to public and private enterprise were often lawyers. One distinguished jurist from the late nineteenth and early twentieth century, Guillem Brocà, began his career as secretary at the Bank of Barcelona. Estate administration was another viable option. For example, Francesc Romaní, one of the most active members of the Academy of Jurisprudence during the 1880s and 1890s, was not considered a "practicing lawyer." Rather than living off lawsuits, he ministered to the legal needs of the truly wealthy. He was the estate administrator for Claudio López, the Marquis of Comillas, one of the richest man in Spain, whose prize assets in the 1880s included the Hispano-Colonial Bank, the Trans-Atlantic Steamship Company, and the Philippines Tobacco Company. The estate covered some 50,000 acres of land and numerous palaces, homes, and real-estate investments scattered throughout the country. In 1886 Francesc Romaní founded the periodical *Regional Spain*, a mouthpiece of political regionalism, which was backed by the textile industrialist Eusebi Güell, one of the city's richest men. Surely, Romaní, the son of a paper manufacturer, was quite good at what he did, for few men enjoyed the patronage of the Güell and López families. Although his career was exceptional, it was indicative of numerous lawyers of lesser renown who worked in similar capacities by managing smaller estates or a number of smaller estates.[113]

For men with legal education and training, business opportunities grew increasingly attractive during the century. Rafael Degollada was a pioneer, teaming up with another lawyer and other investors to found a chemical plant in the 1840s.[114] Antonio Font del Sol, a onetime College of Lawyers dean, joined family members and an industrial engineer named David Alexander to recruit investors for an iron foundry in the 1850s.[115] Ferran Delàs, the son of a titled aristocrat, labored in the law for more than twenty years, before abandoning practice in the late 1870s to run the fire insurance company, "La Catalana."[116] As capitalism grew more gentlemanly, men with law degrees found it easier to pursue careers in business. The "lawyer-millionaire" trio of Darius Rumeu, Josep Nadal, and Josep Espinós, all of whom were Bank of Barcelona board members in the 1890s and dynastic party politicians, was exemplary.[117] In the mid-nineteenth century, a businessmen with a law degree, though by no means unheard of, was a rarity; by the outset of the twentieth century, it was common. As could be expected, not all who tried their hand were successful. Luis María Camino, the "most obligatory lawyer for large mercantile enterprises" in the 1880s, fell into such debt because of stock market speculation that he was forced to sign over his life insurance policy to the Bank of Barcelona, an act that caused him to suffer great public humiliation. Pedro del Balzo struck it rich in the market before going bust in the 1880s as well. After his disgrace, he suffered a stroke. As Joan Maluquer observed, "His wife, a saint, accompanied him by the arm through the streets of the city, until God took him."[118]

For young men with political ambitions, law was also the profession of choice. The parliamentary leader of Catalan nationalism in the twentieth century, Francesc Cambó, made the decision to study law as a boy because "almost all first-rate politicians were lawyers."[119] A well-trodden career path was available: as a university student or neophyte lawyer, a young man with such ambitions would affiliate himself with a political party, write and edit periodicals, and join associations with the goal to court the attention of party notables. If fortunate, he could apprentice in the law office of a politician. Once he had earned a reputation as a competent lawyer, he could run for political office. Taking this road, lawyers served as deputies in provincial deputations, city councilmen, and congressmen or senators; a select few became ministers of state, presidents of provincial deputations, or mayors. Those in executive positions usually hired their apprentices or colleagues as assistants or secretaries. Compared to other countries, the Spanish parliament harbored a high percentage of lawyers. What is more, the proportion climbed steadily. During the early decades of the nineteenth century, some 10 to 20 percent of deputies to the Congress of Deputies were lawyers; by midcentury, this figure rose to beyond 30 percent; and by the early twentieth century, more than 80 percent of all deputies held law degrees. Provincial and municipal assemblies exhibited similar proportions.[120] Barcelona contained a more plural population than the rest of Spain, so percentages of advocates on electoral lists were slightly lower than average. Moreover, lawyers were not as heavily represented in municipal government as they were at higher levels. Differences, however, were not great.[121] In Barcelona, advocates filled the seats of legislatures and served in public administration.

For most who chose this life, politics was an intermittent activity. Some lawyers temporarily closed down their offices while in municipal, provincial, or national government and opened them up upon leaving, but others were able to keep them up and running. For example, one of the most powerful (and hated) lawyer-politicians in the latter decades of the century was Manuel Planas, the Conservative Party boss in Catalonia, an expert electoral fixer. He maintained a functioning practice while serving as the "arbiter of conservative and nonconservative politics" for Catalonia.[122] Even those who headed off to Madrid managed to juggle both activities. Catalan deputies and senators found work taking on Supreme Court appeals coming from the Audiencia of Barcelona.[123] This may have been no more than a hobby to some, but a parliamentarian needed to keep his forensic skills fine-tuned, because he usually had to return to steady practice upon departing government. In the oligarchic world of Spanish politics, many used political connections to reap financial rewards. Interestingly, Francesc Rius i Taulet, mayor of the city during the World Fair of 1888 and one of the few lawyers to make a living from politics alone, vowed to refrain from profiting from his public life. A precursor to the "professional politician" of the twentieth century, he found little time to dedicate to his law practice. The publicity of this pledge obviously meant that others did not do the same. The honorable advocate, however, did not hide his business interests. He was associated with the Iberian Bank.[124]

It is easy to reconstruct the careers of lawyers who became politicians or businessmen, because such individuals fill political and economic histories. Stringing together these biographies, however, can convey the errant impression that law was a springboard to other activities. It was for a few, but most successful advocates were more than content to dedicate their lives to servicing clients, harvesting lawsuits, and winning and losing cases. The bar was populated by lawyers, without political or business ambitions, who spent their finest hours fighting cases on the facts in district courts and disserting on technical points of law at the Audiencia chambers. Such men filled the boards of directors of the College of Lawyers and the Academy of Jurisprudence, constituting an underbelly of power at the bar.

Clients searched out lawyers with reputations that could service their needs and fit their personalities. Valued attributes included erudition, oratory, reason, conciliation, and even hubris and venom. In his memoirs, Joan Maluquer provided portraits of senior practitioners with whom he became acquainted upon beginning practice in the 1870s. The eminent mercantilist and College of Lawyers dean Francesc Barret pronounced advice with the authority of a judicial sentence. Josep Borrell, another dean, was an expert at reaching agreements, the advocate of choice for those who sought a negotiated solution rather than a protracted battle. Alternatively, if a client was pursuing a vendetta, he or she might contact Amador Guerra, "war in name and deed." Eloquence was in high demand, especially for appellate work. Joan Baptista Orriols was said to rival the most celebrated parliamentary orators in the country. Eusebi Jover also had an effective style — patient, insistent, and meticulous. In contrast, some clients and judges might regard a silver tongue with a healthy dose of skepticism. Manuel Anglasell, university professor and procedural expert, was a high earner: his precise attention to detail, cogent reasoning, keen sense of timing, and immaculate orchestration of complicated lawsuits more than compensated for his lack of verbal dexterity. Still, the great speakers had the highest profiles. Joaquim Almeda wielded a superior knowledge of Latin, which allowed him to intimidate judges with ironic, offhand citations to complicated Roman Law axioms. "He spoke with both an elegant and caustic tone, and when he fell in love with a point of view, he knew how to draw blood."[125]

In the nineteenth century, the mercantile and penal law were the two areas of greatest growth. But the civil law remained the backbone of a steady practice. Lawsuits involving wills, inheritance, successions, trusts, and conveyances were the steak and potatoes of many a livelihood. In addition to client recruitment, the maintenance of a viable practice involved long, hard hours dedicated to arduous tasks, in which a practitioner had to pay careful attention to detail. All the same, law could be stimulating at times. Even simple cases unraveled into labyrinthine challenges. Although continually frowned on by the public, dilatory tactics were a routine practice if not a way of life: suits could be joined or separated, parallel suits could be brought, parties could be added or removed, motions could be constantly filed. Amadeu Hurtado shamelessly recalled, "A lawsuit that arrived in straightforward and orderly fashion to a judicial sentence without interceding events was like a cooked dish without sauce. Incidents and recourses that prolonged the process and bewildered the adversary were the tools in which a lawyer's ability and a client's combativeness were measured."[126]

Outside the intellectual challenges of work, other things spiced up an advocate's life. Lawyers doubled as family confidants, privy to a bevy of secrets in a city bristling with rumor and innuendo. Stories of illegitimate children, testamentary fraud, infidelity, and other juicy pieces of gossip then seeping into the romantic novel could make a lawsuit entertaining. Some lawyers, in fact, resembled novelistic characters. One colorful man was Juan Díaz, who entered the bar in the 1840s and ran a successful practice for more than forty years. A native of the Americas, he was nicknamed "the Chinaman" (*el chinito*), probably because he was of mestizo descent. A seductive mel-

Women in a lawyer's office (Sketch by "Avrial," in Burgos, "El abogado"; image courtesy of Biblioteca de Catalunya, Barcelona)

lifluous accent, an impressive top-hat collection, and a penchant for cases involving "passions of love" were his claim to fame. His office was "very well respected and highly considered by strange feminine neighbors."[127] Female clients were common in a law office, especially because widows were often guardians of children destined to receive large inheritances, and they sometimes managed familial assets as owners, usufructuary owners, or beneficiaries of trusts. Some widows were not only rich but also entrepreneurial.[128] Some were also young and beautiful, and, for this reason, appeared as seductresses in popular literature. Writing in the 1920s, Ángel Ossorio instructed practitioners to consider themselves "superior to the yearnings of the passions and the weakness of the flesh." He acknowledged that, "There are cases when the lawyer is not the initiator of the attack, but the victim of a *rapture* previously planned by the client." He counseled his readers to not to be seduced by "sweet feminine tyranny" and advised them "not to look your clients in the face" regardless of their beauty.[129]

In an era in which the popularity of the confessional had long been in decline and the psychiatrist's sofa had not yet come into vogue, law offices were a place where male and female bourgeoisie unloaded their guilt and remorse, seeking the solace of a patient and understanding advocate with an even hand, familiar with overcoming emotion and calmly planning strategy in the Machiavellian worlds of market and family. The harmonious vision of patriarchal society — featuring strong fathers, loving mothers, and obedient and entrepreneurial children — adorned juridical literature. But the hard realities of legal practice were another matter altogether. A lawyer assumed a detached and rational visage while listening to endless stories of duplicity, jealousy, crime, and graft. One can only wonder, in a profession that put a premium on transparency and confidentiality, where advocates sought advice and solace for their own travails? Most likely it was among one another. Mutual consoling and sharing of stress took place in informal gatherings. Despite competition for clients, law was a collegial calling. Friendships forged during university and the early years of practice remained alive among middle-aged and elderly men. This culture of collegiality — sharing confidences and concerns among courtroom adversaries — was ultimately the lifeblood of corporate solidarity.

Overcrowding and the Beginning of Catalanism

When charting the stages of a successful career, it is tempting to arrive at the conclusion that all was well at the bar. Armed with memoirs and biographies of prominent men, it is easy to lay out an archetypical path. A student would excel at university where he would capture his professor's eye and find a law office in which to apprentice. Upon graduation, he would undertake a stint as a public defender, participate in associational life, slog through the lean years, find a suitable partner in marriage, set up his own office within a new family home, and then work to establish a civil-mercantile practice. Once he had earned a reputation by practicing for at least a decade or two, had refined his powers of oral and written persuasion, and had understood how the commercial and political world of Barcelona worked, from the inside where he would be privy to much privileged information, he could capture high-paying work by his early to mid-thirties or forties depending on how things went. If he so desired, he could venture into politics or business, often with the help of his or his wife's savings, inheritance, and family connections, although most were content to practice law and pursue profits without courting public attention. To be sure, centrally located offices of busy advocates formed genuine points of reference, which, in tandem with the college and the academy, were veritable institutions of the bar. However, stories of success, although easily accessible to the historian, can present a distorted image. Those who were less fortunate did not write memoirs, nor were they the subjects of biographies, so their travails can be appreciated only through faceless statistics.

In the latter decades of the nineteenth century, all was not well at the bar. In order to go down the road to success, one usually needed to develop a viable practice. Before an advocate could convert a small office into a multitasking practice that harvested lawsuits, administered estates and trusts, advised companies and families, conducted shareholders and creditors meetings, negotiated deals, and even branched out into politics and business, he first had to establish a sound reputation as a litigator. As Amadeu Hurtado recounted, "The lawsuit was the raison d'être of our profession. Harvesting a lawsuit is what brought one into the professional fold."[130] Once a lawyer was in the fold, he could pursue complementary activities, but it was not easy to become regarded as a midlevel advocate of competence and confidence. As we have seen, at every step of the way, only the dedicated, smart, and hardworking survived. In many respects, attrition had always been a characteristic of the bar. However, by the latter decades of the nineteenth century, competition was stiffer than ever.

Put simply, the problem was that there were not enough civil and mercantile lawsuits to satisfy the needs of the swelling number of university graduates. At the close of the century, the dean of the college, Joaquim Almeda, observed, "The lawsuit is the great umbrella that shelters the entire family of the bar." When he uttered these words, however, he was aware that the umbrella was no longer large enough. Amadeu Hurtado, who entered the bar in the 1890s, claimed that his generation faced "a crisis" of the lawsuit.[131] In fact, the crisis had been going on for some time. The years from the beginning through the middle of the 1880s had been a period of economic boom, called "gold fever" (*febre d'or*) in Barcelona. During this time, it was likely that many persons with troubles breaking into private practice opted to explore opportunities in business. The late 1880s and 1890s, in contrast, coincided with the world's first "Great Depression," which was sharply felt in Barcelona. The Catalan economy suffered more than most, because, in addition to falling demand for textiles, vineyards fell victim to a devastating phylloxera epidemic, which also caused a sharp decline in the production of wine and liquor, the region's chief export.

One way to appreciate the severity of overcrowding is to examine the changing ratio between "practicing" and "nonpracticing" advocates. In 1848, when the legal boom was at its height, before the bar suffered from saturation, the college first divided members into these categories. Out of 346 lawyers, 242 were actively engaged in practice while 104 were not.[132] This means that for every lawyer who was not practicing, more than two were practicing. This likely represents a situation near full-employment, given that many lawyers classified as "nonpracticing" either were working in the law as judges, prosecutors, secretaries, estate administrators, businessmen, and politicians or were retired or ill. By 1860, however, things changed dramatically. For every lawyer who was practicing, another was not practicing. Rising crime would alleviate this situation slightly, because the penal law provided more entry-level work, but improvements were modest. At century's end, the college reported that its membership consisted of 861 lawyers, 433 of whom were practicing, while 378 were not. In empirical terms, the ratio between practicing and nonpracticing lawyers had been cut in half over the course of fifty years.[133] Economic growth had created more jobs outside private practice, but when times were tough, opportunities would be scarce. The threat of "proletarianization" loomed as it did throughout Europe.[134] During the twentieth century, overcrowding reached epidemic levels. Writing in the 1920s, Ángel Ossorio joked that men calling themselves lawyers worked as temporary scribes in town halls, typists in banks, and tram drivers. He sarcastically remarked that inventors of explosives, airplanes, and cough medicine touted law degrees.[135]

Another perspective can be gained by measuring levels of litigation. Figure 1 (in chapter 4), using the Audiencia as a barometer, indicates that levels of civil litigation rose from the mid-eighteenth century through the 1860s. Figure 2, which traces litigation at all levels of professional justice — both in district courts and at the Audiencia — shows that civil and commercial litigation rates did not continue to rise but leveled off. As the number of lawyers increased, there were fewer lawsuits per head. There was indeed a crisis of the lawsuit.

That the numbers of civil and commercial matters were holding steady amid a period of enormous demographic and economic growth was perhaps due to the fewer reasons that people had to sue. Commercial houses often resorted to arbitration in lieu of the courts. Lawyers also dedicated more time to prophylactic measures, as they were increasingly called on to structure successions, deals, and transactions to protect against litigation. This repre-

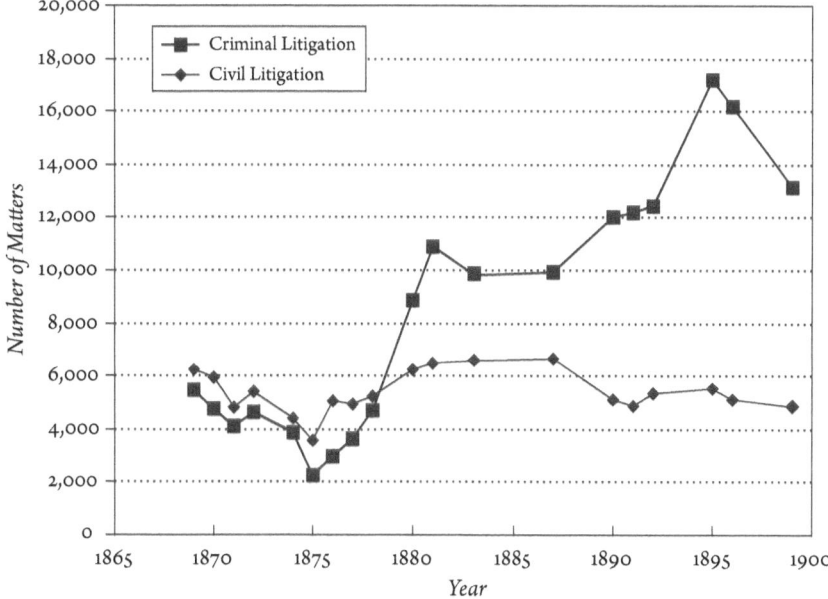

Figure 2. Litigation at Catalan Audiencias and District Courts.
Source: MGJSAT (1869–81, 1883, 1887, 1890–92, 1895–96, 1899).

sented a change from older practices when clients would go to the notary for ordinary needs, while a lawyer would appear on the scene only when the whiff of a lawsuit contaminated (or sweetened) the air.[136] However, the most plausible reason for the stagnation was that district courts were jam-packed and could not adjudicate more civil cases. Legislators saw little need to fund more courts so that lawyers would fill them with suits. In fact, as everyone was well aware, priorities lay elsewhere. Rising crime led statesmen in Spain and throughout Europe to create more penal courts and build more prisons.[137] The coming of the criminal trial in 1882, although endowing defendants with more rights, also streamlined procedures and allowed authorities to incarcerate at a quicker pace. In Barcelona, the criminal chamber of the Audiencia became converted into a criminal *audiencia*, which instead of hearing appeals from all four Catalan provinces, held criminal trials for crimes committed within the province. On the whole, rising crime provided more work at the entry-level, but it was not enough to solve overcrowding. If anything, it contributed to bifurcating the profession between elite civil-mercantile experts who earned enviable livings and those who dedicated much of their practice to poor-paying criminal defenses.

It is probable that overcrowding at the bar — and within the professions as a whole — helped make political Catalanism attractive to many. Young lawyers, faced with difficulties in developing private practices, searched for alternative outlets for work. Business provided a growing number of jobs, but the private sector could not absorb everyone, especially during times of economic sluggishness or downturn. As a result, lawyers looked to the public sector. Writing in Madrid in 1920, Ángel Ossorio ranted that "ninety percent of all apprentices... leave the law office in order to swell the ranks of the bureaucracy or marry rich girls."[138] This flippant accusation, although no doubt an exaggeration, was nothing new. A half century earlier, Benito Pérez Galdós had made a similar claim in his novel *Doña Perfecta* (1871). Echoing popular sentiment, he contended that lawyers fomented *empleomanía*,[139] an expression peculiar to Spain meaning "the quest to create and fill state jobs." Value judgments aside, young Barcelona lawyers clamored for the same opportunities as their Madrid counterparts. They also wished to take state exams for public positions in Barcelona. By decentralizing political authority and devolving administration, more local jobs would become available in the city.

The goal to create a regional bureaucracy centered in Barcelona was one of the central planks of the platform of the Catalan Center. Founded in 1881, the center called for a self-governing legislature and the creation of a Catalan judicial and public administration, including a Supreme Court.[140] From the perspective of struggling lawyers, this promised increased public-sector employment. Home rule also offered the possibility for distinguished lawyers to ascend to high judicial and executive posts.[141] As the president of the Catalan Student Center, Enric Prat de la Riba, aptly stated in 1890:

> The last of the political rights established by the Constitution is the ability to aspire to public careers. Nor have we been allowed to attain this.... Look at the names of the undersecretaries of the ministries, of the captain generals, of the high positions in the army and navy; look at the civil governors, the directors of public institutions, the Council of State, the magistracy, the royal academies, high academia... how few Catalans names can be found.[142]

Discriminatory treatment in the allocation of prestigious posts was visible proof of a widespread phenomenon. Catalans were thought to be underrepresented within the middle and lower levels of the bureaucracy as well.

For their part, lawyers had their own axe to grind. The specific source of their discontent was the "laws of incompatibilities," contained within the Organic Law of Judicial Power of 1870. These rules prohibited anyone from becoming a district or high court judge or prosecutor in the same municipality where they had been born, lived for an extended period, practiced law, or held property.[143] The theory was that nonnative judges and prosecutors would find themselves embroiled in fewer conflicts of interests and would be less vulnerable to the temptations of corruption. As applied to Barcelona, these rules essentially blocked lawyers from ascending to posts in the city. Laws of incompatibility were nothing new, and, although those of the Organic Law were more restrictive than previous versions, they were not controversial at the time. However, as the bar became increasingly saturated, and disputes over the codification of the civil law brought to light other problems, a conflict emerged quite similar to the one that had existed in the eighteenth century when absolutist monarchs had also awarded many such positions to persons from outside the region, presumably to protect against corruption. At the time, lawyers were not aware that a similar dispute had taken place more than a century earlier; if they had known, it would only have fueled their discontent.

Compounding the problem, the laws of incompatibilities were waived in Madrid. This touched a nerve that had long been present, as Barcelona lawyers had periodically groused that their Madrid colleagues were fortunate and undeserving beneficiaries of political centralization. Not only did the capital's lawyers more easily ascend to judicial and political office, but the government regarded its College of Lawyers as a privileged body rather than just one association among many. In the course of one legislative conflict of the early 1860s, the Barcelona college vented its frustration: "We are allowed to fan with palm fronds the illustrious College of Madrid; we can design a crown to be placed on the head of its dignified dean; yet, we are not deemed to possess the requisite sophistication to guarantee the soundness of the legal opinion that we have written."[144] In reference to the laws of incompatibilities, one top mercantilist complained in 1899, "According to the basic principles of the social organism, it is not possible to subject all the colleges of lawyers of the peninsula to one single mold each with all the same rules . . . but for one sole exception in favor of Madrid."[145]

In the course of parliamentary debates over the civil law, lawyers inveighed against the laws of incompatibility and other inequities in the administration of justice. In a speech in the Senate in 1885, Josep Maluquer expounded a series of demands: rules on judicial appointment needed to be changed so that only judges who could speak and read Catalan, and who were versed in Catalan law, should be eligible to serve on the bench. He further recommended that witnesses and defendants should be able address the court using the language in which they felt most comfortable, and that key laws be translated into Catalan. In the realm of education, he called for the creation of a professorship of Catalan law at the University of Barcelona and also insinuated that professors should be allowed to lecture in their native language. To Maluquer, education and justice needed to be reformed to correspond to reality: it was nonsensical that Catalan law was frequently applied in court but barely included in the curriculum; it was unjust that uneducated litigants, witnesses, and criminal defendants, who expressed themselves poorly in Spanish, and who were often scared and dazed by the judicial process, were hauled up before judges and prosecutors who struggled to understand them.[146] These reasons made good sense and were by no means disingenuous. But it cannot be ignored that the proposed reforms promised more jobs to native Catalans in the judiciary and professoriate.

Access to judicial posts was only the tip of the iceberg. Just as entrepreneurs had eyed steam power and brought English machines to Barcelona to reap profits, lawyers and other professionals observed sophisticated civilian bureaucracies in France and Germany and saw the path upon which Spain was destined to tread. Young lawyers, aware of the hazards of developing a successful private practice, aspired not only to become judges and prosecutors but also to staff a civil service in Barcelona. It is no coincidence that many young lawyers clamored for decentralization precisely at the same time that the state was on the verge of expanding significantly. Devolution promised improved employment prospects for educated men who could no longer be protected by the "umbrella" of the lawsuit. Amadeu Hurtado, responding to the dean Almeda, believed that by the twentieth century the bar had replaced the "umbrella" with a "canopy."[147] Just as the market had come to absorb excess lawyers, the state would also fulfill this function. Whether Hurtado realized it or not, the state was the new canopy. By century's end, lawyers throughout Europe sought to expand their influence outside the courtroom, boardroom, and legislature, and into the corridors of state administration. Where the state would be centered, Barcelona or Madrid, or how it would be decentered, was an epochal question that would thereafter dominate much political life in Catalonia for decades to come.

In order to avoid misinterpretation, it must be stressed that the quest to create a Catalan bureaucracy was not necessarily driven by purely corporatist motivations. Political Catalanists did not contend that Catalans had an inherent proprietary right to local jobs. Rather, the argument was that natives and long-term residents could manage local affairs better than central legislators and bureaucrats, given that such individuals were more familiar with regional language, law, and custom and the technocratic needs of an industrial society. As might be expected, stereotype was intertwined with logical reasoning. As Valentí Almirall, the founder of the Catalan Center, stated in 1885, "In a large nation, for example, there are regions that are industrial or agriculture, commercial or mining, etc.; there are those that are more culturally and intellectually advanced. The law can only be just and useful when it is formulated by a group of members who feel similar necessities and find themselves immersed in a similar culture."[148] Two decades later, the lawyer Lluís Duran i Ventosa reiterated this point: "Nations of private enterprise and great industrial development should never be directed by men whose values come from communal living representative of agrarian life and backwardness. This would be equivalent to destining them to ruin."[149] By the later decades of the century, the oligarchic state hardly seemed up to the task of addressing the multiple legislative needs of the industrial region. That an autonomous government with its own bureaucracy, staffed by native sons, could best serve Catalonia was not a contention easily rebutted by even the most skeptical.

It should also be highlighted that lawyers were not only attracted to Catalanism by the prospect of autonomy. This was not the only plank in the platform. Another was the defense of the legal tradition. Alongside the common experience of education, training, practice, and the culture of camaraderie and collegiality, the Catalan law itself was the glue that held the bar together. The government's attempt to promulgate a Spanish civil code in the 1880s became converted into a pitched battle between state legislators and the Barcelona bar, opening the eyes of many to the advantages of home rule. The appeal of a self-governing bureaucracy and judiciary constituted an underlying *material* reason behind the growing popularity of Catalanism, but *ideological* conversion occurred as a result of the conflict over codification of civil law.

6 The Nationalist Profession
LAW AND CATALANISM

> At every opportunity, we must ensure that these small *patrias* — these small nationalities that sustain themselves against the interest of the Motherland — disappear. In this way, we can consolidate a united juridical order, which all good Spaniards so desire.
> ஏ Benito de Ulloa y Rey, Supreme Court magistrate, in the Spanish Senate (1885)

> If this continues, it will not be long before the philanthropic interests of the Castilians succeed in raising us Catalans to their high status. We will be poor like them, lazy like them, braggarts like them.
> ஏ Narcís Verdaguer i Callís, *Veu de Montserrat* (20 April 1889)

> They say it is poorly conceived to maintain different regimes of civil law within a nation, and they are more than correct. For this reason . . . we have become convinced that Spain is not a nation but a state in which various nationalities live, or, better said, die or agonize.
> ஏ Enric Prat de la Riba, "Miscelánea jurídica," *Revista Jurídica de Cataluña* (1896)

DURING THE LAST TWO DECADES of the nineteenth century, Catalanism grew popular among many lawyers. The bar remained diverse, led by high-profile mercantile and civil advocates closely linked to urban and agrarian elites and dynastic political parties. But many members were not content with the overall state of affairs, for individual prospects had not risen in harmony with corporate power. Some advocates were wealthy, but others found it difficult to break into private practice. As the bar grew in numbers and resources, students and practitioners pressured leaders to support projects that would carve out greater space for their realm of expertise. In other countries, the prioritization of corporate concerns led associational representatives to retreat from politics, to exchange their hallowed role as guarantors of liberty, assigned to them since Tocqueville, for the more mundane function as delegates of the special interests of a saturated profession under stress.[1] In Catalonia, things did not play out in this manner. Lawyers did not turn their back on politics but gravitated toward Catalanism.

The growth of Catalanism came from below and took place slowly. By focusing exclusively on leadership, it would be impossible to notice that anything was afoot until very late in the century. In the 1870s, advocates affiliated with dynastic conservative political parties were at the height of their influence. Barcelona's leading conservative lawyers were among the most powerful men in Spain. They had not only maintained control of the College of Lawyers during the tumultuous years of the Democratic Sexennium (1868–74) but had been instrumental in putting an end to Spain's democratic political regime. The college dean Melcior Ferrer and the Academy of Jurisprudence president Manuel Duran headed the League of Social Order, a puissant coterie of Barcelona notables, who, in close cooperation with a similar group of conservative politicians in Madrid, had orchestrated the return of the Bourbons to the Spanish throne in 1875.[2] Another league member, the mercantilist and future college dean Josep Vilaseca, had headed negotiations with Carlist rebels, who had risen up in arms against the democratic regime in 1872. At the behest of the government, he traveled to Peripignan and Switzerland in 1875 and, in a secret agreement, handed over 25,000 French francs in exchange for the promise that the Carlists would renounce a return to the battlefield and agree to participate in elections.[3] The end of the Second Carlist War (1872–75) established an enduring peace that helped consolidate what became known as the Restoration Monarchy (1875–1923), the longest lasting constitutional regime in Spanish history. During the last quarter of the century, the college deans were either Conservative Party militants, largely recruited among former affiliates of the League of Social Order, or advocates who steered clear of the political spotlight but were comfortable with the status quo.[4] As a general rule, the deans kept their distance from the swelling numbers of Catalanists within their ranks.

Over time, the grip of this leadership on juridical associations loosened. During the Restoration, the old Moderates and Progressive parties changed their names to the Conservatives and Liberals in explicit emulation of Britain. But it took some time for the Liberal Party to form and for the constitution to gain legitimacy. Many lawyers of the Left were upset that the bar's leadership had taken such an active role in helping restore the Bourbons to the throne. They had hoped that Spain would become a democratic monarchy or even a republic, as had occurred in France, and were incensed at the return to a parliamentary system with a restricted franchise modeled after Britain. This grand dispute over the country's future was played out in miniature at the college. At first, it took the form of a veiled debate over protocol. At the annual meeting in 1875, the republican Gonçal Serraclara criticized the dean Melcior Ferrer for having sent an official delegation to meet Alphonse XII, the new king of Spain, who had disembarked in Barcelona before heading off to Madrid to occupy the throne. Serraclara contended that the reception violated the bylaws because the college was a "corporation essentially independent from political battles."[5] In 1877 the democratic wing mounted an electoral coup by flooding the annual meeting, ordinarily attended by a few dozen distinguished advocates customarily vested with the authority to elect dean and board. With their ranks swelled by younger men, dissidents ousted Ferrer, who was also president of the provincial deputation and hence one of the most visible representatives of the Bourbon restoration. Victory, however, was fleeting. A year later, conservatives steadied the ship. Ferrer again won elections. The message, though, was not lost. Thereafter, elites confectioned boards reflecting the diversity of the rank and file.[6]

Ideological divisions were nothing new, and the boards of the College of Lawyers had often exhibited a plural composition, but other factors combined to chip away at the hegemony of the leadership. University life, for one, grew more diverse. The hegemony of old Moderate professors, the mandarins of the midcentury bar, slowly wound down. One reason for this was the creation of a parallel degree course in administrative law. Launched in 1857, the degree was not a success, and in 1883 legislators closed it down and merged administrative-law courses into a consolidated curriculum. Spain never created the modern civil service for which these studies were needed, so few students exclusively pursued the degree. Instead, the degree became an additional validation for those students willing to tack a year or two onto their law studies for some additional specialized training.[7] Nonetheless, the reforms had the effect of broadening the curriculum and transfusing the university with new blood, for administrative-law professors tended to be more progressive than their civil-, mercantile-, and canon-law colleagues. Moreover, as different parties alternated in and out of power, appointments were no longer so ideologically monolithic. Not only did the professoriate become more diverse, but relationships grew less hierarchical. Obedient midcentury students gave way to less-deferential young men. During the Second Carlist War (1872–75), students harassed one professor thought to be a Carlist, while a few abandoned studies to fight with the Carlists in the countryside.[8] By the 1880s, the winds of Catalanism entered the cloisters, providing a common cause around which students and professors united. In 1886 law students were the primary movers behind the creation of the Catalanist Student Center, an organization that worked in close collaboration with the Catalan League, in which the civil-law professor Joan Josep Permanyer i Ayats was prominent. That professors incited students to join their causes, and vice versa, likely reduced formality in the classroom.

Two new academies challenged the hegemony of the Academy of Jurisprudence. In 1876 two administrative law professors founded the Academy of Administrative Law, a Barcelona branch of an organization centered in Madrid, where it was headed by the Progressive Laureà Figuerola. This academy never functioned well and was not active for very long.[9] The Academy of Law, however, was more successful. Founded in 1871, it was popular among young lawyers and students and posed a real threat to elder jurists of the Academy of Jurisprudence.[10] The board of the College of Lawyers did not welcome it, and in 1879 evicted the Academy of Law from the premises, alleging that it allowed persons without law degrees to attend sessions and that its heated debates made too much noise.[11] Thereafter, it met at the Association for the Promotion of National Employment (Fomento del Trabajo Nacional), the protectionist lobby for Catalan industry. The Academy of Law would not survive the nineteenth century, but it convened regularly in the 1880s and 1890s.[12] In 1885, it signed a protonationalist manifesto, the *Outline of Grievances*. In so doing, it adopted a more aggressive stance than the cautious Academy of Jurisprudence, whose board did not add its name even though many of its most influential members had done so. The Academy of Jurisprudence would eventually come around to supporting Catalanism, but it would have to be pulled by activist members, younger generations, and its rival academy.

The gradual erosion of the symbolic majesty of the bar also weakened the charisma of the old guard. Associational leaders had successfully promoted — or invented — a classical image of the bar as a pillar of justice, a source of moderation, and a fountain of erudition with its roots in the Middle Ages and Rome. Yet as the profession ballooned in size, membership became more diffuse, customs grew less formal, and the mystique became harder to maintain. Deteriorating conditions in the district courts added to this atmosphere of informality. During the Democratic Sexennium, the government moved the district courts out of the Audiencia Palace and housed them, along with the newly created municipal courts, in the Royal Palace on the Pla de Palau. In theory, this should have allowed for the spacious — if not the smooth — distribution of justice, but on Christmas Day 1875, the Royal Palace burned to the ground under extremely suspicious circumstances.[13] Judges worked out of their own homes for months, before authorities later arranged for makeshift quarters, described as "filthy" by lawyers who roamed their halls for the ensuing thirty-five years.[14] The locations were supposed to be temporary, so few resources were dedicated to upkeep. All courts, including the Audiencia, were to be installed in a Judicial Palace, constructed on the Passeig Sant Joan, the central boulevard of the World Fair. The cornerstone was laid in 1887, a few months before the fair opened, and in 1895 a guidebook reported that the "sumptuous" building was "under construction, and almost complete."[15] The monstrosity, however, did not open its doors until 1911.[16]

Conditions at the Audiencia were much better. The civil and criminal chambers, the regent's chamber, St. George's Room and the Chapel, were beautifully decorated. During a visit in the mid-1880s, the Russian writer Isaac Pavlovski was impressed when he passed through the Orange Tree Patio on his way to the chambers where a "sepulchral silence" reigned.[17] Yet logistical pressures and procedural changes also contributed to a decline in solemnity and formality. By century's end, grand oratorical movements had grown old-fashioned, replaced by a style that put a premium on concision and clarity. The days in which advocates were granted ample license to showcase their erudition came to an end. Magistrates, facing endless backlogs, would extend little rope to a self-important advocate of florid oratory who abused everyone's patience by perorating on juridical science as if in times past. This development was welcomed by many, but it also gave the high court a more bureaucratic feel. The coming of the modern criminal trial in 1882 generated much commotion in the penal chamber, no longer a place for appellate oratory but for emotional pleas of innocence and revengeful accusations of guilt. The advent of the jury in 1888 endowed populist oratory with respectability. Dress became less formal. In court, lawyers shunned full regalia, consisting of black robes and top hats, and donned more comfortable long dark jackets and soft caps. Outside the courtroom, lawyers ceased to wear the top hat, a sign of the decline of gentlemanly status. All this eroded the charisma of the old leadership. The eminent litigator with sonorous oratory, who guided a patient gallery through lulls and crescendos, faded into the past. The elder lawyer who went out in society in a top hat became regarded as a distinguished relic, worthy of respect but not emulation.[18]

Overcrowding, ideological divisions, associational pluralism, and the decline of solemnity in the courtroom and the classroom all contributed to weakening the hegemony of the traditional leadership. Electoral challenges at the college and academy, however, did not come from members of rival academies or from the democratic opposition to the Bourbon restoration. Instead, lawyers associated with political Catalanism united a diverse bar by offering a corporate program that appealed to persons of varying ideological beliefs and juridical expertise. The shift in leadership did not represent the ideological break that democratic lawyers would have liked. Catalanism was more plural than conservatism; by the 1890s, however, its leading lights were also Catholic men of order. The change, though, was not seamless either. Leaders were no longer in lockstep with powerful industrial, financial, and agrarian clienteles and dynastic political parties but instead prioritized the corporate interests of the bar itself. Catalanists proposed that natives and longtime residents staff the bureaucracy and judiciary and also insisted that Catalan civil law should be preserved in its entirety and integrity. The first goal promised to address the problem of overcrowding, while the second ensured that native jurists and professors would remain the custodians of the legal tradition.

In 1896 the Academy of Jurisprudence elected Joan Josep Permanyer i Ayats, university professor of civil law, as president. Permanyer was one of the heads of the Catalanist Union (Unió Catalanista) and had been the lead author of the Manresa Principles (1891), a draft constitution for self-government. Among its various provisions, this charter envisioned the creation of a Supreme Court for Catalonia and demanded that "only Catalans, by virtue of birth or naturalization, can occupy civil service positions in Catalonia."[19] In his inaugural address, he put forward a vision that differed radically from predecessors who had been faithful to the organization of the Spanish state. The only way to ensure that judges were properly versed in the law and could understand witnesses and defendants, he insisted, was for natives to staff an autonomous judiciary. Ridding the land of foreign judges would be the first step in cleansing Catalonia of the "vices of the political organization of Spain." He called on his colleagues to "raise their serene, energetic, and honorable heads without fear, with the persistence of our race, without abdicating their ideas . . . and to fly the flag that I have raised."[20] At the university, the story was the same. The regionalist professor Joan Trias delivered a lecture series on Catalan law in 1897, in which he reiterated the long-standing demand that the curriculum be reformed to reflect the "historical and living reality that our country lives under the empire of its own laws."[21] In 1903 Permanyer i Ayats became dean of the College of Lawyers and remained in the post for eight years.

The ascendancy of Joan Josep Permanyer i Ayats, one of the most visible leaders of the home-rule movement, represented the definitive conquest of the bar by Catalanists. Because he was the son of the onetime overseas minister Francesc Permanyer, it also highlighted a generational change. Older advocates associated with dynastic conservative parties and large financial, agrarian, and industrial interests gave way to younger Catalanists who balanced the concerns of economic actors with those of ordinary lawyers, frustrated with the inadequacies of an overcentralized state. The success of Catalanism at the bar was not the result of an overnight coup. Rather, it had been gaining momentum since the 1880s when a renewed conflict over the coming of the Spanish Civil Code (1889) created space for activists to popularize their agenda. The rest of this chapter explores the defense of Catalan law in the 1880s, which had lasting consequences not only for lawyers but for the region as a whole.

The Defense of Catalan Civil Law

With the benefit of hindsight, it may seem evident that the seeds of hostility present during the civil-law conflicts of the 1880s had been planted decades earlier. As we have seen, the appearance of the draft code of 1851 had infuriated Barcelona lawyers, bewildered by the government's proposal to anchor a civil code in the law of Castile. To them, the legal tradition of Catalonia, the country's richest region, should serve as a baseline for the code's general rules. In debates over the virtues and vices of foral and common law, derogatory and stereotypical images and insults had percolated through scholarly discussions. Common-law jurists insinuated that the Catalan family was characterized by avarice and "paternal despotism," given that its inheritance regime endowed a father with almost unlimited power to distribute his assets as he saw fit and to use his authority to favor a single son to the prejudice of other family members. Catalan jurists, in contract, depicted the Castilian family as lazy and rebellious, given that younger sons and daughters had little incentive to work hard or to obey their parents, because a large portion of their inheritance was guaranteed. From an economic perspective, Catalans insisted that their law created prosperity, because it permitted elective primogeniture, which allowed productive agrarian farms to remain whole rather than be divided into small unproductive parcels by intestate succession. Jurists from each tradition trumpeted the superiority of their respective system. Catalans argued that their law was liberal and promoted economic growth, while common-law jurists contended that theirs was more equitable and fostered tight familial bonds.

At the same time, no one could have foreseen that these stereotypes — diluted within a sea of other legal arguments — would later serve as fodder in a political conflict over the Spanish Civil Code that would reach the front pages of newspapers, mobilize sectors of the Catalan populace, and indeed inaugurate the era of nationalist politics. Even though Catalan and Castilian private laws drew their authority from separate legal traditions, there were many areas in which the law overlapped. Moreover, legal diversity was common throughout Europe and had not become an intractable problem elsewhere. Commissions of codification working within ministries of justices ordinarily resolved regional differences by either imposing a dominant tradition or finding a middle ground. Following the promulgation of the French Civil Code (1804) and sister codes in Belgium (1810), Holland (1838), and a number of Swiss cantons and German and Italian states, civil codes had become uncontroversially regarded as essential companions to constitutions. It was only logical that Spain would follow the example of Italy, which in 1865 promulgated a civil code, largely based on the Napoleonic Code, that resolved the diverse traditions of the former kingdoms in favor of uniform laws. In 1867 Portugal also passed a civil code. The implicit consensus was that sooner or later Spain would follow suit.

In addition to international trends, there were other indicators that jurists in Barcelona and Madrid would eventually overcome differences. After all, Catalan lawyers had historically supported the principle of uniform codification. In the 1760s, Francesc Romà first suggested that a code of laws for all of Spain could be assembled by "selecting the best ones from all the provinces."[22] At the time, he had represented an enlightened vanguard, but during the liberal age, this view won general acceptance. "The most nutritious and delicious fruit coming from the beneficent tree of liberty miraculously planted on our land and watered with the precious blood of our patriotic sons" was how the president of the Academy of Jurisprudence, Josep Bertran, effusively portrayed codes in 1842. A civil code provided "the most solid basis for the immense number of families that constitute the great Spanish family."²³ In 1843 two university professors, Francesc Permanyer and Ignasi Sanponts, wrote, "In the advantageous epoch in which we find ourselves, it is time that the immense accumulation of laws disappear and with them the uncertainties surrounding the law of all Spaniards. All jurists unanimously recognize this, and this general clamor is now heard in all realms of the peninsula. We anxiously await the publication of new codes, which have been promised for some time."²⁴

In fact, other codification projects had been carried out without creating much friction. A Penal Code (1822) and a Commercial Code (1829) had been promulgated during the absolutist era and, although by no means testaments to the beauty and genius of juridical science, were useful enough to remain valid until they were updated later in the century. During the 1820s, some Barcelona lawyers grumbled about a proposal to codify procedural law, fearing that it could alter the substantive law.²⁵ Following the triumph of liberalism, however, procedural codification was no longer deemed threatening. In 1855 a Code of Civil Procedure sailed through the legislature without anyone raising so much as an eyebrow. To be sure, a civil code was a more sensitive enterprise. Penal and commercial law involved only a few persons, namely, those accused of or contemplating the commission of crimes (never a large or influential constituency) and merchants, who had long favored uniform international rules; procedure was an obscure subject, never a concern to anyone but lawyers. Civil codes, in contrast, concerned the lives of ordinary people, with local horizons, more or less aware of the basic rules governing their families and property. The bedrock of all legal systems, civil codes were applicable to all men, woman, and children, and encompassed a complete gamut of issues stretching from cradle to grave: legitimacy, adoption, manumission, marriage, the family economy, tutelage, guardianship, mortgage, contract, property, trusts, testaments, successions. For these reasons, it was logical that the codification of the civil law was a more difficult task and would perhaps take a longer time than other codification projects. Until the 1880s, however, no one prophesied that regional differences would become converted into insuperable hurdles.

In the 1860s a spirit of compromise seemed to be emerging among Spain's elite jurists. Initially, disputes over civil-legal matters soured the air between Barcelona and Madrid. Catalan parliamentarians complained that the Law of Mortgages (1861) and the Notarial Law (1862) ran roughshod over perfectly viable local laws and unnecessarily ate into their local legal regime.²⁶ All the same, these controversies did not occasion any political fallout but became regarded as one of the various setbacks inherent in the parliamentary process. In fact, a year after the promulgation of the Notarial Law, it appeared that an understanding had been reached on civil law. As we have seen, delegates to the Spanish Conference of Jurisconsults in 1863 came to an agreement over the structure of a future civil code: the general laws of the county were to be included in a uniform code, which would contain a list of "special laws" for the foral regions. If the code maintained testamentary liberty, individual property, and emphyteusis within Catalonia, Barcelona lawyers had been grudgingly disposed to accept it. In their hearts, they had felt that these legal institutions should be generalized throughout the country so that all Spaniards could reap the benefits of economic prosperity. In their heads, they knew that a general code with regional exceptions was a clumsy solution that augured endless jurisdictional and choice-of-law headaches. Given that they were in a minority in Spain, though, a compromise was thought to be the only way forward.

At the outset of the Restoration Monarchy, this spirit of compromise initially reigned, as politicians sought to implement the agreement reached at the Conference of Spanish Jurisconsults. On 2 February 1880, the Conservative minister of justice, Saturnino Álvarez, announced that the government intended to recommence the effort to write a civil code. He instructed the Commission for Codes, a body organized within the ministry, to collaborate with named representatives from the foral regions who were given a period of time to submit a list of vital legal institutions that should be preserved as "exceptions." The minister appointed Manuel Duran, a fellow member of the Conservative Party, as Catalan representative. The decree further stated that the draft code of 1851 was to serve as a point of departure: the commission was to revise it after taking into account the reports from the foral representatives in addition to other criticism that had surfaced since its publication.[27] The project was put in the hands of Manuel Alonso Martínez, president of the civil-law section of the commission and a member of the Liberal Party. An author of the Constitution of 1876, he boasted a track record on searching out viable compromises. The theory was that the code was to represent a bipartisan effort that would address the concerns of the Conservative and Liberal parties and jurists representative of the common and foral traditions. In the end, Alonso Martínez smoothly resolved party differences, but he was unable to find a satisfactory answer to the regional question.

In 1881 Manuel Alonso Martínez became minister of justice and presented a draft Basic Law of the Civil Code to the parliament. The "Basic Law" was to contain a broad set of precepts that the Commission for Codes would follow when redacting the document. In 1884 he published a declaration of intentions. In *The Civil Code and Its Relationship to Foral Legislation*, he vowed to write a "national code" that would respect foral traditions to the extent that "was necessary." "Special laws" were to consist of "very few laws," inserted in the back of the code as an "appendix."[28] Foral institutions beneficial to all Spaniards — such as emphyteusis — were to be integrated as general provisions in the code. In this manner, he followed the recommendations of Barcelona jurists who in the 1860s had proposed that some Catalan laws should be applicable throughout the entire country, while others could exist as exceptions. With respect to Catalonia, "exceptional" laws would regulate testamentary donation, the ownership of postmarital assets, marriage contracts, inter-vivos gifts, widowhood, and a few other matters. The author claimed to have fastened upon a compromise. Addressed to an expert audience, the book focused on juridical minutiae. Behind the technical language, however, property interests were paramount. The code was to be written so that it would not upset the balance of entitlements in either the common- or foral-law regions. Essentially, the minister promised to codify the status quo and to avoid property reform. In this way, he hoped it would overcome problems faced by the 1851 draft code, which by attempting to abolish emphyteusis and testamentary liberty was understandably regarded with trepidation in Catalonia.

In Barcelona, it first appeared that the government had struck an acceptable balance. In January 1881, more than one hundred lawyers from diverse district court seats and various economic, juridical, and intellectual associations throughout Catalonia met at the Conference of Catalan Jurisconsults, held at the University of Barcelona. The Barcelona College of Lawyers officially sent eighteen representatives, but practically all delegates were members, even though many attended with credentials from other colleges or associations.[29] The election of delegates at the College of Lawyers had been divisive, as was the conference itself, but supporters of the government project had won a slender majority.[30] The organizers were optimistic that the government had found an acceptable formula. The mission statement announced that Spain should have a "clear, just, and generalized civil law" and stated that the purpose of the conference was to "use the Civil Code of 10 May 1851 as a starting point, and to discuss, vote, and propound, which principles and institutions of foral law were in its opinion of such vital importance that it was indispensable to conserve them as exceptions for Catalonia in the

Spanish Civil Code."³¹ The plan was to dedicate sessions to outlining such "indispensable" principles and institutions, which would be forwarded to Manuel Duran, who would then collaborate with the Commission for Codes in Madrid to ensure that they were properly incorporated. In the opening session, delegates elected Melcior Ferrer, former dean of the college, as conference president. He thought the decree somewhat "premature" but stressed that the most logical manner to proceed was to work constructively with the government.³²

The outcome of the conference, however, demonstrated that opinions had shifted since the 1860s. Things did not go as planned. The majority of delegates repudiated the mission statement and ignored Ferrer's advice. They voted to refrain from even discussing which institutions were "indispensable," because this could be interpreted as furthering the government's objectives. The conference became converted into a sounding board for a categorical protest against the entire initiative. The majority rejected the baseline proposal that Catalan law could be reduced to a series of "exceptions" and insisted that it was an integral whole that could not be chopped up into pieces. Protests came from the Right, Center, and Left. Bellicose metaphors were not lacking. In the press, Lluís Maria de Llauder, a lawyer and Carlist Party chief, argued that accepting the proposal was equivalent to "amputating one's members and laying down one's arms before the powers that threaten."³³ At the conference, Felip Vergés contended that the decree meant "first the mutilation of Catalan law and then its death."³⁴ Joaquim Almeda warned that the end result could be "civil war."³⁵ Josep Maria Vallès de Ribot, leader of the Federal-Republican Party, labeled the idea a "great threat."³⁶ Using this threat as rallying cry, the Catalanist Valentí Almirall proclaimed that Catalan law would survive: "The unanimous opinion of Catalonia will save it, much as unanimous protest has always saved it from those who have attempted to destroy it, from Philip V to the latest unifiers of the law."³⁷

In spite of Almirall's claims, opinions were by no means unanimous. At the conference, a vocal and sizable minority remained faithful to the enlightened ideal dominant earlier in the century that codification signified an unquestionable advance that would augment the happiness of citizens by reducing uncertainty and contradiction in the law. Joan Baptista Orriols, president of the Academy of Jurisprudence and the most eloquent speaker of his generation, declared his "love for Catalan law" but acknowledged that it was "written in a Catalan that nobody speaks, and in a Latin that nobody understands."³⁸ He urged delegates to shift the campaign toward the old goal of fusing the most beneficial laws of Catalonia into a uniform code for all Spaniards. Eusebi Jover regarded the proposal as a perfectly valid compromise. There was a difference, he pointed out, between "unity of codes" and "uniformity of law."[39] In his opinion, the proposal ensured that Spain could have a single code that would respect the cherished diversity of the foral regions. The former September revolutionary Ròmul Mascaró urged his colleagues to rekindle the patriotic spirit of the War of Independence when the "firing squads of Moncloa, the loss of Girona, the defense of Zaragoza, and the glories of Bailén and Bruch, made the hearts of all Spaniards throb with the same sentiment."[40]

The Conference of Catalan Jurisconsults marked a definitive turning point. After the conference, those who represented the majority grew increasingly confident and vocal, while those in the minority either remained silent or became converted to the cause. Some of the minority consisted of dynastic-party politicians, who had more influence within political-oligarchic networks than they did among the independent-minded members of the bar. The leader of the minority, Manuel Planas, the Conservative Party chief in Catalonia, was a political boss (*cacique*) and an expert electoral fixer, the target of frequent caricatures appearing in the satirical press. Although a prominent lawyer, he personally embodied the ills of the Spanish political system in Catalonia and was regarded with quiet derision by many colleagues. One of the opponents, Felip Bertran i d'Amat, had another view. To him, many government supporters were from immigrant families, in other words, "those who by birth or by family are not entirely Catalan."[41] Valentí Almirall did not cast doubt on their origins but their patriotism. He accused them of being a reincarnation of the *botiflers*, the epithet given to the principality's traitors who collaborated with the Crown of Castile during the War of Spanish Succession (1702–14).[42]

In the aftermath of the conference, the legal community reached a consensus, although dissent was always present. It abandoned the idea, present in the 1860s, that foral laws could be blended into a uniform code or be preserved as a series of exceptions. Instead, Catalan law was declared to be an integral whole. At the conference, the Federalist leader and prestigious criminalist Josep Maria Vallès de Ribot put forward the idea that separate codes should govern each of the foral territories.[43] With time, this "Swiss" or "Habsburg" solution would become the prevailing institutional position of the bar. In the aftermath of the conference, the College of Lawyers elected a new dean and board to reflect this consensus.[44] Similarly, the Academy of

Jurisprudence, after much hesitation and handwringing, followed suit. The academy did not "subscribe to the principle of codification," but asserted that "if codification is a current necessity . . . the law should not be united in a single volume, but in a separate volume for each territory."[45] A decade and a half later, Joan Josep Permanyer i Ayats, the author of the academy's declaration, reformulated this in an exclusionary idiom. Speaking at the Atheneum, he announced, "If codification is needed, we will codify for Catalonia and by Catalans, without digesting foreign influences and attending to the aspirations of our people."[46]

The Conference of Catalan Jurisconsults marked the beginning of a decade of protests that took place in the Spanish Cortes, in the press, and eventually in town meetings on streets and squares. It must be highlighted that those who opposed the government's proposal did not necessarily favor political autonomy. Leading Catalanists, such as Valentí Almirall and Joan Josep Permanyer i Ayats, sensed that the conflict represented a golden opportunity to promote home rule. But the protest in the Spanish Cortes was directed by Manuel Duran and other members of the Liberal and Conservative parties. Representative of the bar's traditional leadership and faithful to the Restoration system, deputies and senators did not share in, and in fact repudiated, the goal of political autonomy. Most lawyers who defended Catalan law did not believe that the conservation of private law should give rise to the demand to revive public law and representative institutions. The civil code conflicts, however, opened the door for Catalanists to advertise ideas and convince colleagues and the public at large.

Law and Literary Romanticism

The outcome of the Conference of Catalan Jurisconsults surprised many observers at the time. It gives rise to a number of questions. Why did the Barcelona bar, which had once supported the goal of civil-law codification, come to regard the proposal with such hostility? What happened to the ideas of Josep Bertran i d'Amat, who in the early 1840s had described codes as "the most nutritious and delicious fruit coming from the beneficent tree of liberty miraculously planted on our land and watered with the precious blood of our patriotic sons"? When a code was finally promulgated in 1889, his son Felip Bertran, a prototypical lawyer-millionaire of the era, characterized the document as nothing less than "tyranny" and "horrible absolutism."[47] How did the legal community go from the "tree of liberty" to "tyranny" and "absolutism" from one generation to the next? Why did Catalan legal elites, who in the 1860s had proposed that foral laws be inserted as a series of exceptions to the general rules of a civil code, reject this compromise when legislators offered it two decades later? In short, what occurred between the 1860s and 1880s that caused this volte-face in mainstream opinion?

The most visible reason for this shift of opinion was the coming of romanticism. As we have seen, in the 1860s Catalan jurists began to inject romantic depictions of the *casa pairal* — with its idealized cast of strong patriarchs, loving mothers, entrepreneurial young sons, and hardworking tenant farmers — into juridical discourse. Supported by traditional legal institutions, the agrarian world was said to constitute the moral vertebrae of the region and, along with industry, to be an engine of prosperity. The early disseminators of nascent *pairalisme*, however, did not extend romantic portrayals to the law itself, which they regarded as an inherently rational body of knowledge that should be glossed, interpreted, and updated according to the precepts of juridical science. Overall, they sought to preserve testamentary liberty, individual property, and emphyteusis through concise legal rules, redacted into a uniform code for all Spaniards or conserved as exceptions. At the time, they had shown no inclination to conserve the legal tradition in its entirety or to breathe new life into ancient texts that had suffered from a dearth of commentary since the seventeenth century. By the 1880s, however, romanticism had infused law with such symbolic import that it was considered a treasure in its own right. In short, it was no longer sufficient that specific legal institutions be maintained, but prevailing opinion held that the historic corpus needed to undergird the contemporary law.

How, then, did literary romanticism and the law become so tightly interlaced? Romanticism was not some exogenous phenomenon that seeped into the law through osmosis, but lawyers were the most recognizable sector among intellectuals dedicated to promoting Catalan culture. The Floral Games, an annual poetry competition first held in 1859, was the public face of the movement to revive Catalan literature, which had been moribund since the Middle Ages. The name came from a legendary competition, founded by the Troubadours of Toulouse, which was adopted by Barcelona's count-kings in the late fourteenth century. While many of Barcelona's medieval poets had composed their works in Occitan, their nineteenth-century emulators exclusively used the vernacular. Two poetry anthologies, *The New Troubadours* (1858) and the *Modern Troubadours* (1859), featured a smattering of practicing lawyers.[48] One high-earning litigator, Lluís Pons, published a tragic ode to the Catalan language, which he portrayed as the "Abandoned Queen." In the poem, the queen is no longer welcomed at great balls and ministerial councils or within high society but is left poor and forgotten by the roadside where she showers a sympathetic shepherd with her tearful lamentations.[49] In "Barcelona," Eusebi Pascual, opted for unbridled patriotism. He rhetorically asked, "What has become of your power? / What has become of your independence? / You could be another great power / You will have an honorable revenge / It was not long ago that our forefathers, / with their noble blood sealed / the tomb of our honor."[50]

Distinguished jurists were honored with the presidency of the games. In inaugural ceremonies, they delivered heartwarming speeches that tugged at the emotions of those who yearned for a momentary return to a mythical ancestral past. In 1860 Francesc Permanyer besieged his audience to "Sing in Catalan and drench yourself in the spirit of our forefathers who until now not only spoke but also thought and felt in Catalan." The next year Lluís Pons proclaimed, "Love of language is a guaranty of our being, our history, from where we came, of who we are, and of what we can be." In 1862 the mercantile lawyer and politician Joan Illas praised the sentimental value of the vernacular: "Among strangers and in far-way lands, there is not one day that our language does not appear on our lips, time and time again, always like sweet honey."[51] These homages paid tribute to the timeless beauty of the ancient language, but nobody, at the time, thought to revive Catalan for education, officialdom, pleading, or even prose.[52] Francesc Permanyer wrote and delivered all of his published speeches in Spanish, as did Joan Illas, who incidentally had coauthored a primer on Spanish grammar.[53] These lawyers, like all literate men and women at the time, regarded literature as entertainment or even escapism. Just the same, poetry imbued language with emotion. It would be a short step for something similar to occur to the law. Later generations would tie law and literature closer together.

In addition to poetry, theater also underwent a literary renaissance. Along with cafés and bullrings, theater houses were popular places of recreation. A few lawyers doubled as playwright-producers of comedies, musicals (*zarzuelas*), and dramas. Like poems, plays tended either to celebrate rural customs or to commemorate biblical figures, saints, or patriotic heroes. In 1856 the multitalented Manuel Angelon wrote and produced the first full-length drama in Catalan, *The Virgin of Mercy*, which retold the legend of one of the patron saints of Barcelona. This pioneering work, written in verse, was not a hit, but he soon packed the houses with *Sixteen Judges* (1858), a short one-act *zarzuela*, also in verse, that would be performed on and off into the twentieth century. "Sixteen Judges" referred to a folk expression or tongue twister that was said to have served as a password to enter the city when Barcelona had been under siege by Castile and France in 1714.[54] The play's simple message was nested in an even simpler plot. In a rural town, two young men — one a Castilian soldier and the other a Catalan local — vie for the hand of a young lady. In the end, the native pretender, who speaks "clearly and in Catalan," wins the contest. The fiancée's father, the mayor, celebrates the engagement with the cry: "I want all townspeople, beginning with my daughter . . . to speak and dance in Catalan."[55] The play closes with a customary dance, the *contrapàs*. Enthusiastic audiences were perhaps tempted to carry on prancing into the streets, although it was not likely that many city folks knew the complicated steps. The literary revival would eventually spread to dance, but it would not be until the 1890s when the *sardana* — a dance related to the *contrapàs* but hardly known outside the Empordà region — would become celebrated as the national dance of Catalonia.[56]

Conrad Roure was another practicing lawyer who also made a living as a playwright. Under the pseudonym Pau Bunyegas and later under his own name, the prolific author penned and produced a number of one-act comedies and longer dramas and also wrote lyrics for an opera and a few choral chants. One of his most famous plays was *Clarís* (1879), a three-act tragedy commemorating the life and heroic death of Pau Claris, the political leader of the Catalan revolt against Castile, known as the Reapers' War (1640–52).[57] Roure and his eclectic group went by the nickname the *xarons*, which meant "of bad taste, lacking in art, elegance, or distinction," an ironic phrase that suspiciously echoed the aesthetic manifesto of Flaubert's clique in Paris. The *xarons* strove to popularize "Catalan that is spoken nowadays," which they counterpoised with the pretentious Catalan, disinterred from the Middle Ages and garishly adorned by the baroque poets of the Floral Games.[58] In 1865 this group launched a satirical journal in Catalan, entitled *A Sheet of Paper*, which they followed with a stream of similar periodicals and almanacs that flirted with press laws and, as a result, appeared on and off under different mastheads in the ensuing decades. Valentí Almirall, the founder of political Catalanism, was the most politically driven member of the lot. In 1879 he published the first daily newspaper in Catalan, the *Catalan Daily*, which ran until 1882. Conrad Roure was its literary editor. Within its pages, he displayed his erudition by publishing a Catalan translation of the *Iliad*.[59]

As could be expected, historians enthusiastically contributed to the renaissance. Strictly speaking, historical scholarship was not part of literary revival, given that historians, like practically everyone who wrote prose, usually did so in Spanish. Just the same, narrating the crusades and conquests of counts and kings, and depicting the mythical harmony of medieval society, were essential to the romantic quest to recover and glorify the imperial past. The prominent historians of the 1860s and 1870s, Victor Balaguer and Antoni Bofarull, both held law degrees, although neither actively practiced. These rivals dug into the Crown of Aragon Archive and published multivolume histories of Catalonia that began with prehistoric times, ran up to the nineteenth century, and culminated with the defeat of absolutism and the victory of liberalism.[60] Not content with this denouement, the next generation added an additional chapter. The lawyer-historians Josep Pella and Josep Coroleu coauthored two books on public law, *The Catalan Corts* (1876) and *The Foral Law of Catalonia* (1878). Translating historic texts into a modern idiom, they proposed that Catalonia should not only retain its private law but also recuperate and codify its lost public law as a means of recapturing political autonomy. To Balaguer and Bofarull, ancient Catalan constitutionalism had been a precursor to Spanish constitutionalism. To Pella and Coroleu, the abolition of self-governing bodies in 1716 remained an open wound that could be cauterized only by the restoration of home rule.

Josep Pella was a founding member of "Young Catalonia," a group of romantics who borrowed their name from similar literary associations, some with explicit nationalist objectives, such as Young Italy, Young Poland, and Young Ireland. Their initial goal was to expand the reach of the literary renaissance beyond poetry and theater and bring it into other genres. Catalan was no longer to be considered solely a language reserved for verse, or for portraying town and peasant conversations. Rather, it was deemed appropriate for scholarly prose, short stories, and novels. In 1871 the Young Catalans published the first Catalan-language literary magazine, *La Renaixensa*, which was filled with poetry, vignettes, and essays on history, law, religion, legend, archaeology, folklore, architecture, and other cultural and religious topics. Initially published as a weekly, it began to run as a daily in 1881. Juridical subjects featured prominently. The lead article of the second issue was a historical study of the *Usatges*, a feudal-law compilation that came to be regarded as the Magna Carta of the ancient principality.[61] In the next issue, another article appeared on testamentary liberty and the legal rules governing the *hereu*.[62] In 1879 Josep Coroleu took on the daunting task of trying to explain the historical origins of emphyteusis to a lay audience.[63]

The *Renaixensa* also published vignettes that idealized rural life and spread the myth of *pairalisme* (patriarchism). The naming of a *hereu*, the marriage of a son or daughter, the testament of a patriarch, or a similar legal conundrum was often the fulcrum around which a family drama turned. Some of these read as didactic conversations meant to educate readers and to disabuse them of deprecatory characterizations of Catalan law. One common plot was the triumph of love over family expectation, although, when all was said and done, law and custom prevailed.[64] Law was celebrated not only as a vital element of daily life but as a historic treasure in need of preservation. Recognizing the living value of medieval legal documents and ingrained customs paralleled similar projects to restore Romanesque monasteries and churches, to reedit the poetry of the fifteenth-century crusader Ausiàs March, or to recount the heroic conquests of the Counts of Barcelona.

Renaixença — meaning rebirth — was later used to describe the literary movement as a whole. With time, it resonated among pious Catholics. The "Vic Group" was a coterie of priests, friars, lawyers, notaries, property owners, and other assorted lay and religious professionals and literati from the diocese of Vic. Believing that religion and law constituted the bedrock of society, they were committed to disseminating traditional values as an antidote to the inhumanity of the industrial world. In 1880 the group organized millennium celebrations of the apparition of the Virgin of Montserrat, one of the patron saints of Catalonia; and in 1889 they began the restoration of the Ripoll monastery, the religious heart of Old Catalonia, which housed the tomb of the first Count of Barcelona, Wifred the Hairy. On a practical level, the church had a weighty reason to throw its support behind the campaign to defeat the Spanish Civil Code. Under Catalan choice-of-law rules, canon law, along with Roman law, was applied in court when a statute did not speak directly to, or proved contradictory on, a legal question. At the Conference of Catalan Jurisconsults in 1881, Felip Bertran i d'Amat claimed that "to touch Catalan law is as grave as desecrating the holy grail of our religion."[65] The priest Josep Torras, later the bishop of Vic, inserted a synoptical account of legal history within his *Catalan Tradition* (1892), a manifesto of regionalism: "Catalan jurisprudence was so Catholic and so popular, that liberty and faith have imbued its spirit down to the present day. It could be said that our law was spontaneously identified, at least in spirit, with the law of the church."[66] Not all agreed with the creative coupling of "liberty" and "faith," but Catalan law — like any sophisticated legal tradition — was deep and diverse enough to offer something to anybody.

This overview does not do justice to the diversity of the cultural renaissance, which included numerous associations and periodicals, some secular and others Catholic, scattered throughout towns in the ancient principality. Aside from lawyers, contributors included doctors, intellectuals, architects, librarians, archivists, journalists, administrators of public and private enterprises, artists, priests, monks, and even some businessman.[67] In order to assess the movement's influence on the bar, however, it is also crucial to recognize its limits. First, many lawyers participated in revivalism, but most did not. At the Conference of Catalan Jurisconsults in 1881, the literary-inclined attendees — Lluís Pons, Josep Pella, Josep Coroleu, Gonçal Serraclara, Valentí Almirall, and Conrad Roure — vehemently defended the autonomy of Catalan law. However, other defenders were practical men, who had not been seduced by poetry, theater, history, folklore, or religion, but simply believed that Catalan law should not be reduced to a series of exceptions to general rules. Second, not all revivalists rallied behind the cause. Eusebi Pascual, the previously mentioned author who had published a patriotic ode to Barcelona, opposed the campaign to defeat the civil code. As editor to the daily newspaper *La Publicidad*, he reminded readers that "in addition to Catalan blood ... Spanish and, above all, human blood circulates in our veins."[68] Third, practically all novels and daily newspapers were published in Spanish. In their daily routines, lawyers might flip through the *Renaixensa*, but they always read the mainstream press, which regarded literary revival and Catalanism with a mixture of sympathy, indifference, curiosity, skepticism, and ridicule. In 1889 the Catholic daily, the *Correo Catalán*, joked that some Catalanists butchered the language: "Some write it well; others poorly; there are others who write in a risible fashion."[69]

Finally, the most important limitation of the influence of revivalism on the bar concerned the issue of language itself. As we have seen, lawyers came to advocate reforms that would allow Catalan to be spoken within parts of judicial proceedings, but they never sought to adopt it for all judicial life. It was one thing to recommend that judges, prosecutors, and lawyers *understand* and *speak* the native language so that they could properly investigate crimes and question uneducated and illiterate defendants and witnesses, many of whom struggled to express themselves in Spanish. This argument also strengthened the claim that natives should staff the judiciary, a measure that would theoretically provide increased job opportunities to an overcrowded profession. However, it was quite another thing to propose that lawyers should *write* and *plead* in Catalan. Lawyers had exclusively employed Spanish for their professional duties since the New Foundation (1716), had long been schooled in the language, and could not have shifted to Catalan even if they had been so inclined.[70] What is more, they were not so inclined. It would have been impossible for practitioners to employ Catalan in their motions and briefs or to deliver appellate argument in a language that had not been used for formal oratory or writing since the seventeenth century. To many, the revival of Catalan law within genres such as poetry and theater did not mean that it should be exported into justice, other spheres of officialdom, or business. In short, *literary* revival did not initially mean *linguistic* revival.[71]

In a speech at the Academy of Jurisprudence in 1897, the nationalist Enric Prat de la Riba proposed that "witnesses and criminal defendants" be permitted to testify in Catalan because "many, in fact a majority, do not know Spanish." Such persons tended to come from the lower levels of society "in most need of protection by public authority." He reiterated the long-standing demand that all "civil servants serving in the judiciary need to know the language of the region in order to carry out their functions."[72] But he stopped short of suggesting that judges, lawyers, and proctors use Catalan in their writings, briefs, or speeches. If he had done so, his program would have appealed to fewer lawyers. This was a far cry from an unequivocal call for full linguistic revival.

On balance, it would be erroneous to attribute the opposition to codification solely to the influence of literary endeavor. The trenchant defense of Catalan law was not only an outgrowth of romanticism but also the result of decades of juridical scholarship. Unlike poets and playwrights, jurists did not seek to "revive" a canon that had been dead for centuries; rather, they worked to conserve a tradition that was alive in court. The defense of Catalan law did not spontaneously appear in the 1880s, on the heels of revivalism, but was the consequence of parallel jurisprudential developments. It is not clear whether romantic rebirth influenced the law or if it was the other way around. Suffice it to say that trends in law and literature cross-fertilized one another.

The Making of Catalan Civil Law:
Positive Law and the Historical School

Catalan lawyers did not rally behind their legal tradition because they had been swayed by romanticism or revivalism. Nor were their actions a smokescreen for the defense of the economic interests of rich clienteles; after all, the material interests of property holders, large and small, agrarian and industrial, were perfectly addressed within the government's proposal for a civil code, which promised to codify the status quo without upsetting the balance of property interests or entitlements anywhere in Spain. The primary reason behind the bar's politicization was that Catalan law had become a defining element of corporate identity and power. To shed a comparative light on the matter, the task of codification was perhaps not as difficult as trying to separate London barristers from their attachment to the English common law, but something similar was afoot. In the 1830s a Benthamite movement to codify law in Britain had failed miserably, and in the 1880s the attempt to reduce Catalan law to a series of exceptions to general rules of a Spanish civil code would also fail for the same reason.[73]

The making of Catalan civil law began as a positivistic project, in which lawyers sought to update and rationalize their law for use in daily practice. During the first half of the century, advocates awaited the coming of a Spanish civil code, believing that it would incorporate, or at least preserve, key institutions of family and property in Catalonia. Until this occurred, however, they had no choice but to update and modernize the only regime they had. Despite having suffered scholarly neglect in the eighteenth century, Catalan law governed everyday relationships and was frequently applied in court. It was uncontroversially invoked for issues involving property, inheritance, and the family economy. In the many areas in which Castilian and Catalan law overlapped, such as contract or intestate succession, or in which Catalan law was silent or contradictory, lawyers could rely on *Las Siete Partidas* (1260s), a historic collection of Roman laws for the Crown of Castile, written in Spanish and hence easily applicable in court. This was contained within the *Novísima recopilación* (1805), the most recent compilation of Spanish common law, which also contained various other laws valid in Catalonia. But jurisprudence was divided over the extent to which the *Partidas* could be cited.[74] Furthermore, the *Novísima recopilación* was voluminous and unwieldy; published before the abolition of feudalism, it reeked of the Old Regime. Ultimately, the exigencies of practice did not give lawyers and judges the luxury of sitting back and waiting for a code to appear. Rather they needed practical guidance on how old laws would be applied to everyday legal problems. In response to demand, jurists slowly constructed a "Catalan civil law." This was not an explicit project born out of a manifesto but evolved slowly and picked up pace in the 1880s once political conflicts had begun.

The first major work that can be legitimately associated with legal renaissance was Pere Vives's *Translation into Spanish of the Usatges and Other Laws* of Catalonia. Published between 1832 and 1835, this four-volume compilation was a much-needed update of statutory law, last compiled in 1704 and hopelessly outdated. For his part, Vives followed the chronological structure of the 1704 version. His compilation and translation began with the *Usatges*, continued with collections and commentaries of customs, and culminated with the laws of the old parliament, called "constitutions." In a rather matter-of-fact manner, he included those laws that were still applicable and expunged those that had been derogated or were "notoriously useless."[75] He inserted helpful commentary and translated all laws into Spanish, so that lawyers were spared the tedious task of having to translate them from Catalan one by one. The author did not intend his work to be the first step in the reconstruction of an autonomous tradition but only wished to aid his fellow practitioners in their daily tasks. In fact, Pere Vives looked favorably upon codification and, like practically all advocates of his generation, insisted that some Catalan laws should be incorporated into a general code, while others should be preserved as exceptions.[76] As a code became delayed, though, he saw the need to reedit the compilation. In the early 1860s, some three decades after the appearance of the original edition, he published a revised version. In this way, he was able to incorporate changes to Catalonia's legal regime caused by the Law of Mortgages (1860), the Notarial Law (1861), and other enactments.

If Pere Vives bestowed upon his colleagues an updated "compilation," then Josep Antoni Elias and Esteve de Ferrater gifted them a de facto "code." The *Manual of Civil Law applicable in Catalonia* (1842) adopted the style and spirit of the French Civil Code. Its authors redrafted old laws into short, graspable rules organized into articles, titles, chapters, and books. The *Manual* contained an unideological blend of foral and common law and went to great strides to simplify antiquated customary institutions — later the lifeblood of romanticist authors — in favor of clear and precise laws that could be smoothly applied in court without generating needless controversy. Periodically updated throughout the century, the *Manual* was an essential component of any lawyer's library.[77] A Catalan advocate needed to keep this volume handy, as he did with Vives's compilation and procedural-, civil-, mercantile-, and penal-law codes and guides. In the mid-1870s, Josep Elias published *The General and Foral Civil Law of Spain*, a guidebook for use anywhere in the country. It consisted of an ordered exposition of common-law provisions, but, after each article, it provided, when necessary, a list of exceptions applicable in the foral regions. Elias's motivations were purely practical. He mission was not to strengthen the autonomy of foral traditions but only to reflect accurately the state of civil law in Spain. He criticized those authors who regarded foral regimes as "an antiquated law," on the verge of disappearance and hence undeserving of scholarly commentary. Foral laws, he stressed, were "alive in various rich and populous provinces, the knowledge of which should be important to all, because national unity has created interlocking relationships."[78]

Vives, Elias, and Ferrater were practically minded lawyers and court reporters who never contemplated that their publications would later be seen to have laid the foundation for a "Catalan civil law." Indeed, if a Spanish civil code had been approved in the 1850s or 1860s, their work could just as easily have been interpreted as contributing to a larger project, taking place throughout the country, in which jurists recuperated and renovated the diverse laws of the various regions of the peninsula with the objective of working toward a code that combined "the best ones from all the provinces."[79] History, however, turned out differently. At the university, academics imported a jurisprudential theory that imbued these positivistic projects with political meaning. Professors glossed "historical-school jurisprudence," the legal philosophy of Friedrich von Savigny (1779–1861), the first rector of the University of Berlin and the most highly regarded private-law jurist of his time. In the rest of the continent, Savigny had been influential during the first half of the century when he and his followers had successfully reasserted the importance of jurisprudence during an age when some idealists had erroneously proclaimed that the promulgation of codes had obviated the need for scholarly interpretation. In Catalonia, historicism arrived late, but once it took hold, it was particularly virulent.

Why were Barcelona's jurists so attracted to historical-school jurisprudence? In the first place, Savigny's overriding priority had been to conserve Roman law. His jurisprudential system fit in well in Catalonia, which possessed a Mediterranean legal tradition similar to that of the Baltic cities where he had developed his thought. Despite its name, the historical school did not grant a lawyer or judge license to interpret the law wildly according to individual conceptions of the mandates of history. On the contrary, its operative principle was that law would evolve slowly through commentary, interpretation, and litigation — the cunning of history would reveal law's innate reason. In essence, the historical school defended the methods by which law was practiced before codification and hence justified the maintenance of the status quo in Catalonia. Savigny's philosophy ensured that scholars and professors would retain their custody over interpretation and could continue to write guidebooks, articles, glosses, and commentaries by relying on Roman texts, statutory law, compilations of custom, the treatises of distinguished jurists, and other scholarly sources. The practitioner would employ a range of tools in order to craft arguments on a case-by-case basis.[80] To be sure, the historical school was cast within the corporate interests of bars and professoriates everywhere. Even in countries where civil-law codification had already taken place, scholars relied on Savigny to justify the principle that codes should be interpreted by jurists versed in the subtleties of Roman Law and legal history, standard subjects taught at universities in all of Europe.[81]

The second reason why Barcelona was fertile ground for a reception concerned the debate over codification itself. Savigny had developed his philosophy in response to a proposal to promulgate a single civil code for the German states. Writing in the wake of the expulsion of Napoleonic armies, he had opposed calls to codify law on the French model. In his world-famous pamphlet *On the Vocation of Our Age for Legislation and Jurisprudence* (1814), he had argued that codification was artificial and pathological, an unjustified legislative interference that truncated law's natural evolution. He contended that law should be left in the hands of jurists and professors, who could ensure that law evolved in concert with custom and the spirit of the people, the *Volksgeist*.[82] In this way, old institutions would slowly die out, and new ones would gradually emerge in harmony with society. This was enormously helpful, for it enabled Catalan jurists to defend institutions that were sliding into extinction, such as emphyteusis, by explaining that they should be allowed to metamorphose slowly rather than being radically transformed at the stroke of a pen. Abrupt legislative interference, so the reasoning went, risked creating artificial institutions without proven viability, which could be prejudicial to social welfare and even give rise to agrarian violence. To be sure, the *Volksgeist* endowed the positivistic project to renovate Catalan law with a potent philosophical punch.

Manuel Duran was the chief baton waver in this parade of juridical adulation. He was likely introduced to Savigny by his university colleague Estanislao Reynals who had cited the German jurist in order to marshal authority for the opposition to the draft code of 1851.[83] In a six-month campaign in the *Diario de Barcelona*, the conservative daily newspaper, Reynals had criticized the "modern mania for regulating everything"[84] and praised the value of "custom" over "statute." But Reynals was not versed in the subtleties of the historical school and had cloaked his argument in the rhetoric of pure political reaction. In his speeches at the Academy of Jurisprudence, he had denigrated all "new law," calling it a "fiction," and had insisted that the only "true law" was that of the Roman-ecclesiastical tradition.[85] The most reactionary members of the bar nodded in agreement, but others paid scant attention. At the time, he was the only author who rejected the principle of codification entirely. Moreover, when all was said and done, he expressed visceral dissatisfaction only with a single article of the 1851 draft code — that which abolished testamentary liberty. Once the draft code was defeated, he did not seek to convert his journalism into a jurisprudential treatise.

Manuel Duran was a more sophisticated scholar with wider appeal and tremendous motivational and organizational skills. In 1869, he founded a Barcelona branch of the Berlin-based "Savigny Foundation" and summarized the basic outlines of the historical school in his presidential address at the Academy of Jurisprudence.[86] In 1878 he wrote the introduction to the Spanish translation of Savigny's *Contemporary System of Roman Law*.[87] In 1883 he published his *Outline of the Institutions of Civil Law in Catalonia*, which he submitted as the Catalan representative to the Commission for Codes. In this work, he inveighed against Alonso Martínez's proposed Basic Law of 1881, which sought to make the code as uniform as possible and hence to reduce exceptions to a minimum in order to strengthen national unity. To combat this initiative, Duran glossed the historical school, adjusting its principles to Spanish circumstances. Just as Savigny had contended that the customs of the diverse German states had not evolved together to the extent that could justify uniform codification, Duran made a similar argument: the existence of a multiplicity of customs, laws, and jurisprudential schools in Spain evidenced that time was not ripe for codification: "As long as there exist diverse nationalities, it is absolutely impossible to aspire to civil legal unity."[88] Accordingly, he recommended that all law in Spain should be left uncodified. Manuel Duran did not believe that the quest to conserve Catalan law should give rise to a political movement for self-government. However, once he had popularized German historicism, he had opened a Pandora's box. With time the *Volksgeist* would clear the path for the reception of the Herderian doctrine of national self-determination.[89]

Although some Catalan lawyers were reluctant to embrace wholeheartedly the figure of Savigny, they were receptive to his historicism. In addition to his fame as a venerated scholar, the German jurist had been a controversial public figure, notorious for defending the privileges of the aristocracy and opposing the liberation of the serfs in Prussia.[90] For those uncomfortable with his reactionary reputation, Montesquieu was a fine alternative. In the

Spirit of Law, the enlightened jurist had contended that laws should reflect the geography, climate, and the spirit of the people, and he had praised the existence of legal diversity within a single country. Before the reception of Savigny, Catalan writers had invoked Montesquieu to combat the 1851 draft code, arguing that Catalans, or anyone for that matter, had the right to reject laws foreign to their spirit.[91] To scholars concerned with consistency, Montesquieu had never been a good fit, for he was a notorious critic of Roman law, but ordinary lawyers were not bothered: the broad message of the *Spirit of Law*, like that of the historical school, could be expropriated without having to swallow either jurisprudential system whole. In Barcelona, Savigny and Montesquieu were the intellectual adhesive that fixed "spirit" to "law." They were the equivalent to legal thought to what Marx and Bakunin were to working-class ideology in Barcelona.

The widespread popularity of historicism did not mean that Barcelona lawyers agreed on all matters. Just as jurists were divided over whether Savigny or Montesquieu should be an appropriate guiding light, they argued over multiple substantive issues dividing Right and Left in all of Europe concerning religion and property reform. They even brandished divergent opinions about codification: conservatives maintained that law, whether codified or not, should be left in the hands of university professors and elite practitioners; Federal-Republicans, on the other hand, contended that a democratically elected Catalan legislature should codify and reform it.[92] In spite of such divisions, the bar reached a consensus that Catalan law — regardless of the disputed nature of its contents, influences, and pending reforms — was not an exceptional "foral law" but an independent "civil law," reflective of distinctive spirit and character, the future of which should be decided in Barcelona and not Madrid.

These influences pushed the frontiers of juridical reasoning. Lawyers could still be heard appealing to Enlightenment conceptions such as utility, economy, and happiness, but they bolstered well-worn rational arguments with historicist and organicist ones. The midcentury contention that Catalan law promoted patriarchal authority, family harmony, and economic productivity was fortified by the mystical notion that law reflected the spirit, sentiments, and idiosyncrasies of the people. Rational arguments could be rebutted by counterarguments, but romantic conceptions were more aesthetic and, as such, did not lend themselves to compromise. Josep Maria Vallès de Ribot believed that law was "embodied in popular conscience,"[93] while Lluís Maria de Llauder agreed that it represented "the mold in which the family, the life, and the physiognomy of the Catalan people has been formed."[94] Faithful to Montesquieu's geographic determinism, Valentí Almirall deduced that a "fractured and mountainous country" caused Catalans to exhibit an "egalitarian, reflexive, imaginative, rugged, and independent character," manifest in their civil law.[95] Joaquim Cadafalch observed that laws "have been incarnated in our customs and form a great part of our being."[96] The regionalist priest Josep Torras praised the juridical movement as "the most splendid manifestation of our national character and the most tangible demonstration of the triumph of Catalan spirit."[97]

When mixed with the controversy over codification, romanticism and historicism polarized the images of "Catalan" and "Castilian" law. In the 1830s and 1840s, scholars had attempted to bridge divisions by finding common ground in Roman law. Beginning in the 1880s, most strove to do the opposite. They conjured up theories, laws, and sources in order to buttress the contention that the two traditions were historically and hence scientifically irreconcilable. Vallès de Ribot stated that they were based on "completely antithetical principles."[98] The framers of the *Outline of Grievances* (1885), an early Catalanist manifesto, counterpoised Catalan law, indicative of "the positive and analytic temperament of our people, inspired by the overarching principle of civil liberty," with Castilian law, "inspired by the contrary principle, the predominance of authority."[99] Such derogatory remarks mirrored similar ones coming from Madrid. Alonso Martínez depicted foral laws as "uses, customs, *fueros*, deeds, and whims."[100] Another distinguished jurist claimed that they were "petrified in their old forms, mute and inert witnesses to legal progress, living only as an echo of times past, when necessities and aspirations were quite different from those of modern life."[101] One Supreme Court magistrate characterized Catalan law as nothing more than an "anachronism." "My sweet dream," he declared, "is to erase from the geography of Spain these ridiculous nationalities that through an exaggerated provincialism are constantly promoting conflicts with the rest of the Spaniards."[102]

Historical-school jurisprudence also conditioned the positive law. In 1880 Guillem Brocà and Joan Amell published the *Institutions of Catalan Civil Law*, a new guidebook for practitioners and judges. The *Institutions* covered the same legal regime as its predecessor, *Manual of Civil Law Applicable in Catalonia*. The basic legal rules of the competing guides were essentially the same, but some of the underlying sources were different. The *Manual* held that "civil law" consisted of a combination of "common" and "foral" legal rules; the *Institutions*, in contrast, shunned the foral-common terminology. Elias and

Ferrater had sought to resolve differences between common and foral law by finding common ground when possible. Brocà and Amell did just the opposite: they cast their project with the intention of enabling "Catalan civil law" to stand on its own. Legal realities meant that the latter authors could not avoid some applicable common-law provisions, but they excluded them to the greatest extent possible. Although not as elegant as its predecessor and downright clumsy when it tripped over common-law provisions, the *Institutions* was still a handy tool. The authors sacrificed elegance in drafting in order to deliver an unambiguous political message — Catalan law was not an exceptional "foral law" but an autonomous "civil law." As a result of the conflict over codification in 1880s, the pace of publication picked up, as other jurists published books, pamphlets, and articles. Later, Brocà converted the historical introduction of the *Institutions* into a multivolume *History of Catalan Law* (1918), still one of the paradigmatic works of Catalan legal history today.[103]

In 1895 the young jurist Enric Prat de la Riba, the future ideologue of nationalism, coauthored *A Compendium of Catalanist Doctrine*, in which he sought to standardize a new vocabulary. He insisted that words such as "foral" or "dialect" denoted subsidiarity and hence should not be used to describe Catalan law or language. The authors equated the difference between "common" and "foral" with that between "language" and "dialect": neither was Catalan a dialect of Spanish, nor was Catalan law a foral exception to a common-law norm. Instead, Catalonia possessed an autonomous language and civil law, equivalent to those of any European country.[104] This terminological difference was essential to distinguishing between a "nation" and a "state." As Prat de la Riba wrote: "They say it is poorly conceived to maintain different regimes of civil law within a nation, and they are more than correct. For this reason ... we have become convinced that Spain is not a nation but a state in which various nationalities live or, better said, die or agonize."[105]

This tour through law and jurisprudence explains why Catalan lawyers came to defend their legal tradition so vehemently. We should not discount that literary revival had seeped into juridical reasoning and had soaked law in sentiment. But the legal community had gone down its own road and had come out at a similar place. In the 1830s, Catalan law — like much law throughout Europe — had been in tatters, having suffered scholarly neglect throughout the eighteenth century, gradual encroachment by Spanish common law, and massive legal changes due to the abolition of feudalism and the reorganization of property. By the 1880s, however, Catalan law was no longer in a decadent state but had been updated and modernized. In response to practical needs and following continental trends, scholars had converted a "foral" into a "civil law." Historical-school jurisprudence had anointed professors and practitioners as guardians of the tradition. Everyone equated law with spirit. Hence, when Spanish legislators recommenced efforts to codify civil law in the 1880s, they confronted a more highly developed legal tradition; romantic intellectuals and practicing lawyers who considered law a regional treasure and an organic expression of collective values and spirit; and, not to be forgotten, a bar that had augmented its wealth, corporate power, confidence, and influence.

In the end, Catalan jurists constructed or "made" a civil law in much the same way a French, Spanish, or German civil law was made. As elsewhere, this undertaking was subjective, fraught with cultural and political assumptions, as well as borrowed law and jurisprudence.[106] It was not carried out by a legislative commission but by practitioners and professors who wrote books and articles on institutions, historic texts, and jurisprudential trends and published guidebooks that doubled as de facto codes. Catalan law was not "reborn" — literally raised from the dead — as was the literary tradition; nor was it "invented" like choral chants and dances were.[107] To be sure, though, if neither reborn nor invented, Catalan law was reworked and remade. The closest parallel to law was language. Both had been decadent for centuries, but both remained omnipresent in the daily lives of Catalans. Just as Catalan law remained applicable in court and was frequently used in notarized documents, Catalan language was still the dominant conversational medium among natives. However, the juridical movement predated what was known as the "linguistic campaign." Legal guides and compilations had been circulating for decades when the linguist Pompeu Fabra published the first outline of Catalan grammar, *An Essay on Modern Catalan Grammar* (1891). Fabra did not publish the first treatise on spelling until 1913, and a complete dictionary of the Catalan language did not appear until 1917. Lawyers defended their regional legal regime in the Spanish legislature long before linguists and teachers insisted that Catalan language be taught in primary and secondary school. To be sure, the civil code conflict was to be the first political dispute of the nationalist era.

The Political Conflict and Nascent Nationalism

The university professor and commercial lawyer Manual Duran headed the parliamentary protest in Madrid. The first extended legislative debate occurred in 1885 when the Conservative Party introduced a new Basic Law to the Spanish Congress of Deputies. This replaced the previous one of 1881, drafted by Manual Alonso Martínez. The minister of justice, Francisco Silvela, claimed to have forged a new compromise that addressed the concerns of Catalan lawyers. Instead of reducing foral law to a single appendix, he promised that each foral region would have a separate appendix. Moreover, until the Commission for Codes wrote such appendixes, he pledged to conserve all foral-law regimes in their present state. However, he did not seek to dislodge Alonso Martínez from his role as author of the code nor was he receptive to the idea of promulgating an independent volume for each foral region. Unsatisfied with what were thought to be minimal concessions, Manuel Duran broke party ranks to oppose the Basic Law.[108] In 1885 he was elected dean of the College of Lawyers.

In the Congress of Deputies, Manuel Duran adjusted his scholarly beliefs to political realities and international developments. By the 1880s, Germany could no longer serve as an exemplar. Following unification, the old rivalry between "Romanist" and "Germanist" schools had come to an end, and the Reich's jurists had performed nothing short of hermeneutical magic by reinterpreting Savigny to be compatible with codification.[109] In fact, Spanish supporters of uniform codification applauded the case of Germany. Commenting on one of the German draft codes, one advocate of uniform codification had praised the "truly patriotic enthusiasm of German lawyers" who had agreed to "sacrifice the traditional civil laws of the empire's territories" in order to work toward "a future civil code."[110] In Madrid, the ferocious determination of Manuel Alonso Martínez and the Commission for Codes meant that codification was imminent. Assessing the terrain, Duran realized that a categorical protest against the principle of codification was bound to fail. After hesitating, he followed the recommendations of the Conference of Catalan Jurisconsults and the Academy of Jurisprudence. In the Spanish parliament, he suggested that Catalan law be preserved not as an "appendix" but as "independent laws" to be codified by a commission of jurists, the majority of whom would be Catalan. To him, this would be an appropriate compromise. The suggestion, though, found no support whatsoever, and his proposed amendment to the Basic Law was roundly defeated.[111]

Manuel Duran and his entourage were active in juridical conferences, believing perhaps naively that their opinions could gather momentum and eventually prevail in a marketplace of ideas. In 1886 he and a number of other

Catalan lawyers attended a second Spanish Juridical Conference in Madrid. The impassioned legislative protests of 1885 had succeeded in dragging out debate, derailing the approval of the Basic Law. An outbreak of cholera and the illness of the king had caused the Spanish Cortes to close prematurely with the Basic Law hanging in the air. Given this atmosphere, it is possible that they marched into conference with the optimistic but illusory hope that they could seize the atmosphere of insecurity to bury the project. They reiterated what had become the institutional position of the Barcelona bar — different codes should exist for each of the foral regions. The suggestion again fell on deaf ears. At the conference, a slender majority agreed to preserve some foral institutions, and an overwhelming majority voted that "national unification" was the overriding purpose of codification.[112] Incensed by the adverse result, Duran and the three juridical academies (Jurisprudence, Law, and Administrative Law) sponsored a Barcelona Juridical Conference, held at the Palace of Sciences during the World Fair of 1888. Opponents of the government's plans came from all over Spain to express their collective discontent, mull over alternatives, discuss a number of other juridical issues, and, of course, enjoy the fair in their free time.[113]

Despite his vaunted reputation as a prolific scholar and a powerful commercial lawyer, Manuel Duran failed to impress where it mattered most — in the Spanish Cortes. At every step of the way, he confronted the code's author, Manuel Alonso Martínez, who also had a reputation as an eminent litigator, an erudite jurist, a shrewd politician, and a reasonable man. There was never any love lost between the two. Duran defiantly confessed to the congress, "There is a complete disagreement between the criteria of Mr. Alonso Martínez and my own. There is a divergence of principles, there is a divergence of schools of thought."[114] In the end, Duran convinced very few outside Catalonia. Even many politicians from other foral regions considered the government compromise adequate and the Catalan position intransigent. In 1885 Liberals returned to power and Alonso Martínez became minister of justice for the second time in the decade. In 1888 he resubmitted the Conservative-proposed Basic Law to the Cortes, with some amendments concerning civil marriage, and picked up debate from where it had been abandoned. Using this controversial and arguably unconstitutional procedure, he avoided having to revisit the issue of the relationship between common and foral law and rammed the bill through the Spanish Cortes with limited discussion.[115] In October, the ministry began to publish the Civil Code in serial form. This was not the end of the affair. The appearance of the code caused an uproar. Practitioners, students, and professors associated with regionalist and Catalanist political organizations took the lead in the ensuing protest.

In assessing the effectiveness of the parliamentary opposition, it is important to recognize that Manuel Duran and his colleagues, though dissatisfied with the result, had won two major concessions. First, the Basic Law of 1881 had proposed to include all foral-law exceptions in one appendix, while that of 1888 guaranteed that each region would have its own separate appendix. This left the door open to discussions over the content, length, and scope of such an appendix: a long and detailed appendix could resemble a code or volume of independent laws, whereas a short number of concise rules would look more like a list of exceptions. In short, the debate was far from closed. Second, the proposed Basic Law of 1881 had promised to preserve only the statutory law of the foral regions; in contrast, that of 1888 also maintained the validity of all supplementary sources applied according to choice-of-law rules. This meant that the code was to be applied only in the last resort — that is, if no Catalan statutory laws or its traditional set of Roman-canonical complements addressed an issue. As stated in Article 12 of the code itself, until the appendixes were written, foral law was to be conserved "in all its integrity." At the same time, the Catalan caucus did not manage to stop codification or ensure that Catalan law would be contained in an independent volume written by its native sons. Most ominously, the Civil Code conserved foral law only "for the time being," a turn of phrase that sounded like a death knell to many.[116] Taken as a whole, the end result was ambiguous, leaving the future of Catalan law up in the air. Catalan deputies and senators had not gotten their way but had at least achieved a stalemate.

In the eyes of many, however, a stalemate was not good enough. Political Catalanists had long been convinced that leaving the matter to parliamentarians, members of dynastic political parties, was doomed to failure. Regardless of how many oratorical points could be scored, regardless of how well impassioned speeches read in the Barcelona press, regardless of whether all of Catalonia believed that Manuel Duran had a superior juridical mind to that of Manuel Alonso Martínez, Catalan deputies and senators were bound to get, and did get, outvoted. To Catalanists, it was not acceptable to chalk up the adverse result to the nature of the political process. The civil law was more important than budgets, tariffs, or other matters pending before the Spanish Cortes and could not be simply dismissed as one of the numerous casualties of majority rule. Once a code went into effect, it would immediately condition behavior. Unlike other pieces of legislation, a code could not be repealed, or easily amended, by ensuing governments. Given this situation, Catalanists perceived that getting bogged down in legislative debates and scholarly conferences only delayed the inevitable and was destined to result in, and did result in, an unsatisfactory compromise. In 1887 the law student Enric Prat de la Riba, then president of the Catalan Student Center, criticized "the spirit of collegiality that has produced such awful results." "This spirit of collegiality," he wrote, "threatens to bury our civil law, which embodies all that is good and flourishing in our fatherland."[117] Instead of polite debate, he favored the use of modern propaganda techniques to put external pressure on the government.

Even before the publication of the code in 1888, Catalanists had employed more aggressive tactics. They stirred up passions, excoriated the malevolent intentions of politicians, bypassed the Cortes by petitioning the monarchy, and brought the controversy out of the legislature and its backrooms and into the public spotlight. They adopted new methods of organization, soon to be characteristic of the era of mass politics, by staging meetings, protests, marches, and picnics. In their public speeches, they did not limit themselves to criticizing the proposals of central legislators but took advantage of public outrage to popularize parallel goals. At the top of their agenda was the need to "Catalanize" the judiciary and bureaucracy, a measure that would improve the accessibility of public careers for natives holding law degrees. In addition, they demanded that judges be versed in the language, that courses on Catalan law be incorporated into the curriculum, and that defendants, litigants, and witnesses be permitted to testify in Catalan. They delivered their speeches and published their manifestos in the vernacular. To these campaigners, the maintenance of Catalan law was the first step that would culminate in home rule or at least a significant degree of administrative and juridical devolution.

The first sign that Catalanists were disposed to adopt aggressive tactics occurred in January 1885. A number of activists from the "bar, industry, letters, and science"[118] met at the Llotja Palace to launch a formal protest against two hostile measures proposed by the Conservative government — to lower tariffs and to codify the civil law. In the *Outline of Grievances* (1885), the authors appealed directly to King Alphonse XII (who had the constitutional power to dissolve a government if he found one minister in agreement), requesting that he put a stop to those who threatened to damage the "moral and material interests" of Catalonia. In 1885 the young king fell ill and died, but the protest continued. During the Floral Games held at the World Fair in 1888, Joan Maluquer presented the queen regent Maria Christina with a manifesto, the *Message to the Queen Regent*. More radical than the *Outline*, the *Message* put forth an ambitious program of self-government. Addressing the concerns of the bar, it railed against foreign judges who "neither understand our language nor can comprehend those with whom they have to deal" and who were "unfamiliar with our venerated laws and, upon learning them, consider them repugnant." Consistent with the interests of young professionals facing depressing job prospects, it insisted that "Catalans name those who occupy public positions of the Catalan nation, ensuring that all judicial, administrative, and teaching positions are given to Catalans."[119] Hundreds of signatories urged her to follow the example of her Habsburg relative Franz Joseph I, who in 1867 had granted autonomy to Hungary.

The loudest protest took place in the wake of the publication of the code. In October 1888 the Ministry of Justice began to publish it in serial form. Following the appearance of the first few articles, many came to the conclusion that the bar's leadership had failed. Article 12 promised to preserve Catalan law "in all its integrity," but it also included the ominous phrase that this was "for the time being." The commission was later to reduce Catalan law to an appendix. Even more scandalous, the code contained a truly nasty provision, Article 15, which was portrayed as an underhanded maneuver intended to inflict serious damage on all foral-law regimes. In essence, Article 15 was a choice-of-law provision that determined to whom the Civil Code applied and to whom foral law applied. As read by many, though, it essentially governed citizenship. This was because a person would be considered "Catalan" if he or she was governed by Catalan law.[120] As written, Article 15 applied Catalan law only to residents who had been born in Catalonia and who were children of two Catalan parents. This clashed with an older medieval law, used to determine who was a "native" for public employment, according to which long-term residents, all persons born in Catalonia, and even those born outside Catalonia to a Catalan father or grandfather were "natives." In concrete terms, the Civil Code threatened to apply Catalan law to a limited number of persons. Given migration and intermarriage, Catalan law was destined to lose applicability over time. The number of "Catalans" for the purposes of applying the civil law would become fewer and fewer.

In response, campaigners organized a series of town meetings. At each meeting, speakers from Barcelona traveled to a city or town where they joined local notables. In their speeches, they conveyed the baleful consequences of the civil code by distilling legal technicalities into an intelligible and forceful narrative laden with organicist arguments that stressed the relationship between the health of law and the vitality of the Catalan people. They didactically explained legal technicalities in intelligible terms, inveighed against the government, and channeled the crowd's ire over Article 15 to promote other goals. In retrospect, it may be difficult to envision the existence of public rallies over issues so theoretically cerebral, and so out of the reach of the general populace, as civil law. In no other place in the world did this occur. But, as hard as this is to imagine, this is what happened. Beginning in February and lasting to June 1889, twenty major demonstrations took place, the largest of which numbered between three thousand and five thousand people.[121] Held in town squares, they were staged amid a celebratory atmosphere in the spirit of a local fete. Juridical, economic, and intellectual associations and numerous town halls also convoked well-attended meetings covered by the press. In total, thirty-six petitions reached the floor of the Congress of Deputies, and other complaints were forwarded to the Senate and the Ministry of Justice.[122]

From the start, the Article 15 campaign had a generational air about it. The chief organizer of the meetings was the young lawyer Narcís Verdaguer, the founder of the Catalan Student Center in 1886. Many of the most fiery speakers and writers were young lawyers as well. In 1889 the Student Center circulated a petition, calling the code a "tyrannic act," which came to collect 340 signatures from the schools of law, medicine, and engineering. Hundreds more students and seminarians from other places of advanced study outside Barcelona also added their names.[123] On 7 April, students sponsored a march that began at the university, went down the Ramblas Boulevard, continued along the port, turned into Citadel Park, proceeded up the Passeig Sant Joan, and culminated at the foot of the statue of Rafael Casanovas, the leader of the Catalan resistance during the War of Spanish Succession. Once there, one of the organizers exclaimed: "Until now, men of judgment and experience have spoken; today, the heart that represents the new generation speaks without any other ideals than to defend the rights of Catalonia."[124]

The incendiary tone of the town meetings and the attendant parliamentary protest was a sea change from the polite rhetoric of previous debates. No longer did lawyers survey international developments to emphasize that Spain could follow the example of Austria-Hungary or Switzerland rather than France or Italy. Nor did they descend into laborious explanations on the economic and moral virtues of testamentary liberty and emphyteusis. Nor did they bother to deliver exhaustive expositions on the elegance and beauty of Roman law, the dialectics of legal evolution, and the relationship between custom and statute. Nor did they waste their time by resuscitating the age-old debate over historical versus philosophical jurisprudence. Although some speakers maintained a measured tone by versing on the *ius sanguinis* and the *ius soli* and discussing the symbolic and material importance of the Catalan law, the most convincing orators and writers employed an arsenal of nationalist rhetorical conventions, which discarded nuance, thrived on insult, and surveyed new concepts such as race and ethnicity. Narcís Verdaguer published a series of articles in the *Voice of Montserrat*, a mouthpiece of regionalism, that shocked the polite sensibilities of elder jurists. He claimed that the "Catalan race" differed from the "Castilian race," which in turn descended from the "African race" and, for this reason, had a bellicose and heavy-handed temperament. If the Civil Code was applied in Catalonia, he cried, "We will be poor like them, lazy like them, braggarts like them."[125]

In the Spanish Congress, Joan Maluquer, one of the youngest deputies in the Cortes, was almost as vituperative. At the time, Maluquer was writing a treatise on the civil law of Barcelona, but his fury led him to discard his scholarly style.[126] He forgot any personal debt he may have owed Alonso Martínez, in whose law office he had apprenticed when he had been a doctoral student in Madrid. Having scoured similar laws in all of Europe and even the "semibarbarous" laws of Asia, he was able to find only one provision similar to Article 15 — a French law that ascribed French citizenship to children of French women impregnated by Algerian natives. He ironically quipped, "It is truly very sad that Basques and particularly Vizcayans, Navarrese, Aragonese, Majorcans, and Catalans have to travel in the company of Africans, according to the second provision of Article 15." If the Civil Code and Article 15 came into force, he lamented, "Catalonia loses its civil legislation . . . loses its children. . . . Catalans are going to be true foreigners within their own land."[127]

The most consistent and forceful message was that Article 15 would tear apart the family. If one of the two spouses were not "Catalan," the protestors reasoned, the children would not be Catalan; if children were born outside the region, they would not be considered Catalan. In such cases, multiple legal regimes could operate within a single household, creating enormous confusion and sowing the seeds of a future inheritance dispute. In the Congress of Deputies, Frederic Pons claimed that a husband would be forced to prohibit a pregnant wife from traveling in common-law regions for fear that the family would be subject to a bewildering mixture of law should she accidentally give birth on the journey.[128] Verdaguer contended that "a Catalan man who married a Castilian woman will not have the liberty of making Catalan children."[129] Llucià Ribera, lead editorialist of the conservative newspaper *Diario de Barcelona*, asserted that a Catalan man who married a Castilian woman would "occupy a secondary position within the family undeserving of its head." The only persons favored by Article 15, he retorted, were the "pretty and not-so-pretty girls of our region," who would have a greater possibility of encountering a Catalan spouse because "Catalan grooms would have to feel an exceptional passion before marrying a young Castilian bride."[130] The Catalan League resorted to scaremongering: "Catalans: The new Civil Code will cause great familial disruption and will impoverish you with an abundance of lawsuits, and before this deplorable situation ends, there will no longer be Catalans within our territory."[131]

When the dust had cleared, the protestors accomplished much more than the limited goal of forcing the government to amend Article 15. This was undertaken without much fanfare. The members of the Commission for Codes had long denied the existence of a devious scheme but had insisted that the entire uproar was due to an innocent drafting error that had been blown out of proportion. The government remanded the code for revision and fixed Article 15 in addition to a number of other poorly worded articles.

The government was, in fact, correct. The organizers of the protests never had the limited intention of simply reforming Article 15. This could have been accomplished with a few high-level meetings in Madrid. Rather, the purpose was always to use the civil code controversy as a launching pad for further demands. In the end, the town meetings and public outcry had two more important consequences. First, legislators were put on notice that further incursions into Catalan law would trigger a similarly hostile response; consequently, the commission made no serious attempt to reduce Catalan law to an "appendix." This left Catalan law uncodified. Compilations, guidebooks, and juridical commentary and decisions remained authoritative; jurists, law professors, and judges retained their role as custodians and interpreters. Second, the entire controversy added momentum to the ambitious goal of self-government. In the prophetic words of Narcís Verdaguer, the Article 15 protest constituted the "first victory of Catalanism."[132] Many associations created as a result, or in the wake, of the town meetings coalesced with others to form the Catalanist Union, a confederation of diverse associations that met in a different town every year. During these assemblies, running from 1892 to 1904, lawyers and notaries constituted some 30 percent of delegates.[133]

In the first meeting in 1892, the union promulgated the Manresa Principles, a draft constitution for an autonomous Catalonia.

As a consequence of the Article 15 campaign, ordinary lawyers warmed to the strident messages of Catalanists, who before the civil code conflicts had been considered a fringe element of the bar. Dominated by elder jurists, the Academy of Jurisprudence had initially been cautious, believing that the conundrum of codification would be worked out through debate and negotiation. It had suggested that codification be shelved or, in the alternative, that each foral region be provided with its own separate volume. After the code was published, and it had become evident that the government had not been willing to entertain either proposal, the academy radicalized its demands. In the 1890s it joined the campaign to "Catalanize" the judiciary. In 1892 it dispatched a proposal to the Ministry of Justice in which it requested that legislators annul the laws of incompatibilities, which prohibited persons from assuming positions as judges or prosecutors in places where they had been born or had resided for an extended period of time. The academy recommended in its place the implementation of an appointment policy that would give preference to candidates from the jurisdiction of the vacancy.[134] In 1896 it sent another proposal, calling for legislation that would grant defendants and witnesses the right to use Catalan in court.[135] As a result, judges and prosecutors would have to be Catalan. As the president of the Academy of Jurisprudence, Joan Josep Permanyer i Ayats proclaimed, "Nobody, absolutely nobody can be a priest in a religion he does not profess. Hence, Catalans have to be . . . those in Catalonia who administer justice and apply the law."[136]

Another major consequence was that the next generation of lawyers became indoctrinated in the tenets of Catalanism. In 1904 the leadership of the first nationalist political party, the Regionalist League, was placed in the hands of three young lawyers, Lluís Duran i Ventosa, Enric Prat de la Riba, and Francesc Cambó, who had begun their political careers as leaders of the Catalan Student Center and had become politically awakened as law students during the Article 15 campaign and its aftermath.[137] Son of Manuel Duran, Lluís Duran i Ventosa was yet another visible example of generational change. In many respects, the activism of these young men grew out of the typical frustrations of an idealistic youth upset with the overly pragmatic approaches of their fathers and mentors. However, there was also a materialistic source to their discontent. These individuals grew up in an atmosphere in which law students faced an overcrowded bar and cloudy horizons and were incensed at the lack of dynamism and opportunity within an oligarchic state, which had produced such obtuse pieces of legislation as the Civil Code with its odd combination of general rules and exceptional appendixes. The central government was not equipped to handle the more pressing needs of industry. As Lluís Duran i Ventosa wrote in 1905, "He who does not know, who does not feel, who does not live the life of industry and of commerce, cannot pretend to solve its conflicts."[138]

The successful defense of Catalan law set the stage for other professions to push forth parallel demands. Lawyers had developed a potent formula, which pedagogues, priests, doctors, and architects were eager to emulate. During the World Fair of 1888, eight professional conferences convened in Barcelona, an occurrence that evidenced the presence of a vibrant civil society capable of challenging the long-established pact between Catalan industrial interests and state oligarches.[139] Whereas official celebrations praised the progress and ingenuity of the nation of Spain, the professional meetings relayed a more ambiguous message. At the National Conference on Pedagogy, for example, a few teachers proposed the need to incorporate Catalan language instruction into the classroom.[140] By the late nineteenth century, professional elites no longer only stood shoulder to shoulder with business and political leaders but responded to the concerns, pressures, and demands of their rank and files, the professionalized middle classes who increasingly faced problems of employment, found little official outlet for their concerns, and were warming to proposals to decentralize the state. In 1890 linguists launched the "linguistic campaign" in the magazine *L'Avenç*, in which they expressed the need to write dictionaries and grammar books and to publish technical studies that could establish uniform standards and reduce local variation.[141] In the *Revindication of Language in Primary Education*, Sebastià Farnès, a lawyer and an amateur folklorist, who had been active in the literary renaissance and the Article 15 campaign, explained that neither romantic revival nor scholarly studies could alone ensure the survival of language: it was also necessary to pressure Madrid to revise education laws so that Catalan could be taught in primary school.[142] Interestingly, it was the church that first entered into a protracted political conflict over language. In 1900 the bishop of Barcelona issued a pastoral, instructing priests to preach and to teach the catechism in Catalan language, sparking debates in the Spanish Cortes, reactions in the press, and a diplomatic row with the Vatican.[143]

Analyzing what occurred in Catalonia can help shed light on the emergence of nationalism elsewhere. Literary revival is often regarded as the first step of a nationalist movement — the so-called phase A, to borrow Miroslav

Hroch's terminology. However, this does not mean that romanticism teleologically evolves into nationalism. Not all cultural renaissances move into phase B, the organization of political parties able to contest elections and gain representation. For every such revival that grew into a full-fledged political movement, another remained stillborn.[144] Revivalism in Wales, Cornwall, Brittany, Occitania, and numerous other places never gave birth to political parties capable of convincing much of the populace of their mission. To be sure, organizations of romanticist intellectuals do not spawn nationalism by magically seizing the minds of a populace who, convinced by the power of the written word, imagine a community in order to overcome the isolating and atomizing experience of modernity.[145] Rather, nascent expressions of cultural nationalism must be carried forth by interested groups who have something to gain by it, and who possess the motivation, the access to resources, the prestige, and the skills to vie for control — or to demand a reorganization — of state.[146] In Catalonia, this is what occurred. Catalanism was, in many respects, a corporatist initiative, led by lawyers and like-minded professionals who converted a literary movement into a political one. Having done so, they dragged the rest of the middle classes in their wake.

7 Conclusion and Epilogue
THE SILVER AGE OF THE PROFESSION

> Lawyers have been involved in all the movements of political society in Europe for five hundred years. Sometimes they have served as instruments of political power, sometimes they have taken political power as an instrument.
> ∽ Alexis de Tocqueville, *Democracy in America* (1835)

> If the legal profession of the present day manifests at all typical ideological affinities to various power groups, its members are inclined to stand on the side of "order," which in practice means that they will take the side of the "legitimate" authoritarian political power that happens to predominate at any given moment. In this respect, they differ from the lawyers of the English and French revolutionary periods and of the period of the enlightenment in general.
> ∽ Max Weber, "Economy and Law (Sociology of Law),"
>   in *Economy and Society* (1914)

Conclusion

Looking back on the history of Barcelona lawyers over the long nineteenth century, even the most skeptical cannot help but take notice. When Charles III ascended to the throne in 1759, the bar was a shadow of its old self: a few dozen litigators discreetly went about their business, representing clients in court, conscious that better days lay in the past. A century later, lawyers had regained much of their lost power, prestige, and influence. Practitioners of diverse though broadly liberal beliefs, led by conservative men of order, exploited opportunities in the industrial city and projected their image back in time as curators of the laws and customs of the ancient principality. Success brought its attendant problems. A legal career appealed to persons from various walks of life, swelling ranks and increasing competition. Faced with adverse circumstances, lawyers looked beyond the courtroom to the market and the state for work and used corporate associations to defend interests and to seek new opportunities. By the turn of the twentieth century, a new generation headed an emerging nationalist movement that strove to conquer significant levels of self-government for Catalonia. To be sure, the bar never reached the lofty heights of the seventeenth century when lawyers had constituted a larger percentage of population, when lawsuits had been a more common means of dispute resolution, and when elite advocates and judges had formed the bulwark of a *noblesse de robe*. However, by all accounts, the nineteenth century was a veritable "silver age."

In many respects, the history of Barcelona lawyers paralleled that of their colleagues elsewhere. The evolution of the bar from liberalism to conservatism to corporatism broadly reflects the history of the bar in western continental Europe. In many countries, the bar found itself at a historical nadir under absolutism when royal administrators, many recruited from the army, usurped various areas of dispute resolution previously undertaken by courts. Lawyers, however, reacted to this decline in power. They abandoned their exclusive preoccupation with traditional sources, incorporated philosophical ideas about utility and happiness into legal reasoning, and endowed practical jurisprudence with scholarly prestige. They divorced themselves from the stale idea of urban nobility and exchanged it for a professional ethos of probity, expertise, reason, and talent. During the revolutionary era, many lawyers sensed opportunities and positioned themselves as spokesmen of the people and technocrats of the state. With liberal reforms, they reaped rewards. Procedural codes gave lawyers a greater latitude to make their cases and allowed them to enter forums where their presence had been previously resented and resisted. The increased use and importance of public hearings raised their profile. The reorganization of the judiciary created more courts, staffed with full-time salaried personnel, able to accommodate more lawsuits.

If the revolutionary era was the stage upon which the liberal profession emerged in Europe, then industrialization and the consolidation of the constitutional state was the backdrop for the rise of a conservative one. During the mid-nineteenth century, lawyers everywhere recuperated lost prestige and reinvented a historic image of the bar as a beacon of order, a fountain of erudition, and a guardian of justice and liberty. Leading advocates depicted this newfound charisma as an everlasting feature of the profession, originating in Rome and continuing through the Middle Ages and the Renaissance; by so doing, they erased the problematic epochs of absolutism and revolution from institutional memories. With respect to legal knowledge, jurists reasserted their monopoly on interpretation after it had been temporarily threatened by the codification movement, which in its heyday had boldly (and erroneously) proclaimed to have obviated the need for jurisprudence. The law itself was portrayed as fostering social harmony and economic development, even though daily practice — evictions, bankruptcies, partnership disputes, inheritance battles, labor conflicts, unjust convictions and acquittals, and the like — taught contradictory lessons. Despite frequent ridicule and critique, a legal career appealed to children of the growing middle classes and other walks of life, causing the profession to become saturated. In response to limited opportunities in the courtroom, lawyers developed careers in business, politics, and public and private administration. In the meantime, associations shifted priorities from upholding the humanist heritage of the bar and protecting the liberty of citizens to defending and promoting the corporate interests of its members. This broad history describes not only the Barcelona bar but also those of western Europe.

In light of these conclusions, it is worth revisiting the theories of Max Weber, which still constitute a baseline for the analysis of law and lawyers in the modern age. How do Weber's ideas stack up against this history of advocates in western continental Europe? In his *Economy and Society* (1914), Weber presented a brief but penetrating account of the political evolution of the bar. His narrative is similar to what has been presented in these pages, although his reasons for the transformation are quite different. To Weber, lawyers had constituted a "strong opposition to patriarchal powers" during "bourgeois revolutions of modern times." In a like manner, he recognized the bar had turned conservative thereafter; by the outset of the twentieth century, it had come to support "'legitimate' authoritarian political power." To account for this metamorphosis, he explained that lawyers had joined revolutionary causes throughout the continent because they had been propelled by their ingrained belief in "formal equality of the law." This, in turn, grew out of law's formal rationality that had crystallized in the early modern period. Weber also recognized that a lawyer was "a private person working for a living" who possessed diverse clienteles and a "fluctuating social status." Because of their place in society and the imperatives of the law itself, lawyers were dedicated to ensuring the "security of the individual" and defending "liberty." Once a constitutional state had secured individual rights and liberties, however, lawyers naturally aligned themselves with "order."[1]

As Weber himself was certainly aware, the history of lawyers was more dialectical than he suggests, so it would be unfair, and rather uninformative, to recur to the predictable attack of insisting that the path to modernity was sinuous rather than straight. His analysis can be critiqued on two more fundamental grounds. First, Weber did not appreciate the importance of politics and chose to ignore the strained relationship between advocates and absolutism. During the eighteenth century, the bar witnessed many of its previous functions usurped by the royal bureaucracy and the army, which arguably wielded bodies of knowledge that were just as formally rational as the law, and from whom lawyers doubtlessly learned much. During the late eighteenth century, reformers throughout Europe lumped the bar together with the aristocracy as components of the "unproductive classes" and designed policies aimed to constrict their independence. In response, lawyers abandoned their myopic preoccupation with traditional sources and authorities, advertised the utility of advocacy in society, engaged in economic and philosophical debates, and entered the political arena and the public sphere. Tocqueville was keenly aware of this history when he contended that French lawyers had become "active agents of revolution" because they had been excluded from politics under absolutism. To Tocqueville, lawyers throughout all of Europe had the potential to take "power as a political instrument" when it was in their interests.[2] To be sure, the revolutionary activities of so many students and lawyers, in towns and cities throughout continental Europe and the Americas, was not due to an unshakable belief in formal equality — a principle that was arguably congruent with enlightened absolutism — but was a consequence of the bar's increasingly hostile relationship with the absolutist state and its awareness of the vast opportunities available under a constitutionalist one.

Second, Weber's contention that procedural equality made lawyers predisposed to defend liberty and order is false. Although the continental legal tradition was more formalistic than its rivals, there does not appear to be any inherent link between proceduralism and liberalism. To cite the most obvious comparison, continental lawyers were not more liberal than English or North American ones despite the fact that continental legal systems were far more formal and proceduralistic. What is more, Weber overplayed the influence of formalism in continental law. During the eighteenth and nineteenth centuries, utilitarianism, historicism, and even romanticism wormed their way into and ate away at rule-based adjudication. In courtroom practice, these influences loomed in the background even when they could not be articulated in briefs or decisions. Outside the courtroom, they were a central feature of debate and discussion. It must also be stressed that lawyers grew to accept the most formally rational innovation of them all — codes — only after they had been assured that codification would be undertaken in consonance with the historical foundations of the legal tradition and not derived from philosophical axioms. Following the promulgation of codes, jurists and practitioners throughout Europe successfully conserved their coveted positions as interpreters rather than succumbing to an assigned role as positivists applying rules. Finally, it is worth mentioning that Weber's contention that the structure of legal knowledge made lawyers and bureaucrats reflexively inclined to defend liberty and order would be tragically undermined in the twentieth century when cold-blooded, procedural rationality was the dominant mode of reasoning behind what Hannah Arendt would famously describe as the banality of evil.

Weber's observation that the lawyer was a "private person working for a living" with a "fluctuating social status" was more important than what he perceived. As emphasized throughout this book, it is necessary to analyze the social history of lawyers, from where they came and how they engaged with political power, in order to understand the evolution of bar. With respect to legal knowledge, Weber can arguably be turned on his head. If anything, lawyers were able to adapt, better than any other profession, to epochal changes within society, politics, and economy because of the flexibility, and not the rigidity, of jurisprudence. The hallowed place of interpretation within the Western legal tradition — despite the continent's putative dependency on statute — allowed lawyers to survive and thrive during an era of tremendous transformations in the organization of knowledge. Lawyers were not wedded to objective formalism but, on the contrary, were remarkably adept at reconciling law with the changing exigencies of society in the long nineteenth century. They adroitly reinterpreted law to make a smooth transition from feudalism to capitalism and propounded a whole series of reforms, which would become centerpieces of the constitutionalist state. The bar produced elites able and eager to fill roles in various regimes, ranging from closed liberal systems with restricted franchises to open and democratic ones. During the twentieth century, lawyers remained flexible and proved themselves mildly comfortable within authoritarian (although not totalitarian) dictatorships.

EXCEPTIONALITY AND NATIONALISM

In many respects, Barcelona has been an ideal place to examine the history of a continental bar. It was a city that experienced the telltale signs of modernity. It was obviously not as enlightened as Naples or Edinburgh, but educated classes received secular and scientific ideas and blended them with traditionalist and religious sources of knowledge. Spain did not undergo as utopian a revolution as France, but it did suffer an agonic and prolonged period of revolution and reaction. Catalonia was not as industrialized as Lancashire, but it was one of the more industrialized regions on the continent. Barcelona was not the center of such a vast empire as were London and Paris, but it was the chief economic contact with Cuba, perhaps the most lucrative colony of any European country in the nineteenth century. Catalan nationalism would never shake the international order to the extent of Italian, German, Polish, or Serbian nationalism, but it proved to be an everlasting, nonviolent movement. In sum, Barcelona lawyers experienced a complete gamut of societal changes in the nineteenth century, and for this reason, their study has provided a window into viewing the history of lawyers on the continent.

The history of Barcelona advocates also exhibited many distinguishing features. As would be the case upon examining any group of advocates, it is easy to trawl through the narrative and pick out characteristics that appear exceptional rather than typical. For example, during the Old Regime, lawyers had long been accustomed to working within an atmosphere of open competition given that a guild had not existed since the fourteenth century. This distinguished them from those bars in Europe with *numeri clausi*. The weight of tradition was reflected in the professoriate's love of Roman law, but, taken as a whole, the bar entered the modern era with light historical baggage and burdened by little ritual. With respect to the revolutionary era, it is not clear the extent to which the lawyer-militiaman appeared elsewhere. A lawyer in uniform touting a bayonet was probably not so frequent a sight outside Iberia, Mediterranean Europe, and the Americas. It was quite common in the United States, though, where men like Andrew Jackson took up arms and law; English barristers, in contrast, would be caught with rifle in hand only when off shooting grouse. In the nineteenth century, there do not appear to be many jural cultures where law became so imbued with romanticism. All the same, these remain open questions. Until further studies appear on lawyers during the Old Regime and revolution, and on the influence of romanticism on legal knowledge, or so many other subjects for that matter, it is difficult to ascertain whether Barcelona lawyers were truly exceptional in these regards.

The single characteristic that distinguishes the history of Barcelona lawyers from others, however, is their nationalism. Nowhere did lawyers defend a "native" body of private law from uniform codification and then launch a political movement in its wake. Linguistic and religious conflicts often bred nationalist movements, but legal disputes did not usually take off in this direction. However, when understood in a broad context, events in Catalonia seem less surprising. In England, Germany, France, and other countries, jurists and political theorists had long linked law to history, identity, and ethnicity. According to Hotman and Montesquieu, French law was said to derive from the historic liberties of the Gauls and Franks. To Blackstone and generations before him, English law had its roots in the ancient constitution of the Britons, Saxons, and Danes. To Savigny, German law and custom evolved in harmony with *Volksgeist*.[3] These theories, today discredited by legal philosophers and historians but still echoed by lawyers and laypeople alike, were tremendously appealing in the nineteenth century.[4] Scholars, practicing lawyers, and all sorts of people bandied about sophisticated and hackneyed ideas about law, spirit, and nation. Lawyers not only claimed to uphold universal, rational principles of justice and to constitute an independent arm of constitutional political systems that shielded society from despotism but also portrayed themselves as the curators of laws, practices, and customs that maintained the vitality, health, and ingenuity of the nation.

Barcelona jurists imbibed these influences. If they departed from the script, it was because they framed generalizations and stereotypes within the history of the principality of Catalonia rather than the monarchy of Spain. This outcome was not inevitable. The legal histories of Castile and Catalonia consisted of a similar mélange of so-called Roman and Germanic sources, which could have been read, and were read from time to time, to be complementary. But disagreements over the contents of a Spanish civil code concerning sensitive issues of family, inheritance, and property, combined with the quotidian exigencies of legal practice, led jurists to compile laws, write guidebooks, and ultimately "construct" a Catalan civil law. By the 1880s, many lawyers contended that Catalan and Castilian law were polar opposites or, at the very least, irreconcilable. The ensuing political conflict was exceptional but was the result of a clash of some rather banal conceptions that had been floating around Europe for some time. In retrospect, it is perhaps surprising that such disputes did not erupt elsewhere, but it is possible to point to cases where something similar was afoot. The Austrians, for example, imposed their code throughout the empire, and, when given the chance, Venetian and Hungarian jurists instantly exchanged it for what they believed to be more authentic "Italian" and "Hungarian" legal traditions. In Britain, the existence of Scots law was always an underlying source of tension.[5] In these places, juridical conflict was latent. In Spain, it was patent.

In Catalonia, overcrowding contributed to nationalism's appeal. As we have seen, the Barcelona bar became saturated by the latter decades of the nineteenth century. Overcrowding was particularly acute during times of economic downturn, such as the 1890s, when the market proved less capable of absorbing university graduates, and it likely reached epidemic proportions in the twentieth century. To many young lawyers experiencing troubles breaking into private practice, the prospect of self-government proved enticing, because it promised to erect a future Catalan bureaucracy centered on Barcelona, which, in the long run, would offer public-sector jobs to men with legal education. Elite practitioners, for their part, could also look forward to the increased availability of executive and magisterial posts. This is not to say that the drive for home rule solely responded to corporatist concerns. Lawyers and others believed that persons familiar with the language, laws, and customs of the region, and with the complex needs of an industrial society, could better address the moral and material interests of Catalans than politicians, bureaucrats, and Supreme Court magistrates of the oligarchic state centered in Madrid. Whether they were correct is a matter of opinion, but the contention is not easily rebutted.

Overcrowding did not lead to nationalism everywhere, but it did entail recognizable consequences that will need to be studied on a country-by-country basis. The theme has periodically surfaced within sociology and social history. In 1937 the sociologist Walter Kotschnig's *Unemployment in the Learned Professions* argued that a sea of frustrated unemployed university graduates fueled the spread of Nazism in Germany.[6] More than three decades later, the historian Lenore O'Boyle pointed out that an "excess of educated men" had been identified as a problem in all of continental Europe since much earlier; during the Revolutions of 1830 and 1848, many observers put forward the theory that out-of-work lawyers and other university students were the chief agitators.[7] In Spain, the novelist Benito Pérez Galdós portrayed the existence of excess lawyers as an infectious social disease. He reasoned that lawyers who were unable to find lawsuits to make a living were not predisposed to enter society's productive or entrepreneurial ranks, but instead sought to create and fill state jobs, swelling the ranks of the bureaucracy and becoming an intolerable financial burden to the populace. When this was not enough, they stirred up trouble and engendered revolutions.[8]

Before drawing conclusions, a more thorough study of surpluses is needed. A civilian imperial administration in Britain appears to have provided outlets for lawyers and young professionals.[9] In Spain, where colonial governance in the nineteenth century (unlike during the early modern period) was primarily a military enterprise, few public posts were available for lawyers or other professionals overseas. On the basis of the experience of Barcelona lawyers, a working hypothesis could be that excess practitioners initially found work in business, whereas by the late nineteenth century the universities' capacity to churn out men with law degrees outpaced the market's ability to absorb them. By the twentieth century, lawyers and other professionals looked to the state, in addition to the market, to solve the problem of middle-class employment. This had different consequences. In Germany, Hungary, France, and elsewhere, it contributed to anti-Semitism, xenophobia, and misogyny. In the 1920s and 1930s, many students and lawyers felt threatened by the presence of Jews, women, and the children of immigrants at the bar, and they joined political movements that pressured governments to limit the access of these "minorities" to universities, licenses, and state jobs.[10] Overcrowding not only bred discrimination but also had more socially beneficial consequences. The rise of the welfare state was not unrelated to the demands of lawyers, doctors, architects, psychologists, teachers, and engineers, who lobbied legislators to expand public works, education, housing, health, and legal aid. In so doing, professionals presented themselves as experts with the requisite scientific knowledge able to minister to society's welfare if given lifetime jobs and pensions within state-run institutions (schools, hospitals, rehabilitation clinics, legal aid centers, courts, etc.).[11]

When examining a legal profession anywhere, a parallel list of peculiarities would no doubt arise. In one respect, this history may appear to be hyperbolic. During the eighteenth century, the Barcelona bar was numerically decimated by the onslaught of absolutism; during the revolutionary era, lawyers turned overwhelmingly liberal; in the industrial age, the leadership grew quite conservative; in the late nineteenth century, romanticist and historicist theories led to a very explicit form of juridical nationalism. Obviously, the experience of lawyers cannot be separated from the peculiarities of Catalan history. After all, Barcelona was the traditional capital of an ancient principality where much old law and custom were still alive. It was a revolutionary and liberal city amid a traditionalist countryside undergoing tremendous social upheavals as a result of industrialization. It was a southern European city that experienced a northern European pattern of economic development.

A Mediterranean port with strong commercial ties to the Atlantic world, it was surrounded by the foothills of the Pyrenees where Ultramontanism flourished. While educated urban dwellers looked to Paris as a model, much of society was pulled by the antagonistic influences of Manchester and Rome. To appreciate such stark contrasts, one only has to gaze at the creations of fin-de-siècle architects such as Antoni Gaudí and Lluís Domènech and observe the juxtaposition of exalted Gothic spiritualism with the iron, glass, and mathematical precision of the industrial age. Architectural aesthetics had much in common with legal ones. Nonetheless, until further social histories of lawyers are written, we can only guess at what they have in store. In the end, this history of the Barcelona bar — its evolution from liberalism, to conservatism, to corporatism — likely reflects that of others in Europe.

Epilogue: The End of the Silver Age?

Because we have come this far, it is worth providing a broad overview of the twentieth century, even if this leaves as many questions unanswered as answered. In 1901 the conservative nationalist party, the Regionalist League, first contested elections and won four out of six seats from Barcelona to the Congress of Deputies. In 1906 the part-time juridical writer and full-time political organizer and propagandist Enric Prat de la Riba published *Catalan Nationality*, which became recognized as the bible of the movement. Within its pages, the influence of juridical ideas abounded. It paid homage to historical-school jurisprudence, bristled with romantic and medievalist visions of an idealized patriarchal agrarian society, and reasoned that the continued vitality of law and language constituted living proof of the strength and durability of national spirit. It based the demand for self-government on logic derived from the Herderian theory of national self-determination, and added new fin-de-siècle "sciences" of the nation into the mix.[12] Many of these latter ideas had first appeared in the *Catalan Juridical Review*, a scholarly journal founded in 1895. Within its pages, his column "Juridical Miscellanea" introduced his colleagues at the bar to quasi-biological theories of the nation — Scipio Sighele's collective psychology, Herbert Spencer's social Darwinism, and Vacher de Lapouge's racial anti-Semitism.[13] In the early twentieth century, Catalan nationalism became infested with biological conceptions of race and ethnicity, incorporated the myth of decadence and pangenesis, and regarded imperialism as its historic mission.[14] All the same, it maintained a citizenship ideal that privileged the *ius soli* over the *ius sanguinis* and remained undergirded by historicist and broadly liberal ideas.[15]

The Regionalist League was the dominant nationalist party for the remainder of the Restoration Monarchy (1876–1923). Lawyers, priests, linguists, architects, professors, pedagogues, and industrialists no longer had to carry on isolated protests to make their voice heard in Madrid but could filter demands through the league and other nationalist parties, which could negotiate an array of concerns with the central government. Accomplishments were modest but steady. In 1907 Enric Prat de la Riba, then president of the Barcelona deputation, founded the Institute of Catalan Studies, which sponsored projects to promote and to modernize language, law, and history and to conserve and restore the region's archaeological and artistic patrimony. In 1912 the deputation inaugurated a school of public administration, the purpose of which was to train technocrats for a future Catalan bureaucracy. And in 1914 the Spanish Cortes sanctioned the creation of a Catalan Mancomunitat. This consisted of an amalgamation of the powers of the four provincial Catalan deputations. Although a far cry from an autonomous parliament and executive, it did have the symbolic effect of restoring Barcelona as the capital of Catalonia rather than of merely a province. During the Spanish Second Republic (1931–36), Catalonia first acquired political autonomy.

During the twentieth century, the bar came under intense pressure as Barcelona experienced massive demographic growth and severe episodes of industrial violence. A handful of advocates who represented workers, trade unions, students, and nationalists were persecuted by civil and military authorities during the Restoration Monarchy and the dictatorships of Miguel de Primo de Rivera (1923–29) and Francisco Franco (1939–1975). College deans were called on to mediate disputes, to defend the ability of counsel to carry out duties, and to address delicate situations when advocates were censured, suspended, or jailed for overzealous defenses, illicit affiliations, client meetings that doubled as unauthorized political assemblies, or perfidious ideas. Military regimes harnessed the College of Lawyers and audited its activities. This was arguably a professional in addition to a political conflict: lawyers lost their political preeminence to army officers, who had proclaimed themselves society's new guardians against the twin threats of Bolshevism and peripheral nationalism. The college did not make any heroic institutional stands to defend liberty in the face of dictatorship. At times, it offered some symbolic but perfunctory gestures. In 1924 the dean Amadeu Hurtado resigned after refusing to publish the *Judicial Guide of Catalonia* in Spanish language. In the 1960s the dean Frederic Roda refused to attend a dinner in which he and other municipal dignitaries were invited to meet Francisco Franco; he left his seat empty so that the dictator would be forced to take notice of the protest.[16] As the Francoist regime was on its last legs, the college began to open space to young democratic (and communist, socialist, nationalist, and feminist) lawyers to carry out meetings dedicated to human rights issues and in defense of imprisoned regime opponents. In 1970, for example, the college voted to lend tepid support to lawyers participating in a statewide strike against the Tribunal of Public Order, then the chief judicial arm of the Francoist repression.[17]

As could be expected, the Spanish Civil War (1936–39) was a bleak time for justice. Barcelona and Catalonia were within the Republican zone, dominated by a communist-led Popular Front government. As the war dragged on, the bar disintegrated. Some lawyers worked within revolutionary courts and the bureaucracy, while others joined the republican war effort in one capacity or another, and some skipped over to the other side. Most sought shelter or fled into exile. The communist secret police arrested a few lawyers, associated with "bourgeois" political parties. These individuals had to defend themselves against accusations of spying or harboring counterrevolutionary sympathies.[18] One advocate observed that of 973 lawyers who had been on college lists in 1936, only around 100 were still enrolled in 1938.[19] Of those who remained in practice, a few found work by taking on defenses of men and women accused of political crimes. This was treacherous activity, for defense lawyers feared becoming targets of accusations themselves. Revolutionary courts were staffed with ambitious and cruel prosecutors and judges, responsible for the imprisonment and murder of many. Flimsy evidence, fabulous testimony, contrived procedures, and stacked juries were the order of the day. Although defense lawyers won some favorable verdicts and secured some hard-earned pardons amid trying circumstances, many innocent men and women were sent to prison or died by firing squad. Gabriel Avilés, a liberal agnostic, initially supported the Republic and labored as a defense lawyer during the war. His experience left him so stunned and distraught that he welcomed the arrival of Francoist armies in 1939, unaware that the Generalissimo was about to carry out abominations of justice on an even grander scale.[20]

Upon his victory, Franco imposed martial law to adjudge "crimes" committed during the war. As might be expected, few procedural safeguards existed in military tribunals designed to prosecute persons considered "leftists," "extremists," "separatists," "reds," "sacrileges," and other enemies of the nation. Military defense lawyers had neither the means nor the will to mount adequate defenses and often limited their actions to requesting the judge to lighten the expected penalty. Hearings were often cursory affairs, and it was commonplace for defendants to be adjudged and executed en masse. Unfortunately, no one ever came forward to publish a book, to confess his sins, to detail the futility of his efforts, or to expose the fallaciousness of the proceedings. Ordinary lawyers were prohibited from taking on defenses, although it appears that some military courts in Spain hired a few civilian advocates to fill out a repressive apparatus that was quickly overwhelmed by the sheer volume of its caseload. Postwar judicial and extrajudicial assassinations, together with prison deaths, numbered in the thousands in Catalonia. In the early 1940s, however, the killings began to wind down; and by the mid-1940s, many death sentences had been commuted and almost all political prisoners had been paroled.[21]

At the College of Lawyers, the Francoist regime appointed a dean and board in ideological harmony with the fascist party, the Falange. Upon taking office, the board issued a statement, honoring "colleagues and friends who died in defense of God and Fatherland in the battlefield and to others who were vilely assassinated by the red hoard of the Marxist domination." It later dispatched a telegram to Franco, in which it expressed its adhesion to "The Victorious National Army and its glorious *Caudillo*, the head of New Spain."[22] From March to June 1940, the college was forced to operate a Decontamination Tribunal to adjudge whether practitioners were morally fit to return to practice. Of the forty-five advocates whose licenses it revoked, it appears that most, if not all, were already in exile or jail, although it did hand out temporary suspensions to a few individuals who would have been free to practice had they not been betrayed by colleagues for suspect morals. The tribunal was less invasive than that of the College of Doctors, where many more perfectly qualified professionals, who were not otherwise subject to Francoist justice, had their licenses suspended. Among those on the decontamination list was Lluís Companys, an esteemed labor lawyer and republican politician, president of the autonomous government of Catalonia during the Second Republic and Civil War. Found hiding in Vichy France, Companys was returned to Barcelona where he faced a military tribunal in 1940 and, like many before him, was adjudged guilty and shot.[23]

Following the allied victory in the Second World War, international pressure forced Franco to whitewash the regime's image and soften its governing ideology. As a result, he appointed more moderate deans to the Barcelona College of Lawyers as he did with other colleges and similar associations throughout Spain. As a result, the Falangist board was replaced by one more representative of the rank and file. One lawyer described the postwar bar as dominated by liberals who considered Francoism the lesser of two evils, but he also remarked that a group of Falangists still wielded some influence as late as the 1960s. In the early 1970s, Falangist lawyers still made much noise at meetings with their typically crude and provocative tone. Regime opponents, who began to enter the college in droves in the late 1950s, were initially treated with disdain, ridicule, and paranoia. Attempts to speak Catalan at meetings were initially met with derisive whistles.[24]

Young lawyers began showing democratic colors in the late 1950s in concert with much of the urban middle classes. One lawyer, who described herself as apolitical, remembered that the law school, by the mid-1950s, was "one-quarter Francoist, one-quarter apolitical, and one-half leftist."[25] The regime first permitted elections to the college deanship in December 1958. In these elections, the professor Josep Pi, an affable man of liberal-democratic tendencies, trounced the incumbent dean, Francesc Condomines, a Franco appointee of moderate sensibilities. The next elections in December 1962 were also telling. In a contest depicted by activists as a choice between "fascism" and "democracy," members elected Frederic Roda, a visible opponent of the dictatorship. His board of directors included Miquel Roca, a high-profile organizer of the student movement (and later an eminently successful mercantilist and centrist-nationalist politician), and Montserrat Avilés, probably the first woman to serve on any law college board in Spain. In tandem with her husband, Albert Fina, and other colleagues from the Communist Party, Avilés was then starting what would become a large and influential labor practice. Avilés and Fina emerged as leaders of the labor movement and the anti-Francoist dissent, suffered spells in prison, and were targets of frequent persecution. In the months preceding the death of Franco, their law firm went by the name "October."[26] The dean Frederic Roda died in 1968 amid a judicial conflict typical of the period. He had spent the afternoon at the Palace of Justice, arguing with a judge on behalf of a group of lawyers seeking access to seventeen university students arrested for participating in a nationalist-democratic sit-in. After proving unsuccessful, he left exasperated. While driving home, he suffered a heart attack.[27]

In the twentieth century, the relationship between Catalan civil law and the Spanish Civil Code remained an ongoing point of discord. The civil code conflicts of the 1880s did not settle matters but inaugurated an epoch in which much juridical debate was expressed through a nationalist idiom. In the 1890s a series of controversial Supreme Court decisions paved the way for many provisions of the code to be applied in Catalonia as a "supplement."[28] In 1920 one commentator counted that the court had applied some 730 out of 1,976 articles of the code in Catalonia. In 1958 another divined that more than half were in force.[29] In 1960 a regime-appointed commission of Catalan jurists published an official "compilation," which was roughly a compromise between an "appendix" and a "volume" of independent laws. Since the death of Francisco Franco in 1975 and the transition to democracy, Catalan private law and public law have undergone a sweeping transformation. In a referendum in 1979, Catalans resoundingly approved a Statute of Autonomy. The autonomous government, the Generalitat, constitutionalized the compilation in 1984 and later replaced much of it with a Successions Code (1991), a Family Law Code (1998), and other selected pieces of legislation. Today, the Generalitat is in the process of promulgating a full Catalan Civil Code in piecemeal fashion. Parts are already operative, and the rest will come into force shortly.[30] The new Statute of Autonomy (2006) grants the Generalitat full legislative authority over all civil material.

Since the advent of democracy, the College of Lawyers has elected deans ideologically compatible with the dominant parties in Catalonia, the liberal-conservative nationalists (CiU) and the socialists (PSC). In accordance with the Statute of Autonomy of 1979 and subsequent linguistic normalization laws, Catalan and Spanish are now the official languages of administration and justice, and civil-service candidates for the Generalitat are required to pass a Catalan-language exam. Litigants, witnesses, judges, and lawyers are permitted express themselves in the language of their choice, and translation services exist to address linguistic difficulties. These laws, however, have not produced the results that many had wished. Writing in the mid-1980s, one lawyer lamented that Catalan was barely used in judicial proceedings.[31] Today, generations trained under linguistic normalization have caused the situation to evolve slowly, but Spanish still dominates over Catalan in courts in Barcelona. The administration of justice remains a competency of the state rather than of the autonomous community. Even today, the majority of laws applied in Catalan courts are Spanish laws, judges are recruited from all over Spain, many litigants do not speak Catalan well, and some do not speak it at all. At Barcelona universities, even native law students still prefer to write exams in Spanish.³² With the arrival of growing numbers of immigrants from Latin America, Europe, and North Africa, who also prefer Spanish to Catalan, issues of language and justice promise to be a permanent feature of the political landscape.

The most obvious change in the composition of the bar during the twentieth century was the presence of women. The first women with law degrees graduated from the University of Barcelona in the early 1880s, but they were not allowed to enroll in the College of Lawyers or appear in court.³³ In the 1920s, Spain followed European trends and permitted women to practice law as well as other professions. The first woman matriculated in the Barcelona College in 1926, and, during the Second Republic, there were a half dozen at the bar, a few of whom continued to practice after the Civil War. All were low earners, and we know nothing about any of them. Two women deputies to the Cortes, the lawyers Clara Campoamor and Victoria Kent, were leading socialists, but we do not have information on such women in Barcelona. Still, one cannot help wondering what the practicing lawyer in Barcelona with the intriguing name Llibertat (Liberty) García was engaged in during the Republic.³⁴

Under Franco, women could attend university and practice law, but they were not permitted to serve as judges until 1961. Regime propaganda discouraged girls from pursuing a career, deluging them with guilt-ridden reminders of their obligation to become obedient wives and loving mothers.³⁵ Against the grain of social expectation but supported by open-minded families, some attended university and went on to develop working law practices. They were a true minority. Women who entered the University of Barcelona law school in the mid-1950s numbered less than a dozen per cohort. The trailblazer was Carmen Moreno, who enrolled in the College of Lawyers in 1951, penetrated the middle echelons of the bar, and successfully practiced for more than a half century. She began her career defending "small-time crooks and dregs"³⁶ but, through persistence, earned a reputation as a formidable adversary and fine defense and labor lawyer. The most famous was Lidia Falcón, who graduated from law school in 1960 and went on to be a women's rights lawyer, political activist, playwright, and prolific author. Her early works included *Civil Rights of Women* (1963), *Labor Rights of Women* (1965), *Women in Society* (1973), and *In Hell: A Woman in the Prisons of Spain* (1977). In 1976 she founded the periodical *Vindicación Feminista* and in 1979 launched the Feminist Party of Spain. Still an activist, she has recently declared, "The [judicial] system is catastrophic. It is classist, misogynist, and racist."³⁷

Women who entered the bar in the 1950s and 1960s did not face overt discrimination, outside the frequent sexist remark, and some recall being treated well by judges and colleagues. Penal, labor, and family law were their preferred (and expected) destinations.[38] Ridicule, however, took place behind their backs. One lawyer recalls that Carmen Moreno was rumored to have participated in "perverse acts, the majority of a sexual nature . . . with her clients, which out of respect for her and for women in general, I will not recount."[39] Another recalls that another woman lawyer was sneered at for appearing in court while pregnant in the 1960s.[40] Of the pioneers, some practiced alone, others did so in tandem with husbands, and others benefited from the support and tutelage of a father, sibling, or other family member. For those who did not seek to develop a private practice, some entered the judiciary, worked for the municipality, or chose business. Lidia Falcón remembers being one of three female sole practitioners when she enrolled in the college in December 1960. The college was supportive, awarding her a prize that served to waive the exorbitant matriculation fee.[41] In 2006 the college elected its first woman as dean, and today women lawyers are found in the upper echelons of the judiciary, academia, and politics. Still, a glass ceiling exists. No woman lawyer heads a top mercantile law firm in Barcelona today.[42]

Whether the silver age has continued is a matter for debate. On one level, practicing lawyers face many of the same stresses as in the nineteenth century. As retiring advocates publish their memoirs, the bar remains caught in a familiar ideological net. One left-wing lawyer thinks that many of his colleagues discredit the honor of the profession. The "advisers to the rich, the heads of large law firms," he claims, "confuse their calling with that of capitalism and usury." "They only seek to make money without being worried by the fate of their victims."[43] In contrast, a successful mercantilist insists that "the lawyer is, by definition a defender of liberty. . . . Every lawsuit is an act of liberty. Every contract, a manifestation of liberty of commerce. . . . Every agreement, a triumph of the autonomy of will."[44] Meanwhile, the structure of the bar has changed drastically. Overcrowding has become endemic. Since the 1950s, the growth in the number of lawyers has outpaced that of the general population in all of Europe, and Barcelona is no exception. The latest list of college members exceeds 33,500. The perception is that the gap between highly paid mercantile and civil advocates and the rank and file dedicated to public defenses and low-paying work continues to widen.

In the twentieth century, the bar everywhere became converted from a "general estate to special interest" and no longer carries such influence outside matters that do not directly affect corporate concerns. Lawyers came to constitute a piece within the more complex mosaic of "professional" society.[45] They learned to share space with other professionals who had copied their methods of recruitment and training, their organizational strategies, and the cultural and discursive conventions inherent in the client-practitioner relationship in order to secure state-sanctioned licensing, to reduce competition, and to augment status, security, and profits. In the nineteenth century, doctors were the first to do so, and architects later came on board. Today, engineers, accountants, managers, brokers, teachers, realtors, bureaucrats, consultants, technicians, and a welter of others have carved out niches of expertise, leading to what has been convincingly labeled as the "professionalization of everyone."[46] Lawyers were forerunners. They designed behavior toward the state and the market. If their influence has become diluted with the emergence and heightened sophistication of other professions, and the increased popularity of law as a career choice has led to a bloated and consequently less agile membership, then they have plainly been victims of their own success.

Notes

ABBREVIATIONS

Archives

ACA   Arxiu de la Corona d'Aragó (Archive of the Crown of Aragon, Barcelona)
ACA, RA   Arxiu de la Corona d'Aragó, Real Audiència (Archive of the Crown of Aragon, Collection of the Royal Audiencia, Barcelona)
ACMJ   Archivo Central del Ministerio de Justicia (Ministry of Justice Archive, Madrid)
AGHUB   Arxiu General i Històric de la Universitat de Barcelona (Archive of the University of Barcelona, Barcelona)
AHMB   Arxiu Històric Municipal de Barcelona (Municipal Archive, Barcelona)
AHPB   Arxiu Històric de Protocols de Barcelona (Notarial Archive, Barcelona)
ANC   Arxiu Nacional de Catalunya (National Archive of Catalonia, Sant Cugat del Vallès)

Official Periodical Reports, Minutes, and Recorded Proceedings

CABAJD   Colegio de Abogados de Barcelona, Actas de la Junta Directiva (Minutes of the Board of Directors Meetings of the College of Lawyers, Barcelona)
CABAJG   Colegio de Abogados de Barcelona, Actas de la Junta General (Minutes of the Annual Meetings of the College of Lawyers, Barcelona)
CL   *Colección de las Leyes, Decretos y Declaraciones de las Cortes y de los Reales Decretos, Órdenes, Resoluciones, y Reglamentos Generales* (Collection of Laws, Royal Decrees, Royal Decrees, Orders, Resolutions and General Rules)
CPE   Comisión de Estadística, *Censo de población de España*; and Instituto Geográfico y Estadístico, *Censo de población de España* (Population Census of Spain)
DSC   *Diario de las Sesiones de Cortes* (Spanish Cortes, Record of Proceedings)
DSCCD   *Diario de las Sesiones de Cortes. Congreso de Diputados* (Spanish Cortes, Congress of Deputies, Record of Proceedings)
DSCS   *Diario de las Sesiones de Cortes. Senado* (Spanish Cortes, Senate, Record of Proceedings)
EACIC   Dirección General de Contribuciones, *Estadística administrativa de la Contribución Industrial y de Comercio* (Administrative Statistics for Taxes on Industry and Commerce)

GJC Guía judicial de Cataluña and Guia judicial de Catalunya (Judicial Guide of Catalonia)
IPBM Instituto Provincial de Barcelona, Memoria (Annual Report of the Public Secondary School of the Province of Barcelona)
LACB Lista de los abogados del Ilustre Colegio de la Ciudad de Barcelona (List of the Lawyers of the Illustrious College of Barcelona)
MGJSAT Ministerio de Gracia y Justicia. Solemne apertura de los Tribunales (Ministry of Justice, Opening Ceremonies of the Judicial Year)
UBMIP Universidad de Barcelona, Memoria del estado de instrucción pública (Annual Report of Public Education, University District of Barcelona)

Spanish Archival Terms

caja(s) caja(s) (boxes)
exp(s) expediente(s) (files)
leg(s) legajo(s) (bundles)
reg(s) registro(s) (registries)

CHAPTER 1

1. See Burke, *Royal College of San Carlos*; Ramsay, *Professional and Popular Medicine*; and Porter and Porter, *Patient's Progress*.
2. For Catalonia, see Puigvert, *Església, territori i sociabilitat*.
3. For Barcelona, see Bonnassie, *Cataluña mil años atrás*, 340–46; Freedman, "Catalan Lawyers and the Origins of Serfdom"; and Bensch, *Barcelona and Its Rulers*, 234–76. For Europe as a whole, see Brundage, *Medieval Origins of the Legal Profession*.
4. Martines, *Lawyers and Statescraft*; Bouwsma, "Lawyers and Early Modern Culture"; Prest, *Lawyers in Early Modern Europe*; Amelang, "Barristers and Judges"; and Leuwers, *L'invention du barreau français*.
5. For English lawyers, see Duman, *English and Colonial Bars*; Prest, *Rise of the Barristers*; Brooks, *Pettifoggers and Vipers of the Commonwealth* and *Lawyers, Litigation and English Society*; Lemmings, *Professors of the Law*; and May, *Bar and the Old Bailey*.
6. For France, see Berlanstein, *Barristers of Toulouse*; Fitzsimmons, *Parisian Order*; and Bell, *Lawyers and Citizens*. For Russia, see Huskey, *Russian Lawyers and the Soviet State*. For Germany, see Jarausch, *Unfree Professions*, and Ledford, *From General Estate to Special Interest*. For Hungary, see Kovács, *Politics of the Legal Profession*.
7. Some studies have traversed the nineteenth century. However, these are broad sociological overviews (rather than social histories) that focus on institutions, origins, and regulations. For Germany, Italy, and Switzerland, see Siegrist, *Advokat, Bürger und Staat*. For France, see Halpérin et al., *Avocats et notaires*, and Karpik, *French Lawyers*.
8. Polanyi, *Great Transformation*.

9. For an overview of the historians' critique of the sociological field of professionalism (with ample attention paid to the legal profession), see Burrage, "Introduction: The Professions in Sociology and History."
10. For some examples of this approach, see Siegrist, "Juridicalisation, Professionalisation, and the Occupational Culture of the Advocate," and Konttinen, "'Finland's Route of Professionalisation and Lawyer-Officials."
11. Weber, "Economy and Law (Sociology of Law)."
12. Bourdieu and Passeron, *Reproduction in Education, Society and Culture*, and Larson, *The Rise of Professionalism*.
13. Larson, "The Changing Functions of Lawyers," 446.
14. Althusser never addressed "professionals" or "intellectuals," as did Gramsci, but included them within the broad rubric of the "bourgeoisie." See Althusser, "Ideology and Ideological State Apparatuses," and Gramsci, "The Intellectuals."
15. Halliday and Karpik, "Politics Matter," 16.
16. Durkheim, *Professional Ethics and Civil Morals*.
17. Halliday and Karpik, "Politics Matter," 50.
18. De Vries, "The Industrial Revolution and the Industrious Revolution."
19. For a broad overview of Barcelona history from the Middle Ages to the present, see Fernández-Armesto, *Barcelona*.
20. For population, see table 1 in chapter 2.
21. Pella y Forgas, *Llibertats y antich govern de Catalunya*, 61.
22. Standard histories of European law routinely recognize the importance of the *Usatges* and the *Consolat del Mar*. See Berman, *Law and Revolution*, 310, 340–41; and Robinson, Fergus, and Gordon, *An Introduction to European Legal History*, 156–61, 201. English translations exist: *The Usatges of Barcelona* and *Consulate of the Sea*.
23. For the publications of Catalonia's medieval and early modern jurists, see Brocá, *Historia del derecho de Cataluña*, 386–404, 411–43.
24. For the number, size, and location of factories, see Thomson, *A Distinctive Industrialization*, 227–34.
25. Young, *Travels*, 40.
26. Bourgoanne, *Travels in Spain*, 1:291.
27. For a summary of the size of the midcentury industry, see Barnosell, *Orígens del sindicalisme català*, 117–32; and Garcia Balañà, *La fabricació de la fàbrica*, 15–55.
28. Moreno Fraginals, *El ingenio complejo*, 536.
29. The commercial foundation for industrial takeoff is explained in depth in Fradera, *Indústria i mercat*. For a nice summary of triangular trade routes, see Pascual, *Agricultura i industrialització a la Catalunya del segle XIX*, 196–97.
30. For figures and the geographical sources of migration, see Termes, "La immigració a Catalunya." For population figures, see Figuerola, *Estadística de Barcelona*, 34–37; and CPE (1857).
31. CPE (1897).
32. Rahola, "Comerç i indústria de Catalunya," 323.
33. For the army and civil governance in the province of Barcelona, see Risques

Corbella, *El govern civil de Barcelona*; and Risques, Duarte, Riquer, and Roig Rosich, *Història de la Catalunya contemporània*, 103.

34. For the economic problems of Catalonia, see Nadal, *El fracaso de la revolución industrial*, 118–225; Pascual, *Agricultura i industrialització*; Shubert, *Social History*, 119–23; and Tortella, *Development of Modern Spain*, 75–82, 168.
35. Nadal, "La indústria cotonera," 61; and Pascual, *Agricultura i industrialització*, 203–4.
36. Maluquer de Motes, "The Industrial Revolution in Catalonia," 182.
37. For an overview of the strengths and weaknesses of Spanish liberalism during this period, see Jacobson and Moreno Luzón, "The Political System of the Restoration."
38. Maluquer de Motes, "The Industrial Revolution in Catalonia," 172.
39. Garcia Balañà, *La fabricació de la fàbrica*, 15–24.
40. Marshall, *Travels*, 79.
41. Young, *Travels*, 38.
42. Cited in Permanyer, *Cites i testimonis*, 41.
43. Swinburne, *Travels*, 23–24.
44. For the Liceu and the culture of the high bourgeoisie, see McDonogh, *Good Families*, 185–201.
45. Cited in Permanyer, *Cites i testimonis*, 109.
46. Resina, "From Rose of Fire to City of Ivory," 85.
47. For competing urban designs, see Segarra, "Política urbanística," 189–216.
48. Sánchez, "Manchester español, Rosa de Fuego, París del sur . . .," 21.
49. For population densities and property values, see Garcia Espuche and Guàrdia i Bassols, *Espai i societat*, figs. 57, 71, 72, 88.
50. The first list of lawyer addresses can be found in *Kalendario [sic] y guía de forasteros*, 165–80. For the location of lawyers' residences in 1841, see Garcia Espuche and Guàrdia i Bassols, *Espai i societat*, fig. 87. For a description of the location of lawyer residences in the 1870s and 1880s, see Maluquer i Viladot, *Les meves noces*, 30; for the 1890s, see Hurtado, *Quaranta anys d'advocat*, 1:13. For lawyers' offices in the late nineteenth and early twentieth centuries, see Garcia Espuche et al., "Barcelona," 80–81.
51. I have translated the Spanish word *procuradores* as "proctors" and, by so doing, have followed terminology used in English civil and ecclesiastical courts, where legal professionals were similarly divided into "advocates" and "proctors." I prefer "proctor" to "attorney" or "solicitor," because these latter terms, when used in English, usually refer to legal professionals who underwent a marked expansion in the scope of their activities and came to garner a higher status than continental proctors. In England and Wales, the "solicitor" came to conduct the brunt of legal business that took place outside the courtroom, hence fulfilling many of the roles occupied by advocates and notaries on the continent. In places such as Germany and the United States, the "attorney" is still a synonym for a lawyer who undertakes the dual roles of pleading and procedure.
52. In 1898 there were approximately 634 practicing lawyers registered in Catalonia,

of whom 417 had addresses in Barcelona. In contrast, of 140 notaries, only 25 lived in Barcelona. *GJC* (1898).
53. The ability of notaries to defend Old Regime monopolies in the modern era is the subject of an interesting study: Suleiman, *Private Power*.
54. Capmany, *Centinela contra franceses*, 94.
55. Bergueño Rivero, "La divisió territorial."
56. Pi y Margall, *Las nacionalidades*, 25.
57. Coroleu e Inglada and Pella y Forgas, *Las Cortes Catalanas* and *Los fueros de Cataluña*.
58. Almirall took his name off the list of practicing lawyers in 1881. See ANC, Fons Col·legi d'Advocats, Valentí Almirall.
59. Almirall, *Lo catalanisme*.
60. In its extreme form, this argument held that Spanish blood had been polluted by Arab, Berber, and Mongoloid races, whereas Catalan blood was purer. See Gener, *Cosas de España*, 43, 229.
61. For what could be termed the "primoridalist school," see Balcells, *Catalan Nationalism*, and Simón i Tarrés, *Construccions polítiques i identitats nacionals*. For what could be termed the "modernist school," see Marfany, *La cultura de Catalanisme*, and Ucelay-Da Cal, *El imperialismo catalán*. For an attempt at a middle ground, see Riquer i Permanyer, *Identitats contemporànies*.

CHAPTER 2

1. For this argument, see Larson, *Rise of Professionalism*.
2. The latest version of this debate concerns whether the profession first began to emerge before or after the reception of Roman law. See Reynolds, "The Emergence of Professional Law," 346–36; and Radding, "Legal Theory and Practice," 377–82.
3. The debate and its resolution on professionalism is explained in Burrage, "Introduction: The Professions in Sociology and History," 1–23.
4. For professionalization in the eighteenth century at the French bar, see Leuwers, *L'invention du barreau français*. Another fine study that locates the birth of modern professionalism in the eighteenth century is La Vopa, *Grace, Talent, and Merit*.
5. Brooks, "The Decline and Rise of the English Legal Profession, 1700–1850," in *Lawyers, Litigation, and English Society*, 125–47.
6. For England, see Brooks, *Lawyers, Litigation and English Society*, 27–62, 129–147; and Lemmings, *Professors of the Law*, 61–106, 320–21. For France, see Colin Kaiser, "The Deflation in the Volume of Litigation." Richard Kagan has observed that dwindling litigation rates paralleled economic decadence and population deflation in Castile during the seventeenth century. Kagan, *Lawsuits and Litigants*, 220–35.
7. The importance of "jurisdictional jockeying" to early modern litigation is explored throughout Benton, *Law and Colonial Cultures*.

8. Domínguez Ortiz, *Sociedad y estado*, 247.
9. Swinburne, *Travels*, 61.
10. Ibid., 27.
11. Townsend, *Journey through Spain*, 132.
12. For lawyers and juridical disputes between crown and parliament during the early modern period, see Palos, *Els juristes*.
13. See Maza, *Private Lives and Public Affairs*, and Bell, *Lawyers and Citizens*, 67–104.
14. *Ordenanzas de la Real Audiencia*, ord. 336.
15. Amelang, *Honored Citizens of Barcelona*, 68–73.
16. ACA, RA, regs. 1666, 1687, 1688.
17. Cited in Amelang, "Barristers and Judges," 1264.
18. Bourgoanne, *Travels in Spain*, 2:178.
19. For the authorship of the document, see Lluch, *Las Españas vencidas*, 233.
20. "Memorial de Greuges de 1760," in *Projectes i memorials*, 4–19 [4].
21. Ibid., 8.
22. The framers did not cite figures for Latin America, but their assertions were correct. According to statistics compiled by the historians Mark Burkholder and D. S. Chandler, not a single Audiencia magistrate from 1713 to 1777 possessed a degree from the University of Cervera. Incidentally, things did not improve much. From 1778 to 1808, they record only one from Cervera. Burkholder and Chandler, *From Impotence to Authority*, app. IV.
23. "Memorial de Greuges de 1760," in *Projectes i memorials*, 4–19 [12].
24. Ibid.
25. See Mann, *Sources of Social Power*.
26. Pedro Molas has noted that from 1716 to 1808 Catalans composed only 38 percent of criminal magistrates and 32 percent of civil ones in Catalonia. There was no noticeable change in this appointment policy during the monarchy of Charles III. See Molas Ribalta, "Las audiencias borbónicas en la Corona de Aragón," 132.
27. In 1881 Josep Pella, a lawyer and historian, attributed this observation to the former chancellor of the University of Cervera, the jurist Ramon de Dou. *El Diluvio*, 29 January 1881, p. 338.
28. P.N.A., *Conversa verdadera*, 13.
29. Cited in Karpic, *French Lawyers*, 32.
30. Leuwers, *L'invention du barreau français*, 154–73.
31. Out of the 182 lawyers for whom I have been able to locate the residences, 129 of them lived in this central administrative neighborhood. Another 23 lived in what could be described as the commercial zone, an elongated area stretching from the Pla de Palau to the Convent of Santa Caterina and running along the Carrer Argentaria. Another 30 lived in the neighborhoods where manufacturing was heavy: 21 in the Raval, and 9 on the streets branching out from the parish of Sant Pere de les Puelles. See *Kalendario [sic] y guía de forasteros*, 165–80.

32. ACA, RA, leg. 68, "Carta Acordada, Madrid, 25 de Agosto de 1770"; and ACA, RA, leg. 70, "Papel de Su Excelencia, 29 de Maio de 1771."
33. For a thorough discussion of the *ius commune* and *ius proprium*, see Bellomo, *The Common Legal Past of Europe*. For an overview of legislation on legal education and training during this period, see Peset Reig, "Derecho Romano y Derecho Real."
34. ACA, RA, exp.(1826), caja 63, no. 702; ACA, RA, exp. (1830), caja 22, no. 103; ACA, RA, exp. (1833), caja 135, no. 436.
35. ACA, RA, reg. 1686, "Acuerdo de la Real Audiencia, 2 de Maio de 1716"; and ACA, RA, reg. 1688, "Instrucción que deben observar los examinados para abogados en la relación del proceso, explicación de su dictamen, o sentencia, y diligencias que practiquen."
36. Real Orden 26 enero 1837, *CL* 22 (1837): 28–29.
37. ACA, RA, reg. 1210, p. 290.
38. ACA, RA, reg. 933, p. 65.
39. ACA, RA, reg. 1210, p. 453.
40. ACA, RA, reg. 1210, pp. 481, 709.
41. ACA, RA, leg. 153, "Acuerdo de la Real Audiencia, 5 Marzo 1801."
42. ACA, RA, reg. 931, p. 86.
43. For the original and appellate jurisdiction of the Audiencia in criminal and civil cases, see Dou y de Bassols, *Instituciones del derecho público*, 2:153–61.
44. For Old Regime civil procedure, see ibid., vol. 6. The ensuing discussion in the text is based on this volume as well as an examination of cases found in ACA, RA, Pleitos Civiles, some of which are cited in the footnotes that follow.
45. For an example of multiple supplications in one suit, see ACA, RA, Pleitos Civiles, no. 1624: Cabildo de canónigos de la Catedral de Barcelona contra Magín Planas y Pi.
46. Incidentally, if the supplicant prevailed, the court refunded 500 doblas of the original fee. For a sample case that runs through a full gamut of appeals, supplications, and second supplications, see ACA, RA, Pleitos Civiles, no. 14631: Mariano Carabent contra Jacinto Carabent y Jacinta Carabent.
47. The extent to which torture was still being used in the late eighteenth century is still an open question. For some thoughts on this matter, see Tomás y Valiente, *La tortura judicial en España*, 130–36.
48. For a thorough explanation of Old Regime criminal procedure, see Dou y de Bassols, *Instituciones del derecho público*, vol. 8.
49. Frederic Camp y Llopis, *Contribución al estudio de la administración de Barcelona por los franceses (1808–1814)* (Barcelona: Escuela Salesiana, 1920), 155, cited in Ramisa, *Els catalans i el domini napoleònic*, 210.
50. *Kalendario [sic] y guía de forasteros*, 101–4.
51. For a description of the workings of this court, see Marquès, "Tribunals peculiars eclesiàstico-civils de Catalunya."
52. Moreu Ros, "La actividad del Tribunal de la Inquisición en Barcelona."
53. For the evolution of the commercial law from the Middle Ages to the nine-

teenth century, see Petit, "Derecho mercantil." For a detailed study of legal changes at a commercial consulate during the late eighteenth and early nineteenth centuries, see Adelman, *Republic of Capital*, 141–64. For the presence of lawyers at the commercial consulate in Barcelona, see Espuny Tomás, "El Real Consulado de Comercio," 123–25, 280.

54. I borrow the term "lawyerization" from Langbein, *Origins of the Adversary Criminal Trial*. He stresses that the penal law became "lawyerized" in eighteenth-century England. The same could be said for the commercial law in much of the world as well.
55. Rojo, "José Bonaparte (1808–1813) y la legislación mercantil," 121–82 (139).
56. Quotation by Vicente González Arnao, a lawyer from Madrid, cited in Espuny Tomas and Sarrión Gualda, "El Tribunal de Alzadas," 161.
57. *Ley de Enjuiciamiento sobre los negocios y causas de Comercio*, art. 38.
58. In 1787 census takers counted 390 lawyers in Catalonia. In the year, the Audiencia counted 195 lawyers on court rolls. The *Guía Judicial de Cataluña* (1898) reveals that there were approximately 634 practicing lawyers registered in Catalonia, of whom 417 had residences in Barcelona. Floridablanca, *Censo español*, table VI; ACA, RA, leg. 148, "Lectura de las Rs Ordenanzas, 7 de Enero de 1787"; and *GJC* (1898).
59. Cots i Castañé, "Aproximació a l'estudi dels conflictes senyorials," 244–45.
60. Dou y de Bassols, *Instituciones del derecho público*, 2:107–12 (baronial jurisdictions), 3:7 (lawyers as advisors).
61. Technically, it was only required that a "lawyer" serve as an adviser when the judge or baron was "unlettered," but barons routinely hired lawyers to instruct (prosecute and adjudge) these cases. Tos y Urgellés, *Tratado de la cabrevación*, 6, 14.
62. There is an extensive bibliography on the interesting subject of aristocratic reaction, peasant resistance, and emphyteutic litigation. The key studies are Vilar, *Cataluña en la España moderna*, 2:398–419; Caminal et al., "Moviment de l'ingrés senyorial"; Carbonell i Esteller, "Plets i lluita antisenyorial"; and Arnabat Mata, "Protesta i resistència antisenyorial al Penedès (1758–1808)."
63. For a complete guide to the ins and outs of emphyteutic litigation, see Tos y Urgellés, *Tratado de la cabrevación*. For some sample cases, see ACA, RA, Pleitos Civiles, 14792: Conde de Peralada contra Jaime Sibecas; ACA, RA, Pleitos Civiles, 15804: Eulalia Oliveras (viuda de Sebastián de Granollers) contra Manuel Argemir (administrador de temporalidades de los Jesuitos expulsos); ACA, RA, Pleitos Civiles, 1624: Cabildo de canónigos de la Catedral de Barcelona contra Magín Planas y Pi.
64. For eighteenth-century litigant profiles, see Cots i Castañé, "Els litigis judicials," 407–8, 503–5. According to his statistics, the nobility and the church composed slightly more than 25 percent of eighteenth-century litigants. He also observed that this percentage decreased slightly over the course of the century. We do not have statistics for Barcelona for earlier periods, so it is difficult to make comparisons. However, Richard Kagan has studied litigant profiles in Valladolid during the sixteenth and seventeenth centuries. He has observed

that the church and the nobility composed a larger percentage of legal business. Kagan, *Lawsuits and Litigants*, 220–35.

65. *Ordenanzas de la Real Audiencia*, ord. 325. For fees, see Dou y de Bassols, *Instituciones del derecho público*, 3:12–13; and Vives y Cebriá, *Los Usages y demás derechos de Cataluña*, 1:266–68.
66. For an example of a lawsuit in which litigants were considered "poor" and sued for the ownership of valuable property holdings in an inheritance dispute, see ACA, RA, Pleitos Civiles, 14631: Mariano Carabent contra Jacinto Carabent y Jacinta Carabent.
67. These averages were calculated from information contained in AHMB, Cadastre (1823), Indústria i Comerç, sèrie 9, vol. 8.
68. Campomanes's opinions on legal and university reform are expressed in his *Reflexiones sobre la jurisprudencia española*.
69. These reforms are neatly summarized in Ledford, *From General Estate to Special Interest*, 31–35. For their effects on the subsequent evolution of the structure of the profession in the nineteenth century, see John, "Between Estate and Profession," 162–97.
70. Romá y Rosell, *Las señales de la felicidad*, 54–55.
71. *Ordenanzas de la Real Audiencia*, ords. 301–40.
72. "Memorial de Greuges de 1760," in *Projectes i memorials*, 4–19 [12].
73. Berní y Català, *Resumen de los privilegios*.
74. For the decreasing use of Latin in pedagogy, see Sarrailh, *La España ilustrada*, 197–98.
75. Pérez Villamil, *Disertación sobre la libre multitud de abogados*, 74.
76. Ibid. 34–35.
77. Cited in Vives y Cebriá, *Los Usages y demás derechos de Cataluña*, 3: 181.
78. For an extensive summary and analysis of D'Aguesseau's influential speech, see Karpik, *French Lawyers*, 52–55. For the influence of Salutati, see Amelang, *Honored Citizens*, 105.
79. D'Aguesseau, *Discurso de la independencia del abogado*.
80. Barba y Roca, *Discurso sobre los pleytos*, 1, 5, 22.
81. Ibid., 23.
82. Magarola, *El abogado perfecto*, 23, 31–32.
83. Ibid., 18, 30.
84. I have not found a historical explanation of the etymology of the word "profession" in Europe. It is certain that it existed in France in the seventeenth century, because D'Aguesseau used it. For an interesting discussion of the evolution of the word "liberal profession" in Britain and France, see Goldstein, *Console and Classify*, 10–15.
85. For the use the term "classes" in the eighteenth century, see Floridablanca, *Censo español*.
86. The word "profession" also came to be used colloquially to describe manual occupations, but official censuses distinguished between the "learned profession" and the "manual arts": *EACIC* (1857, 1877, 1887, 1897).
87. Barba y Roca, *Discurso sobre los pleytos*, 3.

88. Berlanstein, *Barristers of Toulouse*, 93–122.
89. Prest, "Law, Lawyers and Rational Dissent"; Pue, "Lawyers and Political Liberalism"; and Lemmings, *Professors of the Law*, 318.
90. These circles are vividly illustrated in Finestres, *Epistolari*.
91. Prats, *La Universitat de Cervera*, 293–97.
92. For the official Enlightenment in Barcelona, and some information on these individuals, see Lluch, *Las Españas vencidas*, 182–84; and Moreu Rey, *El pensament il·lustrat*, 117, 121.
93. Lluch, "La pràctica econòmica de la Il·lustració," 700.
94. For some interesting thoughts on the limits of the Enlightenment in Barcelona, see Amelang, "Comparing Cities."
95. For some notes on Romà's career, see Lluch, "La Catalunya del segle XVIII."
96. Townsend, *Journey through Spain*, 118–19.
97. Coroleu, *Memorias de un menestral*, 19–52.
98. Swinburne, *Travels*, 68.
99. Young, *Travels*, 40. For a general description of Inquisition activities, see Moreu Ros, "La actividad del Tribunal de la Inquisición."
100. For the widespread circulation of banned books and the granting of licenses, see Defourneaux, *L'Inquisition espagnole*, 105–68. For censorship in general, see Domergue, *La censure des livres en Espagne*.
101. For a nice discussion of the influence of Beccaria and Montesquieu in Spain, see Herr, *Eighteenth-Century Revolution in Spain*, 57–62.
102. Lardizábal y Uribe, *Discurso sobre las penas*.
103. Townsend, *Journey through Spain*, 120.
104. "Memorial de Greuges de 1760," in *Projectes i memorials*, 4–19 [6].
105. Barba y Roca, *Discurso sobre los pleytos*, 6.
106. For a discussion of the debate on capital punishment in Spain, see Sarrailh, *La España ilustrada*, 292–307, 538–43; and Sánchez-Blanco, *El absolutismo y las luces*, 192–93.
107. Dou y de Bassols, *Instituciones del derecho público*, 7:87, 98, 117; and 8:280.
108. For Dou and the *Institutions*, see Meilán Gil, "Don Ramón Lázaro de Dou y de Bassols."
109. Tos y Urgellés, *Tratado de la cabrevación*, p. i.
110. Dou y de Bassols, *La riqueza de las naciones* and *Pronta y fácil egecución*.
111. Manuel Sisternes y Felíu, *Idea de la ley agraria*, p. viii. For Romà's views, see Romá y Rosell, *Las señales de la felicidad*, 16–21.
112. For the influence of Bielfeld and Romà in the court of Charles III, see Sánchez-Blanco, *El absolutismo y las luces*, 77.
113. Romá y Rosell, *Las señales de la felicidad*, 137, 153, 154.
114. Domenech y Sabater, *Discurso sobre las obligaciones del abogado*, 30.
115. I have not been able to find a verbatim reproduction on what the Madrid lawyers actually wrote, but this is how it was characterized in the rebuttal by Mujal, *Desengaño al público*, 47.
116. Ibid., 63. For a further exploration of this debate, see Sánchez-Blanco, *El absolutismo y las luces*, 184–86.

117. ACA, RA, Pleitos Civiles, no. 16024: Cabildo de canónigos de la Catedral de Barcelona contra Magín Planas y Pi (labrador).
118. Barba y Roca, *Discurso sobre los pleytos*, 20.
119. Ibid., 19; and Magarola, *El abogado perfecto*, 24.
120. The founders were all lawyers who had recently entered the bar. For the foundation of the academy, see Guàrdia i Canela, "L'acadèmia i el Col·legi d'advocats." For the evolution of *tertulias* into royal academies, see Sarrailh, *La España ilustrada*, 230–32.
121. Excerpts from the original request are reproduced in Antonio M. Borrell y Soler, "Anales académicos. Discurso del Presidente," *Revista Jurídica de Cataluña*, no. 4 (July–August 1955): 394–407 [394].
122. *Ordenanzas de la Academia de Jurisprudencia*. For the requirement that all apprentices attend, see ACA, RA, leg. 86, "Carta Acordada, 30 de Marzo de 1784."
123. These letters are cited in Vilar, "Els Barba, una família il·lustrada," 66, 76.
124. ACA, RA, reg. 933, p. 61.
125. In 1842, Josep Bertran claimed that the academy continued to exist until the French invasion of 1808. See *Acta de la primera sesión inaugural*, 34. It is not clear, however, that this was the case. Any meetings must have been informal, for it had long ceased to operate under its statutes. Audiencia records rarely mention the academy in the 1790s and do not mention it at all during the first decade of the nineteenth century. The last publication that I have found was in 1789: Magarola, *El abogado perfecto*.
126. For these figures, see Maza, *Private Lives and Public Affairs*, 87.
127. ACA, RA, reg. 1214, p. 348.
128. *Novísima recopilación*, libro 5, título 22, ley 29. The *Novísima recopilación* included the order reducing the number in Madrid to 200, and lists one other order, dated 1798, in which other high-court seats were required to lower numbers in proportion to population. The specific order of 100 in Barcelona was first issued as on 25 April 1795. This accord is bundled together with subsequent limits of 100 in ACA, RA, exp. (1829), caja 99, no. 155.
129. In order to offset some of the extra time that a student spent at university, the formal apprenticeship was reduced to one year (1802) and then abolished altogether (1807). This did not mean that lawyers stopped apprenticing. Rather, this only meant that at it was not necessary to document an apprenticeship before taking an Audiencia exam. For these laws, see Peset Reig, "La formación de los juristas."
130. Peset Reig, "La recepción."
131. DSC, 10 April 1811, pp. 853–54.
132. ACA, RA, exp. (1829), caja 99, no. 155. In this file, dated 1829, the crown prosecutor at the Royal Council ordered the Audiencia to "establish a College of Lawyers in this city in conformity with that which was agreed in the Accord of 25 April 1795 and repeated on 14 April 1804 . . . stating that the number of lawyers that should compose this College should not be higher than one hundred by order of seniority of those lawyers residing in the city." In this file,

he included copies of the accords from 1795 and 1804. However, neither the registry for 1795 nor for 1804 indicates that these accords had been registered. In the 1830s, Pere Vives also noted that a *numerus clausus* was never enforced. See Vives y Cebriá, *Los Usages y demás derechos de Cataluña*, 1:24.
133. ACA, RA, leg. 156, "Lectura de las Ordenanzas, 2 de Enero de 1808."
134. Peset Reig, "La recepción," 125.
135. Cited in Elliott, *Empires of the Atlantic World*, 395.
136. Cited in del Pozo Carrascosa, "La introducción del derecho francés," 196.
137. Ibid.

CHAPTER 3

1. There has been one attempt at a comparative theory: Burrage, "Revolution as a Starting Point." This article, however, focuses on changing institutional structures rather than on lawyers themselves.
2. Tocqueville, *Democracy in America*, 252.
3. For the subject of lawyers and the French Revolution, see Dawson, "The *Bourgeoisie de Robe* in 1789" and *Provincial Magistrates and Revolutionary Politics*; Berlanstein, *Barristers of Toulouse*, 166–70; Fitzsimmons, *Parisian Order*; Woloch, "Fall and Resurrection of the Civil Bar"; and Leuwers, *L'invention du barreau français*, 231–64.
4. Fitzsimmons, *Parisian Order*, 194.
5. Voltaire, "Law" and "Laws," in *Philosophical Dictionary*, 64–108.
6. DSC, 22 April 1811, p. 910.
7. DSC, 10 April 1811, p. 854.
8. For the influence of Spanish revolutionary liberalism in Europe during the 1820s, see Bayly, *Birth of the Modern World*, 107, 295.
9. For the size of the franchise, see Burdiel, "Liberal Revolution: 1808–1843," 27; and Cruz, "Moderate Ascendancy: 1843–1868," 43. For the "undemocratic" outcome of Spain's liberal revolution, see Ruíz Torres, "Liberalisme i revolució."
10. The classic critique of the expression "bourgeois revolution" with respect to Spain is Álvarez Junco, "A vueltas con la revolución burguesa." For a fine discussion of Spain's "liberal revolution," see Burdiel, "Myths of Failure, Myths of Success." For a nice examination of continuity and change among middle-class groups in Madrid, see Cruz, *Gentlemen, Bourgeois, and Revolutionaries*.
11. Tocqueville, *Democracy in America*, 258.
12. Fitzsimmons, *Parisian Order*, 162.
13. Rojo, "José Bonaparte (1808–1813) y la legislación mercantil," 139–43.
14. For the naming of the "War of Independence," see Álvarez Junco, *Mater Dolorosa*, 119–28.
15. Cited in Ramisa, *Els catalans i el domini napoleònic*, 323.
16. For biographies of Casanova and Madinaveytia, see Riera i Fortiana, *Els afrancesats a Catalunya*, 266–94; and Ramisa, *Els catalans i el domini napoleònic*, 304–6, 322–36. See also J.R.G., *Quadro de horror*.
17. The three were Ramon Banquells, Josep Anglasell, and Pere Nolasc de Salcedo. See Moliner i Prada, *La Catalunya resistent*, 30, 84.

18. Pérez Samper, "La Real Audiencia de Cataluña," 180.
19. *DSC*, 1 March 1813, p. 4761; and *DSC*, 23 June 1811, p. 1312.
20. ACA, RA, leg. 157, "Acuerdo de la Real Audiencia, Tarragona, 15 de Mayo de 1811"; ACA, RA, leg. 157, "Acuerdo de la Real Audiencia, Vich, 29 de Mayo de 1811."
21. ACA, RA, leg. 157, "Acuerdo de la Real Audiencia, Tarragona, 15 de Mayo de 1811"; ACA, RA, leg. 157, "Acuerdo de la Real Audiencia, Vich, 29 de Mayo de 1811"; ACA, RA, leg. 157, "Acuerdo de la Real Audiencia, Vich, 31 de Diciembre 1811" and, "Acuerdo de la Real Audiencia, Manresa, 2 de Enero de 1813"; and ACA, RA, leg. 121, "Real Orden, San Fernando, 16 de Diciembre de 1813."
22. During opening ceremonies held in January 1811 in Tarragona, only fifteen lawyers signed in, indicating that they had taken the oath. Over the course of 1812, thirty-three lawyers signed, and during 1813, the number was twenty-five. ACA, RA, leg. 157, "Tarragona, Acuerdo de la apertura del Tribunal de 1811," "Lista de los abogados que firmaron en 1812," and "Manresa, Acuerdo, 2 de Enero de 1813."
23. The Tarragona Audiencia issued three decisions in 1810 and none in 1811. In 1812, the Audiencia issued thirty-one in Manresa, and in 1813, it published sixty-one from Manresa and Reus. ACA, RA, Conclusiones Civiles, libro 280.
24. ACA, RA, leg. 157, "Reus, 3 de Enero de 1814."
25. ACA, RA, exp. (1821), caja 5, no. 231; ACA, RA, exp. (1823), caja 22, no. 86.
26. For a short biography of Ventosa, see Durán y Bas and Roure, *Sesión celebrada*, 6–7, 19–20.
27. *Diccionari biogràfic*, s.v. "Josep Bertran i Ros."
28. ACA, RA, exp. (1821), caja 2, no. 60; ACA, RA, exp. (1821), caja 3, no. 134.
29. A Napoleonic census estimated that a city of 140,000 persons became reduced to 36,000. The first number may be slightly too high, but there is no reason to doubt the latter figure, because the French would have been in a position to count heads. Ramisa, *Els catalans i el domini napoleònic*, 188.
30. To be precise, the French threatened to march them by foot across the Alps into Italy, which was, in essence, equivalent to a death sentence. After they took the oath, many fled the city. See Pérez Samper, "La Real Audiencia," and D.J.J.O., *Apuntamiento de lo ocurrido*.
31. Other than the court-appointed public defender, Rafael Casejams, only two independent lawyers — Josep Campa de Portoles and Antoni Trilla — signed in. ACA, RA, leg. 177, 2 January 1810.
32. ACA, RA, leg. 158, "Barcelona, 2 de Enero de 1816."
33. ACA, RA. leg. 157, "Reus, 3 Enero de 1814."
34. Jaume Tos enrolled in the bar in 1778, and in 1822 there was only lawyer more senior than him. Tos probably died before 1833, because upon the official foundation of the college in 1833, he was no longer on court rolls. ACA, RA, exp. (1822), caja 10, no. 1; ACA, RA, reg. 1689; and *LACB* (1833).
35. ACA, RA, leg. 157, "Reus, Acuerdo, 3 de Enero de 1814."
36. These declarations were taken in Barcelona, but are inserted in the folder labeled "Reus," where the opening ceremonies for 1814 had taken place. ACA, RA, leg. 157, "Reus, 3 de Enero de 1814."

37. ACA, RA, leg. 158, "Barcelona, 2 de Enero de 1817."
38. ACA, RA, leg. 159, "Barcelona, 2 de Enero de 1819."
39. For Puig, see Riera i Fortiana, *Els afrancesats*, 202–44; and Ramisa, *Els catalans i el domini napoleònic*, 290–312.
40. There were not many. In 1810 the Court of Appeals issued three "sentences" and four "formal orders." The court published all three sentences and the first three orders in Catalan but published the last order in Spanish. ACA, RA, leg. 318.
41. The issue of Catalan language during the War of Independence is concisely discussed in Marfany, *La llengua maltractada*, 361.
42. The sole dissenting vote was probably that of Tomàs Puig, and there are some scholars who claim that he succeeded in translating the French Civil Code into Catalan. For those who claim that he did, see del Pozo Carrascosa, "La introducción del Derecho francés en Cataluña," 197; and Lamarca i Marquès, "L'administració de justícia a Catalunya," 302–3. Marfany casts doubt on these assertions. Marfany, *La llengua maltractada*, 451. I tend to agree with Marfany.
43. P.N.A., *Conversa verdadera*.
44. Ibid., 6–7.
45. Ibid., 11, 13.
46. Ibid., 12.
47. Ibid., 14.
48. Pérez Garzón, *Milicia nacional*, 186–97. Unfortunately, there were not sufficient data to determine how many of these 190 lawyers volunteered. In any case, it can be assumed that a large proportion of them signed up.
49. I have not found specific statistics for the exact size of the Madrid bar during these years. The first published list records that there were just over 500 lawyers in 1851. Given figures for Barcelona, one could expect the size of the bar to be significantly smaller during the 1830s and early 1840s. *Lista de los abogados del Ilustre Colegio de Madrid*.
50. For an examination of the composition of the militias in Catalonia, see Dueñas García, "La milicia nacional local," and Arnabat Mata, *La revolució de 1820*, 111–25.
51. ACA, RA, exp. (1826), caja 56, no. 66.
52. ACA, RA, exp. (1821), caja 3, no. 134.
53. ACA, RA, exp. (1822), caja 16, no. 700; and AHMB: Cadastre (1823), Sèrie IX, Indústria i Comerç, IX-10. Sala describes his activities during the War of Independence in *El mayor despotismo*.
54. ACA, RA, exp. (1830), caja 106, no. 270. For similar testimony, see ACA, RA, exp. (1827), caja 73, no. 873; exp. (1827), caja 78, no. 873; exp. (1829), caja 99, no. 544; exp. (1829), caja 100, no. 617; and exp. (1831), caja 123, no. 794.
55. ACA, RA, exp. (1827), caja 68, no. 25.
56. ACA, RA, exp. (1821), caja 5, no. 245.
57. ACA, RA, exp. (1830), caja 110, no. 535.
58. ACA, RA, exp. (1829), caja 95, no. 103.
59. ACA, RA, exp. (1821), caja 5, no. 231.

60. ACA, RA, exp. (1822), caja 14, no. 14.
61. ACA, RA, exp. (1827), caja 78, no. 802; exp. (1828), caja 86, no. 565.
62. ACA, RA, exp. (1829), caja 95, no. 103.
63. Again, we only have specific statistics for Madrid. During the Regency of Espartero (1841–43), for example, 188 lawyers were targeted for recruitment for a militia that was over 11,000 strong in Madrid. Pérez Garzón, *Milicia nacional*, 426–37. The percentage in Barcelona was probably similar.
64. Coverdale, *Basque Phase*, 3.
65. ACA, RA, exp. (1837), caja 170, no. 1.
66. AGHUB: Antonio Benavent y Perayre, Antonio Carrera de Ortega, Juan Baeza y Canalejo, Luis Roquer y Guitart, Juan de Gispert y Vilar.
67. For secret societies during the Triennium and their compositions, see Arnabat Mata, *La revolució de 1820*, 139–44, 226. For Salvató and the foundation of the Comuneros, see Gil Novales, *Diccionario biográfico*, 603.
68. For Pi i Margall and Roure, see Roure, *Recuerdos de mi larga vida*, 1:241–45.
69. Flaubert, *Sentimental Education*, 301.
70. Rudé, *Crowd in History*.
71. Santirso, "Voluntarios realistas, voluntarios de Isabel II."
72. Sala, *Defensa del ciudadano José Costa*, 17.
73. For a detailed exploration of these events, see Santirso, *Revolució liberal*, 161–74.
74. We do not have a sociological profile of those who committed these acts in Barcelona, because those who were responsible were never prosecuted. However, Anna Maria Garcia has studied the composition of similar anticlerical revolts in Madrid during 1834 and surmised that these must have been similar to those of Barcelona. Garcia Rovira, *La revolució liberal*, 103–5.
75. Parts of Bertran's report are reproduced in Barraquer y Roviralta, *Las casas de religiosos*, 795–98.
76. The disentailment of the monestary is told in detail in Roselló i Cherigny, "El régimen jurídico."
77. The "fear of social violence" is often cited for the reason why liberal revolution turned elitist. See Fradera, *Cultura nacional*, 31; and Ruíz Torres, "Liberalisme i revolució," 63, 71.
78. Balle, *Memoria*.
79. For example, he opposed the outright abolition of the tithes and suggested a middle road, proposing to cut these in half, from 10 to 5 percent, in order not to prejudice recipients of what were known as "aristocratic tithes." Balle, *Informe*. Though published in 1842, this is a copy of a report that circulated in 1837.
80. DSC, 19 October 1820, pp. 1768–82; and DSC, 6 May 1822, pp. 1220–21.
81. For the composition of the gentry, see Congost, *Els propietaris i els altres*; Segura, *Burgesia i propietat*; and Garrabou, Planas, and Saguer, *Un capitalisme impossible?*, 16–23.
82. For the composition of the juntas in 1835, see Garcia Rovira, *La revolució liberal*, 348; and Santirso, *Revolució liberal*, 168. In order to confirm or establish percentages, I have compared their list of junta members against the list of lawyers on the Barcelona bar. See AHMB, *LACB* (1835).

83. For the composition of the juntas of 1842, see Risques, "La insurrecció de Barcelona," 96–97.
84. For the composition of the Junta Oficialista, see Benet and Martí, *Barcelona a mitjan segle XIX*, 335. In order to identify which members of the junta were lawyers, I have run the names against AHMB, *LACB* (1842).
85. ACA, RA, exp. (1822), caja 15, no. 611; ACA, RA, exp. (1822), caja 18, no. 794; and ACA, RA, reg. 1420, p. 395.
86. ACA, RA, exp. (1829), caja 99, no. 555.
87. ACA, RA, exp. (1821), caja 3, no. 134; and Salvató, *Elecciones de 1839*, 30.
88. See Uribe-Uran, *Honorable Lives*, 45–70.
89. ACA, RA, leg. 122, "Real Orden, Madrid, 14 de Marzo de 1814."
90. Castillo, *La Ciudadela inquisitorial*, 54, 60, 63.
91. *DSCCD*, 6 February 1842, p. 776.
92. Real Determinación 8 junio 1826, *CL* 11 (1826): 131–32.
93. Enric Jardí notes that an anonymous, unpublished history of the college written in the 1930s and found in the college library insinuates that Llobet was in agreement with the contents of Constitution of 1812. Unfortunately, the publication, "El Col·legi d'Advocats de Barcelona. Historial de 1832 a 1932," does not appear in the catalog, and neither I nor the college librarians have been able to locate it. Jardí, *Història del Col·legi*, 1:8.
94. ACA, RA, exp. (1829), caja 99. no. 55.
95. Circular del Consejo Real 25 enero 1827, *CL* 12 (1827): 17–18.
96. See, for example: ACA, RA, exp. (1827), caja 72, no. 340; exp. (1828), caja 81, no. 234; exp. (1828), caja 85, no. 614; exp. (1829), caja 99, no. 540; exp. (1829), caja 99, no. 551.
97. ACA, RA, exp. (1831), caja 122, no. 727.
98. ACA, RA, exp. (1827), caja 72, no. 340.
99. Joan Baladia, a notary for the Inquisition, was the signatory for all the certificates coming from the "committee for the purification of individuals of the literary establishments of the territory of the Royal Audiencia of Catalonia." He was the signatory of the certificates cited in the following footnote.
100. ACA, RA, exp. (1832), caja 131, no. 648; exp. (1833), caja 134, no. 1036; exp. (1833), caja 140, no. 703; exp. (1833), caja 139, no. 624; exp. (1833), caja 139, no. 677; exp. (1833), caja 140, no. 703.
101. ACA, RA, leg. 158, "Barcelona, 2 de Enero de 1819"; and ACA, RA, exp. (1825), caja 43, no. 1.
102. For litigation rates, see figure 2 in chapter 5.
103. For biographical information on Salvató, see Lasso Gaite, *El Ministerio de Justicia*, 20–24, 72–73. For the travails of exile and heroic return of a lawyer persecuted in the 1830s, see Degollada, *Memoria del abogado*.
104. ACA, RA, exp. (1831), caja 120, no. 456. For similar utterances, see ACA, RA, exp. (1826), caja 58, no. 273; exp. (1827), caja 73, no. 409; exp. (1828), caja 80, no. 115; exp. (1828), caja 94, no. 17; exp (1830), caja 103, no. 22.
105. These oaths can be found, among various places, in ACA, RA, reg. (1687), pp. 45, 133, and 145; and ACA, RA, exp. (1824), caja 37, no. 972; exp. (1825), caja 128, no. 379; exp. (1832), caja 128, no. 215.

106. ACA, RA, exp. (1825), caja 43, no. 277.
107. ACA, RA, exp. (1826), caja 58, no. 273.
108. ACA, RA, exp. (1826), caja 60, no. 389.
109. ACA, RA, exp. (1823), caja 23, no. 229.
110. ACA, RA, exp. (1830), caja 597, no. 111.
111. ACA, RA, exp. (1826), caja 60, no. 44.
112. Pérez Garzón, *Milicia nacional*, 356–63.
113. Anguera, *Déu, rei i fam*, 230–32. It should be noted that Anguera records that twenty "students" were on police lists. It is conceivable that a few of these could have been law students, but it is a safe guess that most studied theology.
114. Tocqueville, *Democracy in America*, 13.
115. Ibid., 252, 253, 256.
116. Ibid., 251.
117. Charle, *Social History of France*, 169.
118. Bayly, *Birth of the Modern World*, 144, 264 (emphasis added).

CHAPTER 4

1. P.N.A., *Conversa verdadera*, title page and p. 7.
2. For the size of the franchise under the various suffrage laws, see Caballero Domínguez, "El derecho de representación."
3. Ibid., 13.
4. Pere Vives noted that in 1828 the monarchy put judges in twenty-four new towns so that forty-five towns served as court seats. This number roughly corresponds to the forty-three towns listed as having royal courts in a census conducted in 1830. Vives y Cebriá, *Los Usages y demás derechos de Cataluña*, 28–30; and ACA, RA, exp. (1829), caja 99, no. 555.
5. ACA, RA, exp. (1829), caja 99, no. 555; ACMJ, Colegios de Abogados, leg. 306–1; and *GJC* (1898), 114–239.
6. For a vivid example of the inability of Parliament to reform justice in Britain, see Lobban, "Preparing for Fusion."
7. Real Decreto 26 septiembre 1835, *CL* 20 (1835): 396–437.
8. Real Orden 12 noviembre 1855, *CL* 66 (1855): 251–53.
9. *Ley orgánica del Poder Judicial*, arts. 109, 116, 121, 122, 187.
10. According to the regulations of 1835, repeated in 1844, mayors heard small cases that did not exceed 10 duros, in other words, 200 reales (50 pesetas). Upon the promulgation of the Organic Law in 1870, municipal courts heard all cases for less than 250 pesetas (1,000 reales). See Real Decreto 26 septiembre 1835, *CL* 20 (1835): arts. 31, 40; Real Decreto 1 mayo 1844, *CL* 32 (1844): art. 1; *Ley orgánica del Poder Judicial*, art. 270; and *Ley de Enjuiciamiento Civil de 3 de Enero de 1881*, art. 715.
11. *Ley de Enjuiciamiento Civil* (1855), art. 1133. For artisan salaries, see Cerdá, "Monografía estadística de la clase obrera de Barcelona en 1856."
12. A rough idea of lawyers' fees can be traced by examining fee appeals reviewed by the board of directors at the College of Lawyers: see, for example, CABAJD: 6 October 1863, 16 May 1865, 7 November 1865, 27 February 1871, 30 April 1874,

3 January 1876, 17 February 1876, 28 April 1876, 18 February 1879, 25 February 1879, 25 April 1879, 30 March 1885, 10 September 1885, 26 November 1885, 10 September 1885, 26 November 1885, 30 January 1888, 16 April 1888.

13. Civil case records for the nineteenth century have been moved from the Palau de Justícia to the ANC, but they have yet to be cataloged and indexed. Given their quantity, this promises to be a lengthy task. For eighteenth-century litigant profiles, see Cots i Castañé, "Els litigis judicials."
14. Amat y Furió, "Prólogo," 10.
15. Burgos, "El abogado," no page numbers.
16. The Spanish government began publishing statistics in 1869. During the period from 1869 to 1883, municipal courts in all of Spain attended to anywhere from 100,000 to 180,000 matters per year, while the Audiencias and district courts together attended to 40,000 and 50,000. Similar ratios pertain to Catalonia as well. See *MGJSAT* (1869–83).
17. See, for example, Díez de Ulzurrún, "La reorganización," 204–5.
18. See, for example, "La justícia jutjada per Pi y Margall," *La Tramontana*, 5 October 1888, p. 1.
19. *Estat català, Projecte de Constitució*, 5–37.
20. On commoners hiring council in early modern Spain, see Kagan, *Lawsuits and Litigants*, 126; and Behrend-Martínez, "Female Sexual Potency," 298.
21. Real Orden 1 mayo 1844, *CL* 32 (1844): 658–75.
22. The New Foundation (1716) stated that court seats should have prosecutors, and Dou noted that all courts indeed had one. In Barcelona, royal courts of first instance were organized according to the Real Cédula 13 agosto 1769. In addition to a judge, they were equipped with a prosecutor, a secretary, and at least two bailiffs. Dou y de Bassols, *Instituciones del derecho público*, 3:23.
23. Real Decreto 7 marzo 1851, *CL* 52 (1851): 333–34; Real Decreto 18 agosto 1863, *CL* 90 (1863): 223.
24. The inability and unwillingness of political parties to refrain from keeping judicial appointments independent of political affiliation is a recurring them in Paredes, *La organización de la justicia*, 95–180.
25. The use of the jury for press offenses appeared on and off during the nineteenth century. When in power, the Progressive Party would institute juries for press offenses; in contrast, the Moderates, upon coming to power, would abolish them. Marcuello Benedicto, "La libertad de imprenta y su marco legal."
26. Real Decreto 26 septiembre 1835, *CL* 20 (1835): 396–437, art. 51; *Ley de Enjuiciamiento Civil* (1855), arts. 306–13; and *Ley de Enjuiciamiento Civil de 3 de Enero de 1881*, arts. 637–59.
27. Dou y de Bassols, *Instituciones del derecho público*, 6:177.
28. ACA, RA, reg. 1225, p. 602.
29. Maluquer i Viladot, *Les meves noces*, 49; and Hurtado, *Quaranta anys d'advocat*, 1:13–16.
30. Townsend, *Journey through Spain*, 132.
31. Cited in Ramisa, *Els catalans i el domini napoleònic*, 210.
32. Duran y Bas and Roure, *Sesión celebrada*, 18, 20, 27.

33. The difference between the emphyteutic regime in Barcelona and the rest of Catalonia had to do with law governing the "laudemium," a tax paid to the direct owner whenever the usufructuary owner sold a property. The Barcelona laudemium consisted of 10 percent of the price of the transfer, while the laudemium elsewhere was only 2 percent. The 10 percent laudemium, which dated back to the thirteenth century, originally represented a substantial reduction of the previously applicable "feudal" laudemium of 33 percent. In 1836 liberal legislators "defeudalized" the laudemium by reducing it to the "Roman-law" 2 percent, but the Supreme Court later interpreted this law to apply only to the "feudal" laudemium of 33 percent and not to the Barcelona "exception" of 10 percent. This interpretation, solidified by two Supreme Court decisions (30 November 1868; 15 February 1875), was arguably justified by the letter of the law, but it was clearly against the intentions of the framers of the 1837 law who sought to reduce all laudemia across the board to 2 percent. For the history of laws and Supreme Court jurisprudence, see M. Falcón, *Exposición doctrinal*, 367–68.
34. The last edition was Durán y Ventosa, *Instituciones del derecho mercantil*.
35. For short biographies of Ventosa and Martí d'Eixalà, see Durán y Bas and Roure, *Sesión celebrada*, 6–8, 19–20, 24–27.
36. For biographical information, see Durán y Bas, *Ensayo biográfico*.
37. From 1823 to 1844, Francisco Fontanellas was the only single capitalist consistently in the top tax bracket of men of commerce. By 1844 Torres had also risen into the top tax bracket of the legal profession. In a well-publicized criminal case, it emerged that Torres was the legal adviser to the Fontanellas family. See AHMB, Cadastre, Sèrie IX, Indústria i Comerç, vol. VIII-35, vol. IX-8, vol. IX-12; and Ferrater, *Resumen del proceso*, 52–59.
38. Maluquer i Viladot, *Les meves noces*, 44–45.
39. For a list of common critiques leveled against this tribunal, see Pedro Armengol y Cornet, "Necesidad de reformar la actual organización de los tribunales de comercio," *La Gaceta Jurídica*, 19 April 1860, p. 10; 22 April 1860, pp. 17–18; and "Tribunales de comercio," *El Foro*, 30 September 1864, pp. 157–58.
40. Real Orden 1 octubre 1842, *CL* 39 (1842): 358–59.
41. Decreto 6 diciembre 1868, *CL* 100 (1868): 877.
42. For population calculations of Barcelona and Catalonia based on Floridablanca's census, see Iglésies, *El cens del comte de Floridablanca*, 13, 51. For population in 1857, see *CPE* (1857).
43. ACA, RA, leg. 148, "Barcelona 7 Enero de 1787," and *LACB* (1857).
44. Durán y Bas, *Ensayo biográfico*, 13.
45. For his political views, see Vergés y Permanyer, *Oración fúnebre*. For a short biography, see Durán y Bas, *Ensayo biográfico*.
46. Around the time of Vergés's incarceration, the *Diario de Barcelona* reported the existence of Carlist bands around Tortosa, Montblanc, Tàrrega, Figueres, Girona, Granollers, Valls, Vic, Tremp, and La Pobla de Segur. For the details of the Vergés case, see *Diario de Barcelona*, 2 May 1872, p. 4354; 3 May 1872, p. 4362; 10 May 1872, p. 4674; and AGHUB, exp.: Felipe Vergés y Permañer.

47. Garcia Espuche and Guàrdia i Bassols, *Espai i societat*, 62–63.
48. The trial briefs and the court reporter's summary for the appeal were published: Francisco de Paula Vergés, *Alegación en derecho*; Serrahima, *Alegación en derecho*; and Plá y Soler, *Apuntamiento del pleito*.
49. The lawyer and municipal deputy Josep Maria Rufart noted that the state agreed to give the municipality 8 million pesetas, pursuant the "Law of Compensations." As he explained, this was more than enough to cover the 5 million owed to Ayerbe and other claimants. For the final resolution, see *El Diluvio*, 5 July 1892, pp. 5676–77.
50. Ferrer et al., *Dictamen sobre las principales cuestiones* (unpublished document at the Col·legi d'Advocats library).
51. For Barcelona's conservative professional and intellectual circles, see Casassas, *Entre Escil·la i Caribdis*.
52. *Estatutos para el régimen de los Colegios*; Real Orden 29 mayo 1841, CL 27 (1841): 817; and Real Orden 6 junio 1844, CL 32 (1844): 744–77.
53. CABAJD: 36 December 1836, 19 January 1838; and Jardí, *Història del Col·legi*, 1:18–21.
54. CABAJD: 30 April 1843, 22 May 1843; CABAJG: 9 May 1843; and Jardí, *Història del Col·legi*, 1:35–37.
55. Real Orden 6 junio 1844, CL 32 (1844): 744–77.
56. CABAJD: 30 March 1873.
57. CABAJD: 30 November 1876.
58. CABAJD: 18 October 1883, 28 March 1887, 21 June 1891.
59. CABAJD: 27 June 1844.
60. Real Decreto 1 abril 1855, CL 64 (1855): 396.
61. In 1878 the catalog of the library listed more than 6,500 volumes; three decades later, this number had come to exceed 20,000. In 1884, the only larger libraries in Barcelona were those of the university and the Atheneum. The library's expenses and all yearly expenses of the college were included in a short accounting statement inscribed into the minutes of the general assembly. See CABAJG (1875 to 1899); Colegio de Abogados de Barcelona, *Catálogo de las obras* (1878); Colegio de Abogados de Barcelona. *Catálogo de las obras existentes en la biblioteca* (1908); and Roca y Roca, *Barcelona en la mano*, 149, 154, 169, 242–43.
62. In 1840, the academy listed 36 inaugural members and its ranks swelled to 80 by 1842, but it did not register another soul until 1857. In 1893, its registry indicated that some 657 new members had enrolled since it recommenced activities in 1857. Academia de Jurisprudencia. *Registro general de socios* (1820–93). This registry is found in a small archive, literally a closet, kept alongside the academy minutes at the Col·legi d'Advocats.
63. Angelon, *Guía satírica*, 28; and "Academias de Jurisprudencia y Legislación — de Zaragoza y de Barcelona — Diputados Catalanes," *La Gaceta Jurídica*, 13 December 1860, pp. 563–64.
64. One such instance occurred in 1858 when a record-setting 122 members flooded the annual meeting, causing it to be suspended and reconvened. A similar scenario was repeated in 1862, when another record-setting 180 members attended

the annual meeting, which was suspended as well. CABAJG: 5 December 1858, 20 December 1862, 22 December 1862.
65. *Iris Catalán*, 2 April 1857, p. 1; 5 April 1857, p. 1.
66. CABAJD: 5 May 1855, 29 October 1855.
67. The amount in the treasury can be traced by examining the accounts of the college that were submitted for approval at the annual meeting. See, in general, CABAJG.
68. Karpik, *French Lawyers*, 39; and Leuwers, *L'invention du barreau français*, 77–81.
69. There are some scattered entries in the Audiencia registry, which indicate that the society was functioning in the eighteenth century. See ACA, RA, reg. 933, p. 482; reg. 934, p. 181; reg. 1213, p. 43; reg. 1216, p. 385.
70. CABAJD: 22 January 1859, 6 August 1859, 5 January 1860.
71. The financial difficulties of the Mutual Aid Society are detailed in J. Coll y Britapaja, "La Asociación de Socorros Mutuos de los Abogados de Cataluña," *El Derecho*, 1866, pp. 425–430, 433–448, 457–67.
72. The budget of 1871–72 did not included funds for the society for the first time since 1859. See CABAJG: 28 May 1872. For the insolvency of the society, see CABAJD: 28 June 1876.
73. See, for example, Aracil Gómez, "De las penas perpetuas," *La Gaceta Jurídica*, 6 May 1860, pp. 49–50; 17 May 1860, pp. 73–74; Aracil Gómez, "¿La prostitución pública, es un mal remediable ó necesario? Es conveniente ó no su reglamentación?" *El Foro*, 8 April 1861, pp. 37–39; Francisco Oller y Borrás, "Igualdad en los medios legales de defensa," *El Foro*, 26 August 1861, pp. 137–140; Anonymous, "Juzgados de Paz," *El Foro*, 4 November 1861, pp. 185–87; "Defensa de Don Manuel Matamoros García, acusado de pretender abolir o variar en España la Religión Católica Apostólica Romana — Audiencia de Granada," *El Foro*, 14 July 1862, pp. 237–40; 21 July 1862, pp. 246–48; 28 July 1862, pp. 254–56; 4 August 1862, pp. 262–64; and Salvador Balius Bonaplata, "Administración," *El Foro*, 13 April 1863, pp. 121–22.
74. It is unclear for how long the newspaper actually ran. At the AHMB, I have only found numbers running into 1867, although a shaky encyclopedia entry for Josep Maluquer claims that the paper ran until 1869. *Diccionari biogràfic*, s.v. "Josep Maluquer i Tirrell."
75. It is difficult to surmise what was taking place during each directorial shakeup, especially given the reluctance of the college secretaries to spell out in the minutes any of the underlying motivations behind what were usually framed as disputes over procedure rather than substance. Some of these changes are chronicled in Jardí, *Història del Col·legi*, 1:30–35, 49–52.
76. See *Academia de Jurisprudencia y Legislación. Acta de la sesión pública inaugural celebrada en 27 Diciembre de 1868*; *Academia de Jurisprudencia y Legislación de Barcelona. Acta de sesión pública inaugural celebrada en 26 Diciembre de 1869*; *Academia de Jurisprudencia y Legislación de Barcelona. Acta de la sesión pública inaugural celebrada en 20 Diciembre de 1871*; *Acta de la sesión pública inaugural celebrada en la Academia de Legislación y Jurisprudencia de Barcelona. El día 28*

de Diciembre de 1872; Academia de Jurisprudencia y Legislación de Barcelona. Acta de la sesión pública inaugural celebrada en 14 Diciembre de 1873; and Academia de Jurisprudencia y Legislación de Barcelona. Acta de la sesión pública inaugural celebrada en 27 Diciembre 1874.

77. The Moret Law — colloquially called the "Law of Free Wombs" — freed all future children of slaves and prohibited the purchase and transfer of slaves. For the Moret Law, see Scott, *Slave Emancipation in Cuba*, 63–83. For abolition in Spain, see Schmidt-Nowara, *Empire and Anti-slavery*. For the Hispanic Overseas Circle, see Rodrigo y Alharilla, *Los marqueses de Comillas*, 73–75.

78. Roura, *Ramon Martí d'Eixalà*.

79. The lawyer Josep Leopold Feu first coined the term "Catalan school" in the 1860s. See Fradera, *Cultura nacional*, 123–38. The first reference to the "Catalan conservative school" can be found in Durán y Bas, *Noticia de la vida*. This is cited in Riquer i Permanyer, *Identitats contemporànies*, 114.

80. During the course of the entire nineteenth century, only two university professors became college deans. The Romanist Vicenç Rius, by far the least conservative member of the original professoriate, won elections in the early 1860s. Manuel Duran also became dean in 1885. It is difficult to gauge how many tried and lost, because college minutes do not always list all the candidates, but often just record the number of votes received by the winner. However, we are able to chronicle some cases in which professors lost elections: Ramon Martí (1840), Francesc Permanyer (1857), Ramon Roig (1859). CABAJG: 19 December 1840, 7 December 1857, 4 December 1859. There were also numerous instances in which university professors won and lost elections to the various posts on the board of directors.

81. For a brief description of Figuerola's practice in Madrid, see Maluquer i Viladot, *Les meves noces*, 14–15.

82. See Giralt, "El conflicto 'rabassaire'"; Balcells, *El problema agrario*, 27–55; and Ferrer i Alòs, *Pagesos, rabassaires i industrials*.

83. The rights of the *rabassaires* were defended by lawyers who litigated on their behalf. For a summary of some of the arguments made, see Pi y Margall, "La rabassa morta," in *Articles*, 418.

84. The classic Marxist interpretation of the relationship between law and the rise of the "bourgeoisie" can be found in Thompson, *Whigs and Hunters*, 258–69. A fine monograph that has criticized the supposed symbiotic relationship between law, lawyers, and the spread of capitalism is Kostal, *Law and English Railway Capitalism*. The author shows how lawyers used the law to defend traditional property rights and to stymie the steam railway industry.

85. The classic study on the relationship between common and foral law in Spain is García Gallo, "Aportación al estudio de los fueros."

86. For stem and nuclear families in Spain, see Shubert, *Social History*, 36.

87. I explain this in depth in Jacobson, "Law and Nationalism."

88. To be precise, the Catalan law provided that a testator could donate three-quarters of an estate freely; the remaining quarter had to be divided among legitimate children. It was often the case that a child's statutory share was given

to him or her upon marriage, or used to pay for his education. In contrast, Spanish common law mandated that a testator's assets be divided more evenly. It restricted free testamentary donation to one-fifth of an estate, a minuscule amount, while the other four-fifths were to be equally divided among legitimate children. This was modified by another institution — called a *mejora* — which allowed a testator to improve the situation of a preferred child by donating one-third of the assets directly to him or her, and then splitting the rest evenly among all children. The difference between the two systems was subject to endless commentary. It is concisely explained in Alonso Martínez, *El Código Civil en sus relaciones*, 121–45.

89. For the interplay between Catalan customary law, traditional family organization, emphyteutic relationships, and *pairalisme*, see Barrera González, *Casa, herencia y familia*; Congost, *Els propietaris i els altres*, 33–52, 267–69; and McDonogh, *Good Families*, 39–58.
90. García Goyena, *Concordancias, motivos y comentarios*, 326.
91. The draft code's proposed solution on how emphyteutic obligations could be "redeemed" was complicated. If an establishment was permanent, the plan was to convert the usufructuary owner into an alodial owner of properties subjected to mortgages held by the former direct owner. If an establishment was temporary, however, the direct owner would be granted ownership, while the usufructuary owner would be given a leasehold that would expire at the end of the term. For a thorough examination of emphyteusis and debates over its reform, see Clavero, *El Código y el fuero*, 84–154; and Congost, "Sagrada propiedad imperfecta."
92. For a thorough chronicle of the protests, see Lasso Gaite, *Crónica de la codificación*, 241–90.
93. For a thorough analysis of the protest to the 1851 draft code in Catalonia, see Salvador Coderch, *La compilación y su historia*.
94. For this observation, see Garcia Balañà, "Ordre jurídic," 85–111.
95. Cadafalch y Buguñá, *Inconvenientes de la sucesión forzosa* and *¿Conviene uniformar?* For a thorough examination of the various authors who contributed to the debate, see Pérez Collados, "El derecho catalán de sucesiones."
96. Cadafalch y Buguñá, *¿Conviene uniformar?*, 133.
97. Ibid., 76.
98. Ibid., 115, 137, 168.
99. This article was published in *La Patrie* in March 1858 and then later incorporated into his book, *Les ouvriers européens*. Relevant excerpts from the latter are reprinted in Cadafalch y Buguñá, *¿Conviene uniformar?*, 323–63.
100. Cadafalch y Buguñá, *¿Conviene uniformar?*, 151.
101. Agustí Trilla y Alcover, "La llibertat de testa y l'institució d'hereu segons las lleys catalanas," *La Renaixensa*, 1 March 1871, 34–35.
102. The tendency of the Catalan middle classes to spread inheritances out more evenly in the nineteenth century is a recurrent theme in Ponce and Ferrer, *Família i canvi social*.
103. Falguera, *Conferencias*, 13, 17.

104. Durán y Bas, *Memoria*, 218.
105. Ibid., pp. xiv, xciv.
106. *Diario de Barcelona*, 22 January 1881, pp. 908–9.
107. Such artisan and shopkeeper inheritance practices are depicted in the novel Santiago Rusiñol, *L'auca del Senyor Esteve* (1907).
108. Vives y Cebriá, *Observaciones sobre algunos artículos*, 13.
109. Hurtado, *Quaranta anys d'advocat*, 1:17.
110. Almirall, *Las leyes forales*, 112.
111. "Un poco de lógica," *La Publicidad*, 11 January 1881, p. 1.
112. Valentí Almirall, "Discurs en defensa del dret civil de Catalunya," *Diari Català*, 30 January 1881, p. 232.
113. See, for example, Martí de Eixalá, *Tratado elementar [sic]*, and Sanponts y Barba, Martí de Eixalá, and Ferrer y Subirana, *Las Siete Partidas*.
114. Cadafalch y Buguñá, *Inconvenientes de la sucesión forzosa*, 7, 56.
115. Moret y Prendesgast and Silvela, *La familia foral y la familia castellana*.
116. See Giner, *Estudios jurídicos*, 33–49; and Azcárate, *Estudios filosóficos*, 307–58.
117. Ulloa y Rey, *DSCS*, 21 February 1885, pp. 1292–93, 1319. Incidentally, Wifred the Hairy was a real and not a fictional character. The first count of Barcelona, he died in the late ninth century. In any case, Ulloa's invocation of Wifred was meant to be facetious.
118. By the 1860s, only republicans pressed for the abolition of emphyteusis. During the First Republic (1873), legislators promulgated a law that made it possible for emphyteutic establishments to be "redeemed" by owners of the usufructuary interests. It is unclear whether the procedure would have worked, because those seeking to redeem them would have to find the money or have access to credit to pay for the redemption. This issue is moot, though, because the law was abolished in 1874 along with many other laws passed during the First Republic. See Clavero, *El Código y el fuero*, 122–28.
119. Aniceto de Palma y Luján, "Congreso de Jurisconsultos," *Revista General de Legislación y Jurisprudencia* 23 (1863): 272–308 [307]. See also *Congreso de Jurisconsultos*.
120. D.F. de P. y D.J.B.S., *Código Civil Español*, p. x.
121. Vives y Cebriá, *Observaciones sobre algunos artículos*, 3.
122. This custom began in 1887 and was still continuing at the end of the century. CABAJD: 17 May 1886, 10 December 1886, 24 December 1886, 9 December 1890, 23 November 1891, 4 January 1892, 26 November 1892, 19 January 1893, 4 December 1893, 17 December 1894, 2 December 1895, 30 November 1896, 6 December 1897, 6 December 1898. It is not clear how many members actually showed up or for how long it lasted.
123. Durán y Bas, "La escuela jurídica catalana," in *Escritos jurídicos*, 347–74; and Durán y Bas and Roure, *Sesión celebrada*.
124. Prat de la Riba, *Ley jurídica de la industria*, in *Obra completa*, 2:19–256.
125. I have borrowed this argument, and reinterpreted it with respect to law, from Fradera, *Cultura nacional*. He, in turn, is heavily reliant on Raymond Williams's

interpretation of literary conservatism in *Culture and Society, 1780–1950*. I have commented on this in Jacobson, "'The Head and Heart of Spain.'"
126. For the Orléanist period, see Leuwers, *L'invention du barreau français*, 298–330. In the case of France, the traditions and customs of the local bars were "invented" by adopting those of Paris.
127. Emphyteusis cannot be considered liberal, even under the most inclusive of definitions, for two reasons. First, the division of property into "direct" and "beneficial" owners violated the principle of the indivisibility of ownership and simply reeked of feudalism. Second, and more important, emphyteusis bound an individual to the contract of his or her ancestors. This is contrary to the most basic of liberal principles, which would prevent anyone from being bound by an agreement that he or she (or his or her spouse) had not entered into by exercise of his or her own free will.
128. I have also explored the issue of lawyers and liberalism in Jacobson, "Droit e politique dans l'Espagne du XIXe siècle." For a different take, see Harty, "Lawyers, Codification."
129. In an influential book from the late 1960s, the Marxist sociologist Jordi Solé-Tura tried to link nationalism with economic interest. He claimed that Catalanism was a vehicle for industrialists to keep tariffs high and for agrarian elites to maintain their traditional property rights. This does not make sense. Both these demands could have been achieved, and were achieved before nationalism, through ordinary liberal-conservative political channels. A nationalist movement, with all its linguistic and cultural accoutrements, promised to be costly; on its face, it offered few tangible economic benefits. Solé-Tura, *Catalanismo y revolución burguesa*.

CHAPTER 5

1. Parés i Puntas, *Tots els refranys catalans*, chap. 6, nos. 1738, 1742; chap. 8, nos. 1222, 1229, 1241, 1316.
2. Ibid., chap. 6, nos. 622, 1628; chap. 8, nos. 1236, 1246, 1364, 1375.
3. Perez Galdós, *Doña Perfecta*, 56.
4. There is a history of industrial engineers in Barcelona: Garrabou, *Enginyers industrials*.
5. ACA, RA, exp. (1839), caja 188, no. 1.
6. ACA, RA, exp. (1840), caja 197, no. 1.
7. ACA, RA, exp. (1844), caja 236, no. 1.
8. ACA, RA, exp. (1843), caja 228, no. 1.
9. Real Orden 23 enero 1839. Cited in ACA, RA, exp. (1843), caja 228; no. 1.
10. Angelón, *El abogado defensor*, 12.
11. Fors, *De la abogacía*, 29.
12. Balzac, *Colonel Chabert*, 100.
13. D.A.G., *El abogado*, 33–34.
14. Altadill, *Barcelona y sus misterios*, 200, 528.

15. Altadilll, *La ambición en la mujer*, 168, 170.
16. The relationship between literary satire and professional power is explored in Corfield, *Power and the Professions*.
17. For the bar in 1857, I was able to identify the geographic origins of 288 of 459 lawyers. About 44 percent were born Barcelona, while an additional 47 percent were from other areas in Catalonia. With respect to the bar in 1897, I found information on 719 of 796 lawyers. Fifty-two percent came from Barcelona, 37 percent from other areas in Catalonia, and the rest from outside Catalonia. The figures for 1897, however, most likely overstate the percentage of lawyers from Barcelona and Catalonia, and understate those who came from outside the region. This is, because the great majority of those who could not be identified had attended university outside Barcelona and were mostly born outside Catalonia. AGHUB.
18. For 1857 I located the professions of the fathers of 120 of 459 lawyers enrolled in the college. For 1897 I found this information for 367 out of 796 members. The years 1857 and 1897 have no special relevance. They were simply chosen to coincide with years for which censuses were taken.
19. For the social origins of Neapolitan and Florentine lawyers, see Siegrist, "Gli avvocati nell'Italia del XIX secolo," 148. For English and Welsh barristers, see Duman, *English and Colonial Bars*, 17. For attorneys in the province of Hannover, see Ledford, *From General Estate to Special Interest*, 145–49. Other useful studies have focused on law school matriculates and graduates: Harrigan and Neglia, *Lycéens et collégiens sous le Second Empire*, tables 21, 117; and Jarausch, *Students, Society, and Politics*, 152–53. Some authors have compared and digested multiple studies: Charle, "Professionen und intellektuelle," and Banti, "Burgesies de les 'professions,'" 28–29.
20. None of the studies mentioned in the previous footnote cover exclusively an industrial city, except for Duman's work on England, as most barristers lived in London. The other studies examine the origins of lawyers or law students from broader areas (i.e., the countries of France and Germany; the province of Hannover) or less industrialized cities (Naples, Florence). Studies of industrialized cities might yield data that are similar to data of Barcelona. This, however, remains to be seen.
21. There is an interesting biography by his grandchild: Serrahima, *Un advocat del segle XIX*.
22. Altadill, *Barcelona y sus misterios*, 180.
23. Coll i Amargós, *Narcís Verdaguer i Callís*, 30–32; and AGHUB, Narciso Verdaguer y Callís.
24. García Venero, *Rius y Taulet*, 51–52; AGHUB, Francisco Rius y Taulet.
25. The classic study on (downward and upward) social mobility is Kaelble, *Social Mobility*.
26. For university and secondary school fees in 1857, see *Ley de Instrucción Pública (1857)*, 67.
27. For artisan salaries, see Cerdá, "Monografía estadística," 629–40.
28. These calculations were made by tabulating receipts for matriculation and de-

grees present in student files. See AGHUB, exps.: Manuel Llopis y Ameller, Francisco Andreu y Grau, Jaime Barnadas y Fortiana, José Cens y Roquer, José María Vives y Mendoza, José María Vilanova y Santomá, Fernando Coll y Soler, Jaime Vila y Escardó, José Bosch y Avilés, Pío Vilalta y Cardona.
29. Altadill, *Barcelona y sus misterios*, 378.
30. AGHUB, exps.: Francisco Permañer y Tuyet, Felipe Vergés y Permañer.
31. For an interesting case study of such a phenomenon, see Pascual, *Els Torelló*.
32. Barrera González, *Casa, herencia y familia*, 263.
33. Garrabou, Planas, and Saguer, *Un capitalisme impossible*, 51–55.
34. For Bertran, see Garcia Balañà, "Ordre jurídic," 63. For Cadafalch, see Maluquer i Viladot, *Les meves noces*, 45; and AGHUB, exp.: Joaquin Cadafalch y Buguñá.
35. ACA, RA, exp. (1822), caja 14, no. 455.
36. ACA, RA, exp. (1830), caja 110, no. 535. AGHUB, exp.: Francisco Rius y Taulet.
37. This story is told in Serrahima, *Un advocat del segle XIX*.
38. For some interesting information on the Duran family, and some of the other previously mentioned legal families, see Jardí, *1000 famílies catalanes*, 35–54.
39. Alexandre Bacardí was a well-known expert on civil law and colonial law. A few members of the Milà de la Roca family were members of the College of Lawyers upon its foundation in 1833. For Bacardí's publications, see Bacardí, *Manual del derecho civil vigente* and *Nuevo Colon*. These families are studied in McDonogh, *Good Families*, 159, 161.
40. Even in the twentieth century, when it became common for some sons of the "good families," to study law, few pursued a career as a lawyer. McDonogh, *Good Families*, 126.
41. Josep Bertran's son Felip Bertran d'Amat became a distinguished lawyer-financier and politician and president of the Academy of Jurisprudence. Felip married into the Musitu family and his son, Josep Bertran i Musitu married into the Güells. See McDonogh, *Good Families*, 88, 151, 218; Jardí, *1000 famílies catalanes*, 46; and Cañellas and Toran, *El personal polític*, 87, 168.
42. On the baptismal certificate of Melcior Ferrer's son, Ramon Ferrer i Estruch, his grandfather is listed as Ramon Estruch, one of the principal shareholders of the Hispano-Colonial Bank. AGHUB: Melchor Ferrer y Brugada, Ramón Ferrer y Estruch. For the Estruchs, see Cabana, *Bancs i banquers a Catalunya*, 11.
43. The de facto freedom of secondary-school teachers to interpret the curriculum is emphasized in Boyd, *Historia Patria*, 4–40.
44. For 1857 I was able to track the educational background of some 248 of 459 lawyers enrolled in the bar. For 1897 I was able to find information for 583 of 796 lawyers. Because many students alternated between various schools, I have made rough calculations based on where they spent the *majority* of their years of education. Another problem is that records for those who attended secondary school during the Democratic Sexennium (1868–1873) are quite patchy. During this period, most all religious schools were formally closed, but some still operated. To identify whether a school was religious or secular, I used

IPBM (1878–79, 1882–83, 1897–98) and UBMIP (1858–59, 1867–68, 1877–78, 1899–1900).

45. The number of male religious in Spain grew from 1,683 in the 1860 census to 10,745 by 1901. Callahan, *Catholic Church*, 52.
46. IPBM (1896–97), 86–97. For the importance of the Sacred Heart School to elite society, see McDonogh, *Good Families*, 122–25.
47. For the increasing influence of the church in education in Barcelona and its (tragic) political consequences, see Connelly Ullman, *Tragic Week*, 28–38.
48. For this reputation of the Vic seminary, see Ramisa, *Els orígens del catalanisme conservador*, 60; and Coll i Amargós, *Narcís Verdaguer i Callís*, 40.
49. Roure, *Recuerdos*, 1:15–17.
50. AGHUB, exps.: Luis Durán y Ventosa, Raimundo Durán y Ventosa, Juan José Permanyer y Ayats, Ricardo Permanyer y Ayats, Francisco de Paula Vergés y Mas, Felipe Vergés y Mas.
51. Diglossia in Catalonia is explained in depth in Marfany, *La llengua maltractada*, 307–443. For elite linguistic habits in the early twentieth century, see McDonogh, *Good Families*, 115–22.
52. Coroleu, *Barcelona y sus alrededores*, 47–48.
53. In his memoirs, Maluquer recalls various lawyers with whom he spoke only Spanish in the 1870s and 1880s. One was Pedro del Balzo, whom he described as "a Spaniard raised here, in our land"; another was Juan Díaz, who was from the Americas; another was Luis María Camino who he believed, perhaps erroneously, spent time in the Antilles. Maluquer i Viladot, *Les meves noces*, 38, 46, 74.
54. The 1897 bar, for example, consisted of 796 lawyers. Out of this number, I was able to find 719 academic files at the university. Although a few files could have been lost, those that were not found represent lawyers who enrolled in the Barcelona bar but had not attended the university there. Most of these were undoubtedly persons who immigrated to Barcelona. Moreover, according to those files which I have found, about 10 percent of the bar was born outside Catalonia. AGHUB, exps.
55. For Camino's family origins, see AGHUB: Luis María Camino y Alonso del Real; and Maluquer i Viladot, *Les meves noces*, 74.
56. Illas y Vidal and Figuerola, *Elementos de gramática castellana*.
57. *Prospecto y reglamento del Colegio de Valldemia*, 26.
58. See, for example, AGHUB, exps.: Mariano Pons y Tarrech, Pablo Valls y Bonet, Cayetano Martí de Eixalá, Laureano Figuerola y Ballester.
59. AGHUB, exps.: Francisco Barret y Druhet (Alcalá de Henares), José Buigas y Respall (Zaragoza), Fernando de Delás y de Jalpí (Valencia), Francisco Permanyer y Tuyet (Seville).
60. Roure, *Recuerdos*, 1:121–26.
61. Medicine and law were the most popular subjects: the schools of science, pharmacy, and philosophy were smaller. The average number of students matriculated in the various departments between 1858 and 1889 are as follows: medicine (653), law (576), science (264), pharmacy (218), and philosophy (141). *UBMIP* (1858 to 1889).

62. The average number of licentiates in law awarded from 1841 to 1888 was about fifty-two. Some small gaps exist in the records, particularly from 1845 to 1849. See AGHUB, *Registro de títulos espedidos por la superioridad.*
63. Roure, *Recuerdos*, 1:126.
64. For the changing requirements of the law degree in the nineteenth century, see Peset Reig, "Estudios de derecho y profesiones jurídicas."
65. Roure, *Recuerdos*, 1:122–24.
66. Enric Prat de la Riba, "Pròleg," in Duran i Ventosa, *Regionalisme i federalisme*, 24.
67. Benet and Martí, *Barcelona a mitjan segle XIX*, 183–84. AGHUB, exp.: Juan Gualberto Nogués y Mossoll.
68. Serraclara, *La nueva Inquisición*, and DSCCD, 10 November 1869, p. 4166; DSCCD, 18 November 1869, p. 4282; DSCCD, 12 January 1870, p. 4681.
69. Maluquer i Viladot, *Les meves noces*, 38.
70. Corominas, *Els anys de joventut*.
71. This story is told in Hurtado, *Quaranta anys d'advocat*, 1:23–42. Hurtado fails to mention, though, that both he and Corominas flirted with anarchism. For this, see Marfany, *Aspectes del modernisme*, 25–26.
72. Roure, *Recuerdos*, 1:127–33, 239, and 2:57–63; and Serrahima, *Un advocat del segle XIX*, 57–65, 67.
73. Cattini, *Historiografia i catalanisme*, 25–74.
74. Varela, *La novela de España*, 119.
75. Roure, *Recuerdos*, 1:238.
76. The apprenticeship was first abolished in 1807 but resurrected during the return to absolutism in 1823. The Progressives considered it an impediment to freedom of practice and nullified it in 1836. The Liberal Union resurrected a two-year apprenticeship for a short period beginning in 1858. During this latter period, a student could apprentice at the same time as undertaking university studies. For laws reestablishing the apprenticeship requirement, see Real Decreto 14 octubre 1824, *CL* 9 (1824): 230–96; and Real Decreto 11 septiembre 1858, *CL* 77 (1858): 200–210.
77. The Moyano Law (1857) gave the University of Madrid a monopoly on the award of all doctorates. Legislators removed the monopoly during the Democratic Sexennium (1868–73). Many Barcelona lawyers, in fact, took advantage of this to obtain doctorates in this time. See, for example, AGHUB, exps.: Joaquín Almeda y Roig, Ángel Bas y Amigó, Guillermo María de Brocá y Montagut, Ramón Catá de la Torre, Francisco Vergés y Mas, Darío Rumeu y Torrent, Juan José Permanyer y Ayats, Manuel Planas y Casals, Juan Sol y Ortega, José María Vallés de Ribot, Joaquín Vehils y Catá de la Torre.
78. Maluquer i Viladot, *Les meves noces*, 14–16, 53, 98–99.
79. Cambó, *Memorias*, 50.
80. Maluquer i Viladot, *Les meves noces*, 38.
81. Ossorio, *El alma de la toga*, 199.
82. Roure, *Recuerdos*, 1:121, 239.
83. Serrahima, *Un advocat del segle XIX*, 32–38, 55.
84. Durán y Bas and Roure, *Sesión celebrada*, 19.

85. Balzac, *Old Goriot*, 128.
86. From the 1845 to 1890, the college averaged some twenty-five new enrollments per year. The university awarded an average of some fifty-two degrees between 1841 and 1888. CABAJG (1845 to 1890); and AGHUB, *Registro de títulos expedidos por la superioridad*. There are some gaps in the records, particularly from 1845 to 1849, so the degree average is not exact.
87. Angelón, *Guía satírica*, 28.
88. There were other tests used to classify a defendant as "poor." See *Ley de Enjuiciamiento Civil* (1855), art. 182; *Ley de Enjuiciamiento Criminal*, art. 123.
89. "De los honorarios de los abogados," *El Foro*, 23 June 1862, pp. 209–10.
90. The thousands of files of college members are almost exclusively filled with lawyers requesting places as public defenders and notifying the college of their replacements when they are out of town or on vacation. Some files are annotated with calculations in the margins to make sure that no advocate exceeded a combined total of four years. See ANC, Colegio de Abogados, exps.
91. LACB (1833 to 1900).
92. Ossorio, *Mis memorias*, 30.
93. Statistics of crimes and punishments were often compiled at the end of the year. This list of offenses comes from from the most common crimes listed in ACA, RA, exp. (1842), caja 220, no. 1; exp. (1845), caja 252, no. 1.
94. Maluquer i Viladot, *Les meves noces*, 24.
95. Parés i Puntas, *Tots els refranys catalans*, chap. 8, nos. 1232, 1233.
96. Ossorio, *Mis memorias*, 31.
97. *El Foro*, 9 September 1861, p. 149.
98. See, for example, Ventosa and Villalaz, *Acusaciones pronunciadas*.
99. Duran noted that Torres's successes included "Canela... Fiol... Bofill... and others of great fame." Durán y Bas and Roure, *Sesión celebrada*, 18.
100. For this procedure, see *Estatutos para el régimen de los Colegios*, 10. During the course of the century, the college normally reviewed around ten to twenty-five fee-reductions per year. CABAJG (1858 to 1899).
101. Ossorio, *Mis memorias*, 27.
102. Maluquer i Viladot, *Les meves noces*, 58.
103. From 1853 to 1865, lawyers in the lowest tax bracket paid a tax ranging from 270 reales (67.5 pesetas) to 26 escudos (65 pesetas). From 1866 to 1884, this number rose from 60 to 95 pesetas. Compare this to that of a carpenter. In 1846 the average carpenter in Barcelona paid 130 reales (32 pesetas). From 1870 to century's end, an average carpenter paid 50 pesetas. For these figures, see AHMB, Cadastre, Indústria (1853, 1860, 1860–65); and ACA, Hacienda, Inventario, nos. 12.642, 12.672, 12.678, 12.700, 16.505, 16.525.
104. In 1846 the average lawyer from Barcelona paid 290 reales per year in taxes. Other relevant figures include: carpenters (130 reales); architects, doctors, notaries (290 reales). See Real Decreto 27 marzo 1846, CL 36 (1846): 545–47.
105. In 1870 the average lawyer from Barcelona paid 219 pesetas per year in taxes. Other amounts include carpenters, plumbers (50 pesetas); architects, doctors, pharmacists (238 pesetas); notaries (206 pesetas). *Consultor de los Ayuntamientos*.

106. *Ley de Instrucción Pública (1857)*, art. 228. For salaries at the turn of the century, see Villacorta Baños, *Profesionales y burócratas*, 212.
107. "Los promotores fiscales," *El Foro*, 6 January 1862, p. 2.
108. Degollada, *Memoria del abogado*, 5.
109. Serrahima, *Un advocat del segle XIX*, 113.
110. Serrahima's family donated some of his billing records to the National Archive. I have tabulated the following approximate yearly earnings: 1881 (44,000 pesetas), 1900 (51,000 pesetas). ANC, Fons Serrahima, inventari 321, caixes 86, 87.
111. I have extracted these figures from Serrahima's previously mentioned billing records and from those fees audited by the College of Lawyers. See, for example, CABAJD: 6 October 1863, 16 May 1865, 7 November 1865, 27 February 1871, 30 April 1874, 3 January 1876, 17 February 1876, 28 April 1876, 18 February 1879, 25 February 1879, 25 April 1879, 30 March 1885, 10 September 1885, 26 November 1885, 10 September 1885, 26 November 1885, 30 January 1888, 16 April 1888.
112. These observations are based on shareholders lists from a number of companies, in which the notaries recorded occupations. See AHPB, José Manuel Planas Compte (1850), vol. 1, p. 265 (Ferrocarril del Norte); AHPB, José Falp (1852), vol. 1, p. 239 (Ferrocarril de Barcelona a Zaragoza); AHPB, José Manuel Planas Compte (1864), vol. 1, p. 423 (Banco Territorial y de Crédito); AHPB, José Xuriach Fabra (1863), vol. 1, p. 19 (Auxiliar del Ensanche y Reforma de Barcelona). For these companies, persons described as "lawyers" averaged the following amount invested: FBZ (119,660 reales), FN (46,000 reales), BTC (46,580 reales), AERB (69,167 reales). This was significantly less than persons described as "men of commerce" for each of the respective companies: FBZ (163,700 reales), FN (120,000 reales), BTC (102,000 reales), AERB (86,428 reales). The amounts doctors and doctor-surgeons invested were, on the whole, slightly lower than lawyers: FBZ (52,333) (40,000 reales), BTC (n/a) AERB (68,333 reales). This information was accessed and calculated through the database compiled and administered by the Departament d'Història i Institucions Econòmiques de la Universitat de Barcelona, *Empreses i empresaris a la Catalunya del segle XIX*.
113. For Romaní, see Rodrigo y Alharilla, *Los Marqueses de Comillas*, 147. For Brocà, see Maluquer i Viladot, *Les meves noces*, 29.
114. Fontana, *La revolució liberal*, 136–37.
115. For the foundational articles of Font y Alexander y Cia, see AHPB, Salvador Clos Gualba (1853), vol. 3, p. 201. During a shareholders' meeting in 1861, Antonio Font de Sol appeared as the largest shareholder. AHPB, Pedro Pablo Gose (1861), p. 652. This information was accessed through the database, Departament d'Història i Institucions Econòmiques de la Universitat de Barcelona, *Empreses i empresaris a la Catalunya del segle XIX*.
116. For the Delàs family, see Maluquer i Viladot, *Les meves noces*, 51; and AGHUB: Fernando de Delás i de Gelpí.
117. See Jardí, *Història del Col·legi*, 1:77, 84, 87; and Voltes Bou, *La banca barcelonesa*, 103.
118. Voltes Bou, *La banca barcelonesa*, 38.
119. Cambó, *Memorias*, 25.

120. For these figures, see Arnabat Mata, *La revolució de 1820*, 104–5; Benet and Martí, *Barcelona a mitjan segle XIX*, 546; de la Fuente Monge, *Los revolucionarios de 1868*, 186–88; and Gómez-Navarro, Moreno Luzón, and Rey Reguillo, "La élite parlamentaria entre 1914 y 1923," 116. The percentage for Spain appears even higher than those of France and Italy. See Le Béguec, *La république des avocats*, 37–41; and Cammarano, "The Professions in Parliament."
121. For elections to the Cortes, studies of Barcelona show slightly lower figures than the rest of Spain. See Arnabat Mata, *La revolució de 1820*, 104–5; and Janué i Miret, *Els polítics en temps de revolució*, 265–66. At the municipal level, lawyers were not as well represented as commercial and industrial classes. See Fuster i Sobrepere, "Els regidors de Barcelona," 190; and Cañellas and Toran, *El personal polític*, 164–65.
122. Maluquer i Viladot, *Les meves noces*, 48.
123. Josep Maluquer noted that he practiced in Madrid while serving as senator. DSCS, 23 February 1885, p. 1317. His younger cousin, Joan Maluquer, also identified Modest Llorens, Estanislau Figueras, Joaquim Maria de Paz (a senator for life), and Josep Leopold Feu as other Catalan lawyer-politicians who took on appeals in front of the Supreme Court in Madrid. Maluquer i Viladot, *Les meves noces*, 32.
124. Montserrat Llorens, "Francisco de P. Rius i Taulet," in Vicens i Vives and Llorens, *Industrials i polítics (segle XIX)*, 442; and Cañellas and Toran, *El personal polític*, 191.
125. Maluquer i Viladot, *Les meves noces*, 42, 43, 49, 52.
126. Hurtado, *Quaranta anys d'advocat*, 1:14.
127. Maluquer i Viladot, *Les meves noces*, 46.
128. For entrepreneurial widows with fortunes in nineteenth-century Barcelona, see Rodrigo y Alharilla, "Mujeres con fortuna, mujeres afortunadas" (unpublished article cited with the permission of the author).
129. Ossorio, *El alma de la toga*, 231, 239–40 (emphasis in original).
130. Hurtado, *Quaranta anys d'advocat*, 1:13.
131. Ibid., 16.
132. *LACB* (1848).
133. At midcentury, for every nonpracticing lawyer, there were 2.3 who practiced. At century's end, for every nonpracticing lawyer, only 1.15 practiced. *LACB* (1848, 1900).
134. For overcrowding and the threat of proletarianization in Germany, see Siegrist, "Public Office or Free Profession?"
135. Ossorio, *El alma de la toga*, 13–14.
136. These are the reasons invoked by Hurtado, *Quaranta anys d'advocat*, 1:16–17.
137. To this end, in 1882 the government created a vast number of new "criminal *audiencias*," so that two existed in each of the country's forty-nine provinces. This proved too costly, and in 1892 the law was amended so that each province had one such court. For court reforms of the 1880s, Agúndez, *Historia del poder judicial*, 130.
138. Ossorio, *El alma de la toga*, 199.

139. Pérez Galdós, *Doña Perfecta*, 56.
140. Pich i Mitjana, *El Centre Català*, 42–44.
141. During the nineteenth century, only four Catalans ever became ministers of justice: Ramon Salvató (1837), Jacint Felix Domènech (interim minister, 1854), Laureà Figuerola (1870), and Manuel Duran (1899). All four of them served less than a year in office. Lasso Gaite, *El Ministerio de Justicia*, 20–24, 72–73. I have found no Catalans who served as Supreme Court magistrates in the nineteenth century, and only a few Barcelona lawyers who became ministers of state in other areas.
142. Prat de la Riba, "Discurs del President del Centre Escolar Catalanista de Barcelona," in *Obra completa*, 1:131–40 [132–33].
143. *Ley orgánica del Poder Judicial*, art. 117 (rules of incompatibility for judges and magistrates), art. 772 (rules of incompatibility for prosecutors).
144. *La Gaceta Jurídica* (22 July 1860), p. 261.
145. CABAJD, 19 June 1899.
146. *DSCS*, 20 February 1885, pp. 1264–68; 23 February 1885, p. 1321.
147. Hurtado, *Quaranta anys d'advocat*, 1:20.
148. Almirall, *Lo catalanisme*, 144–45.
149. Duran i Ventosa, *Regionalisme i federalisme*, 290.

CHAPTER 6

1. This argument has been made with respect to Germany: Ledford, *From General Estate to Special Interest*, 291–99.
2. For the rise of this group, see Riquer i Permanyer, "La Diputació conservadora: 1875–1880."
3. This interesting story has been revealed recently in "Una revelación histórica. El precio de la paz carlista," *La Vanguardia*, 2 April 2006.
4. The college deans from the outset of the Restoration to the century's end were Melcior Ferrer (1873–1877; 1878–1880), Idelfons Par (1877–78), Francesc Barret (1879–1791), Josep Borrell (1881–85), Manuel Duran (1886–1891), Maurici Serrahima (1891–95), and Josep Vilaseca (1896–1899). Ferrer, Barret, Duran, and Vilaseca were members of the League for Social Order and the Conservative Party. Borrell and Serrahima stayed out of politics, but were men of order.
5. CABAJD, 5 January 1875.
6. For divisions at the college at the outset of the Restoration, see Maluquer i Viladot, *Les meves noces*, 21–23.
7. For the problems with the degree, see Salvador Balius Bonaplata, "Administración," *El Foro*, 13 April 1863, pp. 121–22.
8. Rincón Igea, "La educación en Barcelona," 366–67.
9. The Academy of Administrative Law's first publication was its bylaws, *Academia de Derecho Administrativo de Barcelona. Estatutos y reglamento*. The only other publication I have found is Somoza-Llanos, *Discurso leído*. Following 1880, it never changed its board of directors, a fact that suggests inactivity.
10. *Academia de Derecho. Estatutos y reglamento*.

11. CABAJD: 21 March 1879; 3 May 1879.
12. The last Academy of Law publication that I have found is *Academia de Derecho. Exposición a S.M. La Reina Regente.*
13. For a detailed description of the motivation behind the alleged arson, see Roure, *Recuerdos de mi larga vida: La restauració dels Borbons*, 51–54.
14. Hurtado, *Quaranta anys d'advocat*, 1:13.
15. Roca y Roca, *Barcelona en la mano*, 79.
16. For some insightful comments on the architecture and symbolism of the iconography of this building, see Umbach, "A Tale of Second Cities."
17. Cited in Permanyer, *Cites i testimonis sobre Barcelona*, 109.
18. For changes in dress, oratory, and court location, see Maluquer i Viladot, *Les meves noces*, 49; and Hurtado, *Quaranta anys d'advocat*, 1:13–16.
19. *Unió Catalanista. Bases pera la Constitució Regional*, 8.
20. Juan José Permanyer, "Necesidad de que la vida jurídica de Cataluña sea catalana en todas sus esferas y manifestaciones (Discurso leído en la sesión pública inaugural de la Academia de Jurisprudencia, el día 6 de Marzo de 1896)," *Revista Jurídica de Cataluña* 2 (1896): 161–189 [163, 189].
21. Trías, *Conferencias*, 5–6.
22. Romá y Rosell, *Las señales de la felicidad*, 306.
23. *Acta de la primera sesión inaugural*, 59.
24. D.F. de P. y D.J.B.S., *Código Civil Español*, p. vi.
25. For resistance to procedural codification in the 1820s, see Oliver y Esteller, *Estudios históricos*, 152–68; and Gay Escoda, "Notas sobre el derecho supletorio," 860–61.
26. Riquer i Permanyer, *Identitats contemporànies*, 299–301.
27. The decree is analyzed in Baró Pazo, *La codificación*, 211.
28. Alonso Martínez, *El Código Civil*, 29, 451.
29. The first vote count at the Conference of Jurisconsults listed ninety-three persons in attendance, while the last vote count numbered eighty-nine members, although an additional six members later tried to register their vote. Of these latter ninety-five members, only thirteen did not appear on the list of the College of Lawyers of Barcelona. See "Segona sessió del Congrés Català de Jurisconsults," *Diari Català*, 4 January 1881, p. 22; "Congrés Català de Jurisconsults, sessió d'ahir, dia 25," *Diari Català*, 26 January 1881, p. 198; and "Congrés Català de Jurisconsults, sessió d'ahir, dia 27," *Diari Català*, 27 January 1881, p. 212.
30. CABAJD, 11 December 1880.
31. At the conference, one delegate read the announcement verbatim. Rómulo Mascaró, "Discurso Pronunciado en el Congreso Catalán de Jurisconsultos," *La Publicidad*, 12 January 1881, p. 1. The announcement was also reprinted in *Congreso Catalán de Jurisconsultos, 1880–1881.*
32. *El Diluvio*, 29 January 1881, p. 339.
33. Luis María de Llauder, "Nuestra Legislación Civil," *El Correo Catalán*, 9 January 1881, p. 3.
34. "Congreso Catalán de Jurisconsultos. Sesión del día 25," *El Correo Catalán*, 26 January 1881, p. 3.

35. "Congrés Català de Jurisconsults. Sessió d'ahir, dia 17," *Diari Català*, 18 January 1881, p. 134.
36. "Congres Català de Jurisconsults. Sessió d'ahir, dia 20," *Diari Català*, 21 January 1881, p. 158.
37. Valentí Almirall, "Discurs en defensa del dret civil de Catalunya," *Diari Català*, 30 January 1881, p. 233.
38. "Congreso Catalán de Jurisconsultos. Sesión del día 13," *El Correo Catalán*, 15 January 1881, p. 3.
39. "Congrés Català de Jurisconsults. Sessió d'ahir, dia 17," *Diari Català*, 18 January 1881, p. 134; and "Congreso Catalán de Jurisconsultos. Sesión del día 17," *El Correo Catalán*, 18 January 1881, p. 3.
40. "Discurso pronunciado en el Congreso Catalán de Jurisconsultos por D. Rómulo Macaró," *La Publicidad*, 18 January 1881, p. 1.
41. "Crónica general," *La Publicidad*, 13 January 1881, p. 3.
42. "Crónica general," *La Publicidad*, 28 January 1881, p. 2.
43. "Congrés Català de Jurisconsults. Sessió d'ahir, dia 21," *Diari Català*, 22 January 1881, pp. 166–67; and *Diario de Barcelona*, 22 January 1881, pp. 908–9.
44. CABAJD, 6 May 1881. The new president of the academy, Josep Borrell, had been the vice president of the Congress and was one of the leading opponents of the government's project.
45. *Academia de Jurisprudencia y Legislación de Barcelona. Dictamen sobre la codificación*, 23.
46. *Acta de la sessió pública celebrada en lo Ateneu*, 34.
47. Felipe Bertrán y de Amat, "De la Inclusión en el Apéndice correspondiente del Código Civil de España del derecho particular de Cataluña como individualidad legal propia de este país," in *Academia de Jurisprudencia y Legislación de Barcelona. Acta de la sesión pública inaugural celebrada en 17 de diciembre de 1890*, 37.
48. *Los trobadors moderns*; and Bofarull y Brocá, *Los trobadors nous*.
49. Luis Gonzaga Pons y Fuster, "La reina abandonada," in Bofarull y Brocá, *Los trobadors nous*, 248–357.
50. Eusebi Pascual, "A Barcelona," in Bofarull y Brocá, *Los trobadors nous*, 40–42.
51. Cited in Anguera, *El català al segle XIX*, 82, 83, 140.
52. For this point, see Marfany, *La llengua maltractada*, 481–82.
53. Illas y Vidal and Figuerola, *Elementos de gramática castellana*.
54. The tongue twister begins with "Setze jutges d'un jutjat mengen fetge d'un penjat..." ("Sixteen judges on a tribunal eat the liver of a hanged man...").
55. Angelón, *Setze jutjes*, 29, 31.
56. For how the *sardana* became the national dance of Catalonia, see Marfany, *La cultura del catalanisme*, 322–52.
57. This play ran through four printed editions, the last appearing in 1914. Roure, *Clarís. Epissodi histórich en tres actes*.
58. For this point, see Marfany, "'Minority' Languages and Literary Revivals," 137–67. Much of my discussion of literary revival is based on this article and other cited works by Marfany.

59. *Diccionari biogràfic*, s.v. "Conrad Roure i Bofill."
60. Balaguer, *Historia de Cataluña*, and Bofarull y Brocá, *Historia crítica*.
61. Joaquim Botet i Sisó, "Los Usatjes de Barcelona. Estudis histórichs y crítichs de la primera de compilació de lleyes catalanas," *La Renaixensa*, 15 February 1871, pp. 17–18; 1 March 1871, pp. 29–31; 15 March 1871, pp. 41–43; 2 April 1871, pp. 55–57; 15 April 1871, pp. 73–75.
62. Agustí Trilla y Alcover, "La llibertat de testar y l'institució d'hereu segons las lleys catalanas," *La Renaixensa*, 1 March 1871, pp. 34–45; 15 March 1871, pp. 46–47; 1 June 1871, pp. 113–14; 15 June 1871, pp. 126–29.
63. Joseph Coroleu, "Dels contractes de enfiteusis y a rabassa morta segons l'antiga y la moderna llegislació," *La Renaixensa* 2 (1879): 161–176, 209–25, 257–70.
64. See, for example, Antoni Aulésti i Pijoan, "L'hereu," *La Renaixensa* 1 (1876): 352–61; Joaquim de Negre y Cases, "Donació o heretament en capítols matrimonials. Afers de família," *La Renaixensa* 2 (1876): 110–20; and Sebastiá Farnés, "Refrans catalans: L'Avi Rabassa," *La Renaixensa* 1 (1883): 395–99.
65. *La Publicidad*, 13 January 1881, p. 3.
66. Torras i Bages, *La tradició catalana*, 378.
67. To take one example, Margalida Tomàs has identified forty-one persons associated with Young Catalonia. She described nine of these persons as lawyers, notaries, or law professors. Moreover, many of those whom she classified under other descriptions likely held law degrees. For example, an additional eight persons worked in public or private administration. Other professions included librarians and archivists (three), printing and photography (three), doctors (three), architects (one), banking and business (three), pedagogy (three), building and manufacture (three), journalism and publishing (five). Margalida Tomàs, "La Jove Catalunya," pp. v–xlvi.
68. "Un poco de lógica," *La Publicidad*, 11 January 1881, p. 1.
69. "¿Qué hacen los catalanistas?," *Correo Catalán*, 9 February 1889, p. 6.
70. In fact, some lawyers first began to use Spanish in pleading in the mid-seventeenth century, before they were required to do so. For this, see Laitin, Solé, and Kalyvas, "Language and the Constructions of States."
71. For this crucial distinction, see Marfany, "Renaixença literària i decadència lingüística," 139–52.
72. Prat de la Riba, "Exposición de la Academia de Legislación y Jurisprudencia sobre el uso del catalán en los actos judiciales," in *Obra completa*, 1:405–9 [407, 409].
73. Resistance not only to Bentham's but also to Blackstone's attempts to provide structure to the common law are pointed out throughout Lobban, *The Common Law*. The failure of the codification movement in England is also discussed in Anderson, *Lawyers*, 3–40.
74. For a summary of Supreme Court jurisprudence on this matter, see Brocá and Amell y Llopís, *Instituciones del derecho civil catalán*, 1:108–11.
75. Vives y Cebriá, *Los usages y demás derechos de Cataluña*, title page.
76. Vives y Cebriá, *Observaciones sobre algunos artículos*.

77. The last edition was Elías and Ferrater, *Manual de derecho civil vigente*, ed. Alejandro de Bacardí, 3d ed. (1885).
78. Elías, *Derecho civil general y foral de España*, p. iii.
79. Romá y Rosell, *Las señales de la felicidad*, 306.
80. My interpretation of Savigny's legal philosophy is reliant on Whitman, *Legacy of Roman Law*.
81. This is explained in Kelley, *Historians and the Law*.
82. Savigny's manifesto against codification, *Vom Beruf unserer Zeit für Gesetzgebung und Rechtswissenschaft*, was never translated into Spanish or Catalan in the nineteenth century. There was an English translation: Savigny, *Of the Vocation of Our Age* (1831).
83. For a complete analysis of influences, see Figueres Pàmies, *La escuela jurídica catalana*.
84. "Código Civil en proyecto," *Diario de Barcelona*, 17 June 1852, p. 3556.
85. Estanislao Reynals y Rabassa, "El derecho nuevo," in *Academia de Jurisprudencia y Legislación de Barcelona. Acta de la sesión pública inaugural celebrada en 27 Diciembre de 1874*; and "El derecho cristiano," in *Academia de Jurisprudencia y Legislación de Barcelona. Acta de la sesión pública inaugural celebrada el día 26 de Enero de 1876*.
86. Durán y Bas, "El derecho en las legislaciones civiles del siglo XIX" (1869), in *Escritos. Estudios jurídicos*, 129–53. The Foundation was not very active: Josep Borrell i Soler, "L'escola històrica de Catalunya," *Revista Jurídica de Cataluña* 33 (1927): 293–303 (293).
87. Durán y Bas, "Prólogo," pp. vi–xix.
88. Durán y Bas, *Memoria*, p. ii.
89. Llobera, "La formació de la ideologia nacionalista catalana," and Bilbeny, *La ideologia nacionalista*, 99–107.
90. For a list of criticisms and accusations commonly leveled against Savigny, see Hermann Klenner, "Savigny's Research Program."
91. See, for example, Cadafalch y Buguñá, *Inconvenientes de la sucesión forzosa*, 25–30.
92. See, for example, the utterances of Josep Maria Vallès de Ribot in "El Meeting de la Bisbal," *El Correo Catalán*, 1 May 1889, p. 7.
93. *Diario de Barcelona*, 21 January 1881, p. 868.
94. Luis María de Llauder, "El derecho civil catalán," *El Correo Catalán*, 3 January 1881, p. 2.
95. Valentí Almirall, "Discurs en defensa del dret civil de Catalunya," *Diari Català*, 30 January 1881, p. 232.
96. *Diario de Barcelona*, 16 January 1881, p. 652.
97. Torras i Bages, *La tradició catalana*, 366.
98. *Diario de Barcelona*, 22 January 1881, pp. 908–9.
99. *Memòria en defensa dels interessos morals*, 43.
100. Alonso Martínez, *El Código Civil*, 370.
101. *Congreso Jurídico Español. Tema primero*, 17.

102. *DSCS*, 21 February 1885, p. 1293.
103. For a full survey of nineteenth-century publications on Catalan law, see Brocá, *Historia del derecho de Cataluña*, 424–63.
104. Prat de la Riba and Montanyola, *Compendi de la doctrina catalanista*, 7.
105. Enrique Prat de la Riba, "Miscelánea jurídica," *Revista Jurídica de Cataluña* 2 (1896): 49.
106. Watson, *Making of the Civil Law*.
107. For the "invention of traditions" thesis applied to excursionism, choral chants, dance, and even some vocabulary within language, see Marfany, *La cultura del catalanisme*, 293–352. His analysis is based on the seminal Hobsbawm and Ranger, *Invention of Tradition*.
108. For the Conservative Basic Law, see *DSCCD*, 17 May 1885, appendix 1. Letters between Silvela and Duran over the matter are printed in Riquer i Permanyer, *Espistolari polític*, 315–19.
109. For German codification, see John, *Politics and the Law* and "The Politics of Legal Unity."
110. Oliver y Esteller, *Breve sumario*, 7.
111. *DSCCD*, 8 June 1885, "Apéndice décimo al núm 167," pp. 1–3; and *DSCCD*, 17 June 1885, p. 5176.
112. Durán y Bas, "Estructura más apropiada para un Código Civil Español," in *Escritos. Estudios jurídicos*, 375–92. For vote tabulations, see G.A., "Congreso Jurídico Español," *Revista General de Legislación y Jurisprudencia* 70 (1887): 37–60, 626–27. For a critique of proceedings, see Bofarull y de Palau, *La codificación civil en España*.
113. "Congreso Jurídico de Barcelona," *Revista General de Legislación y Jurisprudencia* 78 (1888): 186–95; and *Actas del Congreso Jurídico de Barcelona*.
114. *DSCCD*, 19 June 1885, p. 5233.
115. The question of whether such a procedure was constitutional or not was subject to a lively debate in the Senate between Alonso Martínez and Vicente Romero Girón. See *DSCS*, 24 January 1887, 108–10.
116. These concessions can be appreciated by contrasting the contents of the draft Basic Law of the Civil Code proposed by Alonso Martínez in 1881 with that which was eventually approved in 1888. For the 1881 proposal, see *DSCS*, 22 October 1881, "Apéndice quinto al número 24," pp. 1–3. For the 1888 law, see *Código Civil Español* (1889), 2–11.
117. Prat de la Riba, "Sistemes de propaganda catalanista. Primera intervenció al Centre Escolar Catalanista en desembre de 1887," in *Obra completa*, 1:113–20 [115].
118. *Memoria en defensa*, 63.
119. *Missatje*, 4, 7.
120. Article 15 did not mention the words "citizenship" but merely provided general rules concerning the applicability of foral and common law. For the specific wording of Article 15, see *Código Civil Español* (1888), art. 15.
121. Maspons i Anglasell counted twenty meetings: see Maspons i Anglasell, prologue to *La primera victòria*, 15. For numbers in attendance, see "La manifes-

tación de Manlleu," *El Correo Catalán*, 25 April 1889, p. 9 (3,000 persons); "El meeting de la Bisbal," *El Correo Catalán*, 1 May 1889, p. 7 (4,500 people at La Bisbal); and *La Veu de Montserrat*, 4 May 1889, p. 143 (5,000 people at La Bisbal). The numbers reflect those reported by a sympathetic press, so they might be slightly inflated.

122. DSCCD, Legislatura 1888–1889, Indíce, pp. 45–46.
123. Cited in Comalada Negre, *Catalunya davant el centralisme*, 221.
124. Coll i Amargós, *Narcís Verdaguer i Callís*, 204.
125. Verdaguer i Callís, "¡Article 15 aprovat! (de *La Veu de Montserrat* del 20 D'Abril de 1889)," in *La primera victòria*, 50–53.
126. Maluquer Viladot, *Derecho Civil especial de Barcelona*.
127. Ibid., 251.
128. "Discursos de D. Federico Pons pronunciados en el Congreso en los días 18, 19 y 20 de Marzo y 5 de abril de 1889," *Colecció de discursos pronunciats*, 198–241 [p. 212].
129. Verdaguer i Callís, "Crit d'alarma (publicat sense títol com a Revista de Barcelona, a *La Veu de Montserrat*, de Vich del 16 de Febrer de 1889)," in *La primera victòria*, 28.
130. Luciano Ribera, "Herida por la espalda," *Diario de Barcelona*, 12 February 1889, p. 1895.
131. "Nova lley y cau de plets per la família catalana," *El Correo Catalán*, 8 April 1889, p. 4.
132. Verdaguer i Callís, "La primera victòria del catalanisme (de *La Veu de Montserrat* del 3 d'Agost de 1889)," in *La primera victòria*, 99–104.
133. Llorens i Vila, *La Unió Catalanista*, 95.
134. *Exposición que la Academia de Jurisprudencia y Legislación de Barcelona ha dirigido*.
135. "Sección de noticias," *Revista Jurídica de Cataluña* 2 (1896): 328–29.
136. Juan José Permanyer, "Necesidad de que la vida jurídica de Cataluña sea catalana en todas sus esferas y manifestaciones (Discurso leído en la sesión pública inaugural de la Academia de Jurisprudencia, el día 6 de Marzo de 1896)," *Revista Jurídica de Cataluña* 2 (1896): 161–189 [185].
137. Molas, *Lliga Catalana. Un estudi de estasiologia*, 180.
138. Duran i Ventosa, *Regionalisme i federalisme*, 290.
139. For this point, see Ucelay–Da Cal, *El imperialismo catalán*, 81.
140. Grau and López, "L'Exposició Universal del 1888."
141. Ferrando Francés and Amorós, *Història de la llengua catalana*, 481–83.
142. Farnès, "La revindicació."
143. For the conflict between the church and state over whether priests were at liberty to preach the catechism in Catalan, see Figuerola i Garreta, *El Bisbe Morgades*, 539–675.
144. For the phases of nationalist revival, Hroch, *Social Preconditions of National Revival*. Note that I do not claim that Hroch argues that "phase A" always evolves into "phase B." However, I do offer a brief explanation of why this occurs in some cases and does not in others.

145. For the imagination of communities, see Anderson, *Imagined Communities*. This analysis convincingly explains why humans imagine communities in the modern world, but, as the author would certainly admit, it does not alone explain why some nationalist movements succeed and others fail.
146. In this respect, my analysis complements that of Breuilly, *Nationalism and the State*. Breuilly posits that nationalism needs to be understood as chiefly a contest for control of the state. Incidentally, Breuilly's list of contestants includes bourgeoisie, traditional elite, and workers, but he does not address professionals.

CHAPTER 7

1. Weber, "Economy and Law (Sociology of Law)," 875–76.
2. Tocqueville, *Democracy in America*, 251–52.
3. For Montesquieu's views, see "On the Origin and Revolutions of the Civil Laws among the French," in *Spirit of the Laws*, 532–601. For Blackstone's, see Blackstone, *Commentaries on the Law of England*, 1:3–37, 63–92. Hotman's theories and their influence in France and England are analyzed in Pocock, *Ancient Constitution*, 1–29. The relationship between national identity and codification is explored in Halpérin, *Entre nationalisme juridique*.
4. Today, the claim that law is organically reflective of the spirit and personality of the nation has been discredited. Watson, *Evolution of Law*.
5. The reasons why Scots law did not contributed to the creation of a nationalist movement are explored in Kidd, *Subverting Scotland's Past*, 144–65.
6. Kotschnig, *Unemployment in the Learned Professions*.
7. O'Boyle, "Problem of an Excess of Educated Men."
8. Pérez Galdós, *Doña Perfecta*, 56.
9. O'Boyle, "Problem of an Excess of Educated Men," 481; and Bayly, *Birth of the Modern World*, 145.
10. For Germany, see Jarausch, *Unfree Professions*, 105; and Jarausch, "The Decline of Liberal Professionalism," esp. 284. For anti-Semitism at the bar in Germany, see also Müller, *Hitler's Justice*, 43, 59–67. In Hungary, Mária Kovács has noted that some of the most forceful supporters of governmental laws of the 1920s limiting the number of Jews in the legal profession were not bar associations but rather student organizations. Kovács, *Liberal Professions and Illiberal Politics*, 57. O. O. Gruzenberg portrays the prerevolutionary Russian bar as an intellectual oasis within an anti-Semitic society. Gruzenberg, *Yesterday: Memoirs of a Russian-Jewish Lawyer*. For the relationship between overcrowding and xenophobia, anti-Semitism, and misogyny at the bar in early twentieth-century France, see Charle, "Le recrutement des avocats, 1880–1914," and Israel, *Robes noires et années sombres*, 45–49, 56–63.
11. For professionals and the development and decline of the welfare state, see Perkin, *Rise of Professional Society*, and *Third Revolution*.
12. Prat de la Riba, *La nacionalitat catalana*.
13. These references can be found throughout the multiple articles contained in Prat de la Riba, *Obra completa*, vol. 1.

14. These tendencies and influences are explored throughout Ucelay-Da Cal, *El imperialismo catalán*.
15. I have addressed the "civic" and "ethnic" attributes of nationalism in Spain and Catalonia in Jacobson, "The Iberian Mosaic."
16. Hurtado, *Quaranta anys d'advocat*, 2:163–213; and Fina, *De la llei i la justícia*, 139–40. For an informative overview of the twentieth-century history of the college, see Jardí, *Història del Col·legi d'Advocats*, vol. 2.
17. L. Falcón, *Memorias políticas*, 141–52.
18. For an account of one such harrowing experience, see Serrahima, *Memòries de la guerra i de l'exili*, 2:91–131.
19. Avilés, *Tribunales rojos*, 36–37.
20. For the travesties of justice, and detailed descriptions of lawyers, judges, prosecutors, and the accused, see ibid. For a portrait of Avilés, see Casarés, *Memòries d'un advocat laboralista*, 500–504, 532–36. The ample bibliography on revolutionary justice is summarized in an introductory essay to a reprint of Eduardo Barrioberos's account of his activities as head of the Barcelona Revolutionary Tribunal in 1936 and 1937. See Eduard Masjuan, "Introducción."
21. Josep M. Solé i Sabaté documents 3,385 postwar judicial executions in Catalonia, 85 percent of which took place in 1939 and 1940. This number does not include extrajudicial killings, persons who died while being interrogated, or prison deaths. Solé i Sabaté, *La repressió franquista a Catalunya*, 10. The juridical dimensions of the Francoist repression in Madrid have also been studied; see Ruiz, *Franco's Justice*.
22. Cited in Jardí, *Història del Col·legi*, 2:67 (emphasis in original).
23. Solé i Sabaté, *La repressió franquista a Catalunya*, 258–60.
24. Fina, *Des del nostre despatx*, 41, and *De la llei i la justícia*, 139; and L. Falcón, *Memorias políticas*, 146.
25. Interview with Carmen Cabrerizo (11 October 2006).
26. These circles are described in fascinating detail in Fina, *Des del nostre despatx*. In addition to describing the risks of practice during the period, it recounts the ongoings of his and his wife's law office amid the major strikes of the day: Rockwell-Cerdans (1967–68), Tranvías de Barcelona (1967), La Maquinista (1971), SEAT (1971), La Térmica (1973), SEAT and Hispano-Olivetti (1974).
27. Jardí, *Història del Col·legi*, 2:273–74.
28. Borrell y Soler, *El Códic Civil a Catalunya*.
29. Franquesa, *La jurisprudencia*, 12–27; Camps y Arboix, *Historia del derecho catalán*, 68–84.
30. For the latest statement of civil law, see Egea Fernàndez and Ferrer Riba, *Codi Civil de Catalunya i legislació complementària*.
31. Fina, *De la llei i la justícia*, 51.
32. Interview with Eudald Vendrell Ferran (3 October 2007), professor of civil law and practicing lawyer. He estimates that courts in Barcelona use about 70 percent Spanish and 30 percent Catalan.
33. Folguera Crespo, "Revolución y restauración," 470–71.
34. The number of women, their names, and their relative status on the earning scale can be traced in *GJC* (1927 to 1945).

35. Scanlon, *La polémica feminista*, 321; and Morcillo, *True Catholic Womanhood*.
36. Loperena, *El circo de la justicia*, 119.
37. "La vida arrebatada de Lidia Falcón," *El Mundo*, 23 November 2003.
38. Interviews with Carmen Cabrerizo (11 October 2006); Montserrat Avilés (24 October 2006).
39. Loperna, *El circo de la justicia*, 119.
40. Interview with Montserrat Avilés (24 October 2006).
41. L. Falcón, *La vida arrebatada*, 302–5.
42. Interview with Eudald Vendrell Ferran (3 October 2007).
43. Ibid., 83.
44. Roca i Junyent, *Sí advocat!*, 65.
45. For "special interest," see Ledford, *From General Estate to Special Interest*. For "professional society," see Perkin, *Rise of Professional Society*.
46. Wilensky, "Professionalization of Everyone?"

Bibliography

PRIMARY SOURCES

Archives and Official Periodical Reports, Minutes, and Proceedings
See the abbreviations list at the beginning of the Notes.

Databases of Primary Source Materials
Departament d'Història i Institucions Econòmiques de la Universitat de Barcelona, *Empreses i empresaris a la Catalunya del segle XIX.*

Newspapers
El Correo Catalán
El Derecho. Revista de Jurisprudencia y Administración
Diari Català
Diario de Barcelona
El Diluvio
El Foro. Periódico de Jurisprudencia y Administración
La Gaceta Jurídica. Periódico de Jurisprudencia y Administración
Iris Catalán
El Mundo
La Publicidad
La Renaixensa
Revista General de Legislación y Jurisprudencia
Revista Jurídica de Cataluña
La Tramontana
La Vanguardia

Books, Articles, and Pamphlets

Academia de Derecho. *Estatutos y reglamento de la Academia de Derecho. Establecida en Barcelona en 1871.* Barcelona: Ortega, 1891.
Academia de Derecho. *Exposición a S.M. la Reina Regente en suplica de reformas en el derecho público de España.* Barcelona: Tasis, 1898.
Academia de Derecho Administrativo de Barcelona. *Estatutos y reglamento aprobados por el Excmo. Sr. Gobernador de la Provincia en 10 de Marzo 1876.* Barcelona: Ramírez, 1876.
Academia de Jurisprudencia. *Registro general de socios (1820–93).*
Academia de Jurisprudencia y Legislación. *Acta de la sesión pública inaugural celebrada en 27 Diciembre de 1868.* Barcelona: Martí y Cantó, 1875.

Academia de Jurisprudencia y Legislación de Barcelona. *Acta de sesión pública inaugural celebrada en 26 Diciembre de 1869.* Barcelona: Martí y Cantó, 1875.

Academia de Jurisprudencia y Legislación de Barcelona. *Acta de la sesión pública inaugural celebrada en 20 Diciembre de 1871.* Barcelona: Martí y Cantó, 1875.

Academia de Jurisprudencia y Legislación de Barcelona. *Acta de la sesión pública inaugural celebrada en 14 Diciembre de 1873.* Barcelona: Martí y Cantó, 1875.

Academia de Jurisprudencia y Legislación de Barcelona. *Acta de la sesión pública inaugural celebrada en 27 Diciembre 1874.* Barcelona: Martí y Cantó, 1875.

Academia de Jurisprudencia y Legislación de Barcelona. *Acta de la sesión pública inaugural celebrada el día 26 de Enero de 1876.* Barcelona: Magriñá y Subirana, 1876.

Academia de Jurisprudencia y Legislación de Barcelona. *Acta de la sesión pública inaugural celebrada en 17 de Diciembre de 1890.* Barcelona: Barcelonesa, 1892.

Academia de Jurisprudencia y Legislación de Barcelona. *Dictamen sobre la codificación propuesta en el Real Decreto de 2 Febrero de 1880.* Barcelona: Barcelonesa, 1881.

Acta de la primera sesión inaugural de la Academia de Jurisprudencia y Legislación de Barcelona. Barcelona: Espona, 1842.

Acta de la sesión pública inaugural celebrada en la Academia de Legislación y Jurisprudencia de Barcelona. El día 28 de Diciembre de 1872. Barcelona: Martí y Cantó, 1875.

Acta de la sessió pública celebrada en lo Ateneu Barcelonés lo 17 de Desembre de 1897. Barcelona: La Renaixença, 1899.

Actas del Congreso Jurídico de Barcelona — Septiembre, 1888. Barcelona: Roviralta, 1889.

Alonso Martínez, Manuel. *El Código Civil en sus relaciones con las legislaciones forales.* Reprint, Madrid: Plus Ultra, 1949. Original edition, 1884.

Almirall, Valentín. *Lo catalanisme.* Barcelona: Edicions 62, 1994. Original edition, 1886.

———. *Las leyes forales y el carlismo en Cataluña.* Barcelona: Pedro Casanovas, 1868.

Altadill, Antonio. *La ambición en la mujer.* Barcelona: López, 1865.

———. *Barcelona y sus misterios.* 6th ed. Vol. 2. Barcelona: Torrens, 1885.

Amat y Furió, Vicente. "Prólogo." In Antonio Aguilar et al., *La administración de justicia ante la opinión,* 3–31. Barcelona: Henrich, 1890.

Angelón, Manuel. *El abogado defensor considerado bajo el punto de vista social y en sus relaciones con la civilización.* Barcelona: Pons, 1853.

———. *Guía satírica de Barcelona. Bromazo topográfico-urbano-típico-burlesco.* Reprint, Barcelona: Millá., 1946. Original edition, 1854.

———. *Setze jutjes.* 2d ed. Barcelona: Lo Regional, 1895.

Avilés, Gabriel. *Tribunales rojos (vistos por un abogado defensor).* Barcelona: Destino, 1939.

Azcárate, Gumersindo de. *Estudios filosóficos y políticos.* Madrid: Fé, 1877.

Bacardí, Alejandro de. *Manual del derecho civil vigente en Cataluña o sea resumen ordenado de las disposiciones el derecho real posteriores al decreto llamado de Nueva Planta y de las anteriores así del derecho municipal, como del canónico y romano aplicables a nuestras costumbres por José Antonio Elías y Esteban de Ferrater.* 2d ed. Barcelona: Ramírez y Rialp, 1864.

———. *Nuevo Colon o sea tratado del derecho militar de España y sus Indias.* 3d ed. 3 vols. Barcelona: Ramírez, 1878.

Balaguer, Victor. *Historia de Cataluña y la Corona de Aragón.* 5 vols. Barcelona: Manero, 1860–63.

Balle, Juan de. *Informe que sobre la memoria para la supresión del diezmo leída a las Cortes por el Escmo. Sr. secretario del despacho de Hacienda.* Barcelona: Tomas Gorchs, 1842.

———. *Memoria en demostración del derecho que asiste al escelentísimo Sr. Duque de Medinaceli en el pleito que sigue contra el Administrador Principal de Bienes Nacionales sobre pertenencia del solar que ocupó el convento de Frailes Menores de la regular observancia de San Francisco de Asis en la ciudad de Barcelona.* Barcelona: Garriga y Aguasvivas, 1845.

Balzac, Honoré de. *Colonel Chabert.* Translated by Carol Cosman. New York: New Directions, 1997.

———. *Old Goriot.* Translated by M. A. Crawford. London: Penguin, 1951.

Barba y Roca, Manuel. *Discurso sobre los pleytos. Abertura de la Academia de Jurisprudencia de la ciudad de Barcelona en 30 de Octubre de 1781.* Barcelona: Suriá y Burgada, 1781.

Berní y Català, Joseph. *Resumen de los privilegios, gracias, y prerrogativa de los abogados españoles.* Valencia: Lucas, 1764.

Blackstone, William. *Commentaries on the Laws of England.* Vol. 1. Oxford: Clarendon Press, 1765. Facsimile reprint, Chicago: University of Chicago Press, 1979.

Bofarull y Brocá, Antonio. *Historia crítica (civil y eclesiástica) de Cataluña.* 9 vols. Barcelona: Aleu y Fugarull, 1876.

———. *Los trobadors nous. Col·lecció de poesías catalanas, escullidas de autors contemporáneos.* Barcelona: Manero, 1858.

Bofarull y de Palau, Manuel de. *La codificación civil en España. Consideraciones acerca de la discusión de este tema en el último Congreso Jurídico.* Madrid: Valero, 1887.

Borrell y Soler, Antoni. *El Códic Civil a Catalunya. Estudi crític de les sentències del T.S. de Justícia y de les resolucions de la D.G. dels R. que l'hi apliquen.* Barcelona: Giró, 1904.

Bourgoanne, Chevalier de. *Travels in Spain: Containing a New, Accurate, and Comprehensive View of the Present State of that Country to Which Are Added Copious Extracts from the Essays on Spain of M. Peryon.* Translated from the French. 2 vols. Dublin: William Porter, 1790.

Brocá, Guillermo María de. *Historia del derecho de Cataluña especialmente del civil, y exposición de las instituciones del derecho civil del mismo territorio en relación con el Código Civil de España y la jurisprudencia.* Vol. 1. Barcelona: Gili, 1918. Facsimile reprint, Barcelona: Generalitat de Catalunya, Departament de Justícia, 1985.

Brocá, Guillermo María de, and Juan Amell y Llopís. *Instituciones del derecho civil* catalán vigente, o sea exposición metódica y razonada de las leyes, costumbres y jurisprudencia de los autores y de la antigua Audiencia del Principado; completada con las doctrinas del Tribunal Supremo y precedida de una introducción histórica. 2d ed. Vol. 1. Barcelona: Barcelonesa, 1886.

Burgos, Carmen de ("Colombine"). "El abogado." *Los contemporáneos*, no. 340 (2 July 1915).

Cadafalch y Buguñá, Joaquín. *¿Conviene uniformar la legislación de las diversas provincias de España sobre la sucesión hereditaria y los derechos del cónyuge sobreviviente?* Madrid: Colegio de Sordomudos y de Ciegos, 1862.

———. *Inconvenientes de la sucesión forzosa establecida en el proyecto de Código Civil.* Barcelona: Oliveres, 1852.

Cambó, Francisco. *Memorias, 1876–1936.* 2d ed. Madrid: Alianza, 1981.

Campomanes, Pedro Rodríguez de. *Reflexiones sobre la jurisprudencia española.* In Antonio Álvarez de Morales, *El pensamiento político y jurídico de Campomanes*, 137–83. Madrid: Instituto Nacional de Administración Pública, 1989.

Camps y Arboix, Joaquín. *Historia del derecho catalán moderno.* Barcelona: Bosch, 1958.

Capmany, Antonio de. *Centinela contra franceses.* Valencia: Monfort, 1808.

Casarés, Francesc. *Memòries d'un advocat laboralista (1927–1958). Primera part.* Barcelona: La Campana, 2006.

Castillo, Joaquín del. *La Ciudadela inquisitorial de Barcelona ó las víctimas inmoladas en las aras del atroz despotismo del Conde de España.* Barcelona: Saurí, 1835.

Censo de la población de España en el año de 1797.

Cerdá, Idelfonso. "Monografía estadística de la clase obrera de Barcelona en 1856." In *Teoría general de la urbanización, y aplicación de sus principios y doctrinas a la reforma y ensanche de Barcelona*, 1:629–40. Madrid: Torrija, 1867.

Código Civil Español. Redactado por el Gobierno en cumplimiento de la Ley de 11 de Mayo de 1888, y publicado en virtud de autorización concedida al mismo por Real Decreto de 6 de Octubre del mismo año. Madrid: Góngora, 1888.

Código Civil Español conforme a la edición oficial reformada con arreglo a lo dispuesto en la Ley de 26 de Mayo 1889. Madrid: Revista de Legislación, 1889.

Colecció de discursos en defensa de la legislació civil catalana. Barcelona: Barcelonesa, 1891.

Colegio de Abogados de Barcelona. Catálogo de las obras existentes en la biblioteca. Barcelona: Ramírez, 1878.

Colegio de Abogados de Barcelona. Catálogo de las obras existentes en la biblioteca. Barcelona: Henrich, 1908.

Congreso Catalán de Jurisconsultos, 1880–1881. Barcelona: La Academia, 1880.

Congreso de Jurisconsultos. Reseña de las sesiones celebradas en los días 27 28, 29, 39, 31 de Octubre de 1863. Madrid: Quirós, 1863.

Congreso Jurídico Español. Tema primero: estructura más apropiada para un Código Civil Español. Distinción formal entre leyes obligatorias y leyes supletorias. Madrid: Hernández, 1886.

Consulate of the Sea, and Related Documents. Translated and edited by Stanley S. Jados. Birmingham: University of Alabama Press, 1975.

Consultor de los ayuntamientos. Manuel novísimo del subsidio industrial y de comercio. Madrid: de la Riva, 1870.

Coroleu, José. *Barcelona y sus alrededores. Guía histórica, descriptiva y estadística del forastero.* Barcelona: Jaime Seix, 1887.

———. *Memorias de un menestral de Barcelona, 1792–1854.* Barcelona: Ediciones Betis, 1946. Original, 1864.

Coroleu e Inglada, José, and José Pella y Forgas. *Las Cortes Catalanas. Estudio jurídico y comparativo de su organización y reseña analítica de todas sus legislaturas episodios notables, oratoria y personajes ilustres, con muchos documentos inéditos del Archivo de la Corona de Aragón e el del municipio de Barcelona.* Barcelona: Revista Histórica Latina, 1876.

———. *Los fueros de Cataluña. Descripción comentada de la constitución histórica del Principado; sus instituciones políticas y administrativas y sus libertades tradicionales.* Barcelona: Administración San Pablo, 1878.

Corominas, Pere. *Els anys de joventut i el procés de Montjuïc.* Edited by Max Cahner and Joan Coromines. Barcelona: Curial, 1974.

D.A.G. *El abogado. Comedia en dos actos traducida del francés para el teatro de Barcelona.* Barcelona: Piferrer, 1841.

D.F. de P. y D.J.B.S. *Código Civil Español. Redactado en vista de los diferentes cuerpos del derecho, y demás leyes, decretos, y reales órdenes que se han publicado en España hasta el día.* Barcelona: Torner, 1843.

D.J.J.O. *Apuntamiento de lo ocurrido con los ministros de la Real Audiencia de Barcelona en el día nueve de Abril de mil ochocientos y nueve.* Valencia: Domingo, 1810.

D'Aguesseau, Henrique Francisco. *Discurso de la independencia del abogado compuesto en francés por el celebre canciller de la Francia, el Noble Sr. Henrique Francisco D'Aguesseau.* Translated by Antonio Francisco Puig y Gelabert. Barcelona: Pla, 1785.

Degollada, Rafael. *Memoria del abogado don Rafael Degollada, en defensa de su honor ultrajado. Con las cuatro persecuciones sufridas por sus opiniones políticas desde el mes de Enero de 1836 hasta el de Octubre de 1837, en que fue deportado a la Habana y de allí a Pinos.* Marseilles: Senés, 1839.

Díez de Ulzurrún, Cándido. "La reorganización de la administración de la justicia." In Antonio Aguilar et al., *La administración de justicia ante la opinión*, 197–209. Barcelona: Henrich, 1890.

Domenech y Sabater, Vicente. *Discurso sobre las obligaciones del abogado. Abertura de la Academia de Jurisprudencia Teórico-Práctica de la ciudad en 30 Octubre 1779.* Barcelona: Gibert y Tutó, 1779.

Dou y de Bassols, Ramón Lázaro de. *Instituciones del derecho público general de España con noticia del particular de Cataluña, y de las principales reglas de gobierno en qualquier estado.* 9 vols. Madrid: García, 1800–1803. Facsimile reprint, Barcelona: Banchs, 1975.

---. *Pronta y fácil egecucion del proyecto sobre laudemios, fundada principalmente en una autoridad del Dr. Adan Smith*. Cervera: Casanovas, 1831.

---. *La riqueza de las naciones, nuevamente explicada con la doctrina de su mismo investigador*. Cervera: Imprenta de la Pont. y de la Real Universidad, 1817.

Durán y Bas, Manuel. *Ensayo biográfico del Doctor D. Felipe Vergés y Permanyer y del excelentísimo señor D. Melchor Ferrer y Bruguera, Marqués de Cornellá*. Barcelona: Barcelonesa, 1891.

---. *Escritos. Estudios jurídicos*. Edited by Luciano Ribera. Barcelona: Oliveres, 1888.

---. *Memoria acerca de las instituciones de derecho civil en Cataluña*. Barcelona: Casa de Caridad, 1883.

---. *Noticia de la vida y escritos del Excmo. Sr. Francisco Permanyer y Tuyet*. Barcelona: Diario de Barcelona, 1870.

---. "Prólogo." In F. C. de Savigny, *Sistema del derecho romano actual*. Translated by Jacinto Mesía and Manuel Poley from the French translation of the original German by Ch. Guenoux, 1:vii–xxxix. Madrid: Góngora, 1878–79.

Durán y Bas, Manuel, and Conrado Roure. *Sesión celebrada por el Ilustre Colegio de Abogados de Barcelona, el día 27 de Mayo de 1886 para la inauguración de la Galería de Retratos de Jurisconsultas Catalanes*. Barcelona: Casa Provincial de Caridad, 1887.

Duran i Ventosa, Lluís. *Regionalisme i federalisme*. 2d ed. Barcelona: Editorial Catalana, 1922.

Durán y Ventosa, Raimundo. *Instituciones del derecho mercantil de España por D. Ramón Martí de Eixalá y D. Manuel Durán y Bas*. Barcelona: Sociedad General de Publicaciones, 1911.

Egea Fernàndez, Joan, and Josep Ferrer Riba. *Codi Civil de Catalunya i legislació complementària. Amb notes de concordança i jurisprudència*. 13th ed. Barcelona: EUB, 2006.

Elías, José Antonio. *Derecho civil general y foral de España o sea resumen ordenado de las leyes vigentes en los varios territorios que forman la Monarquía española y de las decisiones del Tribunal Supremo que establecen jurisprudencia con un apéndice sobre las disposiciones del derecho civil que rigen en las provincias del mar*. 3 vols. Barcelona and Madrid: Gómez and Gaspar y Homdedeu, 1875–77.

Elías, José Antonio, and Esteban de Ferrater. *Manual de derecho civil vigente en Cataluña o sea resumen ordenado de las disposiciones del derecho real posteriores al decreto llamado de Nueva Planta y de las anteriores así del derecho municipal, como del canónico y romano, aplicables a nuestras costumbres* Edited by Alejandro de Barcardí. 3d ed. Madrid: López; Barcelona: Llordachs, 1885.

Estat Català, Projecte de Constitució aprobat pe'l Congrés Regional Federalista de Catalunya el dia 2 de maig de 1883. Barcelona: Cuesta, 1908.

Estatutos para el régimen de los Colegios de Abogados del Reino. Madrid: Compañía Tipográfica, 1838.

Exposición que la Academia de Jurisprudencia y Legislación de Barcelona ha dirigido al Excmo. Sr. Ministro de Gracia y Justicia acerca de la necesidad de modificar las disposiciones vigentes sobre incompatibilidades de los funcionarios de las carrera judicial y fiscal. Barcelona: Barcelonesa, 1892.

Falcón, Lidia. *Memorias políticas (1959–1999)*. Barcelona: Editorial Planeta, 1999.

———. *La vida arrebatada*. Barcelona: Editorial Anagrama, 2003.

Falcón, Modesto. *Exposición doctrinal del derecho civil español, común y foral*. 5th ed. Vol. 2. Barcelona: La Publicidad, 1897.

Falguera, Félix María. *Conferencias de derecho catalán dadas en el Ateneo Barcelonés en 1870 y 1880*. Barcelona: La Anticuaria, 1889.

Farnès, Sebastià. "La revindicaciò del llenguatge en l'ensenyança primària." In *Articles catalanistes (1881–1891)*, edited by Jordi Llorens i Vila, 81–113. Barcelona: Edicions 62, 1982.

Ferrater, Esteban de. *Resumen del proceso original sobre usurpación del estado civil de D. Claudio Fontanellas*. Madrid, Barcelona, and Havana: Librería Plus Ultra, 1865.

Ferrer, Melchor, Manuel Durán y Bas, Ildefonso Par, Luciano Ribera, and José María Vallés de Ribot."Dictamen sobre las principales cuestiones que se debaten en el pleito seguido entre el excmo. Ayuntamiento de Barcelona y excmo. Sr. Marqués de Ayerbe." Unpublished document found at the Col·legi d'Advocats, 1889 or 1890.

Figuerola, Laureano. *Estadística de Barcelona en 1849*. Barcelona: Gorchs, 1849.

Fina, Albert. *De la llei i la justícia*. Barcelona: Editorial Laia, 1987.

———. *Des del nostre despatx*. Barcelona: Dopesa, 1978.

Finestres, Josep. *Epistolari*. Edited by Ignasi Casanovas. 2 vols. Barcelona: Biblioteca Balmes, 1932.

Flaubert, Gustave. *Sentimental Education*. Translated by Robert Baldick. London: Penguin, 1964.

Floridablanca, Conde de. *Censo español executado del orden del Rey*. Madrid: Imprenta Real, 1787.

Franquesa, Joaquín. *La jurisprudencia y el derecho civil de Cataluña*. 2d ed. Barcelona: Bosch, 1925.

Fors, Luis Ricardo de. *De la abogacía y de los abogados*. Barcelona: Ramírez y Rialp, 1865.

García Goyena, Florencio. *Concordancias, motivos y comentarios del Código Civil Español*. Vol. 2. Madrid: Sociedad Tipográico-Editorial, 1852.

Gener, Pompeyo. *Cosas de España: Herejías nacionales. El renacimiento de Cataluña*. Barcelona: Llordachs, 1903.

Giner, Francisco. *Estudios jurídicos y políticos*. Madrid: Suárez, 1875.

Gruzenberg, O. O. *Yesterday: Memoirs of a Russian-Jewish Lawyer*. Translated by Don C. Rawson. Berkeley: University of California Press, 1981.

Hurtado, Amadeu. *Quaranta anys d'advocat. Història del meu temps*. 2 vols. Barcelona: Xaloc, 1956.

Illas y Vidal, Juan, and Laureano Figuerola. *Elementos de gramática castellana. Obra aprobada por el Gobierno con Reales Órdenes de 30 de Junio de 1848 y 20 de Mayo de 1852*. Barcelona: Castaño, 1853.

J.R.G. *Quadro de horror ó sea conducta atroz y criminal de D. Juan Madinabeytia.* Palma de Mallorca: Roca, 1813.

Kalendario [sic] y guía de forasteros en Barcelona. Barcelona: Piferrer, 1787.

Ley de Enjuiciamiento Civil. Edición oficial. 2d ed. Madrid: Ministerio de Gracia y Justicia, 1855.

Ley de Enjuiciamiento Civil de 3 de Enero de 1881 con las reformas introducidas hasta fines de 1898. 6th ed. Madrid: Góngora, 1899.

Ley de Enjuiciamiento Criminal de 14 de Septiembre de 1882. Madrid: Góngora, 1899.

Ley de Enjuiciamiento sobre los negocios y causas de Comercio, decretada sancionada y promulgada en 24 de Julio de 1830. Madrid: Amarita, 1830.

Ley de Instrucción Pública (1857). In *Colección de leyes referentes a instrucción pública y otras que con ésta se relacionan*, 10–67. Madrid: Tello, 1890.

Ley orgánica del Poder Judicial de 15 de Septiembre de 1870 y Ley adicional a la misma de 14 de Octubre 1882. Madrid: Administración, 1902.

Lista de los abogados del Ilustre Colegio de Madrid. Madrid: Semanario Pintoresco y de la Ilustración, 1851.

Lardizábal y Uribe, Manuel. *Discurso sobre las penas: contraído a las leyes criminales de España para facilitar su reforma.* Madrid: Ibarra, 1782.

Loperena, Josep Maria. *El circo de la justicia. Bufonada de togados y otras gentes de mal vivir.* Barcelona: Flor de Viento Edicions, 2007.

Magarola, Miguel. *El abogado perfecto. Discurso inaugural que en la abertura de la Academia de Jurisprudencia teórico-práctica de Barcelona, celebrada el día 21 de Octubre de 1789.* Barcelona: Gibert y Tutó, 1789.

Maluquer i Viladot, Joan. *Les meves noces d'or amb el molt il·lustre Col·legi d'Advocats de Barcelona, 1877–1927. Records de 50 anys professionals polítics i locals.* Barcelona: Altés, 1929.

Malquer Viladot, Juan. *Derecho civil especial de Barcelona y su término.* Barcelona: Imprenta Renaixensa, 1889.

Marshall, Joseph. *Travels through Spain and France in the years 1770 and 1771.* London: G. Corrall, 1776.

Martí de Eixalá, Ramón. *Tratado elementar [sic] del derecho civil romano y español.* 2 vols. Barcelona: Verdaguer, 1838.

Martí y Miralles, Juan. *Estudios sobre el art. 12 del Código Civil.* Barcelona: Doria, 1901.

Maspons i Anglasell, Francesc. Prologue to Narcis Verdaguer i Callís, *La primera victòria del catalanisme*, 7–22. Barcelona: La Revista, 1919.

Memòria en defensa dels interessos morals y materials de Catalunya presentada directament a S.M. lo Rey en virtut d'acort pres en la reunió celebrada en la Llotja de Barcelona, lo dia 11 de Janer de 1885. Barcelona: La Renaixença, 1885.

Missatje a S.M. Donya Maria Cristina de Habsburg-Lorena, Reyna Regent d'Espanya, Comtesa de Barcelona. Barcelona: Renaixença, 1888.

Montesquieu. *The Spirit of the Laws.* Translated and edited by Anne Cohler, Basia Miller, and Harold Stone. Cambridge: Cambridge University Press, 1989.

Moret y Prendesgast, Segismundo, and Luis Silvela. *La familia foral y la familia castellana.* Madrid: Cuesta, 1863.

Mujal, Juan A. *Desengaño al público con pura y sólida doctrina: tratado de la observancia y obediencia que se debe a las leyes, pragmáticas sanciones y reales decretos*. Madrid: García, 1774.
Novísima recopilación de las leyes de España. 5 vols. Madrid: 1805. Facsimile reprint, Madrid: Imprenta Nacional, 1992.
Oliver y Esteller, Bienvenido. *Breve sumario del proyecto de Código Civil de Alemania y del proyecto de ley*. Madrid: Góngora y Alvárez, 1889.
———. *Estudios históricos sobre el derecho civil en Cataluña*. Barcelona: Tasso, 1867.
Ordenanzas de la Academia de Jurisprudencia Teórico-Práctica, establecida en la ciudad de Barcelona. Barcelona: Gibert y Tudò, 1777.
Ordenanzas de la Real Audiencia de el Principado de Cathaluña. Barcelona: Teixidó, 1742.
Ossorio, Ángel. *El alma de la toga*. Madrid: Pueyo, 1920.
———. *Mis memorias*. Madrid: Tebas, 1975.
P.N.A. *Conversa verdadera y de molt profit tinguda entre un pagès nomenat Isidro y lo advocat Doctor Julià. Se publica per ser útil als servils y liberals, als tibis o indiferents, y mes als pagesos que res entenguian en lo del dia*. Barcelona: Tegero, 1821.
Pella y Forgas, Joseph. *Llibertats y antich govern de Catalunya*. Barcelona: Puig, 1905.
Pérez Galdós, Benito. *Doña Perfecta*. Madrid: Alianza, 1983. Original edition, 1876.
Pérez Villamil, Juan. *Disertación sobre la libre multitud de abogados, si es útil al estado o si fuera conveniente reducir el número de estos profesores*. Madrid: Ibarra, 1782.
Pi y Margall, Francisco. *Articles*. Edited by Gabriel Alomar. Barcelona: L'Anuaria, 1908.
———. *Las nacionalidades*. Buenos Aires: Editorial Americalee, 1945. Original edition, 1876.
Plá y Soler, Magín. *Apuntamiento del pleito. Doña Juan Ruíz de Araña. Marquesa Viuda de Ayerbe contra el Ayuntamiento Constitucional de Barcelona*. Barcelona: Ramírez, 1886.
Prat de la Riba, Enric. *La nacionalitat catalana*. 4th ed. Barcelona: Edicions 62, 1998. Original edition, 1906.
———. *Obra completa*. Edited by Albert Balcells and Josep Maria Ainaud de Lasarte. 3 vols. Barcelona: Proa, 1998.
Prat de la Riba, Enric, and Pere Montanyola. *Compendi de la doctrina catalanista*. Sabadell: Lo Catalanista, 1894.
Projectes i memorials. Segles XVIII i XIX. Edited by J. A. González Casanova. Barcelona: Generalitat de Catalunya, Departament de Justícia, 1990.
Prospecto y reglamento del Colegio de Valldemia situado junto a la ciudad de Mataró, provincia de Barcelona, en España, bajo la advocación de Nstra. Sra. De la Luz. Barcelona: Barcelonesa, 1887.
Roca i Junyent, Miquel. *Sí advocat! El que no vaig aprendre a la facultat*. Barcelona: Columna, 1997.
Roca y Roca, J. *Barcelona en la mano. Guía de Barcelona y sus alrededores*. Barcelona: López, 1884.

———. *Barcelona en la mano. Guía de Barcelona y sus alrededores*. Barcelona: López, 1895.
Romá y Rosell, Francisco. *Las señales de la felicidad de España y medios de hacerlas eficaces*. Madrid: Muñóz del Valle, 1768.
Roure, Conrad. *Clarís. Epissodi histórich en tres actes y en vers. Representada per primera vegada en lo Teatro Catalá lo 25 de Novembre de 1879*. 3d ed. Barcelona: Lo Teatro Regional, 1896.
———. *Recuerdos de mi larga vida: Costumbres, anécdotas, acontecimientos y sucesos acaecidos en la ciudad de Barcelona, desde 1850 hasta el 1900*. 3 vols. Barcelona: El Diluvio, 1925.
———. *Recuerdos de mi larga vida: La restauració dels Borbons*. Vol. 8 of *Memòries de Conrad Roure*, edited by Josep Pich i Mitjana. Vic: Eumo and Institut Universitari d'Història Jaume Vicens i Vives, 1998.
Sala, Ramón María. *Defensa del ciudadano José Costa coronel retirado del ejército y del primer regimiento de la milicia nacional voluntaria de Barcelona*. Barcelona: Roca, 1822.
———. *El mayor despotismo acompañado de la más crasa ignorancia*. Palma: Brusi, 1811.
Salvató, Ramon. *Elecciones de 1839*. Madrid: Alvert, 1839.
Sanponts y Barba, Ignacio, Ramón Martí de Eixalá, and José Ferrer y Subirana. *Las Siete Partidas del sabio rey don Alfonso el X con las variantes de más interés, y con la glosa del Lic. Gregorio López del Consejo Real de Indias de S.M., vertida al castellano y estensamente adicionada con nuevas notas y comentarios y unas tablas sinópticas comparativas, sobre la legislación española, antigua y moderna, hasta su actual estado*. 3 vols. Barcelona: Bergnes, 1843–44.
Savigny, Frederick Charles von. *Of the Vocation of Our Age for Legislation and Jurisprudence*. Translated by Abraham Hayward. London: Littlewood, 1831. Facsimile reprint, New York: Arno Press, 1975.
Serraclara, Gonzalo. *La nueva Inquisición. Proceso del diputado Serraclara y sucesos ocurridos en Barcelona el día 23 Setiembre de 1869*. Barcelona: Española, 1869.
Serrahima, Mauricio. *Alegación en derecho por parte del Excmo. Ayuntamiento de Barcelona en el pleito . . . promovido por el Excmo. Sr. Marqués de Ayerbe, sobre reivindicación de derechos reales en la llamada Rodalia de Corbera de esta ciudad*. Barcelona: Ramírez, 1886.
Serrahima, Maurici. *Memòries de la guerra i de l'exili, 1936–40*. Vol. 2. Barcelona: Edicions 62, 1981.
Sisternes y Felíu, Manuel. *Idea de la ley agraria española*. Valencia: Montfort, 1786. Facsimile reprint, Barcelona: Alta Fulla, 1993.
Somoza-Llanos, José. *Discurso leído en la Academia de Derecho Administrativo de Barcelona*. Barcelona: Peninsular, 1880.
Swinburne, Henry. *Travels through Spain in the Years 1775 and 1776*. London: P. Elmsly, 1779.
Tocqueville, Alexis de. *Democracy in America*. Translated by Harvey C. Mansfield and Delba Winthrop. Chicago: University of Chicago Press, 2000.
Torras i Bages, Josep. *La tradició catalana*. Barcelona: Edicions 62, 1981. Original edition, 1892.

Tos y Urgellés, Jayme. *Tratado de la cabrevación según el derecho y estilo del principado de Cataluña, sus utilidades y efectos, del modo de principiar, y seguir las causas de cabrevación, de los privilegios del señor directo, o mediano, y de las excepciones que competen al reo, o enfiteota.* Barcelona: Rubió, 1826. Revised edition of one published in 1784.

Townsend, Joseph. *A Journey through Spain in the years 1786 and 1781 with particular attention to the Agriculture, Manufacturers, Commerce, Population, Taxes, and Revenue of that Country.* Vol. 1. London: Dilly, 1791.

Trías, Juan de Dios. *Conferencias de derecho civil catalán.* Barcelona: La Hormiga de Oro, 1899.

Los trobadors moderns. Col·lecció de poesías catalanas compostas per ingenis contemporáneos. Barcelona: Manero, 1859.

Unió Catalanista. *Bases pera la Constitució Regional Catalana acordadas de delegats celebrada a Manresa.* Barcelona: La Renaixença, 1900.

The Usatges of Barcelona: The Fundamental Law of Catalonia. Translated and edited by Donald J. Kagay. Philadelphia: University of Pennsylvania Press, 1994.

Ventosa, Ricardo, and Demetrio de Villalaz. *Acusaciones pronunciadas en la causa criminal seguida contra Claudio Feliu y Fontanills sobre usurpación del estado civil de D. Claudio de Fontanellas ante la Excma. Sala Tercera de la Audiencia de Barcelona en grado de revista seguidas por la sentencia ejecutoria dictada por la misma Real Sala.* Barcelona: Ramírez y Rialp, 1865.

Verdaguer i Callís, Narcis. *La primera victòria del catalanisme.* Barcelona: La Revista, 1919.

Vergés, Francisco de Paula. *Alegación en derecho que presenta el Excmo. Sr. Marqués de Ayerbe y de Rubí contra el Excmo. Ayuntamiento de Barcelona.* Barcelona: Jepús, 1886.

Vergés y Permanyer, Felipe. *Oración fúnebre que pronunció en las solemnes exequias celebradas en la Sta. Iglesia Catedral de Vich el día 4 de Julio de 1865, con motivo de la colocación de los restos mortales del Dr. D. Jaime Balmes Pbro. En el nuevo monumento levantado en los claustros de la misma Catedral.* Vic: Plaza de las Garzas, 1865.

Vives y Cebriá, Pedro Nolasco. *Observaciones sobre algunos artículos del proyecto del Código Civil de España que tienen mira a la cuota de la legítima y al modo de pagarla.* Barcelona: Plus Ultra, 1862.

———. *Traducción al castellano de los Usages y demás derechos de Cataluña que no están derogados o no son notoriamente inútiles, con indicación del contenido de éstos y de las disposiciones por las que han venido a serlo, ilustrada con notas sacadas de los más clásicos autores del Principado.* 2d ed. 2 vols. Madrid and Barcelona: Font and Plus Ultra, 1861. Facsimile reprint, Barcelona: Generalitat de Catalunya, Departament de Justícia, 1989.

Voltaire. *Philosophical Dictionary.* Translated by Oliver Flemming. Vol. 6, part 1. New York: E. R. DuMont, 1901.

Young, Arthur. *Travels during the Years 1787, 1788, and 1789; undertaken more particularly with a view of ascertaining the cultivation, wealth, resources, and National Prosperity of the Kingdom of France.* 2d ed. Vol. 1. London: W. Richardson, 1794.

Interviews

Avilés, Montserrat, 24 October 2006.
Cabrerizo, Carmen, 11 October 2006.
Vendrell Ferrer, Eudald, 3 October 2007.

SECONDARY SOURCES

Adelman, Jeremy. *Republic of Capital: Buenos Aires and the Legal Transformation of the Atlantic World*. Stanford: Stanford University Press, 1999.
Agúndez, Antonio. *Historia del poder judicial en España*. Madrid: Editorial Nacional, 1974.
Althusser, Louis. "Ideology and Ideological State Apparatuses (Notes toward an Investigation)." In *Lenin and Philosophy*, 127–86. New York: Monthly Review Press, 1971.
Álvarez Junco, José. *Mater Dolorosa: La idea de España en el siglo XIX*. Madrid: Taurus, 2001.
———. "A vueltas con la revolución burguesa." *Zona Abierta* 36–37 (1985): 81–110.
Amelang, James S. "Barristers and Judges in Early Modern Barcelona." *American Historical Review* 89, no. 5 (December 1984): 1264–84.
———. "Comparing Cities: A Barcelona Model?" *Urban History* 34, no. 2 (2007): 173–89.
———. *Honored Citizens of Barcelona: Patrician Culture and Class Relations, 1490–1714*. Princeton: Princeton University Press, 1986.
Anderson, Benedict. *Imagined Communities: Reflections on the Origin and Spread of Nationalism*. London: Verso, 1983.
Anderson, J. Stuart. *Lawyers and the Making of English Land Law, 1832–1940*. Oxford: Clarendon Press, 1992.
Anguera, Pere. *El català al segle XIX. De llengua del poble a llengua nacional*. Barcelona: Empúries, 1997.
———. *Déu, rei i fam. El primer carlisme a Catalunya*. Barcelona: Publicacions de l'Abadia de Montserrat, 1995.
———. *Els precedents del catalanisme. Catalanitat i anticentralisme: 1808–1868*. Barcelona: Empúries, 2000.
Arnabat Mata, Ramon. "Protesta i resistència antisenyorial al Penedès (1758–1808)." In *Moviments de protesta i resistència a la fi de l'Antic Règim*, edited by Ramon Arnabat Mata, 93–110. Barcelona: Publicacions de l'Abadia de Montserrat, 1997.
———. *La revolució de 1820 i el Trienni Liberal a Catalunya*. Barcelona: Eumo Editorial, 2001.
Balcells, Albert. *Catalan Nationalism: Past and Present*. Translated by Jacqueline Hall and Geoffrey J. Walker. Basingstoke: Macmillan, 1996.
———. *El problema agrario en Cataluña. La cuestión rabassaire (1890–1936)*. 2d ed. Madrid: Ministerio de Agricultura, 1980.
Banti, Alberto Mario. "Burgesies de les 'professions' a l'Europa del segle XIX." *Recerques. Història, Economia, Cultura* 28 (1994): 24–41.

Barnosell, Genís. *Orígens del sindicalisme català*. Vic: Eumo Editorial, 1999.
Baró Pazo, Juan. *La codificación del derecho civil en España (1808–1889)*. Santander: Universidad de Cantabria, 1993.
Barraquer y Roviralta, Cayetano. *Las casas de religiosos en Cataluña durante el primer tercio del siglo XIX*. Vol. 2. Barcelona: Altés y Alabart, 1915.
Barrera González, Andrés. *Casa, herencia y familia en la Cataluña rural*. Madrid: Alianza Editorial, 1990.
Bayly, C. A. *The Birth of the Modern World, 1780–1914*. Oxford: Blackwell, 2004.
Behrend-Martínez, Edward. "Female Sexual Potency in a Spanish Church Court, 1673–1735." *Law and History Review* 24, no. 2 (Summer 2006): 297–330.
Bell, David A. *Lawyers and Citizens: The Making of a Political Elite in Old Regime France*. Oxford: Oxford University Press, 1994.
Bellomo, Manlio. *The Common Legal Past of Europe, 1000–1800*. 2d ed. Translated by Lydia G. Cochrane. Washington, D.C.: Catholic University of America Press, 1995.
Benet, Josep, and Casimir Martí. *Barcelona a mitjan segle XIX. El moviment obrer durant el Bienni Progressista (1854–1856)*. Vol 1. Barcelona: Curial, 1976.
Bensch, Stephen P. *Barcelona and Its Rulers, 1096–1291*. Cambridge: Cambridge University Press, 1995.
Benton, Lauren. *Law and Colonial Cultures: Legal Regimes in World History, 1400–1900*. Cambridge: Cambridge University Press, 2005.
Bergueño Rivero, Jesús. "La divisió territorial." In *Transformacions territorials a Catalunya (segles XIX–XX)*, edited by Joan Vilagrasa Ibarz, 239–65. Lleida: Pagès, 2000.
Berlanstein, Lenard R. *The Barristers of Toulouse in the Eighteenth Century (1740–1793)*. Baltimore: Johns Hopkins University Press, 1975.
———. "Lawyers in Pre-Revolutionary France." In *Lawyers in Early Modern Europe*, edited by Wilfrid Prest, 164–80. New York: Homes and Meier, 1981.
Berman, Harold J. *Law and Revolution: The Formation of the Western Legal Tradition*. Cambridge, Mass.: Harvard University Press, 1983.
Bilbeny, Norbert. *La ideologia nacionalista a Catalunya*. Barcelona: Laia, 1988.
Bonet i Baltà, Joan. *L'església Catalana, de la Il·lustració a la Renaixença*. Barcelona: Publicacions de l'Abadia de Montserrat, 1984.
Bonnassie, Pierre. *Cataluña mil años atrás (siglos X–XI)*. Translated by Rodrigo Rivera. Barcelona: Península, 1988.
Bourdieu, Pierre, and Jean-Claude Passeron. *Reproduction in Education, Society and Culture*. Translated by Richard Nice. 2d ed. London: Sage, 1977.
Bouwsma, William J. "Lawyers and Early Modern Culture." *American Historical Review* 78 (1973): 303–27.
Boyd, Carolyn P. *Historia Patria: Politics, History, and National Identity in Spain*. Princeton: Princeton University Press, 1997.
Breuilly, John. *Nationalism and the State*. Chicago: University of Chicago Press, 1985.
Brooks, Christopher W. *Lawyers, Litigation and English Society since 1450*. London: Hambledon Press, 1998.

———. *Pettifoggers and Vipers of the Commonwealth: The "Lower Branch" of the Legal Profession in Early Modern England*. Cambridge: Cambridge University Press, 1986.

Brundage, James A. *The Medieval Origins of the Legal Profession: Canonists, Civilians, and Courts*. Chicago: University of Chicago Press, 2008.

Burdiel, Isabel. "The Liberal Revolution: 1808–1843." In *Spanish History since 1808*, edited by José Álvarez Junco and Adrian Shubert, 18–32. New York: Oxford University Press, 2000.

———. "Myths of Failure, Myths of Success: New Perspectives on Nineteenth-Century Spanish Liberalism." *Journal of Modern History* 70, no. 4 (December 1998): 892–912.

Burke, Michael. *The Royal College of San Carlos: Surgery and Spanish Medical Reform in the Late Eighteenth Century*. Durham, N.C.: Duke University Press, 1977.

Burkholder, Mark A., and D. S. Chandler. *From Impotence to Authority: The Spanish Crown and the American Audiencias, 1687–1808*. Columbia: University of Missouri Press, 1977.

Burrage, Michael. "Introduction: The Professions in Sociology and History." In *Professions in Theory and History*, edited by Michael Burrage and Rolf Torstendahl, 1–23. London: Sage, 1990.

———. "Revolution as a Starting Point for the Comparative Analysis of the French, American, and English Legal Professions." In *Lawyers and Society: Comparative Theories*, edited by Richard L. Abel and Philip S. C. Lewis, 322–74. Berkeley: University of California Press, 1989.

Caballero Domínguez, Margarita. "El derecho de representación: sufragio y leyes electorales." *Ayer* 34 (1999): 41–63.

Cabana, Francesc. *Bancs i banquers a Catalunya. Capítols per una història*. Barcelona: Edicions 62, 1972.

Callahan, William J. *The Catholic Church in Spain, 1875–1998*. Washington, D.C.: Catholic University of America Press, 2000.

Cammarano, Fulvio. "The Professions in Parliament." In *Society and the Professions in Italy, 1860–1914*, edited by Maria Malatesta, translated by Adrian Belton, 276–312. Cambridge: Cambridge University Press, 1990.

Caminal, Monserrat, Esteban Canales, Angels Solà, and Jaume Torras. "Moviment de l'ingrés senyorial a Catalunya (1770–1835)." *Recerques. Història, Economia, Cultura* 8 (1978): 51–72.

Camps i Arboix, Joaquim. *Historia del derecho catalán moderno*. Barcelona: Bosch, 1958.

Cañellas, Cèlia, and Rosa Toran. *El personal polític de l'Ajuntament de Barcelona (1877–1923)*. Barcelona: Publicacions de l'Abadia de Montserrat, 1996.

Carbonell i Esteller, Montserrat. "Plets i lluita antisenyorial. El Ducat de Cardona a les acaballes de l'antic règim." *Pedralbes. Revista d'Història Moderna* 3, no. 3 (1983): 265–78.

Casassas, Jordi, ed. *Entre Escil·la i Caribdis. El catalanisme i la Catalunya conservadora de la segon meitat del segle XIX*. Barcelona: La Magrana, 1990.

———. *Els intel·lectuals i el poder a Catalunya (1808–1975)*. Barcelona: Pòrtic, 1999.
Cattini, Giovanni C. *Historiografia i catalanisme. Josep Coroleu i Inglada (1839–1845)*. Barcelona: Afers, 2007.
Charle, Christophe. "Professionen und intellektuelle. Die liberalen Berufe in Frankreich zwischen Politik und Wirtschaft." In *Bürgerlich Berufe. Zur Sozialgeschichte der freien und akademischen Berufe im internationalen Vergleich*, edited by Hannes Siegrist, 127–44. Göttingen: Vandenhoeck & Ruprecht, 1988.
———. "Le recrutement des avocats parisiens, 1880–1914." In *Avocats et barreaux en France, 1910–1930*, edited by Gilles Le Béguec, 21–34. Nancy: Presses Universitaires de Nancy, 1994.
———. *A Social History of France in the Nineteenth Century*. Translated by Miriam Kochan. Oxford: Oxford University Press, 1994.
Clavero, Bartolomé. *El Código y el fuero. De la cuestión regional en la España contemporánea*. Madrid: Siglo XXI, 1982.
Coll i Amargós, Joaquim. *Narcís Verdaguer i Callís (1862–1918) i el catalanisme possibilista*. Barcelona: Publicacions de l'Abadia de Montserrat, 1998.
Comalada Negre, Angel. *Catalunya davant el centralisme*. Barcelona: Sirocco, 1984.
Congost, Rosa. *Els propietaris i els altres. La regió de Girona, 1768–1862*. Vic: Eumo, 1990.
———. "Sagrada propiedad imperfecta. Otra visión de la revolución liberal." *Historia Agraria* 20 (April 2000): 61–93.
Connelly Ullman, Joan. *The Tragic Week: A Study of Anticlericalism in Spain*. Cambridge, Mass.: Harvard University Press, 1968.
Corfield, Penelope. *Power and the Professions in Britain: 1700–1850*. London: Routledge, 1995.
Cots i Castañé, Albert. "Aproximació a l'estudi dels conflictes senyorials a Catalunya (1751–1808)." *Estudis d'Història Agrària* 6 (1983): 244–64.
———. "Els litigis judicials en la societat catalana del segle XVIII i primera meitat del XIX. Una aproximació a partir dels processos civils de la Reial Audiència de Catalunya." Ph.D. diss., Universitat de Barcelona, 1988.
Coverdale, John. *The Basque Phase of Spain's First Carlist War*. Princeton: Princeton University Press, 1984.
Cruz, Jesús. *Gentlemen, Bourgeois, and Revolutionaries: Political Change and Cultural Persistence among the Spanish Dominant Groups, 1750–1850*. Cambridge: Cambridge University Press, 1996.
———. "The Moderate Ascendancy: 1843–1868." In *Spanish History since 1808*, edited by José Álvarez Junco and Adrian Shubert, 33–48. New York: Oxford University Press, 2000.
Dawson, Philip. "The *Bourgeoisie de Robe* in 1789." *French Historical Studies* 4 (1965): 1–21.
———. *Provincial Magistrates and Revolutionary Politics in France*. Cambridge, Mass.: Harvard University Press, 1972.
Defourneaux, Marcelin. *L'Inquisition espagnole et les livres français au XVIIIe siècle*. Paris: Presses Universitaires de France, 1963.

de la Fuente Monge, Gregorio. *Los revolucionarios de 1868. Élites y poder en la España liberal*. Madrid: Marcial Pons, 2000.

de Vries, Jan. "The Industrial Revolution and the Industrious Revolution." *Journal of Economic History* 54 (1994): 240–70.

del Pozo Carrascosa, Pedro. "La introducción del derecho francés en Cataluña durante la invasión napoleónica." In *El tercer poder: hacía una comprensión histórica de la justicia contemporánea en España*, edited by Johannes-Michael Scholz, 5–35. Frankfurt am Main: Vittorio Klostermann, 1992.

Diccionari biogràfic. Barcelona: Albertí, 1966–1970.

Domergue, Lucienne. *La censure des livres en Espagne à la fin de l'ancien régime*. Madrid: Casa de Velázquez, 1996.

Domínguez Ortiz, Antonio. *Sociedad y estado en el siglo XVIII español*. Barcelona: Editorial Ariel, 1976.

Dueñas García, Francisco. "La milicia nacional local durante el Trienio Liberal (1820–1823)." Ph.D. diss., Universitat Autònoma de Barcelona, 1997.

Duman, Daniel. *The English and Colonial Bars in the Nineteenth Century*. London: Croom Helm, 1983.

Durkheim, Emile. *Professional Ethics and Civil Morals*. Translated by Cornelia Brookfield. London: Routledge, 1957.

Elliott, John. *Empires of the Atlantic World: Britain and Spain in America, 1492–1830*. New Haven: Yale, 2006.

Espuny Tomás, María Jesús. "El Real Consulado de Comercio del Principado de Cataluña (1758–1829)." Ph.D. diss., Universitat Autònoma de Barcelona, 1992.

Espuny Tomás, María Jesús, and José Sarrión Gualda. "El Tribunal de Alzadas o de Apelaciones del Consulado de Comercio de Barcelona: Sus reformas (1763–1813)." *Pedralbes. Revista d'Història Moderna* 8 (1988): 161–80.

Fernández-Armesto, Felipe. *Barcelona: A Thousand Years of the City's Past*. London: Sinclair-Stevenson, 1991.

Ferrando Francés, Antoni, and Miquel Nicolás Amorós. *Història de la llengua catalana*. Barcelona: Pòrtic, 2005.

Ferrer i Alòs, Llorenç. *Pagesos, rabassaires i industrials a la Catalunya central (segles XVIII–XIX)*. Barcelona: Publicacions de l'Abadia de Montserrat, 1987.

Figueres Pàmies, Montserrat. *La escuela jurídica catalana frente la codificación española. Durán y Bas: su pensamiento jurídico-filosófico*. Barcelona: Bosch, 1987.

Figuerola i Garreta, Jordi. *El Bisbe Morgades i la formació de l'església catalana contemporània*. Barcelona: Publicacions de L'Abadia de Montserrat, 1994.

Fitzsimmons, Michael. *The Parisian Order of Barristers and the French Revolution*. Cambridge, Mass.: Harvard University Press, 1987.

Folguera Crespo, Pilar. "Revolución y restauración. La emergencia de los primeros ideales emancipadores (1868–1931)." In *Historia de las mujeres en España*, edited by Elisa Garrido, 454–92. Barcelona: Editorial Síntesis, 1997.

Fontana, Josep. *La revolució liberal a Catalunya*. Lleida and Vic: Pagès and Eumo Editorial, 2003.

Fradera, Josep Maria. *Cultura nacional en una sociedad dividida. Cataluña, 1838–1868*. Translated by Carles Mercadal Vidal. Madrid: Marcial Pons, 2003.

———. *Indústria i mercat. Les bases comercials de la indústria catalana moderna.* Barcelona: Editorial Crítica, 1987.
Freedman, Paul. "Catalan Lawyers and the Origins of Serfdom." In *Church, Law and Society in Catalonia, 900–1500*, 287–314. Aldershot: Valorium, 1994.
Fuster i Sobrepere, Joan. "Els regidors de Barcelona a la Dècada Moderada." In *La ciutat i les revolucions, 1808–1868. Les lluites de liberalisme*, edited by Ramon Grau, 187–201. Barcelona: Ajuntament de Barcelona, 2004.
Garcia Balañà, Albert. *La fabricació de la fàbrica. Treball i política a la Catalunya cotonera (1784–1874)*. Barcelona: Publicacions de l'Abadia de Montserrat, 2004.
———. "Ordre jurídic i trajectòria de l'Acadèmia de Jurisprudència i Legislació de Barcelona, 1840–1931 (a propòsit de la formació i els límits de la política burgesa a Catalunya)." Master's thesis, Universitat Autònoma de Barcelona, 1993.
Garcia Espuche, Albert, and Manuel Guàrdia i Bassols. *Espai i societat a la Barcelona pre-industrial*. Barcelona: La Magrana, 1986.
Garcia Espuche, Albert, Manuel Guàrdia, Francisco Javier Monclús, and José Luis Oyón. "Barcelona." In *Atlas histórico de ciudades europeas. Península Ibérica*, edited by Manuel Guàrdia, Francisco Javier Monclús, and José Luis Oyón, 62–93. Barcelona: Salvat, 1994.
García Gallo, Alfonso. "Aportación al estudio de los fueros." *Anuario de Historia del Derecho Español* 26 (1956): 387–446.
Garcia Rovira, Anna M. *La revolució liberal a Espanya i les classes populars*. Vic: Eumo Editorial, 1989.
García Venero, Maximiliano. *Rius y Taulet. Veinte años de Barcelona (1868–1888)*. Madrid, Editora Nacional, 1968.
Garrabou, Ramon. *Enginyers industrials, modernització econòmica i burgesia a Catalunya (1850–inicis del segle XX)*. Barcelona: L'Avenç, 1982.
Garrabou, Ramon, Jordi Planas, and Enric Saguer. *Un capitalisme impossible? La gestió de la gran propietat agrària a la Catalunya contemporània*. Vic: Eumo Editorial, 2000.
Gay Escoda, Josep Maria. "Notas sobre el derecho supletorio en Cataluña desde el decreto de Nueva Planta (1715) hasta la jurisprudencia del Tribunal Supremo (1845)." In *Hispania. Entre derechos propios y derechos nacionales*, edited by Bartolomé Clavero, Paolo Grossi, and Francisco Tomás y Valiente, 2:806–65. Milan: Giuffrè Editore, 1990.
Gil Novales, Alberto, ed. *Diccionario biográfico del Trienio Liberal*. Madrid: Ediciones El Museo Universal, 1991.
Giralt, Emili. "El conflicto 'rabassaire' y la cuestión agraria en Cataluña hasta 1936." *Revista de Trabajo* 5 (1964): 51–71.
Goldstein, Jan. *Console and Classify: The French Psychiatric Profession in the Nineteenth Century*. Cambridge: Cambridge University Press, 1987.
Gómez-Navarro, José Luis, Javier Moreno Luzón, and Fernando Rey Reguillo. "La élite parlamentaria entre 1914 y 1923." In *Con luz y taquígrafos. El parlamento en la Restauración (1913–1923)*, edited by Mercedes Cabrera, 105–42. Madrid: Taurus, 1998.
Gramsci, Antonio. "The Intellectuals." In *Selections from the Prison Notebooks*,

edited and translated by Quintin Hoare and Geoffrey Nowell Smith, 5–23. New York: International Publishers, 1971.

Grau, Ramon, and Marina López. "L'Exposició Universal del 1888." In *Exposició Universal de Barcelona. Llibre del centenari, 1888–1898*, 347–55. Barcelona: L'Avenç, 1988.

Guàrdia i Canela, Josep-D. "L'acadèmia i el Col·legi d'advocats de Barcelona en els 150 anys de la reorganització d'aquest." *Revista Jurídica de Catalunya* 82, no. 2 (1983): 247–51.

Halliday, Terence C., and Lucien Karpik. "Politics Matter: A Comparative Theory of Lawyers in the Making of Political Liberalism." In *Lawyers and the Rise of Western Political Liberalism: Europe and North America from the Eighteenth to the Twentieth Centuries*, edited by Terence C. Halliday and Lucien Karpik, 15–64. Oxford: Clarendon Press, 1997.

Halpérin, Jean-Louis. *Entre nationalisme juridique et communauté de droit*. Paris: Presse Universitaires de France, 1999.

———. "Les sources statistiques de l'histoire des avocats en France au XVIIIe et au XIXe siècles." *Revue de la Société Internationale d'Histoire de la Profession d'Avocat* 3 (1991): 55–74.

Halpérin, Jean-Louis, et al. *Avocats et notaires en Europe: Les professions judiciaires et juridiques dan l'histoire contemporaine*. Paris: Librairie générale de droit et de jurisprudence, 1996.

Harrigan, Patrick, and Victor Neglia. *Lycéens et collégiens sous le Second Empire. Étude statistique sur les fonctions sociales de l'enseignement secondaire public d'après l'enquête de Victor Duruy (1864–65)*. Lille: Université de Lille III, Maison des Sciences de l'Homme, 1979.

Harty, Siobhán. "Lawyers, Codification, and the Origins of Catalan Nationalism, 1881–1901." *Law and History Review* 20, no. 2 (Summer 2002): 349–84.

Herr, Richard. *The Eighteenth-Century Revolution in Spain*. Princeton: Princeton University Press, 1958.

Hobsbawm, Eric J., and Terence Ranger, eds. *The Invention of Tradition*. Cambridge: Verso, 1983.

Hroch, Miroslav. *Social Preconditions of National Revival in Europe: A Comparative Analysis of the Social Composition of Patriotic Groups among the Smaller European Nations*. Translated by Ben Fowkes. New York: Columbia University Press, 2000.

Huskey, Eugene. *Russian Lawyers and the Soviet State: The Origins and Development of the Soviet Bar, 1917–1939*. Princeton: Princeton University Press, 1986.

Iglésies, Josep. *El cens del comte de Floridablanca 1788 (Part de Catalunya)*. Barcelona: Fundació Salvador Vives Casajuana, 1969.

Israel, Liora. *Robes noires et années sombres. Avocats et magistrats en résistance pendant la Seconde Guerre Mondiale*. Paris: Fayard, 2005.

Jacobson, Stephen. "Els advocats de Barcelona, 1830–1880." *Barcelona. Quaderns d'Història* 6 (2002): 153–72.

———. "Droit i politique dans l'Espagne du XIXe siècle. Les avocats barcelonais at les particularités du libéralisme catalan." *Genèses. Sciences sociales et histoire* 45 (December 2001): 4–26.

———. "'The Head and Heart of Spain': New Perspectives on Nationalism and Nationhood." *Social History* 29, no. 3 (August 2004): 393–407.
———. "The Iberian Mosaic." In *What Is a Nation? Europe, 1789–1914*, edited by Mark Hewittson and Timothy Baycroft, 210–27. Oxford: Oxford University Press, 2006.
———. "Law and Nationalism in Nineteenth-Century Europe: The Case of Catalonia in Comparative Perspective." *Law and History Review* 20, no. 2 (Summer 2002): 308–47.
Jacobson, Stephen, and Javier Moreno Luzón. "The Political System of the Restoration, 1875–1914: Political and Social Elites." In *Spanish History since 1808*, edited by José Álvarez Junco and Adrian Shubert, 93–109. New York: Oxford University Press, 2000.
Janué i Miret, Marició. *Els polítics en temps de revolució. La vida política a Barcelona durant el Sexenni Revolucionari*. Vic: Eumo Editorial, 2002.
Jarausch, Konrad H. "The Decline of Liberal Professionalism: Reflections on the Social Erosion of German Liberalism, 1867–1933." In *In Search of Liberal Germany: Studies in German Liberalism from 1789 to the Present*, edited by K. H. Jarausch and L. E. Jones, 261–86. Oxford: Berg Publishers, 1990.
———. *Students, Society, and Politics in Imperial Germany: The Rise of Academic Illiberalism*. Princeton: Princeton University Press, 1982.
———. *The Unfree Professions: German Lawyers, Teachers, and Engineers, 1900–1950*. Oxford: Oxford University Press, 1990.
Jardí, Enric. *1000 famílies catalanes. La cultura*. Barcelona: Dopesa, 1977.
———. *Història del Col·legi d'Advocats de Barcelona*. 2 vols. Barcelona: Col·legi d'Advocats, 1989.
John, Michael. "Between Estate and Profession: Lawyers and the Development of the Legal Profession in Nineteenth-Century Germany." In *The German Bourgeoisie: Essays on the Social History of the German Middle Class from the Late Eighteenth to the Early Twentieth Century*, edited by David Blackbourn and Richard J. Evans, 162–97. London: Routledge, 1991.
———. *Politics and the Law in Late Nineteenth-Century Germany: The Origins of the Civil Code*. Oxford: Clarendon Press, 1989.
———. "The Politics of Legal Unity in Germany, 1870–1896." *Historical Journal* 28, no. 2 (1985): 341–56.
Kaelble, Harmut. *Social Mobility in the 19th and 20th Centuries: Europe and America in Comparative Perspectives*. Leamington Spa: Berg, 1985.
Kagan, Richard L. *Lawsuits and Litigants in Castile, 1500–1700*. Chapel Hill: University of North Carolina Press, 1981.
Kaiser, Colin. "The Deflation in the Volume of Litigation at Paris in the Eighteenth Century and the Waning of the Old Juridical Order." *European Studies Review* 10 (1980): 309–36.
Karpik, Lucien. *French Lawyers: A Study in Collective Action, 1274–1994*. Translated by Nora Scott. Oxford: Clarendon Press, 1999.
Kelley, Donald R. *Historians and the Law in Postrevolutionary France*. Princeton: Princeton University Press, 1984.
Kidd, Colin. *Subverting Scotland's Past: Scottish Whig Historians and the Creation of*

an Anglo-British Identity, 1689–c. 1830. Cambridge: Cambridge University Press, 1993.

Klenner, Hermann. "Savigny's Research Program of the Historical School of Law and Its Intellectual Impact in 19th Century Berlin." *American Journal of Comparative Law* 37, no. 1 (Winter 1989): 67–79.

Konttinen, Esa. "'Finland's Route of Professionalisation and Lawyer-Officials." In *Lawyers and Vampires: Cultural Histories of Legal Professions*, edited by Wesley Pue and David Sugarman, 124–50. Oxford: Hart, 2003.

Kostal, R. W. *Law and English Railway Capitalism*. Oxford: Clarendon Press, 1994.

Kotschnig, Walter Maria. *Unemployment in the Learned Professions. An International Study of Occupational and Educational Planning*. London: Oxford University Press, 1937.

Kovács, Mária M. *Liberal Professions and Illiberal Politics: Hungary from the Habsburgs to the Holocaust*. Oxford: Oxford University Press, 1994.

———. *The Politics of the Legal Profession in Interwar Hungary*. New York: Columbia University Institute on East Central Europe, 1987.

Laitin, David D., Carlota Solé, and Stathis N. Kalyvas. "Language and the Constructions of States: The Case of Catalonia in Spain." *Politics and Society* 22, no. 1 (1994): 5–29.

Lamarca i Marquès, Albert. "L'administració de justícia a Catalunya durant l'ocupació Napoleònica (1808–1814). La traducció al català del *Code*." *Pedralbes. Revista d'Història Moderna* 15 (1995): 279–307.

Langbein, John H. *The Origins of the Adversary Criminal Trial*. Oxford: Oxford University Press, 2003.

Larson, Magali Sarfatti. *The Rise of Professionalism: A Sociological Analysis*. Berkeley: University of California Press, 1977.

———. "The Changing Functions of Lawyers in the Liberal State: Reflections for a Comparative Analysis." In *Lawyers in Society: Comparative Theories*, edited by Richard L. Abel and Philip S. C. Lewis, 427–77. Berkeley: University of California Press, 1989.

Lasso Gaite, Francisco. *Crónica de la codificación española. Codificación civil*. Vol. 1. Madrid: Ministerio de Justicia, 1970.

———. *El Ministerio de Justicia. Su imagen histórica*. Madrid: Ministerio de Justicia, 1970.

La Vopa, Anthony J. *Grace, Talent, and Merit: Poor Students, Clerical Careers and Professional Ideology in Eighteenth-Century Germany*. Cambridge: Cambridge University Press, 1988.

Le Béguec, Gilles. *La république des avocats*. Paris: Armand Colin, 2003.

Ledford, Kenneth F. *From General Estate to Special Interest: German Lawyers, 1878–1933*. Cambridge: Cambridge University Press, 1996.

Lemmings, David. *Professors of the Law: Barristers and English Legal Culture in the Eighteenth Century*. Oxford: Oxford University Press, 2000.

Leuwers, Hervé. *L'invention du barreau français, 1660–1830. La construction nationale d'un groupe professionnel*. Paris: L'École des Hautes Études en Sciences Sociales, 2006.

Llobera, Josep. "La formació de la ideologia nacionalista catalana. La idea de Volkgeist [sic] com a element definidor." *L'Avenç*, no. 63 (September 1983): 24–35.

Llorens i Vila, Jordi. *La Unió Catalanista i els orígens del catalanisme polític*. Barcelona: Publicacions de l'Abadia de Montserrat, 1992.

Lluch, Ernest. "La Catalunya del segle XVIII i la lluita contra l'absolutisme centralista. El 'Proyecto del abogado general del público' de Francesc Romà i Rosell." *Recerques. Història, Economia, Cultura* 1 (1970): 33–50.

———. *Las Españas vencidas del siglo XVIII. Claroscuros de la Ilustración*. Translated by Rosa Lluch. Barcelona: Crítica, 1999.

———. "La pràctica econòmica de la Il·lustració: el valencià Manuel Sisternes i Feliu i els seus dictàmens com a fiscal de l'Audiència de Catalunya (1776–1779)." In *Primer Congreso de Historia del País Valenciano*, vol. 3 (Valencia: Universidad de Valencia, 1976), 695–706.

Lobban, Michael. *The Common Law and English Jurisprudence, 1760–1850*. Oxford: Clarendon Press, 1991.

———. "Preparing for Fusion: Reforming the Nineteenth-Century Court of Chancery." *Law and History Review* 22, nos. 3–4 (2004): 389–428, 565–600.

Maluquer de Motes, Jordi. "The Industrial Revolution in Catalonia." In *The Economic Modernization of Spain, 1830–1930*, edited by Nicolás Sánchez Albornoz, 169–90. New York: New York University Press, 1987.

Mann, Michael. *The Rise of Classes and Nation States*. Vol. 2 of *The Sources of Social Power*. Cambridge: Cambridge University Press, 1993.

Marcuello Benedicto, Juan Ignacio. "La libertad de imprenta y su marco legal en la España liberal." *Ayer* 34 (1999): 65–92.

Marfany, Joan-Lluís. *Aspectes del modernisme*. Barcelona: Curial, 1990.

———. *La cultura del catalanisme*. Barcelona: Empúries, 1995.

———. *La llengua maltractada, el castellà i el català a Catalunya del segle XVI al segle XIX*. Barcelona: Editorial Empúries, 2001.

———. "'Minority' Languages and Literary Revivals." *Past and Present* 184, no. 1 (August 2004): 137–67.

———. "Renaixença literària i decadència lingüística." *Barcelona. Quaderns d'Història* 6 (2002): 139–52.

Marquès, Josep M. "Tribunals peculiars eclesiàstico-civils de Catalunya. Les contencions i el Breu." *Pedralbes. Revista d'Història Moderna* 13, no. 2 (1984): 381–92.

Martines, Lauro. *Lawyers and Statescraft in Renaissance Florence*. Princeton: Princeton University Press, 1968.

Masjuan, Eduard. "Introducción" to Eduardo Barriobero y Herrán, *El Tribunal Revolucionario de Barcelona, 1936–37*, 9–41. Reprint, Seville: Espuela de Plata, 2007.

May, Allyson N. *The Bar and the Old Bailey, 1750–1850*. Chapel Hill: University of North Carolina Press, 2003.

Maza, Sarah. *Private Lives and Public Affairs: The Causes Célèbres of Prerevolutionary France*. Berkeley: University of California Press, 1993.

McDonogh, Gary Wray. *Good Families of Barcelona: A Social History of Power in the Industrial Era*. Princeton: Princeton University Press, 1986.

Meilán Gil, José Luis. "Don Ramón Lázaro de Dou y Bassols y sus Instituciones de derecho público." In *Actas del I Symposium de Historia de la Administración*, 343–80. Madrid: Instituto de Estudios Administrativos, 1970.

Molas, Isidre. *Lliga Catalana. Un estudi de estasiologia*. Vol. 1. Barcelona: Edicions 62, 1972.

Molas Ribalta, Pedro. "Las audiencias borbónicas en la Corona de Aragón." In *Historia social de la administración española. Estudios sobre los siglos XVII y XVIII*, edited by Pedro Molas Ribalta et al., 116–64. Barcelona: CSIC, 1980.

Moliner i Prada, Antoni. *La Catalunya resistent a la dominació francesa (1808–1812)*. Barcelona: Edicions 62, 1989.

Morcillo, Aurora G. *True Catholic Womanhood: Gender Ideology in Franco's Spain*. Dekalb: Northern Illinois University Press, 2000.

Moreno Fraginals, Manuel. *El ingenio complejo económico social cubano del azúcar*. Barcelona: Crítica, 2001.

Moreu Rey, Enric. *El pensament il·lustrat a Catalunya*. Barcelona: Edicions 62, 1966.

Moreu Ros, Carmen. "La actividad del Tribunal de la Inquisición en Barcelona entre 1759 y 1786. Las proposiciones erróneas." *Pedralbes. Revista d'Història Moderna* 8, no. 2 (1988): 503–12.

Müller, Ingo. *Hitler's Justice: The Courts of the Third Reich*. Cambridge, Mass.: Harvard University Press, 1991.

Nadal, Jordi. *El fracaso de la revolución industrial en España, 1914–1913*. Barcelona: Ariel, 1975.

———. "La indústria cotonera." In *Indústria, transports i finances*, 13–85. Vol. 3 of *Història econòmica de la Catalunya contemporània*, edited by Jordi Nadal i Oller, Jordi Maluquer de Motes, Carles Sudrià i Triay, and Francesc Cabana i Vancells. Barcelona: Enciclopèdia Catalana, 1988–94.

O'Boyle, Lenore. "The Problem of an Excess of Educated Men in Western Europe, 1800–1850." *Journal of Modern History* 42, no. 4 (December 1970): 471–95.

Palos, Joan Lluís. *Els juristes i la defensa de les Constitucions. Joan Pere Fontanella (1575–1649)*. Vic: Eumo Editorial, 1997.

Paredes, Javier. *La organización de la justicia en la España liberal. Los orígenes de la carrera judicial: 1834–1870*. Madrid: Civitas, 1991.

Parés i Puntas, Ana. *Tots els refranys catalans*. Barcelona: Edicions 62, 1999.

Pascual, Pere. *Agricultura i industrialització a la Catalunya del segle XIX. Formació i desestructuració d'un sistema econòmic*. Barcelona: Editorial Crítica, 1990.

———. *Els Torelló. Una família igualadina d'advocats i propietaris. Liberalisme, conservadorisme i canvi econòmic i social (1820–1930)*. Barcelona: Editorial Rafael Dalmau, 2000.

Pérez Collados, José María. "El derecho catalán de sucesiones en vísperas de la codificación." *Anuario de Historia del Derecho Español* 125 (2006): 331–67.

Pérez Garzón, Juan Sisinio. *Milicia nacional y revolución burguesa. El prototipo madrileño, 1808–1874*. Madrid: CSIC, 1978.

Pérez Samper, María Angeles. "La Real Audiencia de Cataluña durante la Guerra de la Independencia." *Pedralbes. Revista d'Història Moderna* 2 (1982): 177–209.
Perkin, Harold. *The Rise of Professional Society: England since 1880*. London: Routledge, 1989.
———. *The Third Revolution: Professional Elites in the Modern World*. London: Routledge, 1996.
Permanyer, Lluís. *Cites i testimonis sobre Barcelona. La ciutat viscuda i jutjada per personatges no catalans al llarg de 2000 anys*. Barcelona: La Campana, 1993.
Peset Reig, Mariano. "Derecho romano y derecho real en las universidades del siglo XVIII." *Anuario de Historia del Derecho Español* 54 (1975): 273–339.
———. "Estudios de derecho y profesiones jurídicas (siglos XIX y XX)." In *El tercer poder: hacía una comprensión histórica de la justicia contemporánea en España*, edited by Johannes-Michael Scholz, 349–80. Frankfurt am Main: Vittorio Klostermann, 1992.
———. "La formación de los juristas y su acceso al foro en el tránsito de los siglos XVIII a XIX." *Revista General de Legislación y Jurisprudencia* 62 (1971): 605–672.
———. "La recepción de las Órdenes del Marqués de Caballero de 1802 en las Universidad de Valencia. Exceso de abogados y reforma en los estudios de leyes." *Saitabi. Revista de la Facultad de Filosofía y Letras de la Universidad de Valencia* 19 (1969): 119–48.
Petit, Carlos. "Derecho mercantil. Entre corporaciones y códigos." In *Hispania. Entre derechos propios y derechos nacionales*, edited by Bartolomé Clavero, Paolo Grossi, and Francisco Tomás y Valiente, 1:347–80. Milan: Guiffrè, 1989.
Pich i Mitjana, Josep. *El Centre Català. La primera associació política catalanista (1882–1884)*. Barcelona: Editorial Afers, 2002.
Pocock, J. G. A. *The Ancient Constitution and the Feudal Law: A Study of English Historical Thought in the Seventeenth Century*. 2d ed. Cambridge: Cambridge University Press, 1987.
Polanyi, Karl. *The Great Transformation: The Political and Economic Origins of Our Time*. Rev. ed. Boston: Beacon Press, 2001. Original edition, 1944.
Ponce, Santi, and Llorenç Ferrer, eds. *Família i canvi social a la Catalunya contemporània (s. XIX–XX)*. Vic: Eumo Editorial, 1994.
Porter, Dorothy, and Roy Porter. *Patient's Progress: Doctors and Doctoring in Eighteenth-Century England*. London: Polity Press, 1989.
Prats, Joaquim. *La Universitat de Cervera i el reformisme borbònic*. Lleida: Pagès Editors, 1993.
Prest, Wilfrid. "Law, Lawyers and Rational Dissent." In *Enlightenment and Religion: Rational Dissent in Eighteenth-Century Britain*, edited by Knud Haakonssen, 169–92. Cambridge: Cambridge University Press, 1996.
———. *The Rise of the Barristers: A Social History of the English Bar, 1590–1640*. Oxford: Clarendon Press, 1986.
———, ed. *Lawyers in Early Modern Europe and America*. New York: Holmes and Meier, 1981.
Pue, W. Wesley. "Lawyers and Political Liberalism in Eighteenth- and Nineteenth-

Century England." In *Lawyers and the Rise of Western Political Liberalism: Europe and North America from the Eighteenth to the Twentieth Centuries*, edited by Terence C. Halliday and Lucien Karpik, 167–206. Oxford: Clarendon Press, 1997.

Puigvert, Joaquim M. *Església, territori i sociabilitat (s. XVII–XIX)*. Vic: Eumo Editorial, 2000.

Radding, Charles M. "Legal Theory and Practice in Eleventh-Century Italy." *Law and History Review* 21, no. 2 (Summer 2003): 377–82.

Rahola, Frederic. "Comerç i indústria de Catalunya." In *Geografia general de Catalunya: Barcelona*, edited by Francesch Carreras i Candi, 323–464. Barcelona: Martín, 1913–18.

Ramisa, Maties. *Els catalans i el domini napoleònic*. Barcelona: Publicacions de l'Abadia de Montserrat, 1995.

———. *Els orígens del catalanisme conservador i "La Veu del Montserrat," 1878–1900*. Vic: Eumo Editorial, 1985.

Ramsay, Mathew. *Professional and Popular Medicine in France, 1770–1830: The Social World of Medical Practice*. Cambridge: Cambridge University Press, 1988.

Resina, Joan Ramon. "From Rose of Fire to City of Ivory." In *After-Images of the City*, edited by Joan Ramon Resina and Dieter Ingenschay, 75–122. Ithaca: Cornell University Press, 2003.

Reynolds, Susan. "The Emergence of Professional Law in the Long Twelfth Century." *Law and History Review* 21, no. 2 (Summer 2003): 346–66.

Riera i Fortiana, Enric. *Els afrancesats a Catalunya*. Barcelona: Curial, 1994.

Rincón Igea, Benito de. "La educación en Barcelona durante el Sexenio Revolucionario (1868–1874). Las escuelas municipales, el Instituto Provincial y las facultades universitarias." Ph.D. diss., Universitat de Barcelona, 1991.

Riquer i Permanyer, Borja de. "La Diputació conservadora: 1875–1880." In *Història de la Diputació Diputació de Barcelona*, edited by Borja de Riquer i Permanyer, 1:245–63. Barcelona: Diputació de Barcelona, 1987.

———. *Identitats contemporànies. Catalunya i Espanya*. Vic: Eumo, 2000.

———, ed. *Epistolari polític de Manuel Duran i Bas (Correspondència entre 1866 i 1904)*. Barcelona: Publicacions de l'Abadia de Montserrat, 1990.

Risques Corbella, Manel. *El govern civil de Barcelona al segle XIX*. Barcelona: Publicacions de l'Abadia de Montserrat, 1995.

———. "La insurrecció de Barcelona pel novembre de 1842. La seva dinàmica social." *Recerques. Història, Economia, Cultura* 10 (1980): 93–112.

Risques Corbella, Manel, Angel Duarte, Borja de Riquer, and Josep M. Roig Rosich. *Història de la Catalunya contemporània*. Barcelona: Pòrtic, 1999.

Robinson, O. F., T. D. Fergus, and W. M. Gordon. *An Introduction to European Legal History*. Abingdon, Oxon: Professional Books, 1985.

Rodrigo y Alharilla, Martín. *Los Marqueses de Comillas, 1817–1925*. Madrid: LID, 2000.

———. "Mujeres con fortuna, mujeres afortunadas. Roles sociales y funciones públicas de las mujeres burguesas en Barcelona (1840–1900)." Unpublished article cited with permission of author.

Rojo, Angel. "José Bonaparte (1808–1813) y la legislación mercantil e industrial española." *Revista de Derecho Mercantil* 143–44 (January–June 1977): 121–82.
Roselló i Cherigny, Elena. "El régimen jurídico de la desamortización en Barcelona: el caso del Convento de St. Josep / Mercado de la Boqueria." Master's thesis, Universitat Pompeu Fabra, 2005.
Roura, Jaume. *Ramon Martí d'Eixalà i la filosofia catalana del segle XIX*. Barcelona: Publicacions de l'Abadia de Montserrat, 1980.
Rudé, George F. E. *The Crowd in History: The Study of Popular Disturbances in France and England, 1730–1848*. New York: Wiley, 1964.
Ruiz, Julius. *Franco's Justice: Repression in Madrid after the Spanish Civil War*. Oxford: Oxford University Press, 2005.
Ruíz Torres, Pedro. "Liberalisme i revolució a Espanya." *Recerques. Història, Economia, Cultura* 28 (1994): 59–71.
Salvador Coderch, Pau. *La compilación y su historia. Estudios sobre la codificación y la interpretación de las leyes*. Barcelona: Bosch, 1985.
Sánchez, Alejandro. "Manchester español, Rosa de Fuego, París del sur . . ." In *Barcelona, 1888–1929. Modernidad, ambición y conflictos de una ciudad soñada*, edited by Alejandro Sánchez, 15–22. Madrid: Alianza Editorial, 1994.
Sánchez-Blanco, Francisco. *El absolutismo y las luces en el reinado de Carlos III*. Madrid: Marcial Pons, 2002.
Santirso, Manuel. *Revolució liberal i guerra civil a Catalunya*. Lleida: Pagès, 1999.
———. "Voluntarios realistas, voluntarios de Isabel II y milicia nacional, o en la guerra también hay clases (Cataluña, 1832–1837)." *Historia Social* 23 (1995): 21–40.
Sarrailh, Jean. *La España ilustrada de la segunda mitad del siglo XVIII*. Translated by Antonio Alatorre. Mexico, DF: Fondo de Cultura Económica, 1957.
Sarrión Gualda, José, and M. Jesús Espuny Tomás. *Las Ordenanzas de 1766 del Consulado de Comercio de Cataluña y el llamado Proyecto de Código de Comercio de 1814 de la Diputación Provincial de Cataluña*. Vol. 16 of *Documentación Jurídica* (April–June 1989). Madrid: Secretaría General Técnica del Ministerio de Justicia, Gabinete de Documentación y Publicaciones.
Scanlon, Geraldine M. *La polémica feminista en la España contemporánea (1868–1974)*. Translated by Rafael Mazarrasa. Madrid: Siglo XXI, 1976.
Schmidt-Nowara, Christopher. *Empire and Anti-slavery: Spain, Cuba, and Puerto Rico, 1833–1874*. Pittsburgh: University of Pittsburgh Press, 1999.
Scott, Rebecca. *Slave Emancipation in Cuba: The Transition to Free Labor, 1860–1899*. Reprint, Pittsburgh: University of Pittsburgh Press, 2000.
Segarra, Ferran. "Política urbanística i creixement urbà." In *La ciutat industrial*, 189–216. Vol. 6 of *Història de Barcelona*, edited by Jaume Sobrequés i Callicó. Barcelona: Enciclopèdia Catalana, 1995.
Segura, Antoni. *Burgesia i propietat de la terra a Catalunya en el segle XIX. Les comarques barcelonines*. Barcelona: Curial, 1993.
Serrahima, Maurici. *Un advocat del segle XIX. Maurici Serrahima i Palà (1834–1904)*. Barcelona: Horta, 1951.
Shubert, Adrian. *A Social History of Modern Spain*. London: Unwin Hyman, 1990.

Siegrist, Hannes. *Advokat, Bürger und Staat: Sozialgeschichte der Rechtsanwälte in Deutschland, Italien und der Schweiz (18.–20.Jh.)*. 2 vols. Frankfurt am Main: V. Klostermann, 1996.

———. "Gli avvocati nell'Italia del XIX secolo. Provenienza e matrimoni, titolo e prestigio." *Meridiana. Rivista di Storia e Scienze Sociali* 14 (1992): 145–81.

———. "Juridicialisation, Professionalisation and the Occupational Culture of the Advocate in the Nineteenth and the Twentieth Centuries: A Comparison of Germany, Italy and Switzerland." In *Lawyers and Vampires: Cultural Histories of Legal Professions*, edited by Wesley Pue and David Sugarman, 101–23. Oxford: Hart, 2003.

———. "Public Office or Free Profession? German Attorneys in the Nineteenth and Early Twentieth Centuries." In *German Professions, 1800–1950*, edited by Geoffrey Cocks and Konrad H. Jarausch, 46–65. New York: Oxford University Press, 1990.

Simón i Tarrés, Antoni. *Construccions polítiques i identitats nacionals. Catalunya i els orígens de l'estat modern espanyol*. Barcelona: Publicacions de l'Abadia de Montserrat, 2005.

Solé i Sabaté, Josep M. *La repressió franquista a Catalunya, 1938–1953*. Barcelona: Edicions 62, 1985.

Solé-Tura, Jordi. *Catalanismo y revolución burguesa*. Madrid: Edicusa, 1970.

Suleiman, Ezra N. *Private Power and Centralization in France: The Notaires and the State*. Princeton: Princeton University Press, 1987.

Termes, Josep. "La immigració a Catalunya. Política i cultura." In *La immigració a Catalunya i altres estudis del nacionalisme català*, 123–93. Barcelona: Editorial Empúries, 1984.

Thompson, E. P. *Whigs and Hunters: The Origin of the Black Act*. London: Allen Lane, 1975.

Thomson, J. K. J. *A Distinctive Industrialization: Cotton in Barcelona, 1728–1832*. Cambridge: Cambridge University Press, 1992.

Tomàs, Margalida. "La Jove Catalunya: Entre la literatura i la política." In *La Jove Catalunya. Antologia*, edited by Margalida Tomàs, pp. v–xlvi. Barcelona: Edicions La Magrana, 1992.

Tomás y Valiente, Francisco. *La tortura judicial en España*. Reprint, Barcelona: Crítica, 2000.

Tortella, Gabriel. *The Development of Modern Spain: An Economic History of the Nineteenth and Twentieth Century*. Translated by Valerie J. Herr. Cambridge, Mass.: Harvard University Press, 2000.

Ucelay-Da Cal, Enric. *El imperialismo catalán. Prat de la Riba, Cambó, D'Ors y la conquista moral de España*. Madrid: Edhasa, 2003.

Umbach, Maiken. "A Tale of Second Cities: Autonomy, Culture, and the Law in Hamburg and Barcelona in the Late Nineteenth Century." *American Historical Review* 110, no. 2 (2005): 1–39.

Uribe-Uran, Victor M. *Honorable Lives: Lawyers, Family, and Politics in Colombia, 1780–1850*. Pittsburgh: University of Pittsburgh Press, 2000.

Varela, Javier. *La novela de España. Los intelectuales y el problema español*. Madrid: Taurus, 1999.
Vicens i Vives, Jaume, and Montserrat Llorens. *Industrials i polítics (segle XIX)*. Barcelona: Ediciones Vicens Vives, 1958.
Vilar, Pierre. "Els Barba, una família il·lustrada de Vilafranca del Penedès." In *Assaigs sobre la Catalunya del segle XVIII*, translated by Eulàlia Duran, 59–82. Barcelona: Curial, 1979.
———. *Cataluña en la España moderna. Las transformaciones agrarias*. Translated by Laura Roca. Vol. 2. Barcelona: Crítica, 1987.
Voltes Bou, Pedro." *La banca barcelonesa de 1840 a 1920*. Vol. 12 of *Instituto Municipal de Historia. Documentos y estudios*. Barcelona: Ayuntamiento de Barcelona, 1965.
Villacorta Baños, Francisco. *Profesionales y burócratas. Estado y poder corporativo en la España del siglo, 1890–1923*. Madrid: Siglo XXI, 1989.
Watson, Alan. *The Evolution of Law*. Baltimore: Johns Hopkins University Press, 1985.
———. *The Making of the Civil Law*. Cambridge, Mass.: Harvard University Press, 1981.
Weber, Max. "Economy and Law (Sociology of Law)." In *Economy and Society: An Outline of Interpertative Sociology*, edited by Guenther Roth and Claus Wittich, translated by Ephraim Fischoff et al., 2:641–900. Berkeley: University of California Press, 1978.
Whitman, James Q. *The Legacy of Roman Law in the German Romantic Era: Historical Vision and Legal Change*. Princeton: Princeton University Press, 1990.
Wilensky, Harold J. "The Professionalization of Everyone?" *American Journal of Sociology* 70 (1964): 138–58.
Williams, Raymond. *Culture and Society, 1780–1950*. New York: Columbia University Press, 1958.
Woloch, Isser. "The Fall and Resurrection of the Civil Bar, 1789–1820s." *French Historical Studies* 15, no. 2 (Fall 1987): 241–62.

Index

Absolutism, 6, 14, 15, 32, 51, 69, 122; decline of bar under, 30, 33, 35–36, 96, 240, 242, 247; persecution of bar under, 96–105, 242
Academy of Administrative Law, 201, 229
Academy of Jurisprudence, 14, 156, 174, 178, 187; in eighteenth century, 51, 54, 59, 61, 63–64; as conservative association, 126–32, 134, 146; and codification, 139, 205, 209–11, 222–23, 228, 229; and Catalanism, 201, 203, 218, 236
Academy of Law, 201, 229
Administrative law, 128, 133, 200
Advocates. *See* Lawyers
Ahrens, Henri, 144
Alcaldes mayores, 41, 44, 47, 78, 108–9; corruption of, 34–35; and purification proceedings, 99–101
Almeda i Roig, Joaquim, 188, 191, 209
Almirall i Llozer, Valentí, 25, 26, 143, 197, 209–11, 214, 217, 225
Alonso Martínez, Manuel, 175, 207–8, 223, 225, 228–30, 234, 294 (nn. 115, 116)
Alphonse XII, 231
Altadill, Antoni: *Mysteries of Barcelona*, 154, 155, 162, 173; *Ambition of a Woman*, 155
Althusser, Louis, 4
Anarchism, 15, 172
Angelon i Broquetas, Manuel, 151, 153, 179, 213
Angoulême, Duke of, 89
Aquinas, Thomas, 133, 146
Arendt, Hannah, 243
Army, 15, 35, 93, 98; exemption from draft into, 88, 103, 162
Artisans, 17, 21, 38, 57, 87, 92, 96, 98, 110, 117, 157, 159, 161–62, 167; taxation of, 50, 182–83

Attorneys, 260 (n. 51); in Prussia, 51, 71. *See also* Lawyers; Proctors
Audiencia of Barcelona, 32, 38, 118, 122, 134, 153, 202; location of, 19, 37; jurisdiction and organization of, 41–47, 109, 113, 119, 193; regulation of lawyers by, 51–52; during War of Independence, 74–81. *See also* Judges and magistrates
Avilés, Gabriel, 250
Avilés Vilà, Montserrat, 252

Bailiffs, 34, 111
Bakunin, Mikhail, 224
Balle, Joan de, 76, 94–95
Balzac, Honoré de: *Colonel Chabert*, 151, 154; *Old Goriot*, 177
Bankers, 17, 95, 156, 164–65, 184–85
Bank of Barcelona, 115, 185–86
Bank of Spain, 117
Bar: in England, 2, 5, 30, 51, 56, 113, 135, 158, 219, 239, 244; in early modern Europe, 2, 30–32, 120, 240; autonomy and independence of, 4, 5, 8, 51, 72, 96, 125, 126; meritocratic nature of, 5, 30; in France, 5, 35–36, 51, 55–56, 70, 91, 104, 113, 127, 135, 148, 158, 177, 239, 247; in Germany, 5, 158, 247; corporatist nature of, 7, 8, 14, 148, 150, 156, 169, 172, 178–79, 184, 199, 203, 240, 246–47; overcrowding at, 7, 8, 150, 156, 190–97, 203, 217, 236, 246–47, 255; humanism and, 7, 52, 113, 141; misogyny, anti-Semitism, and xenophobia of, 8, 247, 255, 296 (n. 10); diversity of, 14, 30, 73, 83, 85, 127, 128, 143, 157, 158–59; camaraderie and collegiality of, 14, 157, 170, 190, 197; transformation in structure of, 14, 193; size of, 30–31, 47, 65, 101, 119, 177, 192, 255; number of calls to, 33; examination, 40–41; numerical

limitations and, 41, 51, 53, 65, 71, 96, 99, 244; eighteenth-century reform of, 51, 52, 64–65; in Valencia, 51, 52, 65; in Madrid, 51, 61, 65, 135, 176, 194, 195; in Prussia, 51, 70, 71; in United States, 72, 86, 104, 244; historical memory of, 146, 148, 150, 201, 240; Catalanism and, 150, 198–204, 211, 236–37, 240; in Naples and Florence, 158; social mobility and, 159–62; endogeny of, 163–64; specialization of, 178; dictatorship and, 243, 249–50; women at, 254, 255. *See also* College of Lawyers of Barcelona; College of Lawyers of Madrid; Lawyers
Barba i Roca, Manuel, 28, 54–55, 59, 63, 64, 75
Barcelona, 2, 3, 8–23 passim, 31–32, 37, 114–15, 154–55, 158–59, 243–44, 247–48; population of, 9, 11–12, 31, 114, 119; province of, 12, 23, 249; as "industrious city," 32, 57; Enlightenment in, 56–58; Napoleonic occupation of, 66, 73–84 passim, 113; revolution in, 91–96; absolutist repression of, 98; municipality of, 121–22, 124; schools in, 165; linguistic habits of residents, 167–68. *See also* Catalonia; Industrialization
Barons, 47–48, 93–95, 138
Bayly, C. A., 105
Beccaria, Cesare, 58, 59
Bentham, Jeremy, 56, 219
Berlanstein, Lenard, 55
Bertran i d'Amat, Felip, 210, 211
Bertran i Ros, Josep, 78, 93–94, 163, 164, 165, 205, 211
Bielfeld, Baron von, 61
Blackstone, William, 56, 245
Bonaparte, Joseph, 73, 82
Bonaparte, Napoleon, 70, 73, 140
Bonapartism, 23, 74, 105
Borrell i Soler, Josep, 164, 187, 289 (n. 4), 291 (n. 44)
Bourdieu, Pierre, 4
Brocà i de Montagut, Guillem, 185, 225–26
Brooks, Christopher, 30
Bureaucracy. *See* Public administration

Cadalfach i Buguñà, Joaquim, 139–42, 144, 163, 225
Cambó i Batlle, Francesc, 175, 186, 236
Camino y Alonso del Real, Luis María, 168, 175, 186
Campomanes, Pedro Rodríguez de, 51, 56
Càncer, Jaume, 146, 164
Canon law, 45–46, 49, 118, 120–21; as supplement to Catalan law, 216. *See also* Roman-ecclesiastical tradition
Capital punishment, 59
Capmany i Montpalau, Antoni de, 22, 57
Carlist War: First (1833–39), 15, 89, 90, 94, 104, 106, 124, 169, 170, 172; Second (1872–75), 15, 121, 125, 199, 201
Casanova, Ramon, 74–75, 82
Castells, Miquel de, 77, 78, 146
Castilian law. *See* Spanish common law
Castilians, derogatory characterizations of, 66, 140, 145, 197–98, 204, 234
Catalan Center (Centre Català), 24, 25, 26, 194, 197
Catalanism: history of, 22–27; and law, 135, 145, 215; conversion of bar to, 150, 198–204, 211, 236–37, 240; relationship to corporatism, 156, 194–97, 199, 203; citizenship and, 248–49. *See also* Catalanists; Nationalism; Regionalism
Catalanist Student Center (Centre Escolar Catalanista), 26, 194, 201, 233, 236
Catalanist Union (Unió Catalanista), 203, 235
Catalanists: ridicule of, 217; defense of Catalan law by, 231–37
Catalan language: not used in court, 10, 34, 60, 220; and revivalism, 24–25, 212–18, 227, 237; and War of Independence, 82–83; lawyers' use of, 167–69, 171, 252; attempts to incorporate in judicial proceedings, 196, 217–18, 231–32, 236, 253; derogatory characterizations of, 209; distinguished from dialect, 226
Catalan law: defense of, 7, 23, 26, 27, 150, 197, 204–11, 217–37 passim, 245; medieval origins of, 9; central juridical institutions of, 134–43; derogatory characterizations of, 143–44, 148, 204, 225; as proposed appendix to civil code,

145, 208, 228, 230, 235, 253; teaching of, 171, 196, 231; influence of romanticism on, 212, 215–16; supplements to, 216, 230; as civil law, 218–27; citizenship provisions of, 232; codification of, 253. *See also* Emphyteusis; Foral law; Testamentary liberty

Catalan League (Lliga de Catalunya), 26, 201, 235

Catalans: praise for, 10, 17, 18, 32; as Spanish patriots, 22, 74; ethnic roots of, 26; discriminated against, 34, 194; derogatory characterizations of, 66, 145, 204; innate sense of liberty and patriarchy, 141; legal definition of, 232

Catalonia, 8–15, 157, 191; population of, 13, 89, 119; divided into provinces, 23; and War of Independence, 74–81; and First Carlist War, 89–90; secondary schools in, 165–66; historiography of, 215; autonomy of, 249, 253; civil war and repression in, 250–51, 297 (n. 21). *See also* Barcelona; Crown of Aragon; Industrialization

Causes célèbres, 122, 128, 181

Charles III, 33, 34, 35, 61, 64, 75, 89, 108, 126; reform of bar under, 51

Charles IV, 81, 99, 170; reform of bar under, 64–65

Church, Roman Catholic: disentailment and sale of properties of, 14, 72, 84, 85, 107, 147; and Catalan law, 216; and Catalan language, 237. *See also* Canon law; Clergy; Tithes

Citadel fortress, 32, 121, 122

Civil codification, 8, 63, 136–45, 171, 197, 204–11, 219–32, 241–43, 253; in Germany, 228; in Austria, Italy, and Hungary, 245–46

Civil law and procedure, 42–44, 49, 110–15, 179–80, 188–89, 240. *See also* Catalan law; Civil codification; Spanish Civil Code

Civil liberty, 142, 148, 225

Clergy, 1, 15, 17, 55, 57, 86, 88, 121, 151, 152; as lawyers, 45, 103, 121; revolution and, 92, 93, 94; and Catalanism, 216–17, 237, 249

Clients, 115, 123, 133, 134, 147, 149, 150, 154, 181–84, 187–89, 193, 218. *See also* Lawyers; Litigants

Codes: of commercial procedure (1830), 47, 115; of civil procedure (1855), 110, 112, 206; of criminal procedure (1882), 112; of commercial law (1829), 206; of penal law (1822), 206; of civil procedure (1881), 274 (n. 6). *See also* Spanish Civil Code

College of Lawyers of Barcelona, 14, 123–30, 153, 156, 172, 187; location of, 20, 123, 129; deans of, 78, 81, 88, 116, 123, 129, 145, 159, 163, 199, 204, 228, 249, 250, 252, 253, 255, 289 (n. 4); foundation of, 96, 179, 180; political neutrality of, 124–26, 200; conservative takeover of, 129, 132, 134; and fee reductions, 182; and Bourbon Restoration, 199–200; and defense of Catalan law, 208, 210; and civil war and Francoism, 249–52. *See also* Bar; Lawyers

College of Lawyers of Madrid, 61, 195, 270 (n. 49)

Commercial Consulate, 115; location of, 19, 46; abolition of, 117

Commercial law and procedure, 46–47, 49, 67, 73–74, 115, 141. *See also* Mercantile lawyers

Companys i Jover, Lluís, 251

Congress of Vienna, 78, 84

Conservative Party, 22, 187, 199, 207, 211, 228–29

Conservatism: among lawyers and law professors, 4–7, 94, 116, 132–34, 155, 173, 200; and bar, 104–6, 145–50, 240–41, 247; at academy and college, 122–32, 199; and judiciary, 132; and legal tradition, 134–35; relationship to liberalism, 148–49; and codification, 224

Constitutional assemblies: of Cadiz, 65, 70, 71, 76; of Bayonne, 73

Constitutions: of 1812, 70, 71, 76, 84, 103, 108; of 1837, 71; of 1845, 107; of 1876, 207

Consulat del Mar, 9

Contingency fees, 49, 50

Coroleu i Inglada, Josep, 25, 57, 173, 215

Corominas i Montanya, Pere, 172

Corruption: of *alcaldes mayores*, 34, 35; of courts, 35, 66, 96, 108, 111, 195; of lawyers, 42, 66–67, 149, 155, 187
Costa Martínez, Joaquín, 173
Crime rates, 192–93
Crimes, 44, 109, 128, 171, 180
Criminal law. *See* Penal law and procedure
Crown of Aragon, 8, 25, 28, 33, 34, 39, 56
Crown of Castile, 8, 9, 34, 39, 135, 210

D'Aguesseau, Henri, 53–54
Dalí, Salvador, 172
Danton, Georges Jacques, 91
Decretals, 9, 146
Degollada, Rafael, 98, 184, 185, 272 (n. 103)
Deseze, Romain, 153
Dickens, Charles: *Great Expectations*, 91; *Bleak House*, 152, 154
District courts, 108, 109, 110, 187; volume of litigation in, 192–93, 274 (n. 16); poor condition of, 201–2
Doctors and surgeons, 1, 50, 55, 56, 100, 151, 152, 165, 183, 217
Domènech i Montaner, Lluís, 18, 248
Dou i de Bassols, Ramon de, 59, 60, 76, 113, 146
Duhesme, General Guillaume-Philibert, 79, 81
Duran i Bas, Manuel, 114, 116, 117, 164, 176, 181, 199, 289 (n. 141); and historical school jurisprudence, 23, 223; and conservatism, 129–31, 145–46, 289 (n. 4); and civil code conflicts, 207, 211, 227–30
Duran i Ventosa, Lluís, 164, 197, 236–37
Durkheim, Émile, 4

Ecclesiastical law. *See* Canon law; Roman-ecclesiastical tradition
Education: reform of, 52, 65, 161–62, 170; cost of, 161–62; secondary school, 165–67. *See also* Law degrees; Law professors; Law students; Moyano Law; University of Barcelona
Elias, Josep, 87, 90, 93, 97
Elias i d'Aloy, Josep Antoni, 220, 221, 225
Emphyteusis, 48–49, 60–62; survival of, 95, 114–15, 275 (n. 33), 280 (n. 118); and *rabassa morta*, 134; and Catalan law, 137–38, 215, 222, 233; and codification, 139, 143, 144, 207, 208, 212, 279 (n. 91); contrary to liberal doctrine, 149, 281 (n. 127)
Engels, Friedrich, 13
England: common law of, 135, 219; influence of Roman law in, 142; organization of courts in, 109. *See also* Bar
España, Count of, 98
Exalted Liberals, 90, 92, 94, 95, 100, 101, 102

Fabra i Poch, Pompeu, 227
Falcón O'Neill, Lidia, 254, 255
Families: stem versus nuclear, 136. *See also* Castilians, derogatory characterizations of; Catalans: derogatory characterizations of; Inheritance; Property: individual versus community
Farnés i Badó, Sebastià, 237
Federal-Republicans, 24, 25, 90, 111, 172; and Catalan law, 142, 143, 209, 210, 224
Ferdinand VI, 34
Ferdinand VII, 81, 84, 89, 101; persecution of lawyers by, 98–99
Ferrater, Esteve de, 220, 221
Ferrer i Bruguera, Melcior, 129, 130, 164, 165, 199, 209, 289 (n. 4)
Feu i Palau, Josep Leopold, 116, 117, 278 (n. 79)
Feudalism: associated with Catalan law, 138, 140, 144, 148, 149
Feudal law and jurisdictions, 47–48, 60, 94. *See also* Emphyteusis
Figuerola i Ballester, Laureà, 133, 168, 183, 201, 289 (n. 141)
Fina Sanglas, Albert, 252
Finestres i de Monsalvo, Josep, 56
Flaubert, Gustave, 214; *Sentimental Education*, 91, 173
Floral Games, 212–13, 232
Fontanella, Joan Pere, 9, 146, 164
Foral law: relationship to Spanish common law, 135–36, 204, 220, 221, 225–27; and codification, 144, 208, 229, 230; teaching of, 171. *See also* Catalan law; Spanish Civil Code
Fradera, Josep Maria, 280 (n. 125)
France, 16, 17; "100,000 Sons of St. Louis,"

89; organization of courts in, 109. *See also* Bar; Bonaparte, Napoleon; French Civil Code; French Revolution; War of Independence
Franchise, size of, 71, 108, 120, 130, 132; in Britain and France, 71
Franco y Bahamonde, Francisco, 249, 250, 251, 254
Frederick the Great, 51, 59, 61
Freemasons. *See* Secret societies
French Civil Code, 135, 143, 205, 220; influence on draft code of 1851, 138–39; and inheritance, 140, 142
French Revolution, 2, 13, 37, 66–67, 85, 86; and emphyteusis, 62, 95; affect on Charles IV, 64; participation of lawyers in, 69, 91; legislation on legal profession during, 70–71, 91

Gaudí i Cornet, Antoni, 18, 248
Germanic law, 136–37, 140, 144
Germany, 2, 16; codification in, 222, 228. *See also* Bar
Gramsci, Antonio, 4
Grotius, Hugo, 9, 58, 63
Guilds, 5, 37, 49; lack of among Barcelona lawyers, 41, 50, 244; abolition of, 70, 107, 117

Halliday, Terence, 4
Herder, Johann Gottfried, 26, 223, 248
Hereu, 137–38, 143, 147, 162–63, 215, 216
Hispanic Overseas Circle, 130
Hispano-Colonial Bank, 115, 185
Historical-school jurisprudence, 24, 221, 222, 225, 227, 248. *See also* Savigny, Friedrich von
Historicism, 24, 27, 133, 223, 224, 225, 242, 247
Hotman, François, 245
Hroch, Miroslav, 237–38
Hurtado i Miró, Amadeu, 143, 188, 191, 196, 249, 288 (n. 136)

Illas i Vidal, Joan, 116, 117, 168, 213
Industrialization: in Barcelona and Catalonia, 3, 10–13, 16; and affects on bar and legal practice, 14, 67, 106, 114, 115, 118–19, 147, 148, 149, 191, 240: relationship to professionalization, 28–30
Inheritance, 49, 50, 147, 188; and Catalan law, 137–44, 162, 164, 204, 207, 208, 216, 234, 278–79 (n. 88); in England and France, 140–41, 143
Inquisition, 37, 46; and censorship, 34, 58; abolition of, 85–86, 101
Ius commune, 39, 59, 97. *See also* Roman-ecclesiastical tradition; Roman law

Jackson, Andrew, 86, 244
Jesuits, 56, 78, 97, 166
Judges and magistrates, 21, 110, 130, 192; and Catalan language, 34, 196, 203, 217, 218, 231, 232, 253; and bar exams, 40, 41; municipal, 42, 109, 110, 111, 128, 182; and procedure, 43–46, 202; criticism of lawyers by, 53, 55, 153; during War of Independence, 74, 75, 76, 78, 79, 82; and liberal revolution, 90, 93, 95, 96, 101, 102; district-court, 109, 111, 177; salaries of, 183
Judiciary: independence of, 4, 5, 8, 72; appointments to, 10, 36, 72, 96, 100, 101, 111–12, 120, 132, 194–95, 213, 262 (nn. 22, 26); calls to "Catalanize," 34–35, 196, 203, 217–18, 231, 232, 236; organization of, 41–47, 109–12, 130, 240. *See also* Corruption; Judges and magistrates
Juntas: presence of lawyers on, 76, 95–96
Juridical conferences: Conference of Spanish Jurisconsults (1863), 144–45, 150, 207; Conference of Catalan Jurisconsults (1881), 208–11, 216, 217, 228; Barcelona Juridical Conference, (1888), 229; Spanish Juridical Conference (1885), 229
Juridical periodicals, 128–30, 248
Juries, 105, 112, 202
Jurists. *See* Law professors; Lawyers
Justices of the Peace, 109–10

Kagan, Richard, 264–65 (n. 64)
Kant, Immanuel, 60
Karpik, Lucien, 4
Krausism, 144

Langbein, John, 264 (n. 54)
Larson, Magali Sarfatti, 4, 261 (n. 1)
Latin, 60, 188, 209; decline of, 52
Law: sociology of, 3–4, 241–43; and national identity, 7–8, 245–46; and philosophy, 60–61, 63, 67, 240; and capitalism, 135
Law apprentices, 14, 41, 87, 122, 169, 170, 174–77, 186, 194; rules governing, 39, 51, 64, 113, 174, 267 (n. 129), 285 (n. 76)
Law degrees: bachelor's, 39, 65; doctorate, 39, 175, 285 (n. 77); of laws and canons, 45, 117; licentiate, 65, 117; of jurisprudence, 117; numbers awarded, 169; of administrative law, 200
Law of Mortgages, 23, 206, 220
Law professors, 100, 116, 170, 188; in Cervera, 56, 62; oblige students to join university militia, 89; and conservatism, 121, 126, 132–34, 173, 200; and defense of Catalan law, 171, 203–4, 230; salaries of, 183; and historical-school jurisprudence, 221–24
Laws of incompatibility, 112, 195
Law students, 113, 157, 168–79 passim, 242; during War of Independence, 77–78; and liberal militias, 86–90; and purification proceedings, 100–101; as absolutists, 103–4, 125, 201; as dandies and bohemians, 173; and defense of Catalan law, 201, 230, 231, 233, 236; during Francoism, 252; women, 254
Lawsuits, 32, 42, 48–49, 108, 151, 152, 177, 188; length of, 43, 44, 113; monetary amounts of, 110, 184; crisis of, 191–92, 196
Law Unifying Jurisdictions, 117–18
Lawyers: as liberals, 2, 4–7, 13, 72, 76, 83–97 passim, 100–6, 120, 121, 239; and revolution, 2, 13, 30, 69–73, 84–97, 104–6, 116, 147, 152, 240–42, 246; nobility of, 2, 28, 33, 35–36, 38, 39, 52–55, 65, 104, 159, 165, 240; and Enlightenment, 2, 29, 30, 31, 33, 51, 52, 54–67 passim, 74, 75, 82, 111, 133, 146; as political elite, 2, 64, 70, 72, 93–96, 104, 116, 127, 133, 149, 172, 175, 186, 187; and nationalism, 3, 8, 26, 245, 246, 248; as conservatives, 4–7, 94, 116, 132–34, 155, 173, 200; as absolutists, 13, 61, 78, 83, 94, 103, 104, 121, 125, 146, 209; and religion, 14, 21, 165, 166; social origins of, 14, 37–39, 52, 67, 157–66; and associational life, 14, 51, 104, 123, 126, 127, 156, 157, 165, 174, 177, 186, 190; location of homes and offices of, 19–20, 37, 262 (n. 31); secret societies, as members of, 21, 90, 100, 101, 102, 103, 106, 174; as playwrights and poets, 21, 173, 212–14; as estate administrators, 21, 177, 185, 191, 192; as businessmen, 21, 177, 185–86, 187, 190, 191, 192, 241; Catalanism, 22–27, 194–99, 203, 204, 211, 231–37; as historians, 25, 215; education and training of, 29, 39, 64, 65, 165–81 passim; dilatory tactics and unscrupulous behavior, 42, 52, 55, 110, 153, 155, 188; corruption of, 42, 66–67, 149, 155, 187; as clergy, 45, 103, 121; and feudal disputes, 48–49, 62–63; earnings and fees of, 49–50, 110, 177, 181–84; taxation of, 50, 52, 125, 127, 182–84; as radicals and republicans, 63, 90, 92, 97, 102, 104, 171–72; and French Revolution, 66, 69–71, 91, 104, 148, 153; and War of Independence, 73–84, 87; as *afrancesats*, 74–75, 82–83; on *juntas*, 75, 76, 95, 96; as democrats, 75, 104, 147, 174; as militiamen, 86–93, 99, 100, 103, 104, 106, 125, 156, 170, 244; as participants in patriotic clubs or *tertulias*, 88, 91, 101, 106; and progressivism, 94, 127–28; exile and imprisonment of, 97, 98, 101–2, 172, 249–52, 254; persecution of, 97–104, 251; and public administration, 100, 101, 120, 186, 194, 196, 241, 246–47; execution of, 101, 251; as ministers of state, 102, 116, 133, 146, 186, 289 (n. 141); and big business and agriculture, 117, 123, 133–34, 149, 150; and working class, 125, 134, 147, 171, 249, 251, 252, 297 (n. 26); and trade protectionism, 133–34, 150; ridicule and satire of, 152, 155; adages about, 152, 162, 163, 181; as family confidants, 155, 188–90; and café life, 156, 169; as gentlemen, 156, 170, 202; secondary schooling of, 157, 165–68; geographical

origins of, 157, 167, 282 (n. 17); dynasties of, 163–64; linguistic habits among, 167–68, 217–18; non-practicing, 177, 179, 192; investments of, 184, 185, 287 (n. 112); "proletarianization" of, 192; and revivalism, 212–17; as Falangists, 251, 252. *See also* Bar; Judges and magistrates; Law apprentices; Law professors; Law students; Legal practice; Mercantile lawyers; Oratory; Prosecutors; Public defenders; Secretaries
Ledford, Kenneth, 289 (n. 1), 298 (n. 45)
Legal practice, 21, 42–43, 122–23, 178–91, 193, 241, 242; minimum age for, 98, 101, 170
Legal profession. *See* Bar; Professionalization
Lemmings, David, 56
Le Play, Frédéric, 140–41, 144
Liberalism: and proceduralism, 3, 4, 6–7, 241–43; and oligarchy and corruption, 14–16, 106–8; as revolutionary ideology, 71–72, 76, 84–86; and elitism, 71–73, 104–6; and property reform, 94–95; as political culture, 120–21; and Roman law, 132, 137; and Catalan law, 140, 148–49. *See also* Lawyers; Liberal revolution
Liberal Party, 22, 175, 199, 207, 211, 229
Liberal revolution, 13, 69, 72, 73
Libri Feudorum, 9
Litigants, 29, 49–50, 110, 264–65 (n. 64), 274 (n. 13)
Litigation rates, 30, 31, 67, 118–20, 192, 193, 274 (n. 16)
Litigiousness, 119
Llauder i de Dalmases, Lluís Maria de, 209, 224
Llobet, Miquel de, 81, 96, 99, 146

Madinaveytia, Juan, 74, 75
Magarola, Miquel, 54, 55, 63
Maluquer de Motes, Jordi, 16
Maluquer family, 164, 175
Maluquer i de Tirrell, Eduard, 175
Maluquer i de Tirrell, Josep, 128, 195–96, 288 (n. 123)
Maluquer i Viladot, Joan, 168, 175, 182, 186, 232, 234

Manresa Principles, 203, 236
Marfany, Joan-Lluís, 270 (n. 42), 291 (n. 58), 294 (n. 107)
Maria Christina (queen regent), 232
Martí d'Eixalà, Ramon, 116, 117, 132, 143, 146, 278 (n. 80)
Mascaró, Ròmul, 172, 210, 290
Medinaceli, Duke of, 60, 80, 94
Mercantile law. *See* Commercial law and procedure; Mercantile lawyers
Mercantile lawyers, 14, 46, 47, 115–17, 133, 149, 175, 200, 255. *See also* Commercial law and procedure
Message to the Queen Regent (1888), 232
Mieres, Tomàs, 146
Military tribunals, 98, 172, 251
Militias, 86–90, 93, 98–104, 106, 124, 125
Ministry of Justice, 233, 236; Commission for Codes of, 207–9, 228, 235; conflicts with College of Lawyers, 125–28, 195
Moderate Party, 22, 90, 94, 95, 109, 116, 132, 199, 200; legislation of, 23, 111, 124–25, 183; and trade protectionism, 133; and draft code of 1851, 139
Montesquieu, Baron de, 4, 51, 56, 58, 59, 61, 66, 223–24, 245
Moreno, Carmen, 254, 255
Moret Law, 130
Moret y Prendergast, Segismundo, 144
Moyano Law, 161, 170, 175, 183
Municipal courts, 109, 110, 182, 274 (n. 16); corruption of, 111
Mutual Aid Society for Catalan Lawyers, 128, 132

Napoleonic Wars. *See* War of Independence
Nationalism, 3, 22, 249; and law, 7, 8, 244–45; and ethnicity and race, 26, 248; theory of, 237, 238, 281 (n. 129), 296 (n. 146). *See also* Catalanism; Catalanists; Prat de la Riba, Enric; Regionalism
Natural law, 56, 64
New Foundation (1716), 10, 25, 41, 218, 274 (n. 22)
New Model Prison, 20
Notarial Law, 23, 206–7, 220

Notaries, 21, 22, 37, 43, 50, 115, 126, 183, 216
Novelists, depictions of lawyers by, 91, 151–55
Novísima recopilación, 219, 267 (n. 128)
Nueva Planta. See New Foundation

Oaths, 40, 68, 79, 103
O'Boyle, Lenore, 246
One-Hundred Thousand Sons of St. Louis, 89
Oratory, 43, 113–14, 168, 181, 188, 202, 209
Organic Law of Judicial Power (1870), 109, 195, 273 (n. 10)
Orriols i Comas, Joan Baptista, 188, 209
Ossorio y Gallardo, Ángel, 176, 181, 182, 189, 192, 194
Outline of Grievances (1885), 201, 225, 231

Pairalisme (patriarchism), 138, 147, 149, 164, 212
Pascual i Casas, Eusebi, 213, 217
Patriotic *tertulias* and clubs, 88, 91, 100, 101, 106
Peguera, Lluís, 146, 164
Pella i Forgas, Josep, 25, 215, 217, 259 (n. 21)
Penal law and procedure, 14, 44–45, 53, 121, 147, 179–81, 206, 250; enlightened reform of, 56, 58–59; liberal reform of, 111–12, 128, 130, 132, 193, 202; and language of defendants and witnesses, 196, 217–18
Penyafort, Ramon de, 9, 146
Pérez Galdós, Benito: *La fontana de oro*, 91; *Mendizábal*, 91; *Doña Perfecta*, 151, 152, 194, 246
Pérez Garzón, Juan Sisinio, 86, 270 (n. 48), 271 (n. 63)
Pérez Villamil, Juan, 53
Permanyer i Ayats, Joan Josep, 201, 203, 204, 211, 236
Permanyer i Tuyet, Francesc, 114, 116, 117, 145, 146, 162, 164, 167, 204, 206, 213, 278 (n. 80)
Philip V, 10, 26, 30, 32, 34, 121, 209
Piarists, 165, 166
Picasso, Pablo Ruiz, 18
Pi i Margall, Francesc, 24, 90, 274 (n. 18), 278 (n. 83)
Planas i Casals, Manuel, 187, 210

Pons i Fuster, Lluís, 212, 213, 217
Practical jurisprudence, 2, 29, 36, 39, 59, 60, 63, 240
Prat de la Riba, Enric, 236; on labor law, 147; on Catalan law, 171, 198, 226; on public offices, 194, 248; on language, 218; on nationalism, 249
Priests. *See* Clergy
Primo de Rivera, Miguel, 16, 249
Primogeniture, 137–38, 141
Proctors, 20, 21, 37, 43, 123, 152, 218, 260 (n. 51)
Professionalism, ethos of, 2, 29, 30, 31, 36, 50–55, 123, 240
Professionalization: history and sociology of, 3, 6, 28–30, 256; and welfare state, 247
Progressive Party, 22, 94, 127, 133, 199, 201; legislation of, 109, 117, 124, 125, 183
Pronunciamientos, 84, 86, 98, 106
Property, 14, 49, 114; conveyancing of, 22, 188; individual versus community, 136, 141–43, 207, 212; and civil codification, 208, 219. *See also* Emphyteusis
Prosecutors, 21, 45, 72, 96, 109, 110, 111, 177, 192, 195; salaries of, 183; and Catalan language, 196, 217
Prostitution, 128
Protestantism, 121, 128
Public administration, 128, 200; calls to "Catalanize," 194–96, 203, 232, 236–37, 246, 249
Public defenders (*abogados de pobres*), 14, 45, 96, 125, 179–81, 190, 250
Public hearings, 32, 45, 112–14, 240
Pufendorf, Samuel, 58, 63
Puig i Cadafalch, Josep, 18
Puig i Gelabert, Antoni, 54
Puig i Puig, Tomàs, 82, 83, 270 (n. 42)

Reapers' War, 10, 214
Regionalism, 22, 26, 27, 82, 83, 216, 230, 236. *See also* Catalanism; Nationalism
Regionalist League (Lliga Regionalista), 236, 248
Renaixença, 25, 215–17. *See also* Revivalism; Romanticism
Representation to Charles III, 28, 33–36, 42, 52, 67; influence of Montsesquieu on, 59

Revivalism, 24–25, 211–18, 237, 238
Revolutionary violence, 62, 76, 78, 86, 92–93, 102, 148
Revolutions: of 1835, 17, 92, 93, 95, 146; of 1854, 18, 129; of 1848 in Europe, 23, 91, 246; of 1830 in France, 71, 98, 246; of 1820, 84; of 1868, 117, 122, 129, 159, 173; of 1842, 124. *See also* French Revolution; Juntas, presence of lawyers on; Lawyers; Liberalism; Liberal revolution
Rey, Joaquim, 95
Reynals i Rabassa, Estanislao, 222–23
Richelieu, Cardinal, 62, 66
Ripoll, Acacia, 146, 164
Rius i Roca, Vicenç, 88, 128, 129, 163, 278 (n. 80)
Rius i Taulet, Francesc, 161, 163, 187
Robespierre, Maximilien, 64, 86, 91, 140
Roca i Junyent, Miquel, 252, 288 (n. 44)
Roda i Ventura, Frederic, 250, 252
Romà i Rosell, Francesc, 28, 33, 51, 57, 61, 205, 293 (n. 79)
Roman-ecclesiastical tradition, 2, 56, 59, 133, 223
Romaní i Puigdengolas, Francesc, 185
Roman law, 29, 39, 49, 60, 63, 188, 234, 224, 244; associated with liberalism, 132, 148; distinguished from Germanic law, 136–37, 140, 142; associated with absolutism and despotism, 139, 148; and codification, 144, 225; as supplement to Catalan law, 216, 230; and historical-school jurisprudence, 221–22
Romanticism: and cultural and literary renaissance, 24–25, 212–15; influence on forensic oratory, 114; influence on law, 212, 224, 225, 227, 242, 244, 247
Roure i Bofill, Conrad, 90, 167, 169, 170–71, 173, 174, 176, 214, 217
Rousseau, Jean-Jacques, 56, 133
Royal Council (Council of Castile), 38, 39, 44, 81, 99, 100, 113
Rudé, George, 91

Sala, Ramon Maria, 87, 92
Salutati, Coluccio, 53
Salvató, Ramon, 90, 95, 97, 102, 146, 289 (n. 141)
Sanponts i Barba, Ignasi, 145, 206, 280 (n. 113)
Savigny, Friedrich von, 8, 24, 245; and historical-school jurisprudence, 24, 221–24, 248
Scots law, 246
Scottish school of common sense, 133
Secretaries: of courts, 21, 72, 109, 111, 177, 192; of public and private enterprise, 21, 177, 185
Secret societies, 90–91, 100, 101, 103, 106, 155, 174
Seigneurs. *See* Barons
Seminaries, 165–67; and defense of Catalan law, 233
Serraclara i Costa, Gonçal, 172, 200, 217
Serrahima i Bofill, Maurici, 297 (n. 18)
Serrahima i Palà, Maurici, 159, 161, 164, 173, 176, 184, 289 (n. 4)
Sharecroppers, 134, 138, 139
Siete Partidas, 219, 280 (n. 113)
Silvela y de Le Villeuze, Luis, 144
Silvela y de Le Villeuze, Francisco, 228
Sisternes i Feliu, Manuel, 57, 61
Slavery, 11, 147, 149; abolition of, 130
Smith, Adam, 60
Solé-Tura, Jordi, 281 (n. 129)
Spain: creation of, 8; empire of, 11; population of, 13; and "black legend," 66; restoration of Bourbons in, 78, 199
Spanish: as language of courts, 10, 25, 60, 220; as language of education, writing, and formal oratory, 82–83, 167–69, 217–18; at twentieth-century bar and judiciary, 251–52
Spanish America, 8, 11; judicial appointments in, 34, 266 (n. 22); persecution of lawyers in, 97–98
Spanish Civil Code: protests against, 7, 24, 26, 197, 204, 205, 207–9, 216, 231–36; draft of 1851, 23, 138, 139, 144, 204, 207, 208, 222, 223; Basic Law of, 207–8, 223, 228–30; property interests and, 208, 219; support for, in Catalonia, 209–10; derogatory characterizations of, 211, 234; Article 12 of, 230, 232; Article 15 of, 232–36; as supplement to Catalan law, 252

Spanish common law, 135–37, 144; as basis of civil code, 139, 145, 208; derogatory characterizations of, 140, 142, 204, 205; applied in Catalonia, 219, 220, 225, 226

Spanish Cortes: lawyers as deputies and senators in, 94, 95, 116, 133, 172, 186, 288 (n. 123); percentage of lawyers in, 186, 288 (n. 120); debates over civil codification in, 227–30, 233–35

Successions. *See* Inheritance

Sue, Eugène: *Mysteries of Paris*, 154

Supreme Court, 109, 111, 187; decisions concerning Catalan law, 114, 115, 134, 136, 253, 275 (n. 33)

Swinburne, Henry, 17, 32, 58

Testamentary liberty, 140–44, 148, 207, 223, 233

Thompson, E. P., 135

Tithes, 62, 63; abolition of, 85, 93, 107, 271 (n. 79)

Tocqueville, Alexis de, 4, 7; on lawyers in France and United States, 69, 72, 104–6, 239, 242

Torras i Bages, Josep, 216, 225

Torres i Torres, Manuel Josep de, 88, 114, 116, 117, 129, 146, 181

Torture, 44, 263 (n. 47); abolition of, 59, 71, 111

Tos, Jaume, 60, 80, 81, 94, 146

Townsend, Joseph, 32, 57, 113

Trade protectionism, 16, 26, 133–34, 150, 231

Trials, 111, 112, 202

Trias i Giró, Joan, 203

Ucelay-Da Cal, Enric, 295 (n. 139), 297 (n. 14)

Ulloa y Rey, Benito de, 198, 225, 280 (n. 117)

United States, 24, 69; lawyers in, 72, 86, 104, 244; inheritance practices in, 137, 142, 143

Universities, 39, 56, 65, 99, 169, 170. *See also* Law degrees; Law professors; Law students

University of Barcelona: as liberal institution, 57, 89, 97, 132; calls to create chair of Catalan law at, 125, 196; law school, 169–71, 201, 252; teaching of Catalan law at, 171, 204; calls to "Catalanize" professoriate, 232; women at, 254; number of matriculants at, 284 (n. 61)

University of Cervera: moved to Barcelona, 39, 89, 97, 116, 169; and traditionalism, 56, 57, 62, 64, 132

University of Salamanca, 56, 66

Usatges, 9, 215, 219, 220

Vallès de Ribot, Josep Maria, 142, 172, 209, 210, 224, 293 (n. 92)

Ventosa i Palaudaries, Josep, 78, 114, 116, 117, 164, 176

Verdaguer i Callís, Narcís, 161, 175, 198, 233, 234

Vergés i Mas, Francesc, 122

Vergés i Permanyer, Felip, 121, 162, 164, 167, 209

Vilaseca i Mogas, Josep, 164, 172, 199, 289 (n. 4)

Vives i Cebrià, Pere, 145, 146, 164, 176, 219–21, 268 (n. 132)

Volksgeist, 24, 223

Voltaire, 54, 58, 59, 63, 70

Vries, Jan de, 6

War of Independence, 13, 37, 66, 69, 72–84, 87, 94, 97, 210

War of Spanish Succession, 9, 32, 121, 210, 233

Weber, Max, 3, 4, 7, 135, 239, 241–43

Wifred the Hairy, 144, 216

Witnesses and defendants: examination of, 43–45, 112; and language of testimony, 196, 217–18, 231–32, 236, 253

World Fair of 1888, 18, 122, 161, 187, 229, 232

Young, Arthur, 10, 17, 58

Young Catalonia, 25, 215, 292 (n. 67)

www.ingramcontent.com/pod-product-compliance
Lightning Source LLC
Chambersburg PA
CBHW021817300426
44114CB00009BA/215